Financial Accounting

A User's Approach

Volume 1

Fourth Edition

Vernon Kam, PhD, CPA
Micah Frankel, PhD, CPA
Diane Satin, PhD

California State University, Hayward

The McGraw-Hill Companies, Inc.
Primis Custom Publishing

New York   St. Louis   San Francisco   Auckland   Bogotá
Caracas   Lisbon   London   Madrid   Mexico   Milan   Montreal
New Delhi   Paris   San Juan   Singapore   Sydney   Tokyo   Toronto

McGraw·Hill

A Division of The **McGraw·Hill** Companies

Financial Accounting: A User's Approach
Volume 1

McGraw-Hill's Primis Custom Publishing consists of products that are produced from camera-ready copy. Peer review, class testing, and accuracy are primarily the responsibility of the author(s).

1 2 3 4 5 6 7 8 9 0 DEH DEH 9 0 9 8

ISBN 0-07-043459-X

Editor: Todd Bull
Cover Design: Maggie Lytle
Printer/Binder: DeHart's Printing Service

CONTENTS

Chapter 3 – The Income Statement...................................... pg 111

Problems with Inventory

<u>Risks of holding inventory</u>
    Inventory errors
    Obsolescent inventory
    Inventories and fraud
    Inventory and internal control

<u>Inventory Valuation and Financial Statement Analysis</u>
    The financial statements
    Financial ratio analysis

Chapter 1

Role of Accounting

LEARNING OBJECTIVES

After studying this chapter, you should be able to:

- Describe what accounting is.
- Indicate the relationship between accounting and other areas in a business firm.
- List who the users of accounting information are.
- Describe what kind of information the different users want.
- Describe what generally accepted accounting principles are.
- Identify the four most important authoritative bodies in accounting.
- Describe the standard-setting process.
- Explain why establishing international standards is difficult.
- Recognize that some "ethical" problems in accounting exist.

Everyday we take risks. Just about everything we do involves risk. And because of that, the decisions we make, whether they be significant or routine, include an assessment of the risks we face. Taking a risk is to take a chance, the chance that the outcome will not be good. For example, when you put your clothes on this morning, you had to decide what to wear. The risk you faced was that your choice of clothes would not look good on you. Although such a risk may not seem crucial, if the occasion is important, such as a job interview, the outcome could be disastrous. Another example is what you eat. The risk is that there may be something in the food that will make you sick. And we all know that driving a car anywhere involves the risk of getting into an accident.

As in everyday life, business involves many risks. Those who run a business face the ultimate risk of losing money. And those who deal with a business firm also stand the chance of making a loss. They need information to help them assess risk. That is where accounting comes in. Accounting provides people with financial information to assess risk. In this course, you will be introduced to business and accounting concepts and practices so that you will learn how to use accounting information to assess risk.

PURPOSE OF ACCOUNTING

• Apple Computer Company •

It takes inspiration and nerve to start a new business. We admire those who are willing to take the risk to make their dream come true, such as Steve Jobs and Steve Wozniak, co-founders of Apple Computer Company. They designed the Apple I computer in Jobs' bedroom and built the prototype in his garage. To start their company, they raised $1,300 by selling their most prized possessions, Jobs' old Volkswagen bus and Wozniak's Hewlett-Packard scientific calculator. Jobs was 21 and Wozniak 26. In 1976, their first year, they sold about 150 Apple I computers to their big customer, the Byte Shop. Armed with an upgraded model, the Apple II, the next year, they sold 2,500 computers. Business was picking up. In 1980, the company went public. On the first day of trading, all of the 4.6 million shares were sold, with the price jumping from $22 a share to $29. The company was now worth $1.2 billion. Those who purchased the shares had to assess the risk, the risk that this young company would not do well. Obviously, they decided that the risk was worth taking. What information did they have to make their decision? Accounting provided the information that earnings had increased by 700% in 3 years.

• What Is Accounting? •

Accounting is a system that exists in an entity. The objective is to gather, summarize and report financial information to various groups of people who are interested in the entity, called "users."

The information is for decision-making purposes, or put another way, for assessment of risk.

There are people within and outside the entity who are interested in what is going on. **Figure 1.1** illustrates what we have said.

As you can see, certain data are fed into the accounting system which processes the data to derive the desired information that users want. The information is in the form of "financial statements." In this course, the focus will be on the financial statements; however, to understand the statements and their limitations, you need to know something about what goes on in the "accounting system box."

Figure 1.1

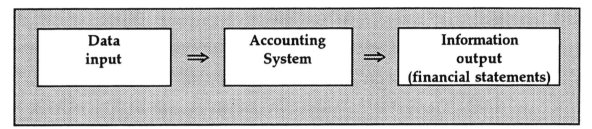

Based on what we said accounting is, we identify three relevant areas which we will discuss further in this chapter. These three areas are (1) the *entity* in which the accounting system is in, (2) the **users** of accounting information and what they want, and (3) the *principles* accountants follow in gathering, summarizing and reporting information.

Steve Jobs (standing) and Steve Wozniak in the early years of Apple. *(Courtesy of Apple Computer, Inc.)*

THE ENTITY

The accounting system resides in an entity. The entity could be a governmental unit, a nonprofit organization such as a church or university, or a business firm. Governmental units and nonprofit entities use a different type of accounting from that employed by business firms called "fund" accounting. Although there are many similarities with business accounting, there are enough differences to warrant a separation. In this book, we will concentrate on accounting for profit-making business firms.

• Accounting Within A Business Firm •

A business firm is in business to make a profit. It must organize itself in such a way so that it can effectively accomplish its purpose. Most firms find it advantageous to arrange their activities into several distinct departments, such as Production, Accounting and Finance, Marketing, Human Resources, and Computer Information Systems. Overseeing all these areas is top management.

–Relationship of accounting with other areas–

Every area in the firm is working to help attain the goal of making a profit. That is why accounting relates to all activities and departments in the firm. When money is involved, accounting is needed.

Accountants work with the _**Production**_ department to set specific production goals each period, and to keep track of the costs of production. What those in the Production department want is for the company to produce the "right" quantity of the product at a low cost and of high quality. The _**risk**_ is that the outcome may not be what is desired. Accounting information is especially helpful in keeping track of the quantity of production and controlling costs.

In many companies, those in _**Finance**_ often do similar work as accountants. Their specialization, however, is in the area of financing and investing. What those in the Finance department want is to obtain financing for the company at a low cost, and to make investments that will provide a good return. The _**risk**_ is that what is desired will not happen. They need information not only on the present financing arrangements and investments but also on the returns and costs, and this information is furnished by accountants.

Those in _**Marketing**_ are especially concerned about the sales of the products of the company. What they want is for the company to have a high amount of sales. The _**risk**_ is that this will not happen. They need information on present and past sales and estimates about the future. This information is supplied by accountants.

The department of _**Human Resources**_ wants to ensure that the company maintains the "right" number of employees at a level of cost that it can afford. Morale and efficiency of employees must also be considered. The *risk* is that what is desired will not happen. Those in this department need information on the number of employees and their compensation, including wages and salaries, medical and pension benefits. This information is provided by accountants.

Much of the information that is needed in the firm is channeled through a computerized system. In order to establish the system and to make sure that it works well, those in the *Computer Systems* area need to know what kind of information is desired and the cost of producing the information. Accountants provide most of the information.

The top *management team* is responsible for the well-being of the company. For them, the *risk* is that the company will not do well. Information is needed on all aspects of the company for purposes of planning and control, including an evaluation of the financial position and profitability of the firm. This information is furnished by accountants. As can be seen in **Figure 1.2**, accounting is involved in all facets of a firm. Therefore, studying accounting provides a good background in all areas of business.

Figure 1.2

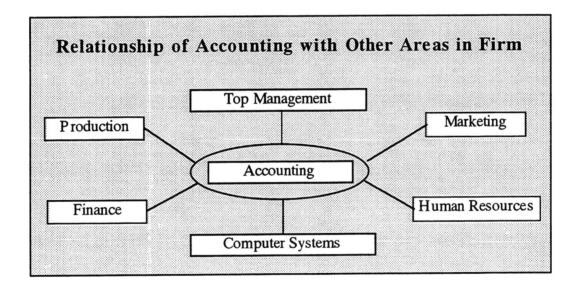

• The Accounting Profession •

Accounting has existed since the times of the Babylonians and Egyptians 5,000 years ago. Over the years, a distinct, definable profession has arisen to serve individuals, business firms, government and other non-profit entities. What accountants do for these different entities relates to the objective of accounting, which is to provide financial information.

–The business firm–

The accounting system is the primary source of information in the firm. To provide the necessary information, typically the work of accountants is divided into several categories.

First, we have financial accounting. Accountants in this area are responsible for preparing the financial statements for "external" users. In this regard, certain rules and standards must be followed. For example, financial statements for stockholders must conform with generally accepted accounting principles, which are discussed later in this chapter. For financial statements to certain regulatory agencies, such as the Securities and Exchange Commission, the accountant must comply with the rules of those agencies.

Second, there is the area of managerial accounting, which relates to the kinds of information needed by the different areas within the firm which we discussed previously. Cost analysis is an important function.

Third is the field of internal auditing, which concerns internal controls. Accountants in this area are responsible for establishing and checking the procedures to safeguard a company's assets and to promoting efficiency of the accounting system.

Accountants working in industry can apply to be a Certified Management Accountant (CMA). Those in internal auditing can apply to be a Certified Internal Auditor (CIA). For both, a person must pass an examination and meet the work requirement to be certified.

–Public accounting–

An area of accounting that affects a company, but is not a part of it is public accounting. This is the domain of the certified public accountant (CPA). Normally, a CPA firm offers three types of services to clients: auditing, management advisory, and tax. From the auditing department, an auditor will examine the financial statements of a company to determine that they conform with generally accepted accounting principles. The CPA is considered an independent third party who must decide that the financial statements are based on transactions that have been properly recorded. The CPA renders an opinion in a formal report.

The area of management advisory services is very broad, and is growing rapidly. It deals with whatever a client wants to know that affects his or her business. Included are the many different aspects of a client's business, such as accounting, production, marketing, financing, and computers. For example, the managers of a company may ask a CPA firm to advise them on what they need to do to have greater sales revenue or to operate more efficiently. Small companies find this area of the CPA firm especially useful.

Tax services involve more than preparation of tax returns. Advice on compliance with tax laws and ways to minimize taxes are important tasks.

To be a licensed CPA, one must be a college graduate, pass the CPA exam and meet the work requirement of the particular state issuing the certificate.

–Government–

Similar to business and CPA firms, governmental units also use accounting and auditing. Regulatory agencies at the local, state, and federal levels employ many auditors.

–Positions–

The different levels of accounting positions in an entity depend on its size. Normally, for the corporation and CPA firm, as illustrated in **Figure 1.3**, one would find the following:

Figure 1.3

<u>Corporation</u>	<u>CPA Firm</u>
Vice-President/treasurer	Partner
Controller	Manager
Senior Accountant	Senior Accountant
Staff Accountant	Staff Accountant

A common fallacy is that accountants need not relate to people because they work with numbers. Whatever the entity, the accountant is a member of a team, and to be effective must know how to work with people. Because a CPA firm serves clients, those in the firm must know how to deal with people. Communication skills are considered an important attribute.

USERS OF ACCOUNTING INFORMATION

Users want accounting information about a given entity, because they will be making decisions concerning their relationship with the entity.

• For A Business Firm •

Suppose the entity is XYZ Corporation. Who are the external groups of people who are interested in XYZ Corporation? We can identify a number of users.

–Stockholders–

One major group of users is present and potential stockholders of the corporation. To buy the stock of any company is taking a big _**risk**_. There is always a chance that the price will go down and a loss will be sustained when the stock is sold. No one wants to make a loss. But on the other hand, if you want to make a profit in the stock market, you must take the risk of buying stock.

Present stockholders of XYZ Corporation need information to decide whether they should sell their stock or buy more. Potential stockholders may be thinking about buying stock in the company and need information to make that decision. They are also interested in receiving dividends from XYZ and need information to assess the likelihood of receiving a certain amount of dividends in the future. They rely on accounting information.

–Creditors–

Another important group of users is present and potential creditors. When creditors sell things on credit to XYZ Corporation, they are taking a _risk_. The risk is that they will not be paid. When banks lend money to XYZ or bondholders buy the bonds of XYZ, they run the same risk. The corporation may not pay them back.

The present creditors need information to determine if the company is in a financial position to pay them so that they should continue to grant credit to XYZ. Potential creditors want to know if they should get involved with XYZ. For example, a bank may want information to decide whether to loan money to the company. They rely on accounting information.

–Others–

Other groups of users are employees, customers, and financial analysts. Employees and their labor unions are interested in the ability of the company to pay wages and salaries and the possibility of an increase in compensation. Customers, especially commercial customers, want information to determine whether the company will continue to exist for them to do business with. Financial analysts want information about the company so they can advise investors appropriately. Certain governmental agencies (such as the Internal Revenue Service) are also interested in XYZ Corporation and have their own rules by which the company must comply with in furnishing information to them.

–Managers–

Notice that all the users we have mentioned so far can be categorized as "outsiders." In contrast, those within a company, internal users, need a lot more information than the others. Managers of a company need information to run the business efficiently. They need a constant flow of information, while the others only need information periodically.

Because of the special needs of managers, accounting for managers is separated from the accounting for external parties. Managers need to make decisions, such as: Should the company buy or lease a building? Should the company sell its product in a new territory? Should the company lay off some of its employees to cut costs? These are not the kinds of decisions which external users need to make.

When the accounting system is geared to providing information to managers, this is called "management" or "managerial" accounting. When the accounting system is aimed at providing information to external parties, this is called "financial" accounting. We have mentioned these terms before, but to illustrate the difference more vividly, **Figure 1.4** is presented. As we saw earlier, both types of accounting exist side by side in a company. This book is one in financial accounting.

Figure 1.4

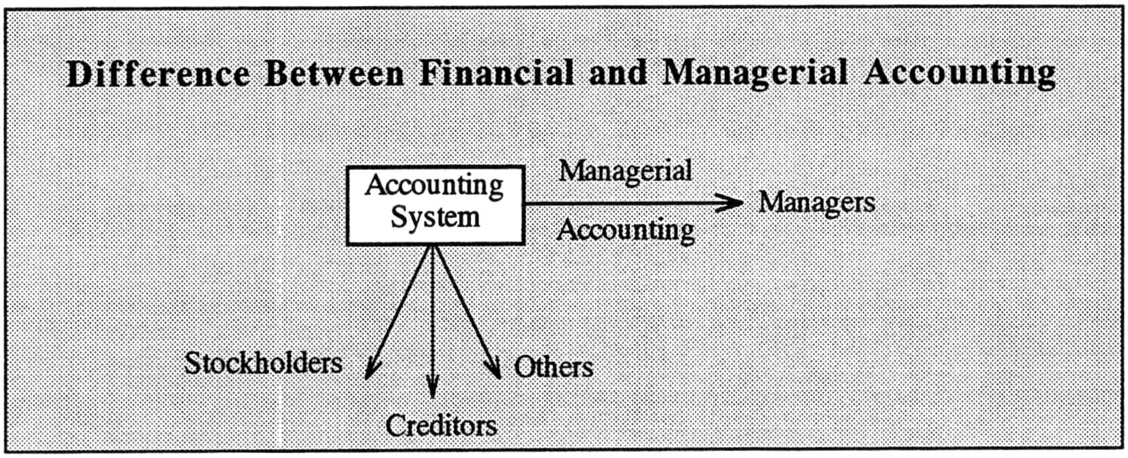

Difference Between Financial and Managerial Accounting

• Uses of Accounting Information •

We have discussed in a general way why users want information about a business firm. We said that they need information for decision-making purposes. The two primary users of accounting information about a specific business firm, present and potential stockholders and creditors, need to decide whether they want to get involved with the company or continue or terminate their relationship with the company. What kind of information do they want?

Both stockholders and creditors want information so that they can make predictions about a company. What predictions are they making?

–Information for stockholders–

A stockholder wants to predict the future price of the stock of the company and also predict whether he/she will be receiving a cash dividend that is considered acceptable. If the price is expected to decline, the stockholder may sell his shares now. If the price is expected to rise, the stockholder may decide to purchase more shares. What factors affect the price of a stock?

The price of a particular stock in the stock market is affected by a number of variables. The expectations of investors have a lot to do with the ups and downs of the price of a stock. Their expectations have to do with assessing the risks involved in investing in a particular stock. In the case of Apple in 1980, the expectations were very positive.

The market is made up of many different buyers and sellers. Why each person buys or sells depends on his/her personal expectations and objectives. We assume that the objective of an investor is to make a profit or minimize a loss. Expectations of an investor about a given company and its stock depend on both general and company-specific factors, as illustrated in **Figure 1.5**. These factors help investors assess the _risk_ of the stock they wish to purchase.

General factors include such components as economic conditions, a war or the political climate. These are beyond the control of a company. For Apple, when it went public in 1980, the American people were ready for something exciting that they could believe in. They wanted to forget the disastrous 1970s, with the Vietnam War and its protests, and the Watergate scandal. Personal computers caught the imagination of the public. It was the right time for Apple to sell shares.

Figure 1.5

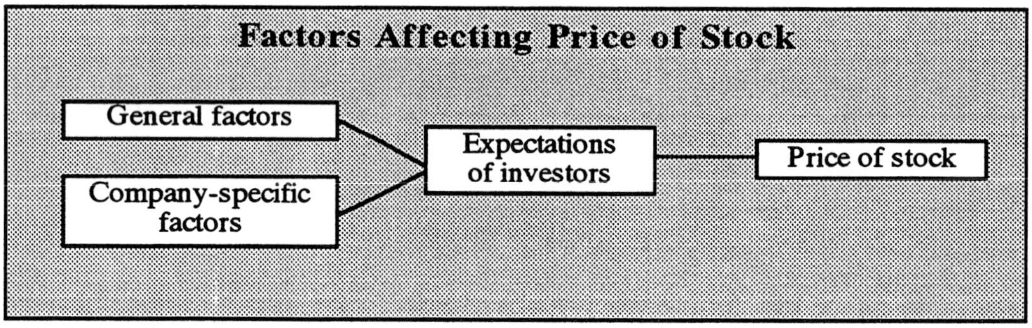

Company-specific factors include the profitability or expected bankruptcy of a company. It is in this latter realm that accounting information plays a role. Investors want information especially on profitability to help them predict whether the price of the stock of a company will increase or decrease. Information about the financial position of a company, on whether it has enough money to pay its debts is also necessary. It is no use investing in a company that is going to go bankrupt. Investors depend on accounting to provide information about the profitability and financial position of a company. For Apple in 1980, with its dizzying growth rate, investors were impressed. In 1977, when the Apple II was first sold, the company sold 2,500 of them; in 1979, they sold 35,000. People were willing to accept the risk of investing in a young company, because they believed demand for personal computers would grow considerably in the future.

–Information for creditors–

Creditors are not as concerned as stockholders about the price of the stock of a company. For stockholders, their gain or loss is derived mainly from receiving dividends and selling the stock for a higher price than the original price. That is why stockholders have a great interest in predicting the price of the stock. For creditors, their gain or loss is derived from receiving interest, if applicable, and collecting the principal; therefore, their focus is on whether the company can pay them. They must predict whether the company will have sufficient cash to pay them any applicable interest and the principal amount when due. In accounting terms, this has to do with the financial position of a company.

–Information on profitability and financial position–

As it turns out, although the type of predictions creditors are making is different from that of stockholders, the kind of information they want is basically the same. Stockholders want information mainly on profitability so they can predict the future price of the stock of a company, while creditors want information to predict whether the company can pay what is due them. Profitability is a measure of the "success" of a company, of how well it is doing. It is not likely that an unprofitable company will have enough cash to pay creditors; therefore, creditors need information on profitability. Likewise, it is not likely that the stock of a company will rise if it is experiencing financial problems; therefore, stockholders need information on the financial position of a company. Accounting theory assumes that both stockholders and creditors want information on the profitability and financial position of a company.

• Accounting and Risk Assessment •

Based on our discussion about the objectives of stockholders and creditors, both present and potential, we can express what they want to know in the form of two questions:

1. How much risk is the company faced with?

2. How good is the company in "managing" risks?

The first question deals with identifying the risks, and the second concerns the strategies a company formulates to handle the risks.

We can categorize the risks a company encounters as general and company-specific.

–General type risks–

A company does not have much control over general types of risk. We identify the following general types, which are not necessarily mutually exclusive:

1. Economic risk. This is the risk that pertains directly to the world or national economy. The risk is created by factors that have a negative impact on a company, such as a recession. The negative effect would be on the company's income, and thus on the price of its stock. The negative impact may cause a company to have difficulty paying its debts.

In a note in its 1997 financial statement, Apple speaks of global market risks, which are beyond its control.

Apple Computer Company

> • **Global Market Risks** •
>
> A large portion of the Company's revenue is derived from its international operations. As a result, the Company's operations and financial results could be significantly affected by risks associated with international activities, including economic and labor conditions, political instability, tax laws, and changes in the value of the U.S. dollar versus the local currency in which the products are sold.

2. Capital market risk. This risk relates to the securities market. For whatever reason, the prices of stocks and bonds may go down. This may be due to the threat of war, or the health of the president, or rumors of a coming recession.

3. Interest rate risk. This risk relates directly to bonds. When market interest rates go up, the price of bonds drops. If interest rates go down, the price of bonds increases. Companies do not have control over the rise and fall of interest rates in the market.

–Company-specific risks–

We identify the following types of risks in this category:

1. Industry risk. This risk pertains to a specific industry and not to the economy as a whole. For example, bad weather may cause problems for certain kinds of agricultural products. Middle East tensions may cause difficulties for the oil industry.

2. Company risk. This risk concerns problems that a particular company may face, such as a labor strike, or the loss of an important government contract, or a new product by a competitor.

3. Credit risk. This risk pertains to the ability of a company to pay its debts. Having too much debt increases this risk for a company. Creditors of a company are especially interested in this type of risk.

–Strategies to manage risks–

For a firm, just to be in business involves all the risks mentioned above. What is the company doing about it? For general risks, companies may not be able to do much to minimize their effect. For company-specific risks, they can. It is useful to categorize their strategies to cope with company-specific risks in terms of the kinds of information stockholders and creditors want, which is financial position and profitability.

1. Financial position. We want to know what strategies a company develops to cope with the risk of not being able to pay its debts. This area concerns a company's plans to manage its assets and liabilities. To a large extent, accounting information can tell us something about this.

2. Profitability. We want to know a company's strategy to generate revenues and control costs. This may involve creating new products, diversifying its product mix, combining with another company, or laying off employees. Accounting information can be of great help in this area.

Many of the chapters in this book will discuss the ways companies manage their assets and liabilities to cope with risk.

• Allocation of Resources •

Up till now, we have discussed the uses of accounting information for different groups of individuals. In a broader sense, accounting information is also useful in helping allocate resources efficiently in the economy. **Figure 1.6** illustrates the point.

–Capitalistic economy–

The economic system in the United States is called "capitalism." Sometimes it is referred to as a free market economy. The reason for the term "capitalism" is that it refers to the fact that it takes "capital" to run a business. In economic theory, capital refers to the factors of production (such as money, land, equipment), and a capitalist is the person who provides money, and often ideas, to get the enterprise started.In the case of Apple, Steve Jobs provided the charisma and the drive. He had a vision where a personal computer in the home would be as common as the TV. Steve Wozniak provided the technical skills. It was he who really created Apple I and Apple II. What they lacked was money to break out of the hobbyist market and into the big time. They found their money in 1977 in the person of Mike Markkula, a former executive of Intel, who invested $91,000 in cash and gave a guarantee to a bank for a line of credit of $250,000.[1]

Figure 1.6

```
┌─────────────────────────────────────────────────────┐
│  Usefulness of Accounting Information                 │
│                                                       │
│  Micro Level:                                         │
│      To:                                              │
│      Stockholders                                     │
│      Creditors                                        │
│      Government regulators                            │
│      Others (employees, consumers, financial analysts, etc.) │
│                                                       │
│  Macro Level:                                         │
│      To:                                              │
│      The economy                                      │
└─────────────────────────────────────────────────────┘
```

–How the system operates–

The capitalistic system can be seen as one large market which basically is regulated by a price mechanism. This price mechanism is made operative by the forces of demand and supply. Just about every good and service, including labor services and capital, is bought and sold in the market. Income is derived from the sale of goods and services in the market. For example, people sell their labor services to a company and earn an income for themselves, and business firms sell goods or services to earn an income also.

An economic system cannot avoid being part of the political system, and therefore political issues are raised that are economic in nature. Capitalism is "free" because people and firms have the right to own property and to do what they wish with their property, as long as it is legal. These freedoms are to be contrasted with other economic systems where personal freedom and property rights are sacrificed in the interest of the State. Under capitalism, people and firms are free to enter and exit the market. In this way, the market is not only free but also competitive.

–Efficient economy–

For the economy to work well it must be efficient; that is, people and firms in the economy must operate capably. If the economy is not working well, then one result will be high prices paid by consumers for goods and services, and these goods and services may not be of good quality. Ideally, when the market is competitive, business firms that are not efficient will be driven out. This will occur because they will not be profitable and/or in good financial position. They will not be profitable

---

[1] Jeffrey Young, *Steve Jobs: The Journey in the Reward* (Scott Foreman, 1988), p. 129.

because consumers will not want to buy their products or services at a price in excess of costs. Only the efficient firms will survive in a very competitive market. To be able to survive, a firm must be able to compete with other firms. It will be competitive if it offers a product that is of good quality at a reasonable price. In the personal computer market, names that once were known are no longer present, such Commodore, NorthStar, Franklin. Competition proved too much for them, and they fell on the wayside.

Today, companies must compete on a global scale. Economic theory takes the position of the rational consumer. This consumer wants a good quality product at a reasonable price and does not care whether the product is from a domestic or foreign company. Because in the real world imperfections exist in markets so that they are not completely free (such as monopolies, government-subsidized products, tariffs, barriers set up to exclude imports, etc.), global economic issues arise that have generated heated political debates in every country. Many domestic firms (including farmers) are concerned that they will not make a profit (or as big a profit as they want) because of foreign competition. Workers are concerned that they will not have jobs because unprofitable companies will not provide work. Regardless of the political-social issues, economic theory is clear that an efficient economy will be, on balance and in the long-run, beneficial for a country, its consumers and firms.

–Accounting at the micro level–

At the "micro" level, the level of the individual firm, you can see how accounting can be of great help to the firm. First, it provides information on profitability. Accounting keeps track of sales revenues and costs. This information tells the managers of a firm about the activities that create profits. A firm needs to keep track of its costs, because costs affect the selling price of its product. If costs are controlled, then the firm can establish a low selling price for its product, which will be attractive to consumers. If costs are kept under control and demand for its product is high, then the company will make a profit. The lower the costs and the higher the demand for the product, the larger the profit.

Second, accounting provides information on a firm's ability to pay its debts, which relates to its "financial position." This includes information on the resources a firm has to run its business and its obligations. Information on its regular operating activities that generate cash and require the use of cash (such as payments for salaries and wages), its financing activities and financial arrangements, and its investments are also helpful to a firm in making sure that it is in good financial position.

–Accounting at the macro level–

Investors will want to put their money into companies that are profitable and in good financial position. Thus, companies doing well will attract capital, as we saw in the case of Apple in 1980 when it first sold shares publicly. In this way, capital will be allocated efficiently because capital will move in the direction of the efficient, profitable firms. In time, those that are not efficient and therefore not profitable will be driven out for lack of capital.

At the "macro" level, the level of the whole economy, the role of accounting is to provide relevant and reliable information on the profitability and financial position of companies so that investors can make intelligent decisions about where to put their money. You can see therefore that accounting information plays an important function in society. You can see also that if accounting information is not correct, investors will be misled about companies, and therefore capital will not be allocated efficiently. Over time, this could lead to consequences that are devastating to the economy.

ACCOUNTING PRINCIPLES

The foregoing discussion shows how important accounting information is at both the micro and macro levels. For the information to be useful, it must be relevant and reliable. How do accountants know what the proper rules and procedures are to derive information that is considered relevant and reliable? For internal purposes, that is, information for management use, accountants depend mainly on theory. For external purposes, that is, information for use by stockholders, creditors, and other outside parties, accountants depend on generally accepted accounting principles (GAAP). This is another major distinction between managerial and financial accounting. Information for external users (financial accounting) is governed by GAAP. Although companies have some discretion, they must follow the prescriptions of GAAP. On the other hand, information for managerial use depends on whatever managers want.

What are generally accepted accounting principles? Who formulates them? GAAP consists of the concepts and procedures that are required to be followed in practice. Three different areas can be identified as the sources of authority for determining acceptability of accounting principles (sometimes called standards). These three are: authoritative bodies, accounting theory, and convention. They are not necessarily mutually exclusive. **Figure 1.7** illustrates the point.

Figure 1.7

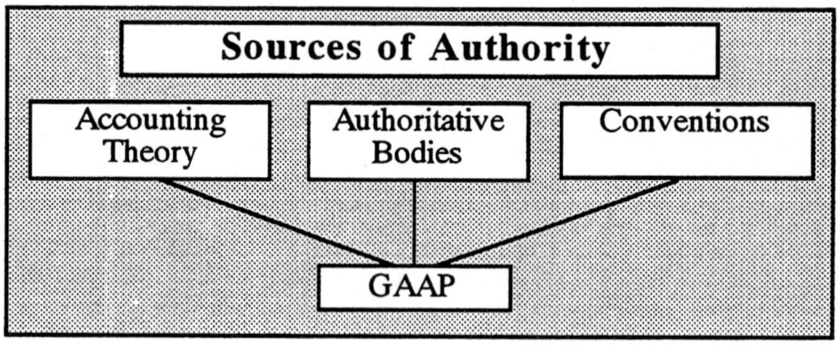

• Authoritative Bodies •

One of the unique features about accounting is the existence and influence of authoritative bodies in establishing accounting principles. In other fields, this is not the case. For example, in physics there is no authoritative body that determines what theories or principles should be accepted by physicists. In the U.S., in medicine, there is the American Medical Association, but it does not tell physicians what medical treatments should or should not be used. However, in accounting there exist authoritative bodies that prescribe to accountants what should or should not be done.

Where do these authoritative bodies get their power? The answer is: either by law or by agreement among accountants. In the U.S., there are numerous regulatory agencies that have the power to prescribe accounting rules for entities under their jurisdictions. There are also private organizations that express their opinions on various accounting issues. We will focus our attention only on the four most important authoritative bodies. They are: the Securities and Exchange Commission, the Financial Accounting Standards Board, the Governmental Accounting Standards Board, and the American Institute of Certified Public Accountants.

–Securities and Exchange Commission–

This Commission, often referred to simply as the SEC, is the most powerful authoritative body in accounting. It is an independent regulatory agency of the federal government established by the Securities Act of 1934. Its primary function is to regulate the securities market. In doing so, it has been given the power to dictate to companies under its jurisdiction the accounting standards and procedures to be followed. Any company that issues securities to the public or whose stock is listed on a stock exchange is automatically under its domain. The main concern of the SEC with respect to accounting information is for "full and fair disclosure." The SEC sees its task as the protection of investors. To protect investors, by law, companies under the SEC must have their financial statements approved by an independent auditor, that is to say, a certified public accountant (CPA). In accordance with the desire of the SEC, approval of the financial statements by a CPA means that they are "fair."

Companies must submit Form 10-K to the SEC. On this form, the following information must be provided: (1) description of the business, (2) the properties the company possesses, (3) legal proceedings by or against the company, (4) a list of anyone owning more than 5 percent of the voting shares and a list of the directors and managers who own shares in the company, (5) the market for the company's stock, (6) selected financial data for 5 years, (7) management's discussion and analysis of the financial condition and profitability of the company, including some financial ratios, (8) the auditor's report and the financial statements of the company, which are those issued to the company's stockholders and focused upon in this book, (9) a list of the directors and executive officers, (10) the remuneration of the directors and officers of the company, and (11) any exhibits and financial statement schedules.

Historically, because of certain events in the United States and the distaste of business firms for "governmental interference," the SEC has allowed accounting principles to be established in the private sector. Although it has the legal power to establish accounting principles, it has deferred to the authoritative body in the private sector, which currently is the Financial Accounting Standards Board (FASB). The SEC sees its role as "overseer" of the procedures prescribed by the FASB.

–Financial Accounting Standards Board–

The FASB became operative in 1973. Its task is to establish accounting standards. It consists of seven members, each of whom represents a particular group of people who have an interest in accounting principles for business firms. The following interest groups are represented: CPAs, financial analysts, industrial accountants, corporate executives, investment bankers and brokers, accounting educators, and governmental accountants. The basis of the membership of the FASB is that, in a democratic society, those who must abide by rules imposed on them should have a voice in the establishment of those rules.

The power of the FASB is derived from two sources. First, the SEC recognizes the FASB as the entity that is to formulate accounting principles. Second, by agreement, CPAs accept the prescriptions of the FASB; therefore, they abide by the decisions of the FASB when they examine the financial statements of companies. Knowing that their financial statements will not be approved by a CPA unless they conform with the accounting procedures established by the FASB, companies will therefore also follow the FASB rulings.

–Governmental Accounting Standards Board–

Similar to the FASB, this board (referred to as the GASB) formulates accounting standards, but for governmental units. In this course we will focus mainly on business firms; therefore, we will not have any occasion to deal with the rulings of the GASB.

–American Institute of CPAs–

The Institute, commonly referred to as the AICPA, is the national organization of CPAs. Before the FASB began its work in 1973, the authoritative bodies which formulated accounting principles were part of the AICPA. The AICPA still wields considerable influence, because it establishes the procedures for conducting an audit by CPAs and it issues guidelines on accounting problems not covered by any FASB ruling.

• Accounting Theory •

Accounting theory provides the rationale for what is done in practice. We speak of accounting theory as though there existed one large overall theory. But this is not the case. Although there is a framework that gives us a general notion of the important components and what we want to accomplish, the fact is that there is no one comprehensive theory but instead many "little" theories. Each one provides an explanation of why something should be done. For example, theory tells us that the pension plan a company has is a liability and therefore should be recorded. Many theories are proposed, but not all become part of GAAP.

How does a theory become part of GAAP? Unlike the natural sciences, there are very few theories in accounting that have been validated by persuasive empirical evidence. Empirical evidence is based on actual, "real world" experience gained through scientific means. Today, academic accountants are doing a great deal of empirical research to find answers to accounting questions, such as the ability of accounting information to predict the bankruptcy of a company, or why managers when given a choice select one accounting method rather than another. However, there is still insufficient evidence to decide on the validity of most theories. Presently, therefore, a theory becomes part of GAAP when it is accepted by an authoritative body in accounting or by convention.

The FASB has formulated a "conceptual framework" in which the fundamentals of financial accounting are expressed. Many of the concepts will be discussed in this book.

• Conventions •

Conventions play a key role in accounting. When a procedure is undertaken for a long period of time, even though there is no authoritative statement supporting it, there is a presumption that practitioners must find it useful and workable and therefore it becomes part of accepted practice. Because theories and standards tend to be very general, conventions are often relied upon for deciding how a specific item should be treated. For example, when a company buys new tires for one of its trucks, by convention this expenditure is considered an expense.

–Conservatism–

A convention that has persisted over many years is that of conservatism. Faced with uncertainty about how to account for something, accountants have decided to take a conservative posture. This translates to a less optimistic view of things. Practically speaking, if an accountant is uncertain about recording a transaction or the value of an item, then he or she should undertake the alternative that is less beneficial to the company. For something that is "positive" for a company, such as revenues, then the lower choice should be taken. For something that is "negative" for a company, such as expenses, then the higher choice should be accepted. For example, if the accountant is uncertain about the amount of a gain (something that is positive), then the accountant should record the lowest amount. If the accountant is faced with two possible figures for an expense (something negative for the firm) and is uncertain which is correct, then the accountant should select the higher figure.

• Standard Setting •

As mentioned earlier, the FASB has the responsibility of setting accounting standards. How should a particular standard be formulated? First of all, the objective of accounting must be considered, which is to provide useful information to users. A standard can be seen as a solution to an accounting problem. In effect, the correct solution represents the "truth" that we want to follow in order to achieve the objective. It seems reasonable to assume that based on accounting theory, the "truth" can be ascertained. The problem is that there is a lack of empirical evidence to support accounting theory so that what constitutes useful information is not clear. This deficiency in accounting hinders the work of the FASB. What is "truth" and what is "useful" are a matter of opinion. What is truth to one group may not be considered so by another. Users perceive truth according to their personal interests.

–Political process–

The FASB was organized in such a way as to make the standard-setting process democratic. When compared to a field such as physics, we can see how different this mode of operation is. In physics, a committee does not meet to vote on whether a certain theory should be accepted or not. There is no democracy. Truth is based on the empirical evidence in support of a theory or principle. But in accounting, the recognition of truth is not clearly demonstrated. Because of this and because users have a stake in the outcome of the standard-setting process, a democratic "due process" approach has been instituted by the FASB. This due process gives all interested parties an opportunity to be heard and to "lobby" for what they want. Therefore, the nature of standard setting has become political.

–Considerations in establishing standards–

Establishing an accounting standard cannot be accomplished purely on the basis of what is implied by accounting theory. For political reasons, besides theory, the FASB must consider the following before making a decision about a standard:

1. What are the costs compared with the benefits? Obviously, in the opinion of the FASB the benefits must be greater than the costs. Benefits are almost impossible to quantify, but the costs can be estimated. If the implementation of a proposed standard for a business firm appears to be too costly, then the proposal may have to be altered or abandned.

2. Who are the various users who will be affected by the standard and what is the possible economic impact on each? For example, the amount of debt for certain companies may increase

tremendously because of the proposed standard, which will make it difficult for them to obtain capital funds. Despite the consequences, the FASB may still prefer to issue its proposed standard, but it should be aware of the repercussions.

3. Is there an alternative solution that is acceptable? A compromise may still achieve the objective and be agreeable to most users.

In this political process, the FASB insists that it must be as neutral as possible, not favoring one group of users over another, and it must not forget its mission, which is to improve the relevance and reliability of accounting information. For a standard to be enacted, a majority of 5 of the 7 votes of the board must be obtained.

• International Standards •

As financial markets have become increasingly international and as business firms have crossed national boundaries, the need for global accounting standards has received considerable attention. Dissimilar accounting practices make comparisons among firms difficult. International companies find compliance with the standards of different countries very troublesome. Because U.S. standards tend to be more stringent than those of other countries, some argue that U.S. companies are placed at a competitive disadvantage in world markets.

In response to the cry for harmonization of standards, the International Accounting Standards Committee (IASC), with headquarters in London, was formed in 1973. Over 100 accounting bodies from about 80 countries are members. In the U.S., the AICPA is a member. The FASB is not a member but has joined the Committee's consultative group. Members are not required to accept the standards of the IASC, but agree to work toward acceptance. The IASC and the International Organization of Securities Commissions (IOSCO) have a joint project to produce a set of common accounting standards. The IOSCO is made up of governmental bodies in charge of securities, such as the SEC.

–Response of U.S.–

Both the SEC and the FASB are aware of the importance of harmonization of accounting standards and are working toward it. For harmonization to take place, the FASB believes the following four questions must be answered:

1. What is the objective of financial reporting? In the U.S., it is commonly accepted that the objective is to provide useful information, but "useful" means different things to people in different countries.

2. How specific should standards be? In the U.S., standards tend to be detailed. In many other countries, standards are very broad and can be interpreted in different ways. The SEC believes that some of the current international standards are too broadly stated. Presently, it is possible for a company to show one set of results on its financial statements and claim conformity with international accounting standards, and yet it can show a completely different set of results and still claim conformity with international standards.

3. What is the extent of disclosure? In the U.S., the objective is to disclose information so that a prudent investor can make intelligent investment decisions. Compared with many other countries, the extent of disclosure in the U.S. is much greater.

4. How are international standards to be established? That is, what authoritative body should formulate standards, what is the process by which a standard is formulated, and what should be the effect on member nations?

–Obstacles to harmonization–

Nationalism is a formidable force that makes harmonization of accounting standards very difficult. Accountants of most countries have grown accustomed to their own practices and believe their standards to be appropriate.

Two different philosophies can be identified concerning the financial statements. One is that they should be "fair," as in the U.S., and the other is that they be "correct" in the legal sense. Culture is the root of this difference. Four factors can be distinguished as causing this cultural difference. They are the legal system, the major providers of capital, tax laws, and the strength of the accounting profession.[2]

–Legal system–

On the one hand, we have countries that subscribe to the "common law" legal system, which had its beginning in England, where statute law is extended by interpretations by the courts, such as the UK, the USA, Canada, Australia, New Zealand, Ireland, and India. These countries permit flexibility and give companies choices among accounting procedures. On the other hand, we have countries that follow the Roman legal system, where laws are based on notions of justice and morality and are highly codified, such as Italy, Germany, Spain, and France. Although some countries may not have been directly influenced by the Roman legal system, they follow the same philosophy, such as Japan. In these countries, accounting standards are very detailed and permit few choices.

---

[2] C. Nobes and R. Parker (eds.), *Comparative International Accounting*, (Prentice-Hall, 1991).

–Providers of capital–

In some countries, such as France and Italy, the government and banks are the primary providers of capital for business firms. There are therefore few investors and they usually are close to the firm so that they receive sufficient information. In other countries, such as the UK and the U.S., providers of capital are varied and include many investors. Because of this, there is concern for the individual investor that he/she receive "fair" disclosure of information.

–Tax laws–

For countries that follow the Roman legal system, tax laws have a substantial impact on accounting principles. For countries that adhere to the common-law system, usually tax laws have little influence on accounting principles.

–Accounting profession–

Where the accounting profession is strong, such as in the U.S., the private sector wields considerable influence on the setting of accounting standards. In countries where the accounting profession is weak, the government plays a decisive role in establishing accounting principles.

ETHICAL ISSUES

Ethical behavior by business firms has always been an issue, but especially so in the past 20 years. Questions about pollution, unsafe working conditions, deceptive advertising, unsafe products, and misleading financial information are but a few of the problems that have generated controversy. In our capitalistic economy, business firms are the primary means by which production and distribution of the goods and services desired by those in society are provided. Society expects firms to accept moral responsibility. Since firms are not human, but artificial persons, obviously then it is the people who make decisions for companies that society expects to act in a responsible manner.

• Meaning of Ethics •

The context of ethics in business is the relations between the firm and different groups of people. First of all, there are ethical questions concerning the firm and society. Second, there are ethical questions pertaining to the firm and various "stakeholders," such as owners of the firm, creditors, employees, and customers. These relations are illustrated in **Figure 1.8**.

There is a variety of meaning on what constitutes ethical behavior, because ethics have to do with accepted norms and values. However, most would agree that the following behaviors are unethical: cheating, lying, stealing, deceiving. And most would agree that the following words connote ethical conduct: fairness, justice, honesty, integrity.

Ethics pertain to making decisions about what is right or wrong, good or bad, that have a moral dimension. Whenever we make a value judgment, we need standards that tell us what is good or bad. Ethical standards are somewhat subjective because they relate to the norms and values in which people believe. No comprehensive theory exists to rationalize ethical behavior. Yet, people do have expectations about ethical conduct.

Figure 1.8

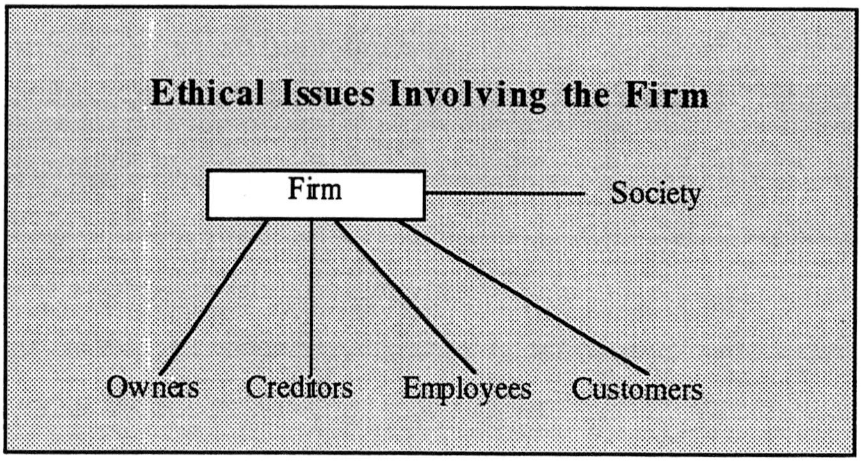

Ethical Issues Involving the Firm

Firm — Society

Owners Creditors Employees Customers

• Ethical Standards •

–Old standards–

The following ethical standards have been advanced in the past.

1. What is _legal_ is ethical, and what is _illegal_ is unethical.

Critics of this standard agree that laws should provide the boundaries within which firms should operate, but they contend that there are many situations where the law has nothing to say but an ethical decision must be made. For example, the manager of a corporation with many stockholders decides to buy merchandise from a firm owned by his brother at a price higher than normal. No law is broken, but is it ethical?

2. What is best for the company and its owners in terms of _making a profit_ is ethical, and what is detrimental to the company is unethical. Managers of companies are "agents" of the stockholders, and they should act in the best interest of the stockholders and the company.

Critics charge that doing what is profitable for a company is certainly the job of managers, but such a standard may involve unethical actions. For example, a firm may be polluting a river to dispose of its waste to save on costs, but is it ethical? Or a company may resort to deceptive means to sell its product to make a profit, but is it ethical? Therefore, doing what is profitable for a company cannot alone be an ethical standard.

For a business firm which is in business to make a profit, what incentive is there to abide by ethical standards? The benefit to firms is the preservation of the free market economy. Participants in the economic system should abide by the "rules of the game," otherwise, the system will become corrupt and may collapse. An analogy would be playing football. Participants are expected to follow certain rules of the game. If they resort to "playing dirty," in time these practices will undermine the whole game. People expect players to do their best to win, but within the rules. Likewise, society expects firms to do their best to make a profit, but within the law and within the framework of accepted ethical standards.

–What society expects–

Although imprecise, the following standards appear to be what society expects firms to follow:

1. Consideration of *social costs and benefits*. The effect on society of a decision must be considered. An action that will produce the greatest net benefits to society is desirable. This standard relates to a firm's relationship with society (see **Figure 1.4**). Examples of social benefits are: conservation of natural resources and energy, recycling of waste materials, employment of handicapped people. Examples of social costs are: air and water pollution, unsafe products.

2. *Rights* and *fair treatment* of individuals. When an action will affect specific individuals, and has little to do with society in general, then the rights of those individuals should be considered. This standard relates to a firm's relationships with its stakeholders, namely, the stockholders, creditors, employees, and customers. Under this standard, it is obvious that behaviors such as lying, cheating, and deceiving are unethical.

An example of a right is that of stockholders who have a right to expect managers to work toward the best interest of the company. There are many questions concerning rights and fair treatment that have no easy answers. Good judgment must be used. For example, if for personal reasons, the president of a company promotes a particular employee, and there are other employees who are more qualified and deserving, is this fair? Doesn't the president have the right to promote whomever he pleases?

–Example case–

Before Apple went public in 1980, the distribution of stock, referred to as "founder's shares," was erratic, based on the whims of Steve Jobs. People who had played a big role in helping the company get on its feet were not able to buy any shares, because they were told by Steve that they were "outsiders." Yet there were in fact some outsiders who bought shares, such as Fayez Sarofim, an Egyptian investor who was a friend of one of the members of the board of directors, Harry Singleton who was chairman of United Technologies, and Ann Bowers, the wife of the vice-chairman of Intel. Some employees received stock options and some did not, depending on how Steve felt about them. Steve was the head of the Compensation Committee that gave the stock options. He denied options to some of his colleagues who had helped him get the company started. In some instances, managers did not receive stock options but employees under them did.[3]

Was it ethical for Steve to sell shares to some but not to others? Was it ethical for Steve to give stock options to some employees but not to others, depending on his personal likes and dislikes? Some say that although he had the legal right to do so, he was not fair to certain outsiders and employees.

• Practical Considerations •

Based on the standards mentioned previously, in business practice, it is desirable to have *"arm's length" transactions* in order to avoid questions of unethical conduct. Such a transaction is one where the parties are looking to their own self interests and decide what is best for themselves. A transaction with a related party, such as buying goods from a firm owned by your brother, creates questions concerning partiality and fairness. An accounting principle for financial statements is that all transactions with related parties must be disclosed.

One should avoid situations where there is a "conflict of interests." One reason for the necessity of auditors is the existence of a possible conflict of interests between the firm and investors. A firm may not want to disclose certain kinds of information or may want to provide misleading information. Managers may wish to do what is best for themselves personally than what is best for the company or stockholders.

• Accounting Ethical Issues •

Accountants cannot help but be involved in ethical considerations of business firms. The report rendered by CPAs in their audit of corporations state that the financial statements "present fairly" the financial position and the results of operations of the firm. An ethical judgment must be made. In fact, accountability is a means by which people are given incentive to keep within ethical bounds. When people know that they must give an accounting of their actions, they are more likely to do what is proper. CPAs subscribe to a code of conduct which mentions an "unswerving commitment to honorable behavior, even at the sacrifice of personal advantage."[4]

The accounting profession has received much criticism in recent years. There are several reasons

---

[3] Jeffrey S. Young, pp. 194-5.

[4] AICPA, *Code of Professional Conduct*, Preamble, ET Section 51.

for this. One is the financial scandals, such as the savings and loan debacle, that have received a great deal of publicity. In some cases, the financial statements of the companies involved were approved by CPAs, which showed the companies to be in good financial condition but further investigation revealed that some of them were actually financially distressed. Another reason is what is termed the "expectations gap." People expect too much from accountants and auditors, because they are not aware of the limitations of accounting and auditing. A third reason is that GAAP may be deficient in some areas so that uninformed investors may be misled by accounting information.

–Motives of management–

Unfortunately, accounting procedures can be manipulated to obtain certain results. The problem is due to the variety of accounting choices that managers have. Because of the diversity in business, accounting for a particular event by one prescribed way may not be the best solution for all firms. In the 1930s, the accounting profession embraced the philosophy that business firms should be given the choice of selecting procedures that are best for them within the framework of broad accepted principles. Although over the years the FASB has reduced the number of choices, it is still true that companies have opportunity to decide among procedures.

Most companies would like to record as few liabilities as possible, and to report an amount of earnings that they feel is proper. To some extent, companies can use accounting methods to achieve their objective. Companies believe that they have the right to "manage" their earnings by employing certain accounting methods. If management believes that earnings for the current year will be smaller than desired, they can use certain accounting methods so that the final reported earnings will be larger than it would have been otherwise. Similarly, if earnings will be much larger than expected, management may wish to use specific accounting methods to reduce the amount. They may wish to do this for fear of criticism about "excess profits" or that labor unions will clamor for higher wages.

Although the procedures selected fall within the purview of GAAP, the question is whether it is ethical to manage earnings. There is no easy answer to the question. Financial analysts accept the practice and see their task as one of determining what the "true" earnings should be by making their own adjustments.

–Auditor independence–

By law, companies under the jurisdiction of the SEC must have their financial statements certified by an independent auditor, which is the CPA. The CPA is to conduct an audit to ensure that the accounting procedures used by a company conform with GAAP. The audit must be in accordance with generally accepted auditing standards. The question is how independent is the CPA? The fee for the audit is paid by the company to the CPA. Auditing is a very competitive profession so that retaining clients is important to a CPA firm.

There are two situations that people have misgivings about. The first is one where the client is using an accounting procedure that is questionable. Some believe that the CPA may not insist on a change for fear of offending and losing the client. The second is one where the CPA furnishes advisory services to the client. Some believe that the CPA cannot impartially audit the accounting system for which the CPA has provided counsel.

The CPA profession argues that despite the appearance of lack of independence, it is able to act with integrity and objectivity in performing an audit. However, the Securities and Exchange Commission, the governmental body which oversees the area of corporate financial reporting, is concerned that auditors may be compromising their work. It recently established a new regulatory board to set standards for auditor independence.

SUMMARY OF KEY POINTS

The following key points were discussed in this chapter:

1. Risk assessment. For a company, just to be in business involves many risks. Stockholders and creditors want to know what specific risks a company faces and what strategies the company has to cope with them. The role of accounting is to provide as much information on this as possible.

2. What accounting is. Accounting is a system in an entity that is concerned with providing financial information to certain users. Users within the entity want the information to assist them in making decisions that will help the entity attain its goal. External users want the information to help them make decisions that will affect their relationship with the entity. All users need accounting information to assess risk.

3. Difference between financial and managerial accounting in a business firm. When the accounting system is geared to providing information to external users, such as stockholders and creditors, then this is called "financial accounting." When the accounting system is aimed at providing information to management, then it is referred to as "managerial accounting." This book will focus on financial accounting.

4. Users of accounting information. The two primary external users of accounting information are stockholders and creditors, both present and potential. Other users are employees, customers, and financial analysts.

5. Uses of accounting information. At the level of the individual firm, users want to make predictions about the firm. Stockholders want to predict the flow of dividends to themselves and the price of the stock. The price of the stock is affected by the profitability of the company. Creditors want to predict whether the firm will have enough cash to pay them. Both stockholders and creditors are taking a risk in their involvement with the firm. They need accounting information to continually assess the risk. The kind of information that both stockholders and creditors need is referred to as profitability and financial position.

At the level of the whole economy, accounting information helps to allocate resources efficiently. Efficient allocation depends on relevant and reliable information given to investors.

6. Generally accepted accounting principles. Accountants depend on GAAP to decide how accounting should be done. Three sources of authority for GAAP can be identified: accounting theory, authoritative bodies, and conventions. The authoritative bodies that are very important are: the SEC, the FASB, the GASB, and the AICPA.

7. Standard setting. Although the SEC has the legal authority to establish accounting standards, it has permitted the FASB to do this. Because accounting standards affect companies, the standard setting process has become political.

8. Need for international standards. Although needed, establishing international standards is difficult, because of nationalism and cultural differences.

9. Ethical issues. Manipulation of accounting methods is possible. Some companies believe in "managed" earnings. The CPA audits a company to ascertain that its financial statements conform with GAAP, but some question whether the CPA is truly independent. CPAs believe they are.

QUESTIONS

1. What is accounting?

2. In a business firm,

a. Indicate the risk each of the following areas faces, and how accounting can be of help in the assessment of the risk:

Production

Marketing

Finance

Human Resources

Computer Information Systems

b. What is the difference between financial accounting and managerial accounting?

c. What does an internal auditor do?

3. For a business firm,

a. Who are the users of accounting information?

b. What kind of information do stockholders want?

c. What kind of information do creditors want?

d. What does a CPA do for a firm that is of importance to users?

4. Give an example of the following types of risk:

a. Economic risk.

b. Market risk.

c. Interest rate risk.

d. Industry risk.

e. Company risk.

f. Credit risk.

5. For the economy as a whole,

a. Describe the "market" in a capitalistic economy.

b. What is one result of an economy that is not efficient?

c. What role does accounting information play in the business firm?

d. What role does accounting information play in the economy?

6. Concerning generally accepted accounting principles,

a. What are they?

b. How are they determined?

7. Regarding authoritative bodies,

a. What is the role of the SEC with respect to accounting information?

b. What is the task of the FASB?

c. What is the relationship between the SEC and the FASB?

d. Where does the FASB receive its authority?

e. Explain why the AICPA has influence in the accounting profession.

8. Explain how accounting theory and conventions play a role in accounting.

9. What is conservatism in accounting?

10. What information must a company submit to the SEC on Form 10-K? How does it compare with the information on a company's financial statements?

11. Concerning standard setting,

a. Why is standard setting a political process?

b. What factors must be considered besides accounting theory?

12. Regarding international standards,

a. Why is there a need for harmonization of accounting standards?

b. What questions does the FASB have concerning harmonization?

c. What are the obstacles to harmonization of standards?

13. Concerning ethical issues,

a. Why is obeying the law insufficient as an ethical standard?

b. Why is pursuing what is profitable an insufficient ethical standard?

c. What standards does society expect a firm to consider?

d. Why has accounting received a great deal of criticism?

e. What does it mean to "manage" earnings? Why is it an issue?

f. Explain what the problem is regarding auditor independence.

14. With respect to Apple Computer Company mentioned in this chapter,

a. In 1976, how did it get started?

b. In 1977, to expand into a larger market, what three individuals acted as "capitalists" for the new company? What did each contribute?

c. In 1980, when the company went public, investors had a favorable view of Apple and purchased all the shares offered. What were the general factors for this favorable view? What were the company-specific factors?

d. Before the company went public in 1980, what is your opinion of the way Steve Jobs distributed stock options to employees?

15. State whether the following statements are true or false. If false, explain.

a. Accounting is able to supply important information to other departments in a business firm.

b. One of the important users of accounting information is stockholders.

c. Nonprofit organizations use the same kind of accounting as business firms.

d. Creditors are especially interested in the price of a company's stock.

e. Stockholders have no interest in the financial position of a company.

f. A capitalistic economy can best be described as one that is regulated by governmental controls.

g. One effect of an inefficient economy is high prices for consumers.

h. Accounting can help a business firm keep track of its costs.

I. Conventions are a source of authority for GAAP.

j. The SEC does not have the legal authority to establish accounting standards for corporations.

k. The FASB follows a "due process" approach in setting accounting standards.

l. The legal system in the U.S. can be described as a "Roman" legal system.

m. The philosophy in the U.S. is that financial statements be "fair."

n. Nationalism is a formidable obstacle to the harmonization of accounting standards in the world.

o. There are hardly any ethical issues in accounting, because companies have no choice but to follow the same accounting methods.

p. The purpose of an audit by a CPA is to ensure that a company has followed the rules set by the CPA for the company.

CASES

Case 1-1

One of your friends is thinking about investing in the common stock of a large corporation, but admits that he knows very little about the stock market. He has been keeping track of the stock price of the company he is interested in and noticed that sometimes the price goes up and sometimes it goes down.

Tell him, as best you can, what you know about this. Include in your answer something about the risks companies take and how this affects the price of their stock.

Case 1-2

Your friend, Jane Lee, mentions to you that she has heard that a number of former communist countries are now interested in a free market economy. She is not sure what that means.

a. Explain to Jane how a capitalistic market economy works.
b. Explain to her why the economy must be efficient.
c. Explain to her the role of accounting information, especially in the capital market.

Case 1-3

Bill White owns a clothing store. Recently, he went to a bank to negotiate a large loan. He brought with him the financial statements of the store, which he had prepared himself, but the bank insisted that he provide financial statements that are in accordance with GAAP. He is confused about GAAP and asks you the following questions:

a. What is GAAP?
b. How do they arise?
c. Why are they necessary?

Case 1-4

ABC Company owns 30 large delivery trucks. Maintenance of the trucks is done monthly, but in December, the trucks are checked thoroughly for any needed repairs and replacements of parts. Usually, the cost of the repairs is about $9,000.

Up till December, earnings for the year, Year 10, had been very low and no improvement could be seen. The president of ABC Company was very concerned, because he was afraid that if earnings were too small the $40,000 loan which he hoped to negotiate with the local bank would be denied. In December, he asked Jim Potter, the company's CPA, what should be done.

Jim suggested that the repairs should be postponed until January of Year 11 so that the $9,000 expense would not further decrease earnings. The company did as Jim suggested. The trucks were not checked in December for repairs. The president was pleased with Jim's suggestion. As a token of appreciation he gave Jim a Christmas gift, a box of expensive wines. Jim was happy to receive it.

In late January, Year 11, when the loan was negotiated, the bank asked for financial statements that were certified, and so Jim did the audit and certified the statements.

Instructions: (The questions below ask for your opinion. There may be no exact right or wrong answers.)

a. Do you think postponement of the repairs until January was ethical? Explain.

b. Was it ethical for Jim to accept the Christmas gift, and to audit and certify the financial statements after giving advice to ABC on what to do? Explain.

Case 1-5

For many years, Jack Felton owned and operated a hardware store. He is now retiring, and a friend of yours, Don Wharton, is thinking of buying the store. Don would like to know whether the store has been successful, but he does not know what to look for. Over the years, Jack kept very informal accounting records and prepared no financial statements.

Instructions: As best you can, write a note to Don explaining to him what he should look for to get a better idea whether he should purchase the store.

Case 1-6

One of your acquaintances, Brian Young, was laid off 3 months ago by the large company he worked for, Compton Company. Brian is bitter, because he had worked for Compton for 20 years and thought he would work there until he retired. Although he is eligible to receive retirement benefits from the company's retirement plan, he feels that he is too young to retire. Brian is 52 years old. He is having a difficult time finding another job.

The reason that was given to Brian for the layoff was a need for "cost reduction." According to the income statements, which had been approved by a CPA, for the past 3 years Compton has sustained a loss. The loss for the past year was extremely large. The officers of the company decided that there are two ways for the company to again make a profit, cut costs and increase sales. Because of the competitiveness of the market, they feel that presently increasing sales is not realistic. Because labor costs are one of the largest costs for the company, the officers decided they had to cut costs by laying off 200 workers. Unfortunately for Brian, he was one the those laid off.

Brian tells you he believes the income statements were "manipulated" in order to justify the layoffs. The CPA denies the charge. Brian also feels that he was laid off because of his high salary, $65,000 a year. He said he wouldn't be surprised if the company later hired a new employee to do his job for half the salary.

Instructions:
1. Present a justification for the layoff that Compton instituted. Your answer should include comments about the capitalistic economy and a response to Brian's charges in relation to GAAP and the work of a CPA.
2. Present an argument on why Brian should not have been laid off. Your answer should include your opinion of a feasible alternative which the company could have taken.

Case 1-7

Consider the following three cases. You are asked to give your opinion in answering the questions.

1. Orville Sampson, who had majored in sociology, had a difficult time finding a job after he graduated from the state university. A friend of his, Brian Kaplan, who had majored in accounting found a job with a CPA firm and told him he was happy with what he was

doing. Orville decided to submit his resume to that CPA firm. To increase his chances of getting an offer, he stated in his resume that he had majored in accounting. Actually, he had only taken one course in accounting. Orville was hired. During the following year, while he was working, he took several accounting courses at night in order to understand accounting better.

According to his supervisor, Audrey Brown, Orville was doing quite well. She said he was a quick learner and knew how to work with clients. Just over a year after Orville was hired, Audrey happened to be talking to Brian Kaplan, who told Audrey how pleased he was that Orville was doing well, especially he said, "for someone who didn't major in accounting." Audrey was shocked. She looked up his personnel file and found his resume in which he stated that he had majored in accounting. She confronted Orville about it. Orville admitted that he had lied because he wanted the job so badly.

A few days later, Audrey asked Orville to see her. She told him that he was fired, because of the false information he had put in his resume. She said the integrety of the firm and its employees were important; the firm could no longer trust him.

Do you think Audrey over-reacted to Orville's untruth in his resume? Explain.

2. From 1970 to 1990, the Hayward Square Bank grew significantly. One reason for its growth was its heavy investment in the real estate market. In order to finance its growth, it had to increase the amount of deposits by depositors. One of its strategies was to offer higher interest rates than those found in the market.

The bank engaged the CPA firm of Pete Marway to be its auditor in 1989. Pete Marway had borrowed money from the bank numerous times in the past. In fact, one of the partners of the firm, Jim Blaney, had a $1,000,000 loan with the bank. Jim said he would feel more comfortable about accepting the bank as a client if the bank would sell the loan to another bank. The bank said it would do so. Actually, the bank did do it, but later repurchased it.

In 1990, the bank failed. The regulators accused Pete Marway of lack of independence in its audit, because one of its partners had a loan with the bank. The firm said the bank had repurchased the loan without its knowledge. The regulators said Pete Marway, being the auditor, should have checked.

Are the regulators correct that there was lack of independence by Pete Marway because of the loan? Was the firm "negligent" in not finding out that the bank had repurchased the loan? Explain.

3. Judy Mason, a senior auditor with the CPA firm, Jason Weston, in the audit of Wedcore Corporation discovered that the company had a large slush fund for its executives to use for "special" expenses. On further investigation, she found that the slush fund was actually used to pay bribes to government officials, especially in foreign countries, in order to obtain contracts. She confronted the executives of Wedcore about it. They told her the slush fund was for use by company officers for special expenses when traveling. No mention was made in the audit workpapers of the existence of the slush fund.

After the audit, Judy resigned from the CPA firm and accepted a high paying position with Wedcore Corporation.

Do you think Judy Mason acted properly in not mentioning the slush fund in her audit? Was it ethical for her to accept a position with Wedcore? Explain.

Case 1-8

The situations below pertain to the problem of proper conduct in business. There are disagreements on what is "proper." Your opinion is solicited. What do you think should be done in each of the following cases? Explain.

1. John Golden owns the Golden Petshop. On March 16, he withdrew $500 to buy a gift for his wife. He told the bookkeeper that it was not necessary to record the withdrawal because he intended to replace the money in a couple of days.

2. Clara Dunn works as a cashier for the Walton General Store. At the end of the day, on May 14, the tape on her cash register indicated that there should be $680.48 in the cash register. There was actually only $671.48. The accountant always got upset when there was a discrepancy, and so Clara decided to put in $9.00 of her own money into the cash register to avoid the fuss.

3. Laurie's Restaurant is a chain of 50 restaurants in California. Every month, financial statements from each of the restaurants are sent to the headquarters office in San Francisco. For the restaurant in Riverside for the month of February a loss was indicated. Bill Clayton, the manager of the restaurant, felt that revenues had been unusually low because it had rained a lot the first week of the month and February is a short month. He felt the loss was not indicative of the business and would give the officers in the San Francisco office the wrong impression. To correct this, he changed the date of the revenues received on March 1

to February 28. By doing this, a small profit was shown for February.

4. The Mayfield Company wants to borrow $250,000 from the National First Bank. The bank insisted that the company furnish it with the latest financial statements indicating the amount of profit from each of its 20 stores, which are scattered throughout the state. Wendy Max, president of Mayfield, was afraid that if the information got into the wrong hands, mainly its competitors, this would be detrimental to the company. She decided that to protect the company, the financial statements given to the bank should show that each store made about the same amount of profit. Actually, 5 of the stores made losses, but the total combined profit of the 20 stores in the statements given to the bank was correct

Case 1-9.

The *Wall Street Journal* had the following heading in one of its articles:[5]

One Messy Store

Chicanery at Phar-Mor Ran Deep
Massaging of Book Masked Losses

Phar-Mor is a discount dry-goods store in the midwest. The article points out that two sets of books were kept, an official one that was manipulated with false entries, and another that kept track of the false entries. The fraud and embezzlement scheme by its top executives caused more than $1 billion of losses for the company. All along, the company's financial statements did not show these losses and were certified by CPAs.

Investigation disclosed the following:

1. CocaCola Enterprises, Fuji Photo Film Co., among others, made payments to Phar-Mor in exchange for Phar-Mor's promise not to deal with rival brands.

2. Phar-Mor helped pay for the construction of a mansion for its president, Mickey Monus.

---

[5] *Wall Street Journal*, January 20, 1994.

3. Phar-Mor paid $16,990 to the father of the president, Nathan Monus, a member of the board of directors, for meals at the Palm Beach Country Club.

4. Phar-Mor purchased merchandise from Jewelry 90, which purchased its goods from a wholesaler in New York. The wholesale firm was owned by a friend of Mickey Monus. Nathan Monus was a paid consultant to Jewelry 90 for 2 years, receiving $354,754 for 6 months in 1992. Investigation discloses that if Phar-Mor had bought its merchandise directly from the wholesaler instead of through Jewelry 90, it could have saved $2.1 million.

5. Phar-Mor sold its investment in Strouss Building Associates, a company owned by Mickey Monus, to a newly found firm controlled by some of the directors of Phar-Mor. If the investment had been kept, Phar-Mor would have made a substantial return.

6. Phar-Mor executives used financial statements showing large profits to obtain more than $1 billion in credit and capital from investors. Actually, Phar-Mor had a $238 million loss in 1992 alone.

7. Phar-Mor paid $80,000 to cover a delinquent account of the now defunct World Basketball League, which was founded by Mickey Monus.

8. Phar-Mor sold sports clothes from the World Basketball League.

9. Phar-Mor put pressure on its suppliers to financially sponsor the World Basketball League.

10. Some of the directors and executives received "stock options," which allowed them to purchase Phar-Mor stock for a reasonable price by a specified date. They were permitted to exercise their options after the expiration date. They did not pay cash which is normal, but gave their promissory notes. At a later date, before the promissory notes were due, they sold their themselves.

Instructions: For each of the foregoing accusations, state whether you believe any unethical conduct was involved. Explain.

(based on article in *Wall Street Journal,* January 20, 1994)

Case 1-10

Dan Kottke worked as a technician for Apple Computer Company in 1980. He was the primary builder of the Apple III prototype circuit board. He was a long-time friend of Steve Jobs, one of the co-founders of Apple. Dan and Steve had gone together once on a trip to India. A couple of times Dan asked Steve about getting some stock options. Steve told him that he had nothing to do with them, and that he should see his supervisor, Rod Holt.

Dan found out that several times Rod had suggested to the Compensation Committee, which was in charge of the distribution of stock options, that Dan be given stock options. But Steve, who was head of the committee, always said no, because Dan was classified as a technician, not an engineer.

Dan went to Mike Scott, the president at that time, to tell him of his unhappiness. Mike granted Dan 2,000 shares.

Instructions: Do you think Steve acted ethically toward Dan? Explain.

(based on excerpt in book by Jeffrey Young on Steve Jobs)

Chapter 2

The Balance Sheet

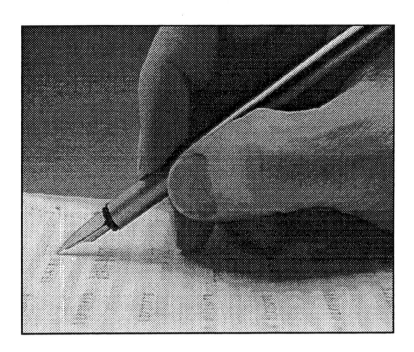

LEARNING OBJECTIVES

After studying this chapter, you should be able to:

• Describe the three basic forms of business organization.

• Describe the balance sheet.

• Define assets, liabilities, and owners' equity.

• Recognize whether assets, liabilities, and owners' equities exist in particular entities.

• Understand the accounting equation and how it relates to the balance sheet.

• Prepare a balance sheet.

• Appreciate the limitations of the balance sheet.

In 1994, the SEC filed a complaint against PNF Industries, Inc., a cellular communications firm operating in New Jersey, accusing the company of materially overstating the assets and stockholders' equity of the company. Because of the inflated values, what should have been a negative balance of $255,361 for stockholders' equity became a positive balance of $16,125,961.[6] To understand the charges, you must know something about the "balance sheet," which is the topic of this chapter.

In the previous chapter, we mentioned that the financial accounting system in a business enterprise is organized to provide information to external users, such as stockholders and creditors. The information is reported in the form of financial statements. There are three primary financial statements: the balance sheet, the income statement, and the statement of cash flows. In this chapter, we will discuss the balance sheet. In the next chapter, we will deal with the income statement. The statement of cash flows will be introduced in Chapter 4, but it is more comprehensible after the specific items on the balance sheet and income statement have been covered; therefore, we will postpone detailed discussion of it until Chapter 14.

Because the form of business organization has an effect on the financial statements, this will be discussed next.

FORMS OF ORGANIZATION

There are three major forms of organization a business entity can have:

(1) a sole proprietorship

(2) a partnership

(3) a corporation

• Proprietorship •

A sole proprietorship is a business with one owner, the proprietor. Starting a sole proprietorship is easy, involving only a few simple legal forms. Usually it will be for a small business enterprise. This form of business organization is very common; about 2/3 of all businesses in the U.S. are sole proprietorships.

A major advantage of this form of business is that the proprietor is his or her "own boss." All decisions are made by the proprietor, such as whom to hire, when to take off from work, how much inventory to purchase. All the profits of the business belong to the owner. For tax purposes, the proprietorship is not recognized as a separate entity and therefore the proprietor pays personal income taxes on the profits, even if they are left in the business.

---

[6] SEC, *Accounting and Auditing Enforcement Release No. 601*, 1994.

A major disadvantage of the sole proprietorship is that the proprietor bears all the risks of the business personally. Therefore, all losses and liabilities are borne by the owner, which means that his or her personal assets are liable to creditors (called "unlimited liability"). Another disadvantage is that raising capital is difficult, because it depends on the owner's ability to receive loans.

• Partnership •

A partnership is a business with more than one owner who are called partners. Usually this form of organization is appropriate for small and medium size businesses. The formation of a partnership does not need approval from the state; an agreement, verbal or written, between two or more people is sufficient. It is of interest to note that Apple Company started off as a partnership in 1976. Steve Jobs and Steve Wozniak signed a 10-page contract to form the partnership. Jobs' friend, Ron Wayne, who was an engineer at Atari, was also a partner, receiving 10 percent ownership. The other two received 45 percent each. Ron later dropped out of the partnership.

A partnership is recognized by law as a separate entity for limited purposes only, such as the name of the business and ownership of property. Because of its limited status as a separate entity, for tax purposes, profits of the business are considered income to the individual partners who must pay income taxes on their share of the partnership profit, whether distributed to them or not.

In most states, the Uniform Partnership Act has been adopted, which specifies the functions and legal requirements for a partnership. A partnership can be either _general_ or _limited_. A general partnership is one that has several partners, each of whom can act on behalf of the firm and is personally liable for the debts of the firm. A limited partnership has at least one general partner and one or more limited partners. The limited partner invests a certain amount into the firm but does not participate in the running of the business. The limited partner is personally liable for the debts of the firm only for a specified amount, usually the amount contributed into the firm.

As you can see, one of the disadvantages of a partnership is that of _unlimited liability_ for a general partner. This means that each general partner is liable for all the obligations of the firm, and this liability can go beyond the amount that is invested in the business and extend to his or her personal assets. Also, the actions of every general partner can bind the firm, even when a partner is acting wrongfully or without authority. However, if the other party knows that a certain partner does not have the authority to act for the firm, then the partnership is not bound. If a partnership is to operate well, partners must have mutual trust in each other. It is desirable to spell out in a written contract what authority and function each partner has and how profits are to be divided.

Recently, a new type of partnership has been approved by the states. This is the limited liability partnership. As stated above, one of the disadvantages of the partnership is that for general partners there is unlimited liability, which means that creditors have access to the personal assets of general partners. For a limited liability partnership, the personal assets would be shielded, but only if the firm went into bankruptcy. However, for a partner who is directly involved in some wrongdoing there is still unlimited liability for him or her.

• Corporation •

A corporation is a business that by law is considered a separate entity. Its existence depends on state law; a group of incorporators (one to three, depending on the state) must obtain a charter from the state. In 1977, wanting to expand their market beyond the hobbyist market, Apple Computer Company became a corporation under the laws of California. Steve Jobs, Steve Wozniak, Mike Markkula, who provided the much needed cash, and Rod Holt, a former Atari engineer who designed the power supply for the Apple II, signed the papers to formally turn the partnership into a corporation.[7]

Because state incorporation laws differ, it is not uncommon for incorporators to look for a state that has few restrictions. Historically, Delaware has had the least restrictive requirements. It is possible to incorporate in one state and operate in others. The corporation is almost like a person; it has the same legal rights as people except voting and marriage. The corporation sells shares of stock and whoever owns the shares is an owner. This form of organization can be used for any size business, but usually large enterprises are corporations. The shareholders elect a board of directors who have the legal responsibility to manage the business. Ordinarily, the board will employ officers who actually run the business.

A major advantage of the corporate form is _limited liability_. The owners of the business, the shareholders, are only liable for the amount invested in the corporation. Another advantage is that a corporation has more _alternatives to raise capital_; it can sell both stocks and bonds. Because the corporation is considered a separate legal entity, it must _pay income taxes_. Stockholders pay taxes only on the dividends they receive from the corporation. Whether this is an advantage or disadvantage depends on the personal situation of a stockholder. The corporation must pay corporate income taxes on its earnings; if those earnings are distributed to stockholders, the stockholders must pay personal income taxes on the same earnings. Because of this "double taxation," in 1982 Congress enacted legislation to permit a small business to be a corporation and yet avoid paying corporate income taxes. Such a corporation is called an "S corporation." A number of restrictions exist for qualification, but the most important is that the S corporation must have no more than 35 stockholders.

A disadvantage of the corporate form is that creating a corporation must conform to specific statutory requirements. The costs of formal incorporation can be large. Also, throughout the life of the corporation, there are many governmental requirements to satisfy.

---

[7] Jeffrey Young, p. 129.

Because corporations play a critical role in the economy, we will discuss them further in Chapter 13.

• Comparison •

A person who is thinking about starting a business, and wondering what the appropriate form of organization the business should take, needs to appraise the major points of the three basic forms. The following points should be considered: the way the business is created, limited or unlimited liability, management of the business, and the tax effect.

COMPONENTS OF THE BALANCE SHEET

Operating a business is a very dynamic process. Something is constantly going on; something is always happening. In one day, a thousand events may occur that affect a particular firm. For example, if we consider a department store on a particular day at a given hour, a few of the many events that may transpire are the following: shoppers are buying goods, a few are returning goods purchased previously, customers are calling in to inquire about certain products, merchandise is being delivered by delivery truck, goods are received in the shipping department, and orders are being placed by the purchasing agents. If somehow we could take a snapshot of the whole business operation on a specific day at a given time, what would we find in our picture?

• Determined By Theory •

The balance sheet is like a snapshot that shows operations at a moment in time. You must remember that the photographer is an accountant. For our department store, out of the many events that occur involving many items, the accountant imposes his/her "categories" on them based on accounting theory to derive a certain order. Only particular events and items are selected. What shows up in this picture is only what accounting theory prescribes. Everything else has been rubbed out.

In accounting terminology, this snapshot of operations of a given moment in time, which is named the ___balance sheet___, consists of a list of three different categories called assets, liabilities, and owners' equity.

Components of the Balance Sheet
Assets
Liabilities
Owners' equity

On the balance sheet, the components are put in the form of an equation, as illustrated in **Figure 2.1.** The equation will be discussed later in the chapter.

Figure 2.1

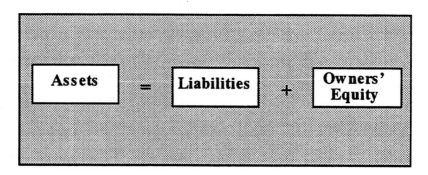

–Example of Apple Balance Sheet–

Notice that the 1997 balance sheet of Apple Company in **Figure 2.2** shows Assets, which total $4,233 million, and Liabilities plus Shareholders' Equity, which also total $4,233 million. The balance sheet is "consolidated," because it also includes the subsidiaries of Apple. Subsidiaries are companies that Apple controls due to its ownership of the majority of the voting shares of those companies. Because Apple is a corporation, the term Shareholders' Equity (or Stockholders' Equity) is used rather than Owners' Equity. Later in the chapter, we will discuss further Apple's balance sheet.

• Assets •

Accounting theory assumes that a business firm cannot operate to earn a profit unless it has assets. It is the assets that help to generate the profit. What are assets? They are economic objects that possess three important characteristics which are discussed next.

–Three characteristics–

__First__, assets are economic objects which have the capability of providing future benefits.[8] For our business firm, the future benefits ultimately relate to the creation of profit for the firm. For example, cash is an asset because we can use it to buy many things. In this sense, it has future benefits. Anything in the future is in the area of "uncertainty," because it has not yet happened.

---

[8] FASB, "Elements of Financial Statements," *Statement of Financial Accounting Concepts No. 6*, paragraph 25, 1985.

Figure 2.2

Apple Computer Inc.
Consolidated Balance Sheets
(Dollars in millions)
September 26, 1997

Assets:
Current assets:

Cash and cash equivalents		$1,230
Short-term investments		229
Accounts receivable, net of allowance for doubtful accounts of $99($91 in 1996)		1,035
Inventories:		
Purchased parts	141	
Work in process	15	
Finished goods	281	437
Deferred tax assets		259
Other current assets		234
Total current assets		3,424
Property, plant, and equipment:		
Land and buildings		453
Machinery and equipment		460
Office furniture and equipment		110
Leasehold improvements		172
		1,195
Accumulated depreciation and amortization		(709)
Net property, plant, and equipment		486
Other assets		323
Total assets		$4,233

Liabilities and Shareholders' Equity:
Current liabilities:

Notes payable to banks	$ 25
Accounts payable	685
Accrued compensation and employee benefits	99
Accrued marketing and distribution	278
Accrued warranty and related	128
Accrued restructuring costs	180
Other current liabilities	423
Total current liabilities	1,818
Long-term debt	951
Deferred tax liabilities	264
Shareholders' equity:	
Series A non-voting convertible preferred stock, no par value; 150,000 shares authorized, issued and outstanding	150
Common stock, no par value; 320,000,000 shares authorized;127,949,220 shares issued and outstanding	498
Retained earnings	589
Other	(37)
Total shareholders' equity	1,200
Total liabilities and shareholders' equity	$4,233

Therefore, for the present, something is an asset if we believe it has the ability to produce future benefits, that is, we expect that it will provide future benefits.

Second, the entity we are concerned with must have "control" over these benefits. There are many assets in the world, but we are only interested in the ones that pertain to our particular entity.

General Motors has a large plant in the Detroit area which is very valuable, but the ABC Shoe Store should not list it as its asset.

Third, the asset must result from a past event that the entity was involved with. If the entity sold merchandise and received $100 cash, the $100 came from a past transaction and therefore it can be listed as an asset. But if I expect to sell merchandise to a customer next month and receive $100, it is not an asset yet because the transaction has not occurred.

To summarize, an asset:
- is an economic object that is expected to provide *future benefits*
- is under the *control* of the entity
- and is the result of a *past event*

The key elements of the characteristics are illustrated in **Figure 2.3**.

Figure 2.3

Asset
1. Future benefits
2. Control
3. Past event

–Illustrations of assets–

Let us apply our definition containing the three characteristics to several situations involving ABC Company to determine what are assets. Notice that an asset arises from a past event, usually a transaction. A transaction is an exchange where something is received and something is given. In the examples below, for every transaction, we would like to know if ABC *received* an asset.

1. ABC Company sold $300 of merchandise to John Young on credit. Did ABC receive an asset?

Although ABC did not receive cash, it did receive John Young's promise to pay. This promise to pay from a customer is usually called "account receivable." This means that we expect to receive cash, which in this case is $300. The account receivable is an asset because it meets the definition of an asset. First, the account receivable is expected to provide a "future benefit," the cash. Cash itself is an asset because we can buy things with it. Second, ABC has "control" over the account receivable and the expected cash. John Young promises to pay ABC, not some other company. Third, the account receivable arose from a "past event," the sale to John Young.

2. On May 1, ABC purchased a used truck from the Acme Trucking Company. ABC gave a down payment of $400 to Acme and signed an agreement to pay $500 every month for the next 3 years. ABC took the truck that day and will be using it in its business. Because ABC did not fully pay for the truck, Acme retained the ownership papers. At the end of the 3rd year, the ownership papers will be transferred to ABC. Is the truck which ABC received on May 1 an asset?

The truck is an asset for ABC on May 1. Why? Because it meets the definition of an asset. First, the truck will provide future benefits. The truck will be providing "trucking services" for the company. Second, although ABC does not have the legal title to the truck, it does have the right to use it now. ABC therefore has "control" over the use, the services, of the truck. The definition of an asset does not say that the entity must possess the ownership papers, but that it has "control" over the benefits. Third, the truck was the result of a "past event," the purchase of it from Acme on May 1.

3. On June 15, ABC Company went to one of its suppliers across town and purchased on credit $600 of merchandise and brought it back to its store. ABC will pay the supplier in 30 days. ABC expects to sell the merchandise to its customers for a higher price. Is the merchandise received by ABC on June 15 an asset?

The merchandise is an asset for ABC on June 15, usually referred to as "merchandise inventory," because it meets the definition of an asset. First, it has "future benefit," because it is expected to be sold to customers for a higher price. Second, ABC has "control" over the merchandise even though it has not yet paid for it. Although the merchandise is not yet paid for, ABC has the right to use it now. Third, the merchandise is the result of a "past event," which is the purchase on June 15.

–Illustrations of events that do not produce assets–

In learning to determine whether an asset has arisen, we need to also learn when they do not.

1. On June 1, ABC Company decides that new equipment should be purchased on July 15. The cost of the equipment is expected to be $4,000.

Although equipment is an asset because it has future benefits, it is not an asset on June 1 for ABC because it has not yet been purchased. The third condition, "result of a past event," is not met. When ABC actually buys the equipment, then it will be an asset for the company.

2. ABC Company has one of its buildings up for sale. It received an offer of $300,000 to purchase the building.

The building is presently an asset for ABC, but not the cash it expects to receive. The third condition, "result of a past event," which, in this case, is the sale of the building, has not yet occurred. The past event should be a transaction, an exchange. ABC received an offer, but it gave nothing for it;

therefore, there is no exchange. ABC cannot consider the offer to be anything that is recordable at this time.

3. ABC ordered $10,000 of merchandise from Lowell Company. It has not yet received the merchandise.

The ordered merchandise is not an asset of ABC. The purchase of the merchandise has not yet taken place, because the relevant "past event," the passing of title, has not occurred. Based on accounting rules, title passes when the goods are "delivered" by the seller and thus "received" by the buyer. Ordering of merchandise does not constitute an exchange. Only when the seller has delivered the goods is there an exchange which will give rise to an asset for ABC, the merchandise.

These three illustrations point out how important the "past event" is in deciding whether a company has an asset.

• Liabilities •

Besides assets, the balance sheet also contains a list of liabilities. What are liabilities? Liabilities are obligations. They represent what an entity owes to some other entity. Liabilities are sometimes referred to as debts or obligations. Liabilities have three important characteristics which will be discussed next.

–Three characteristics–

First, a liability is a *__present obligation.__*[9] The obligation must exist now. An obligation denotes what is owed to another entity. In the example presented earlier of ABC Company purchasing on credit $600 of merchandise, ABC has an obligation to the supplier right now. If ABC expects to buy merchandise next month, then there is no present obligation and therefore no liability.

Second, the entity is required to settle the obligation by giving the other entity an asset or rendering a service at a future date. Usually, cash, which is an asset, will be paid. It may be that the creditor will agree to receive services rather than cash. For example, a law firm may purchase $300 of supplies from ABC Company and agree to render certain legal services to pay off the debt to ABC.

Third, the liability must result from a past event. The liability must arise from a transaction that has already happened, not one that is yet to occur. For example, ABC Company may expect to hire a new vice-president who will be earning a salary of $6,000 a month. ABC does not owe any salary to the vice-president because he hasn't started to work yet.

---

[9] Ibid. paragraph 35.

In summary, a liability:

- is a _present obligation_ of a particular entity to another entity, which requires the entity to settle the obligation at a future date by _conveying assets or rendering services_
- and is the result of a _past event_

The key elements of the characteristics are illustrated in **Figure 2.4.**

Figure 2.4

Liability

1. Present obligation
2. Must convey assets or render services to settle
3. Past event

–Illustrations of liabilities–

Let us apply our definition containing the three characteristics to certain situations encountered by ABC Company to determine if a liability exists. Remember that if a liability exists, this means the company presently _owes_ somebody something.

1. On June 1, ABC purchased on credit $200 of office supplies from National Office Supply Store, which is located a few blocks from the ABC Company. It agreed to pay National in 30 days. In this situation, ABC received an asset, office supplies. Is there a liability for ABC on June 1?

There is a liability for ABC on June 1, which is called "account payable," a promise to pay the creditor, National. The definition of a liability is met. First, on that date, ABC has an obligation to National. It owes National $200 for the office supplies. Second, ABC agrees to pay cash, which is an asset, at a future date. Third, the obligation is the result of a past event, the purchase of the supplies.

2. ABC Company pays some of its employees on a weekly basis, on Fridays. December 31 was on Wednesday and so these employees did not get paid that day. ABC has received the services of its employees for 3 days, but has not paid them yet because payday is on Friday. Is there a liability on December 31 for ABC?

There is a liability on December 31, which is called "wages payable." The definition of a liability is met. First, ABC has an "obligation" to these employees on December 31 to pay them for 3 days of wages. It is due to convenience for ABC that the employees are paid weekly rather than daily. Second, ABC expects to pay the employees in cash, which is an asset. Third, the obligation is the result of a past event, the 3 days of services rendered by the employees.

3. On January 5, ABC borrowed $6,000 from the Continental Bank and signed a 6-month, 8 percent note. The terms are that on July 5, ABC will pay the principal of $6,000 plus 6 months of interest, which is $240 (=$6000 x 8% x 6/12). Does ABC have a liability on January 5?

There is a liability on January 5 for ABC for the amount borrowed of $6,000, which is called "note payable." On January 5, ABC received $6,000 cash from the bank. Obviously, it now owes the bank that amount. The interest of $240 will be discussed later. The note payable is a liability because it meets the definition of a liability. First, on January 5, after receiving the money, ABC has a present obligation to pay Continental Bank. Second, ABC intends to pay the bank in cash, which is an asset. Third, the obligation is the result of a past event, the borrowing from the bank.

What about the $240 interest? Should ABC also record a liability for it? On January 5, there is no liability at the *present* time for the interest. Interest is owed because of the *use* of the money borrowed. ABC just received the money on January 5; therefore, there is no obligation. However, each day thereafter ABC owes one day of interest, which is called "interest payable."

–Illustrations of events that do not produce a liability–

In deciding whether a situation involves a liability, we need to also examine cases where there is no liability.

1. A customer fell down the escalator in the ABC Store. His attorney has contacted ABC, informing the company that the customer intends to file a lawsuit for $500,000.

At this time, there is no liability because the relevant past event has not occurred, which is the point when the company believes that it is probable that it must pay $500,000. The company is required to pay only if it loses the case in court. For lawsuits, the accounting profession has decided that a company should record a liability, even before the case is settled, at the time when it believes it will lose the case and must pay. Presently, no evidence exists to believe that there is a good chance the company will lose the case in court.

2. ABC has just signed an agreement with a contractor for the contractor to build a new building for $1,000,000. Does ABC owe $1,000,000?

At the signing of the contract, there is no liability. There is only an exchange of promises at this point. ABC promises to pay $1,000,000 for a building, and the contractor promises to build the building. According to accounting rules, the relevant event is when the contractor starts construction, which has not occurred. When the contractor starts to build, then the "past event" will have occurred, and ABC will then record a liability for the promised amount.

3. ABC sent an order to Maine Company to purchase on account 100 units of product A for $100 each.

When the order is sent, there is no liability, no accounts payable, at this point, because only an order has been sent. A purchase occurs when "title" to the goods passes from Maine to ABC. Title passes when Maine delivers the goods. In this case, Maine has just been sent the order. The "past event," which is the passing of title when delivery is made, has not occurred.

As with assets, the relevant "past event" is critical in deciding whether a company has a liability to record.

• Owners' Equity •

Besides assets and liabilities, the balance sheet also lists owners' equity. What is it? From the viewpoint of the owners, owners' equity represents their interest or their investment in the firm. From the standpoint of the firm, owners' equity represents the obligation of the firm to the owners. This obligation is referred to by different names, depending on the form of the business organization. Owners' equity has three important characteristics discussed next.

–Three characteristics–

First, owners' equity is a present obligation of an entity to owners.

Second, because the obligation is based on law or by agreement, the entity is required (1) to convey any earnings (positive or negative) to the owners, and (2) in case of liquidation, to give the owners the residual assets. Who are owners? They have the following rights, based on law or by agreement, that pertain to the entity's obligation to them: (a) Owners have the right to run the business or select those who will do so. Because of this right, the earnings of the entity belong to them. For a corporation, paying the earnings to stockholders in the form of dividends is not required by law; however, the unpaid earnings kept in the business remain the possession of the stockholders. (b) If a firm is liquidated, owners have a residual right to the assets. A firm is liquidated when it goes out of business and everything is sold. The cash is divided according to a priority distribution. By "residual," we mean that owners are the last in this priority distribution; they have what is leftover after other "prior" claimants (mainly creditors) get their amounts.

Third, owners' equity is the result of a past event.

In summary, owners' equity:

- is a *present obligation* of an entity to its *owners* which requires the entity to *convey earnings* to the owners, and in case of liquidation to convey the *residual assets* to the owners
- and is the result of a *past event*.

The key elements of the characteristics are illustrated in **Figure 2.5.**

Figure 2.5

> ## Owners' Equity
> 1. Present obligation to owners
> 2. Convey earnings, and in case of liquidation the residual assets
> 3. Past event

–Form of organization–

The way owners' equity is recorded depends on the form of organization, which we discussed earlier in this chapter.

__1. Sole proprietorship.__ Accounting for the owner's equity for a sole proprietorship is simple. If John Anderson is the owner of Anderson Shoe Store, then owner's equity for the store will be called "Anderson, Capital."

__2. Partnership.__ For a partnership, if Laura Lee and Gary Jones are the partners of Unlimited Clothing Store, then owners' equity will be represented by two accounts called "Lee, Capital" and "Jones, Capital."

__3. Corporation.__ For a corporation, as we saw in the case of Apple, owners' equity is also referred to as shareholders' equity or stockholders' equity, and consists of various parts. Two important parts are: capital stock and retained earnings.

Capital stock represents the stock that was issued by the corporation. Those who own shares of stock are legally the owners of the corporation. Every corporation must have common stock. Common stock holders bear the full risk of the company, and in this sense are the "true" owners of the company. Some companies also have "preferred stock." Preferred stock owners are given a "preference" over common stock holders for dividends received and/or assets received in case of liquidation of the company. The stock may be divided between the amount of "par value" and the amount in excess of par value. The par value is the minimum amount, by agreement with the state in which the corporation is established, which a share may be sold for initially.

As mentioned above, the earnings of a corporation belong to the stockholders; however, stockholders do not have personal access to the earnings unless the corporation chooses to pay dividends. Retained earnings represent the amount of accumulated earnings that have not been paid out as dividends. Typically, an analysis of the retained earnings will show the following (with assumed amounts):

Retained earnings, beginning balance	$40,000
Add net income for the period	+23,000
Less dividends	–10,000
= Retained earnings, ending balance	$53,000

–Illustrations of owners' equity–

Let us apply our definition of owners' equity to several cases so that we will have a better understanding of what it is.

1. On April 1, Carol Rodman decided to open a clothing store by investing $10,000 into the business. She will be the sole proprietor of the Rodman Shop. On April 1, does the Rodman Shop have owner's equity?

There is owner's equity for the Rodman Shop on April 1, which will be:

Rodman, Capital $10,000

There is owner's equity, because it meets the definition of owner's equity. First, the shop has an obligation to the owner. Carol Rodman is an owner because (1) she has the right to run the business, and (2) she has, by law, the residual right to the assets of the shop in case of liquidation. Second, the owner's equity is the result of a past event, the establishment of the business represented by the investment of $10,000 into the business by the owner.

2. Kevin Larson and Mary Mayer decided to join together to form an accounting firm, which will be called Larson and Mayer, Accountants. On April 15, by agreement, Larson invested $15,000 into the firm and Mayer invested $1,000. She is a well-known tax accountant and is expected to bring in many clients. On April 15, is there owners' equity for the accounting firm?

There is owners' equity on April 15 for the firm, which will have two accounts:

Larson, Capital $15,000
Mayer, Capital 1,000

The definition of owners' equity is met. First, the firm has an obligation to the partners. They are owners because they possess (1) the right to run the business and receive the earnings, and (2) the right to receive the residual amount, in case of liquidation. Second, the owners' equity is based on a past event, the establishment of the business.

3. On November 12, Nova Corporation sold $20,000 of common stock to a number of investors. How does this event affect stockholders' equity?

The sale of the stock affects stockholders' equity. It wil be listed as:

Common Stock $20,000

There is stockholders' equity because the definition is met. First, based on law the corporation has an obligation to the stockholders, who are the owners. The stockholders are owners because (1) they have the right to vote for the board of directors who oversee the company, and (2) in case of liquidation of Nova, they have a residual interest. Second, the common stock is the result of a past transaction, the sale of the stock.

–Illustrations of events that do not produce owners' equity–

Let us examine a couple of cases where owners' equity is not affected.

1. Mary Hunter and Jane Grandy are planning to open a cothing store, which they will call Mary Jane Clothes. They have consulted an attorney to compose an agreement for their partnership.

At this point, there is no owners' equity for the partnership. There may be an agreement which establishes the partnership, but until the firm receives assets, there is no owners' equity to record.

2. John Francis, president of Francis Company, a small corporation, approached William Bell to become an officer in the company on condition that he purchase 400 shares for a total of $40,000. Bell said he would think about it.

Until Bell purchases the shares, there is no owners' equity involved. The relevant past event for the company is the sale of the shares, which has not occurred yet. When the sale occurs, then the company will record the stock account.

As with assets and liabilities, the "past event" is important in deciding when owners' equity arises.

• Balance Sheet for Sole Proprietorship •

Now that we have discussed the three components of the balance sheet, assets, liabilities, and owners' equity, let us examine a simple balance sheet, one for a sole proprietorship, which is illustrated in **Figure 2.6.**

Notice the following:

1. The date. The balance sheet is for that one day only, that is, at the close of business on that one day. If you remember, we said that it is like a snapshot of a dynamic process. It shows the financial position of the firm as of a moment in time. Referring to the balance sheet for Apple in **Figure 2.2**, you will notice that the date, September 26, 1997 is given. Apple uses a "fiscal year," which is a year that ends other than on December 31. The balance sheet is true for that one day only, September 26, 1997. The numbers would be different the day before, September 25 or the day after, September 27.

2. The assets are listed first on the left side, and then the liabilities and owner's equity on the right side. We have used a "horizontal" display. In **Figure 2.7** we use a "vertical" display, where liabilities and owners' equity are listed below the assets. Apple uses a vertical display. Both forms are acceptable.

Figure 2.6

ABC Company Balance Sheet April 30, 1997			
Assets		**Liabilities**	
Current Assets:		Current Liabilities:	
Cash	$10,000	Accounts payable	$4,000
Accounts receivable	11,000	Notes payable	5,000
Merchandise Inventory	6,000	Wages payable	1,000
Total	$27,000	Total	$10,000
Property, Plant, equipment:		Long-term Liabilities:	
Equipment (net)	35,000	Long-term notes payable	7,000
		Total Liabilities	$17,000
		Owners' Equity:	
		Larson, Capital	$45,000
Total Assets	$62,000	Total Liabilities and owner's equity	$62,000

3. The assets and liabilities are divided into two parts: current and long-term (property, plant and equipment). Because of this, the balance sheet illustrated is often called a "classified" balance sheet. You will notice that Apple divides its assets and liabilities into current and long term. The current and long-term classifications will be discussed in the section to follow.

4. The owners' equity shows whether the company is a sole proprietorship (only one capital account), a partnership (more than one capital account), or a corporation (capital stock is listed).

5. Each side shows the same total balance.

–Current and long-term items–

Current assets are cash and assets that are expected to be used or will be received in cash *within a year* or "operating cycle" if longer. An operating cycle is the time it takes for a firm to go from cash to cash, that is, to purchase inventory, get it sold, and receive the cash from the sale. In **Figures 2.6 and 2.7**, the names of the accounts are the conventional ones employed in practice. Most of the names are self-explanatory. A few, such as prepaid expense, may take a little longer to figure out. As the name indicates, a prepaid expense is an expense that has been paid in advance. Because it is paid in advance, it is an asset. Typical prepaid expenses relate to insurance and rent. If an asset is not current, then it is long-term.

Current liabilities are those that are expected to be paid within an operating cycle or a year, whichever is longer. Most liabilities are current, unless otherwise stated. A few, such as Bonds Payable and Mortgage Payable, are assumed to be long-term unless currently due. In Chapter 11, you will learn of more long-term liabilities.

The order of listing within the current classification is a matter of convention. For current assets, it is done by the *liquidity* of the asset, that is, how close it is to becoming cash. That is why cash is always listed first.

In our example, we had only one long-term asset, equipment. The usual title of this section is: Property, plant and equipment. If an asset is not a current asset, then it is placed in the long-term category.

• Balance Sheet for Corporation •

A balance sheet for a corporation is illustrated in **Figure 2.7**, showing more accounts and classifications than the previous example. In the appendix to this chapter are four balance sheets of actual companies.

We have already discussed the "current" classification.

–Long-term assets–

Typically, as seen in **Figure 2.7**, the long-term assets are classified into four sub-categories:

1. Investments. Examples are securities of other entities expected to be held for over a year, land not currently employed but held for future use, and equipment not utilized in the business.

2. Property, plant and equipment. Examples are land, buildings, and equipment currently used in operations. If not used in operations, they should not be in this category, but in Investments or Other Assets. For buildings and equipment, accumulated depreciation is deducted and so they are stated at their "net" amounts. Land is never depreciated. These assets are sometimes referred to as "fixed" assets.

3. Intangible assets. These are long-term assets that are not "physical." Examples are patents, trademarks, and goodwill.

4. Other assets. This category is for all other long-term assets that do not fit into the other classifications. An example is a long-term receivable.

Figure 2.7

National Company			
Balance Sheet			
December 31, 1997			
Assets		**Liabilities and Stockholders' Equity**	
Current Assets:		Current Liabilities:	
Cash	$56,000	Accounts payable	$45,000
Short-term investment	34,000	Salaries payable	58,000
Accounts receivable	58,000	Interest payable	12,000
Merchandise inventory	96,000	Unearned revenue	10,000
Supplies	7,000	Total current liabilities	$ 125,000
Prepaid expense	8,000		
Total current assets	$259,000		
Investments:		Long-term Liabilities:	
Investment in X Company Stock	156,000	Bonds payable	200,000
Property, plant and equipment:		Stockholders' equity:	
Land	350,000	Common stock, par value $100	600,000
Building	550,000	Paid-in capital in excess of par	400,000
–Less Accumulated Depreciation	–150,000	Retained earnings	230,000
	400,000	Total stockholders' equity	1,230,000
Equipment	340,000	Total liabilities and stockholders' equity	$1,555,000
–Less Accumulated Depreciation	–80,000		
	260,000		
Intangible assets:			
Patents	120,000		
Other assets:			
Long-term receivables	10,000		
Total assets	$1,555,000		

–Long-term liabilities–

Almost all liabilities are current, because most creditors want to be paid within a year. However, if there is a liability which will not be settled, as explained earlier, within a year of the balance sheet date or operating cycle, then it is a long-term liability. For a corporation, which is able to issue bonds, Bonds Payable would typically be listed as a long-term liability. Bonds usually are for a period longer than 5 years.

–Stockholders' equity–

Although not specified, there are two sections in stockholders' equity: Contributed capital and earned capital. Contributed capital is what the stockholders have invested in the company. This consists of all the capital stock and the paid-in capital in excess of par. If there is preferred stock, then that is listed first, followed by common stock. Next is listed the Paid-in Capital in excess of par. There may be other accounts in the contributed capital category, which will be discussed in future chapters. Earned capital is retained earnings.

FINANCIAL CONDITION

In Chapter 1, we mentioned that both stockholders and creditors are concerned about the profitability and financial position of the firm. They want such information so that they can _assess the risk_ involved in their relationship with the company. The big risk is making a loss. The price of the stock may drop and therefore stockholders may sustain a loss on the sale of their stock in the company. The big risk for creditors is that they will not be paid by the company. Accounting information helps them assess the risk, the chance of making a gain or loss. Profitability and financial position are specific aspects of what we may refer to as the "financial condition" of a firm.

Financial condition is a broad concept that encompasses everything a company has and does. We can describe financial condition as the financial "health" of a company. Stockholders and creditors, both present and potential, want to know how well a company has done, is doing, and will be doing. The health of a company has a direct effect on its ability to achieve its purpose, which is to make a profit. As an analogy, consider the health of the quarterback of a professional football team. Suppose that on the day the team is to play, you found out that the quarterback has a mild case of the flu. If you wanted to place a bet on the outcome of the game, you must decide whether the quarterback's illness will affect his performance, and thus the outcome of the game. So also with a firm. Investors want information about the "health" of a company so they can predict what might happen to that company.

• Profitability and Financial Position •

As with a person, there are many facets to the health of a firm. Two important aspects of financial condition are profitability and financial position.

Profitability is important because it tells us something about the performance of a firm. For profitability, a company's revenues, expenses, and income are examined. This will be discussed in the next chapter. For _financial position_, the composition and amounts of assets, liabilities, and owners' equity are studied. The balance sheet is the main source of information for determining the financial position of a firm. The reason for assessing financial position is to ascertain a firm's ability to pay its debts. This has to do with the "solvency" of a firm.

–Working capital–

A company needs cash to pay its debts. But as you can see in the illustrated balance sheets **(Figures 2.6 and 2.7)**, most of the assets of a company typically are in other forms, such as accounts receivable, machinery and buildings. Some assets, although not cash on the balance sheet date, will be cash very shortly, such as accounts receivable. Accounts receivable represent the amount owed to a company mainly by its customers. When customers pay their bills, the company will receive additional cash. Some assets are difficult to convert into cash, such as buildings. Selling a building takes time. As you can see, for assets other than cash, we can have a priority listing of them in terms of how close they are to becoming cash. An asset that is cash or easily converted to cash is referred to as a _liquid asset_. Machinery, land and buildings are not liquid assets, because it is no simple matter to convert (sell) them to cash.

Business analysts have decided that assets that are in the "current" category should be considered liquid assets. Since current liabilities will be paid shortly, usually within a year, it seems feasible to deduct these from the amount of current assets to get a net amount of liquid assets. This net amount of liquid assets is commonly called "working capital." Working capital is defined as the amount of current assets less the amount of current liabilities. It is the amount of funds that a firm can "work" with in the short-run.

–Assessing credit risk in short-run–

Recall that in Chapter 1 we referred to the ability of a company to pay its debt as "credit risk." We want to make an assessment of a company's credit risk especially for the short-run. Most people would say that the short-run is a period of time up to a year. A company can be profitable and yet not have sufficient cash to pay its debts when they fall due. This is also true of individuals. You can have a man earning an income of $100,000 a year, and yet he may not be able to pay his monthly mortgage obligation of $4,000 for the month of November.

To help users assess a company, certain "financial ratios" have been formulated. In Chapter 15, we will present the numerous ratios that can be used. In this chapter, we will present a few ratios that relate to the assessment of a firm's ability to pay its debts. The current ratio and the quick ratio, discussed next, are used to assess a company's credit risk in the short-run.

–Current ratio–

Working capital is a dollar amount. Often, seeing numbers in relation to each other provides more insight. For working capital, such a ratio is the "current ratio."

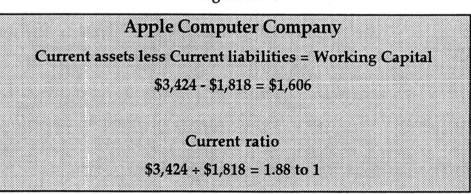

Current ratio formula:

$$\frac{\text{Current Assets}}{\text{Current liabilities}}$$

An illustration is given in **Figure 2.8** based on the amounts for Apple Company in **Figure 2.2**. We see that the current ratio indicates that the amount of current assets is more than twice the amount of current liabilities.

Figure 2.8

Apple Computer Company

Current assets less Current liabilities = Working Capital

$3,424 - $1,818 = $1,606

Current ratio

$3,424 ÷ $1,818 = 1.88 to 1

Is this good or bad? To decide, a comparison should be made with other companies in the same industry and with the company's ratio for the past five years. Some industries traditionally have higher current ratios than others, and some have lower ratios. However, on the average, most business analysts would say that a current ratio of 2 to 1 is sufficiently high. Apple's ratio is slightly less than the standard 2 to 1.

One should not assume that having a very high ratio, such as 10 to 1, is desirable. There is a range of acceptability. If the ratio is too small, then it is an indication that the company may not have sufficient cash to pay its current liabilities. But there is such a thing as having too big a ratio. The reason has to do with putting a company's money where it is most profitable. Placing a great amount of money into current assets is usually not very profitable for a company.

–Quick ratio–

If a company needed to pay off its current liabilities "quickly" (say, within a month), could it do so? The quick ratio is an answer to that question. The ratio is similar to the current ratio except that assets that cannot be quickly converted to cash are eliminated from the amount of current assets. The assets eliminated are merchandise and supplies inventories and prepaid expenses. In other words, the "quick" assets consist of the very liquid assets.

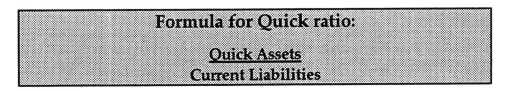

Formula for Quick ratio:

Quick Assets
Current Liabilities

For Apple, the quick assets would be calculated as follows:

Apple Computer Company

Total current assets	$3,424
Less:	
Inventories	–437
Deferred tax assets	–259
Other current assets	–234
Quick assets	$2,494

The calculation is: $2,494 ÷ $1,818 = 1.37 to 1

To decide whether the ratio is good or bad, one should compare it with the industry average and with the company's ratio for the past five years. As a rough rule of thumb, most business analysts would say a ratio of 1 to 1 is sufficient.

• Leverage •

As we mentioned before, investors, especially creditors, are concerned about the amount of debt a company has. Creditors must be paid or a company will be in trouble. If not satisfied, creditors can force a company into bankruptcy and even liquidation. Therefore, debt means **_risk_** for a company. "Leverage" is the term used in finance to signify the level of debt a company has. A highly leveraged company is one that possesses a large amount of liabilities.

–Trading on the equity–

Although the existence of debt means risk for a company, this does not mean that it should have no debts. The reason is due to a financial concept called "trading on the equity." To illustrate, assume that John borrowed $100 from you and promised to pay you back your $100 plus $10 one month from now. With your $100, he invests in the stock market. Let's say that one month later, John sells his stock for $130. To simplify the illustration, let's assume he incurred no expenses. He pays you your $100 plus $10 and gets to keep $20. He has made a gain of $20 using your money. This is trading on the equity. It has to do with using borrowed money to make a profit.

If all of us could do what John did, we would all be rich. But there is a risk. The risk for John was that he might have invested your $100 in a stock and then sell it later for only $85. The difference of $25, which is the amount he owes you ($110) less what he received from the investment ($85), would have to come out of his own pocket. If he did not have the $25, you would be very unhappy with John.

In general, to make large profits one must be bold and take risks. Those who "play it safe" should only expect to make a small return. Whether a company will have a large amount of debt and thereby trade on the equity to a substantial degree depends on the managers. If they are the "daring" type of people, they will; if they are conservative, they will not. Of course, there is also the possibility that adverse circumstances may force a company to be in a highly leveraged position when it really does not want to be in that situation. The preference of investors for companies that trade on the equity significantly depends on how "risk averse" they are.

–Assessing credit risk for the long-run–

A few ratios to assess how much credit risk a company is bearing in the long-run is presented in this section. Both tell the same story but from a different perspective.

1. <u>Debt to Equity Ratio</u> = Total Liabilities ÷ Total Stockholders' Equity

For Apple Company, the ratio is calculated as follows:

$$= \$3,033/\$1,200$$

$$= 252.8\%$$

The ratio shows that for Apple the amount of liabilities is 252.8 percent of the amount of stockholders' equity. A rough rule of thumb is that up to 67% would be considered "conservative." The lesser the percentage, the more conservative (safe) a company is. Obviously, Apple is not a conservative company. But that would be expected of a high-tech company. Such companies are known for taking a lot a risks.

2. Debt to Assets Ratio = Total Liabilities ÷ Total Assets

This ratio is sometimes called the Debt Ratio. For Apple Company, the calculation is:

$$= \$3,033/\$4,233$$
$$= 71.7\%$$

The ratio for Apple shows that total debt is 71.7 percent of total assets. Remember that total assets equal total liabilities + total stockholders' equity. In other words, of the total amount on the right side of the balance sheet, more than half, 71.7% consists of liabilities, and therefore 28.3% is stockholders' equity. A rough rule of thumb is that a ratio up to 40% is considered "safe." Beyond 40%, the larger the percentage, the greater the risk. With 71.7%, Apple is in a risky position. However, although the risk may be high, this does not mean the company is "bad." If the managers are able to handle the risk, this will be very profitable for stockholders. But investors need to know, because they may not want to put money into a company that is risky, even if the returns are high.

3. Long-term Debt to Equity Ratio = Long-term Liabilities ÷ Total Stockholders' Equity

For Apple, the ratio would be:

$$= \$1,215/\$1,200$$
$$= 101.3\%$$

Long-term liabilities and stockholders' equity together are often referred to as a company's "capital structure." This constitutes the long-term commitment of funds into the company. From this perspective, we see that long-term liabilities, in comparison with stockholders' equity, is 101.3% for Apple Company.

The three ratios show that, with respect to leverage, Apple is not a conservative company, but is a company that takes risks.

ACCOUNTING EQUATION

As the illustrated balance sheets show **(Figures 2.2, 2.6 and 2.7)**, the final totals on both sides are exactly equal. For example, in **Figure 2.6**, the total is $62,000. This is not coincidental, but is due to the accounting format that is utilized. The accounting used is called "double entry," and can be cast in the form of an equation. If you look at the numbers on the balance sheet, you will find that they correspond with the following equation:

$$Assets = Liabilities + Owner's\ equity$$
$$\$62{,}000 = \$17{,}000 + \$45{,}000$$

• Background of Double-Entry •

Historical evidence shows that double-entry accounting was first used in Italy in the late 13th century. Since then, every country in the world employs the double-entry principle for accounting. The reason for the popularity of double-entry is that it has proven to be workable and useful, and yet it is basically very simple. Double-entry accounting imposes an order and systematization that give the entity control over all that is recorded. For the business firm, the accounting equation relates all the transactions to the purpose of the firm, which is to make a profit.

• Illustration of Double-Entry Principle •

To understand this equation, let us first depict it another way. Let's say that we are interested in classifying a particular group of college students according to their height and weight. There are 40 students. For height, we want to place each student into one of the following two categories: 5 feet 6 inches and over, and under 5 feet 6 inches. For weight, we want to place each student into one of the following two categories: 130 lbs. and over, and under 130 lbs.

Let's say the conclusions are as follows:

Height		Weight	
5 ft. 6 in. and over	17	130 lb. and over	28
Under 5 ft. 6 in.	23	Under 130 lb.	12
Total	40	Total	40

Is it coincidental that in both lists the total is 40? No, because we are dealing with the same group of students in each case. We do not have 80 people. What we have done is to look at two different characteristics, height and weight, of the same 40 people.

• Double-entry Principle On Balance Sheet •

Similarly, for a business firm, we look at one thing, the total assets, and note two characteristics of it. Let's say we note that ABC Company has a total amount of assets of $62,000. This figure does not tell us much about the company. To be more informative, we will keep track of two characteristics of the total amount of assets: (1) the physical characteristic, and (2) the equity characteristic.

–Physical characteristic–

By the "physical" characteristic of the total assets, we mean the physical trait of each item composing the total, such as cash and equipment. This information tells us a lot more than simply the total of $62,000. In the accounting equation, the physical characteristic is represented by the left side, Assets.

–Equity characteristic–

The term "equity" is a legal term meaning a claim. In our case, a claim on the assets. The "equity" characteristic of the total assets identifies those who have a claim on the total assets. The balance sheet of ABC Company shows that creditors have a claim of $17,000 and the owner, a claim of $45,000. In the equation, the equity characteristic is represented by the right side, the liabilities and owners' equity.

–Characteristics applied to equation–

Figure 2.9 depicts the point we have made.

Figure 2.9

physical characteristic	equity characteristic
Assets	= Liabilities + Owners' equity

You can see therefore that we should always have the same total for the left side of the equation and the right side of the equation. Because it is an equation, it must always be in balance. An equation represents an "identity," that is, the same thing on both sides. As we have explained it, the "same thing" is the total assets. We are simply keeping track of two characteristics of it, because we want that information. As you look at the balance sheet of ABC Company **(Figure 2.6)**, you can see that it gives you a lot more information than simply knowing the total of $62,000.

• Different Views of Equation •

In looking at the accounting equation, there are different ways of viewing it. All of them are correct, but each tells a somewhat different story.

–Abstract view–

One view is to see it as an ***abstraction,*** like a mathematical formula.

Assets = Liabilities + Owners' Equity

–Economic-object view–

Another view, usually that of the firm, is to see the accounting equation in terms of real-world economic objects, as illustrated below. The right side represents the obligations of the firm, and the left side the economic resources. Economic resources provide future benefits. The definitions given in this chapter take this view.

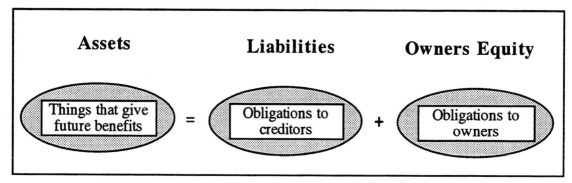

–Financial view–

A financial view, usually taken by investors and creditors, is another perspective. The accounting equation is seen in terms of the funds or capital that have been provided the firm (right side) so that it can invest in the needed resources to create income (left side).

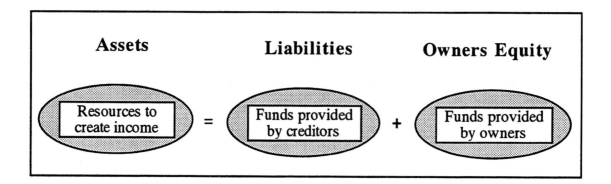

–Legal view–

Another view of the accounting equation is the legal view. Lawyers and government regulators would take this perspective. The right side of the equation represents claims on the firm, and the left side represents the resources available to meet those claims.

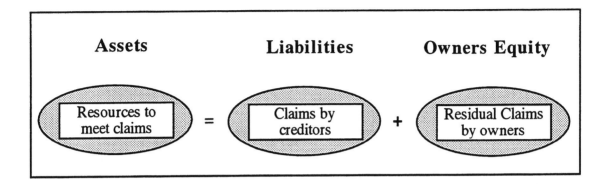

LIMITATIONS OF BALANCE SHEET

The balance sheet informs us of the composition of a firm's assets, the kinds of liabilities it has, and the owners' equity. This type of information is meaningful for stockholders and creditors. It helps them assess the financial position of the company, which has to do with solvency and possible bankruptcy. But in reading the balance sheet, one must be aware that it may not include some important items. The balance sheet does have limitations. We need to be aware of these limitations so that we will not be misled.

• Definition and Recognition •

In this chapter, we have defined assets, liabilities, and owners' equity. We need definitions to help us identify things. As we look at the many and varied economic objects that a firm deals with, classifying them through definition is very helpful. However, concerning definitions, there are two relatable problems we must be aware of:

1. For some items, accountants are uncertain whether they meet the definitions.

2. Not all items that meet the definitions are on the balance sheet.

These two points are discussed next.

–Unsure results from definitions–

With many definitions, it is not always possible to determine whether something in the real world falls within the boundaries of the definitions. For example, it is not always clear whether a certain plant is a bush that happens to be very large, or a tree that happens to be very small. This uncertainty is also true with the definitions in accounting.

For some items, accountants are not sure whether they are assets. As an example, are the employees of a company assets? Or how about the ability of the leaders? Is that an asset? Anyone who is part of an organization knows how important it is to have competent leaders. One very capable person could do remarkable things for an entity; and by the same token, one very inept leader could destroy it. This kind of information is not on the balance sheet because accountants are not sure it meets the definition of an asset.

For some items, accountants are not sure whether they are liabilities. For example, if someone sues the company, is the pending lawsuit a liability? What if in October the company tells its employees that they will receive a Christmas bonus, is there a liability?

For some items, accountants are not sure whether they are owners' equity. For example, if the company issues stock that does not give the stockholder the right to vote, is the stock truly owners' equity?

Because of the uncertainty in applying the definitions, accountants have decided that _recognition_ rules are needed. These rules are based on the objective of providing relevant and reliable information. Accountants believe that if the information is not relevant, then it should not be reported. If the information is not reliable, then it should not be included. Therefore, even if an item seems to meet the definition, it may be excluded because the result is deemed unreliable. Sometimes there must be a "trade off" between relevance and reliability. We discuss next the application of recognition rules.

–Exclusion of some items that meet definitions–

Henry Ford is reputed to have said, "The greatest asset of our company is our employees." According to the definition of an asset, an asset is capable of rendering future benefits to the entity, and the benefits are under the control of the entity, and the asset is the result of a past event. Do employees meet the definition? Many say they do. Employees will render services to the entity; the services are under the control of the entity; and the past event is when they were hired. No business firm could operate without people. Yet no balance sheet of a company includes employees as an asset. Why is that so?

Employees do not meet the recognition rules. A recognition rule tells an accountant when to record an item. There are two reasons why employees are not on the balance sheet as an asset. First, accountants believe that it is very difficult to place a dollar amount on them. To ascertain an amount would be very subjective and arbitrary; therefore, accountants have decided not to recognize employees as an asset because the measure would be unreliable. Second, due to cultural reasons, accountants believe that placing employees on the balance sheet with a dollar amount implies something akin to slavery, and would therefore be offensive to many people.

Thus, even if an item meets the definition of an asset or liability or owners' equity, it may not be recorded because it does not satisfy the recognition criteria. Often, the problem has to do with deriving a reliable measure.

• Measurement •

As you have noticed, not only do we identify an item as an asset or liability or owners' equity, but we also put a dollar amount to it. This is called "measurement" or "valuation." To measure something is to assign a number to it according to certain rules. The pertinent rules for us are the accounting measurement rules.

In future chapters of this book, we will discuss the measurement rules for specific assets, liabilities, and owners' equities. At this point, you should be aware that not only do disagreements exist about the results of the application of definitions and recognition criteria, but also with measurement rules.

A number of measures could be used. They are:

–Expected cash–

This is the amount of cash that is expected to be received or paid for an item. This is used for most current assets and current liabilities.

–Historical cost–

This is the cost that was actually incurred in acquiring an asset or service. In general, accounting rules prescribe that this be used for long-term assets.

–Current cost–

This is the cost of an item that a firm already has that would be incurred if it were purchased currently in the market, given due consideration of the age of the actual item. In general, this is not used for reporting purposes in accounting; however, current cost data may be used as supplementary information.

–Current market value–

This term usually refers to what an item could be sold for if sold now. At times, it may be the same amount as current cost. In general, this is not used for reporting purposes, but there are exceptions, such as securities held as assets for trading purposes. This value may be reported as supplementary information.

–Present value–

This is the amount derived from a mathematical formula for cash sums expected in the future. Bonds are a good example of future cash sums. There is a stream of cash interest payments and a cash principal amount at the end. The future cash sums are "discounted" to derive the value at the present time. This method will be discussed in Chapter 8.

Many disagree with the accounting rule that most of the long-term assets, such as equipment, land, and buildings, should be valued at "historical cost," which is the original amount paid. For example, a company may have purchased land for $50,000 in 1980. On the balance sheet on December 31, 1997, it will still be listed at $50,000. The current market value of the land may be $90,000, but accountants insist that the historical cost be used. Accountants employ historical cost because it is reliable; it is based on a transaction that actually happened. However, for a stockholder or creditor, the $90,000 figure may be more relevant in making predictions about the company.

• Ethical Issues •

It is possible to manipulate documents and accounting methods so that the effect on the balance sheet makes a company appear to be better than it is. Usually, if such an intent exists on the part of management, assets will be overstated and liabilities understated. Practices can range from the fraudulent to that which is legal but questionable. There is often a temptation to "window dress" the balance sheet, especially with respect to current items. In this regard, although legal, the company will attempt to show as much current assets as possible and as little current liabilities as possible. The reason is that the current and quick ratios will look better. For example, on December 31, a company may expect to pay $50,000 in cash for purchases of supplies, payment of salaries and other expenses, but so that the cash amount on the December 31 balance sheet will be as large as can be, it will postpone these payments until after December 31.

For assets, fraudulent practices often pertain to the inventory. Inventory count sheets may have been falsified so that the amount of inventory on the balance sheet is larger than it really is. A questionable accounting practice relates to the loss in value of assets. For instance, old merchandise that is no longer popular with consumers and therefore unsaleable may still be on the balance sheet at their original cost when GAAP calls for its writedown. Another fraudulent practice is to create accounts receivable by fictitious sales transactions.

For liabilities, dates of invoices could be changed so that accounts payable are not recorded in the current period but postponed till the next. Lawsuits against a company in which the probability is great that it will lose or which a judgment against the company has already been determined may not be included as a liability.

The importance of the work of the CPA cannot be overemphasized in ensuring that the balance sheet is reliable.

SUMMARY OF KEY POINTS

The following key points were discussed in this chapter:

1. There are three basic forms of business organization: sole proprietorship, partnership, and corporation. Some important points concerning each are: ease or difficulty in creation, limited or unlimited liability, management of the business, and the tax effect.

2. The balance sheet as a source of information to assess risk. The balance sheet provides information on the "financial position" of the firm. This has to do with the company's "solvency," that is, its ability to pay its debts. All those who deal with the firm are interested in this, but especially creditors. The financial ratios discussed in this chapter help people assess the risk position the firm is in, and therefore the risk they take in doing business with the company.

3. The balance sheet is true as of a moment in time. It is like a snapshot taken of a process that is constantly changing.

4. Composition of balance sheet. The balance sheet consists of a list of assets, liabilities, and owners' equity. You should not be confused by other terms sometimes used.

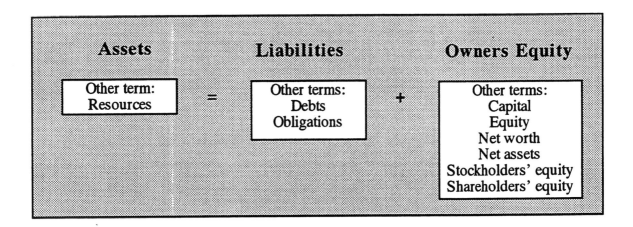

5. Definition of asset. An asset is an economic object which is capable of providing future benefits, which are under the control of a particular entity, and is the result of a past event.

6. Definition of liability. A liability is a present obligation of an entity which requires it to settle the obligation at a future date by conveying assets or rendering services, and is the result of a past event.

7. Definition of owners' equity. Owners' equity is an obligation of an entity to its owners, which requires it to convey earnings to the owners and, in case of liquidation, the residual assets, and is the result of a past event.

8. Financial terms. Terms such as working capital, liquidity, solvency, leverage, and trading on the equity are widely used in business. Be sure that you understand the meaning of these terms.

9. The accounting equation. The balance sheet is based on the accounting equation, which is expressed as:

Assets = Liabilities + Owners' equity

10. Double-entry principle. The accounting equation is based on the "double-entry" principle. The "double" refers to the fact that two characteristics, physical and equity, of the total assets are considered. The physical characteristic is represented by Assets in the equation, and the equity characteristic is represented by the Liabilities and Owners' equity.

11. The balance sheet has limitations. Based on the definitions of assets, liabilities and owners' equity, some items may not appear on the balance sheet, because accountants are not sure that they meet the definitions, or if they do accountants believe their "measurement" to be unreliable. Also, the dollar amounts of some of the long-term assets may not be relevant to users.

12. Ethical issues. The balance sheet can be manipulated. Assets may be overstated and liabilities understated.

APPENDIX

The balance sheets of four actual companies are presented here: a retail company, Gap Inc.; a manufacturing company, Hewlett-Packard; a service company, Delta Air Lines; and a financial service company, Bank of America.

The GAP, INC. and Subsidiaries
Consolidated Balance Sheets

($000)	February 3, 1996	January 28, 1995
Assets		
Current Assets		
Cash and equivalents	$ 579,566	$ 414,487
Short-term investments	89,506	173,543
Merchandise inventory	482,575	370,638
Prepaid expenses and other	128,398	97,019
Total Current Assets	$1,280,045	$1,055,687
Property and Equipment		
Leasehold improvements	736,879	639,801
Furniture and equipment	763,673	620,104
Construction-in-progress	62,030	34,989
	1,562,582	1,294,894
Accumulated depreciation and amortization	(604,830)	(466,117)
	957,752	828,777
Long-term investments	30,370	32,097
Lease rights and other assets	74,901	87,683
Total Assets	$2,343,068	$2,004,244
Liabilities and Stockholders' Equity		
Current Liabilities		
Notes payable	$ 21,815	$ 2,478
Accounts payable	262,505	263,724
Accrued expenses	194,426	185,375
Income taxes payable	66,094	41,156
Deferred lease credits and other current liabilities	6,904	7,127
Total Current Liabilities	$551,744	$499,860
Long-Term Liabilities		
Deferred lease credits and other liabilities	150,851	129,152
Stockholders' Equity		
Common stock $.05 par value(a)		
Authorized 500,000,000 shares; issued 315,971,306 and		
313,945,554 shares; outstanding 287,747,984 shares	15,799	15,697
Additional paid-in capital(a)	335,193	290,565
Retained earnings	1,569,347	1,282,301
Foreign currency translation adjustment	(9,071)	(8,320)
Restricted stock plan deferred compensation	(48,735)	(54,265)
Treasury stock, at cost	(222,060)	(150,746)
	1,640,473	1,375,232
Total Liabilities and Stockholders' Equity	$2,343,068	$2,004,244

The Balance Sheet

Hewlett-Packard Company and Subsidiaries
Consolidated Balance Sheet

October 31

In millions except par value and number of shares

	1996	1995
ASSETS		
Current assets:		
Cash and cash equivalents	$ 2,885	$ 1,973
Short-term investments	442	643
Accounts and notes receivable	7,126	6,735
Inventories:		
Finished goods	3,956	3,368
Purchased parts and fabricated assemblies	2,445	2,645
Other current assets	1,137	875
Total current assets	17,991	16,239
Property, plant and equipment:		
Land	475	485
Buildings and leasehold improvements	4,257	3,810
Machinery and equipment	5,466	4,452
	10,198	8,747
Accumulated depreciation	(4,662)	(4,036)
	5,536	4,711
Long-term investments and other assets	4,172	3,477
Total assets	$27,699	$24,427
LIABILITIES AND SHAREHOLDERS' EQUITY		
Current liabilities:		
Notes payable and short-term borrowings	$ 2,125	$ 3,214
Accounts payable	2,375	2,422
Employee compensation and benefits	1,675	1,568
Taxes on earnings	1,514	1,494
Deferred revenues	951	782
Other accrued liabilities	1,983	1,464
Total current liabilities	10,623	10,944
Long-term debt	2,579	663
Other liabilities	1,059	981
Shareholders' equity:		
Preferred stock, $1 par value		
(authorized: 300,000,000 shares; issued: none)	——	——
Common stock and capital in excess of $1 par value		
(authorized: 2,400,000,000 shares; issued and		
outstanding: 1,014,123,000 in 1996 and		
1,019,910,000 in 1995)	1,014	1,381
Retained earnings	12,424	10,458
Total shareholders' equity	13,438	11,839
Total liabilities and shareholders' equity	27,699	$24,427

78

Delta Air Lines, Inc.
Consolidated Balance Sheets
June 30, 1996 and 1995

	1996 (In Millions)	1995 (In Millions)
ASSETS		
CURRENT ASSETS:		
Cash and cash equivalents	$1,145	$1,233
Short-term investments	507	529
Accounts receivable, net of allowance for uncollectible accounts of $44 at June 30, 1996, and $29 at June 30, 1995	968	755
Maintenance and operating supplies, at average cost	73	68
Deferred income taxes	352	234
Prepaid expenses and other	237	195
Total current assets	**3,282**	**3,014**
PROPERTY AND EQUIPMENT:		
Flight equipment	8,202	9,288
Less: Accumulated depreciation	3,235	4,209
	4,967	**5,079**
Flight equipment under capital leases	515	537
Less: Accumulated amortization	127	99
	388	**438**
Ground property and equipment	2,697	2,442
Less: Accumulated depreciation	1,532	1,354
	1,165	**1,088**
Advance payments for equipment	275	331
	6,795	**6,936**
OTHER ASSETS:		
Marketable equity securities	473	398
Deferred income taxes	415	506
Investments in associated companies	266	265
Cost in excess of net assets acquired, net of accumulated amortization of $84 at June 30, 1996, and $75 at June 30, 1995	265	274
Leasehold and operating rights, net of accumulated amortization of $183 at June 30, 1996, and $165 at June 30, 1995	140	177
Other	590	573
	2,149	**2,193**
	$12,226	**$12,143**

(continued)

The Balance Sheet

LIABILITIES AND STOCKHOLDERS' EQUITY

CURRENT LIABILITIES:

Current maturities of long-term debt	$ 40	$151
Current obligations under capital leases	58	61
Accounts payable and misc. accrued liabilities	1,540	1,473
Air traffic liability	1,414	1,143
Accrued rent	201	235
Accrued salaries and vacation pay	385	378
Total current liabilities	3,638	3,441

NONCURRENT LIABILITIES:

Long-term debt	1,799	2,683
Postretirement benefits	1,796	1,714
Accrued rent	616	556
Capital leases	376	438
Other	425	395
	5,012	5,786

DEFERRED CREDITS:

Deferred gain on sale and leaseback transactions	802	860
Manufacturers' and other credits	96	109
	898	969

EMPLOYEE STOCK OWNERSHIP PLAN PREFERRED STOCK

Series B ESOP Convertible Preferred Stock, $1.00 par value, $72.00 stated and liquidation value; issued and outstanding 6,738,740 shares at June 30, 1996, and 6,786,632 shares at June 30, 1995	485	489
Unearned compensation under employee stock ownership plan	(347)	(369)
	138	120

STOCKHOLDERS' EQUITY :

Series C Convertible Preferred Stock, $1.00 par value, $50,000 liquidation preference; issued and outstanding 13,978 shares at June 30, 1996 and 23,000 shares at June 30, 1995	——	——
Common Stock, $3.00 par value; authorized 150,000,000 shares; issued 72,265,994 shares at June 30, 1996, and 54,537,103 shares at June 30, 1995	217	164
Additional paid-in capital	2,627	2,016
Accumulated deficit.	(119)	(184)
Net unrealized gain on noncurrent marketable equity securities	126	83
Treasury stock at cost, 4,487,888 shares at June 30, 1996, and 3,721,093 shares at June 30, 1995	(311)	(252)
	2,540	1,827
	12,226	12,143

Bank Of America
Consolidated Balance Sheet

(in millions)	Dec. 31, 1996	Dec. 31, 1995
ASSETS		
Cash and due from banks	$ 16,223	$ 14,312
Interest-bearing deposits in banks	5,708	5,761
Federal funds sold	134	721
Securities purchased under resale agreements	7,275	4,962
Trading account assets	12,205	9,516
Available-for-sale securities	12,113	12,043
Held-to-maturity securities	4,138	4,656
Loans	165,415	155,373
Less: Allowance for credit losses	3,523	3,554
Net loans	**161,892**	**151,819**
Customers' acceptance liability	2,861	2,295
Accrued interest receivable	1,441	1,458
Goodwill, net	3,938	4,192
Identifiable intangibles, net	1,616	1,806
Unrealized gains on off-balance-sheet instruments	7,682	7,801
Premises and equipment, net	3,987	3,985
Other assets	9,540	7,119
Total assets	**$250,753**	**$232,446**
LIABILITIES & STOCKHOLDERS' EQUITY		
Deposits in domestic offices:		
Interest-bearing	$ 84,133 $	84,097
Noninterest-bearing	39,694	36,820
Deposits in foreign offices:		
Interest-bearing	42,732	37,886
Noninterest-bearing	1,456	1,691
Total deposits	**168,015**	**160,494**
Federal funds purchased	2,176	5,160
Securities sold under repurchase agreements	7,644	6,383
Other short-term borrowings	17,566	7,627
Acceptances outstanding	2,861	2,295
Accrued interest payable	879	848
Unrealized losses on off-balance-sheet instruments	7,633	8,227
Other liabilities	5,981	5,862
Long-term debt	15,430	14,723
Subordinated capital notes	355	605
Total liabilities	**228,540**	**212,224**

(continued)

Corporation obligated mandatorily redeemable preferred securities of subsidiary trusts holding solely junior subordinated deferrable interest debentures of the Corporation	1,500	——
STOCKHOLDERS' EQUITY		
Preferred stock	2,242	2,623
Common stock	605	602
Additional paid-in capital	8,467	8,328
Retained earnings	11,500	9,606
Net unrealized gain (loss) on available-for-sale securities	32	1
Common stock in treasury, at cost	(2,133)	(938)
Total stockholders' equity	20,713	20,222
Total liabilities and stockholders' equity	$250,753	$232,446

QUESTIONS

1. Concerning a sole proprietorship,

a. How is it formed?

b. Is it recognized as a separate legal entity?

c. Does the proprietorship pay income taxes?

d. What is its major disadvantage?

2. Concerning a partnership,

a. How is it formed?

b. Is it recognized as a separate legal entity?

c. Does it pay income taxes?

d. What is a general partner? A limited partner?

e. What are two disadvantages?

f. What is a limited liability partnership?

3. Concerning a corporation,

a. How is it formed?

b. Is it recognized as a separate legal entity?

c. What is its major advantage?

d. With respect to raising capital, what can it do that the other forms of business organization cannot?

e. Does it pay income taxes?

f. What is an S corporation?

4. By looking at a balance sheet, how can you tell whether the firm is a sole proprietorship, partnership, or corporation?

5. What are the three important characteristics of the following:

a. Assets

b. Liabilities

c. Owners' equity

6. For the following accounts, indicate in what category (Assets, Liabilities, Owners' Equity) it should be placed:

a. Cash

f. Merchandise inventory

b. Notes payable

g. Accounts receivable

c. Lee, Capital

h. Accounts payable

d. Equipment

i. Building

e. Wages payable

7. Concerning financial condition,

a. Describe what the financial condition of a firm is.

b. What is a "liquid" asset?

c. What is "working capital?"

d. What is the formula for the current ratio?

e. Why is the current ratio calculated?

f. What is the formula for the quick ratio?

g. Why is the quick ratio calculated?

h. What is "leverage?"

i. What is the formula for the debt ratio?

8. Concerning the accounting equation,

a. What is the "double-entry" principle?

b. What is meant by the "physical" characteristic?

c. What is meant by the "equity" characteristic?

d. Why should both sides of the accounting equation always be the same amount?

e. What are the different ways of looking at the accounting equation?

9. Concerning the limitations of the balance sheet,

a. Give an example of the unsure results derived from the definitions.

b. Indicate the various measures which could be used. Give an example of the problem of measurement.

c. Give an example of an ethical problem affecting the balance sheet.

10. A business firm has total assets of $1,400,000 and total liabilities of $840,000. Present the owners' equity section of the balance sheet under the following assumptions:

a. The firm is a sole proprietorship owned by James Carter.

b. The firm is a partnership owned by Nancy Cooper, who has a 40 percent interest, and Gail Friedman, who has a 60 percent interest.

c. The firm is a corporation. The shares issued were originally sold for a total price of $280,000. The par value was $200,000. The remainder of owners' equity is earnings that have been retained in the firm.

11. Of the following events, decide whether there is anything to record by the accountant. Explain.

a. Marvel Company hired a new vice-president for $80,000 a year.

b. At a meeting of the officers of the company, Randall Company decided to layoff 10 of its employees. The combined salaries of the employees to be laid off amount to $43,000 a month.

c. Lee Company purchased a new machine, paying $25,000 cash for it.

d. Sherill Company signed a contract with Wooden Company for Wooden to construct a building for $500,000.

12. For each of the following, indicate whether an asset is to be recognized. If so, state the name of the account and the amount:

a. Merchandise inventory for $600 is purchased. No cash is given, but the amount must be paid within 30 days.

b. A check for $1,200 is sent to the landlord as advance payment for 2 months' rent.

c. Merchandise of $100 that had been purchased (see a) was sent back to the supplier because it was defective.

d. An order for $800 of merchandise is received from a customer.

e. U.S. Treasury notes were purchased for $5,000 cash.

f. Machinery is purchased by giving 100 shares of the company's own stock. The stock is selling on the stock exchange for $84 a share.

13. For each of the following, indicate whether a liability is to be recognized by Farber Company. If so, state the name of the account and the amount:

a. At the end of the month, salaries of $4,000 were unpaid.

b. Farber signed a contract for $8,000 with Lenny Advertisement Agency for the agency to develop a 20-second commercial to be shown on TV.

c. A sexual harassment lawsuit for $1,000,000 was filed against the company by a former employee. She charged that the vice-president had made lewd comments to her.

d. A customer incorrectly overpaid his bill by $400.

e. The president announced that employees would receive a Christmas bonus at the end of the year. The accountant estimated the total amount to be $12,000.

f. The company issued 500 shares of common stock with a par value of $100 per share. Each share sells for $110 in the stock market.

g. Farber received a check for $1,200 from a customer as a deposit to purchase merchandise. The merchandise will be sent out next month.

14. Of the following accounts, state what valuation basis should be used according to GAAP. Your answers should be one of the following: expected cash, historical cost, current cost, current market value, present value.

a. Accounts receivable

b. Equipment

c. Supplies

d. Securities held for trading

e. Accounts payable

f. Salaries payable

g. Land

i. Bonds payable

EXERCISES

(See list of key answers at end of chapter)

E2-1

For each of the following, state whether it best describes proprietorships, partnerships, or corporations.

a. Limited liability.

b. One owner.

c. Can be established by an oral agreement.

d. Can sell bonds.

e. Ability to be your "own boss."

f. The business must pay income taxes.

g. Controlled by board of directors.

h. Ownership by stockholders.

i. All the profits belong to the owner.

j. Recognized by law as a separate entity for limited purposes.

k. The majority of business firms are of this type.

l. An owner can be designated as "limited" or "general."

E2-2

Based on the accounting equation,

a. Suppose Haven Company has assets of $55,000 and stockholders' equity of $46,000. What is the amount of the liabilities?

b. Suppose Lin Company has liabilities of $78,000 and owners' equity of $103,000. What is the amount of assets?

c. Suppose Rose Company has assets of $320,000 and liabilities of $65,000. What is the amount of owners' equity?

d. Suppose on July 1, Busch Company had assets of $200,000 and liabilities of $56,000. During July, stockholders' equity increased by $23,000 and liabilities by $12,000. On July 31, what is the amount of the assets?

E2-3

Classify the following items (a to l) as follows:

Current assets

Long-term assets - investments

Long-term assets - property, plant and equipment

Long-term assets - intangible

Current liabilities

Long-term liabilities

Stockholders' equity

Not on balance sheet

a. Accounts payable

b. Cash

c. Equipment

d. Accounts receivable

e. Bonds payable

f. Capital stock

g. Patents

h. Ability of top managers

i. Retained earnings

j. Land

k. Land held as investment

l. Merchandise inventory

E2-4

Use the accounting equation to find the missing amounts for Companies X, Y, Z.

	X	Y	Z
Cash	$2,600	$8,000	$13,000
Accounts receivable	$20,000	$17,000	$6,000
Land and buildings	$80,000	?	$90,000
Accounts payable	?	$7,000	$19,000
Mortage payable	$40,000	$12,000	$23,000
Owners' equity	$60,000	$34,000	?

The Balance Sheet

E2-5

Prepare a balance sheet for Maryann Company for June 30, 1995, using the following classifications: current assets, long-term assets, current liabilities, long-term liabilities, stockholders' equity.

a. Accounts payable $23,000   CL
b. Cash 24,000   CA
c. Equipment (net) 57,000   LA
d. Wages payable 10,000   CL
e. Long-term notes payable 5,000   LL
f. Capital stock 85,000   SE
g. Accounts receivable 8,000   CA
h. Land 55,000   LA
i. Retained earnings ?   SE
j. Notes payable 7,000   CL

E2-6

Of the numbered items below, indicate which of the following classifications the item belongs by writing the letter before the classification:

a. Current assets   f. Current liabilities
b. Long-term investments   g. Long-term liabilities
c. Property, plant, and equipment   h. Stockholders' equity
d. Intangible assets   i. Not on balance sheet
e. Other assets

1. Supplies inventory   9. Retained earnings
2. Common stock   10. Wages payable
3. Land   11. Capital in excess of par value
4. Accounts payable   12. Equipment
5. Bonds payable   13. Goodwill
6. Temporary investments   14. Bank loan payable
7. Land   15. Buildings
8. Accounts receivable   16. Land held for future use

E2-7

Listed below are the account balances for Yamada Company for the month of April, 1996:

Accounts payable	$126,000
Cash	35,000
Wages payable	37,000
Supplies	12,000
Notes payable-long term	740,000
Common stock	600,000
Merchandise inventory	420,000
Land	350,000
Patents	40,000
Accumulated depreciation	310,000
Accounts receivable	94,000
Notes payable-current	50,000
Retained earnings	327,000
Buildings	800,000
Prepaid insurance	22,000
Equipment	450,000
Interest payable	33,000

Based on the information above, compute the following:

a. Current assets

b. Current liabilities

c. Property, plant and equipment

d. Long-term liabilities

e. Total assets

f. Stockholders' equity

g. Total liabilities

h. Working capital

E2-8

What is the effect of the following events on the total assets of ABC Company? Your answer should be "increase," "decrease," or "no effect."

a. Receipt of cash as investment by owner.

b. Purchase of equipment on account.

c. Purchase of equipment for cash.

d. Collection of accounts receivable.

e. Payment of liability.

f. Borrowed money from bank.

E2-9

Western Company was organized on March 1, Year 1. The following events occurred in March:

Issued capital stock for cash, $60,000

Purchased equipment for cash, $25,000

Purchased merchandise inventory on account, $12,000

Sold merchandise on account to customers, $24,000

Paid wages and salaries, $2,000

Collected $4,500 from customers on their accounts

Based on the information given, if you were to prepare a balance sheet for Western Company as of March 31, Year 1, what would be the amount of cash?

E2-10

For each account balance listed below, indicate what the future event is expected to be in terms of either cash flow or use. An example is provided.

Account balance	Future event expected
a. Accounts payable, $56,000	a. $56,000 cash would be used to pay the liability.
b. Accounts receivable, $66,000	b.
c. Notes payable, $35,000	c.
d. Merchandise inventory, $220,000	d.
e. Equipment, $540,000	e.
f. Wages payable, $23,000	f.
g. Prepaid insurance, $12,000	g.

E2-11

Les Santos, accountant for Norton Store, hired Patsy Cline to be his new bookkeeper. In preparing the balance sheet for the month of April, Year 2, she could not get it to balance. Correct the balance sheet for her by placing items in the correct classifications.

Assets		Liabilities and Owners' Equity	
Cash	$18,000	Long-term note payable	$135,000
Accounts payable	19,000	Accounts receivable	18,000
Supplies	13,000	Notes payable	22,000
Equipment	114,000	Inventories	132,000
Norton, Capital	119,000		
Total	$283,000		$307,000

E2-12

As of December 31, Year 9, Northern Pacific Company has the following accounts on its balance sheet:

Cash	$ 40,000
Accounts receivable	39,000
Accounts payable	55,000
Land	125,000
Notes payable	12,000
Buildings (net)	142,000
Retained earnings	80,000
Equipment (net)	56,000
Merchandise inventory	44,000
Notes receivable	21,000
Capital stock	?

Answer the following:

1. What is the amount of the total current assets?
2. What is the amount of the total current liabilities?
3. What is the amount of the total assets?
4. What is the amount of capital stock?
5. What is the amount of stockholders' equity?

6. Calculate the current ratio.

7. Calculate the quick ratio.

E2-13

Mary Segal owns a garment manufacturing company. Lester Company would like to purchase dresses from her for resale. The usual business arrangement is for the customer to purchase on credit. She has asked your advice on determining how good a customer Lester would be; that is, whether Lester can be relied on to pay its bills. Some of the selected information provided by Lester are as follows:

(in thousands)	1996	1995	1994
Current assets	$54	$56	$53
Quick assets	32	39	35
Total assets	240	200	178
Current liabilities	34	23	24
Total liabilities	92	59	41
Total stockholders equity	148	141	137

Instructions: Compute the following ratios for 1996, 1995, and 1994:

(1) current ratio

(2) quick ratio

(3) debt to equity ratio

(4) debt ratio

Based on the ratios, what conclusions can you make concerning the financial condition of Lester?

E2-14

Consider the balance sheet of Apple Company in Figure 2.2.

1. Why is the date September 26, 1997 rather than December 31, 1997?

2. Why is it a "consolidated' balance sheet?

3. What is the composition of property, plant and equipment?

4. What is the current ratio?

5. What is the quick ratio?

6. What is the debt to equity ratio?

7. What is the number of authorized shares?

8. Why isn't there an account called Paid-in Capital in Excess of Par?

9. What is the amount of contributed capital?

10. What is the amount of earned capital?

E2-15

Using the internet, find the balance sheet of Microsoft Company for 1997 (http://www.microsoft.com/msft/ar97/financial/balance.htm). Get a printout of the balance sheet (scale it at 80% to get all the columns) and bring to class.

Instructions: For 1997, (1) compute the current ratio and the debt to equity ratio. (2) What do you think Minority Interest is? (3) Click on Next at the bottom to get further information. How much was the amount of shares repurchased? (4) How much was the preferred stock dividend? (5) What are the Significant Accounting Policies? (6) What was the composition and amounts of Cash and equivalents?

CASES

C2-1

John Morris lost his job with Y Corporation and now wants to open a frozen yogurt shop. His major source of income will be the profits from the shop. He expects to run the shop himself, because he has no other employment and likes the idea of being his own boss. After studying the situation, he finds that it will take an investment of $35,000 to open a yogurt shop, which he has. According to his study, he should make about $40,000 a year in profits.

An acquaintance of John's, Alan Berg, who also lost his job with Y Corporation, heard about what John wants to do and offered to be a partner in the venture. He said he could contribute half of the needed investment and work in the shop as well.

John's wife told him that he should consider incorporating the yogurt shop, because she heard that it is a safer form of business organization.

Instructions: What advice would you give John on the form of business organization for his yogurt shop? Explain.

C2-2

Laurie Randall opened an antique shop. During April, the first month of operations, a few of the events that occurred were the following:

a. Her grandmother gave her an old table that needed to be refinished. Laurie estimated that its value was $150. She estimated that the cost of refinishing the table was $125 and that she could then sell it for $400.

b. She told an antique dealer in another town that she would like to purchase two chairs that she had seen in his shop if he brought the price down to $100 each. He is asking for $150 each. She thinks she can sell them for $175 each.

c. She telephoned the Office Supply Company, which is located across town, to order some supplies. She told the sales clerk to charge her account. The cost is $160. The clerk said the supplies would be delivered in a few days, but Laurie has not yet received them.

d. Laurie hired Sylvia Tong to work part-time in the store. Sylvia's wages are $30 a day. Sylvia is to be paid at the end of each week on Friday. At the end of April, which was a Tuesday, Sylvia had not been paid for that week.

Instructions: For April, based on the information given and the definitions of assets and liabilities, decide for each case whether Laurie has an asset or liability. Explain.

C2-3

Consider the following situations pertaining to Lawson Company:

a. On May 15, at the board of directors meeting, Conrad Johnson, chairman of the board, announced that he will donate a truck, valued at $25,000, to the company.

b. Two months ago, Betty Ward purchased $4,000 of merchandise from the company and charged the purchase to her account. The agreement was for her to pay $4,000 one month ago. On May 18, a letter was sent reminding her that payment is due.

c. On May 20, Lawson received the new computer it had ordered from CompAmerica Company. The cost is $2,500. Payment has not yet been made. A check will be sent next week to CompAmerica Company in full payment.

d. Rita Lee, who had worked as secretary to the president for 25 years, was dismissed a month ago. On May 24, at a press conference, she announced with her attorney that she has filed a lawsuit against Lawson for age discrimination. She is asking for a million dollars.

Instructions: Based on the definitions of assets and liabilities, determine in each situation whether an asset or liability exists for Lawson Company for the date specified. Explain.

C2-4

A few of the events in Year 8 which affected Stanton Department Store are listed below. Stanton has several stores in the midwest.

a. In March, Henry Taylor, the financial officer of the corporation, reported that Horace Department Store, Stanton's chief competitor, is planning to build a new store in the same shopping center as Stanton's in the city of Danville. He estimates that profits could decline by $100,000 next year because of this.

b. On April 14, Judy Caldwell, wife of one of the prominent citizens of Danville, purchased several expensive dresses for a total price of $2,800. The dresses had cost Stanton $1,200. On that day, she took the dresses with her but did not pay for them with cash. Instead of cash, she charged the purchase by using her Stanton credit card.

c. At the board of directors meeting on August 18, Henry Taylor, the financial officer, told the board that the company should sell 1,000 shares of its common stock, par value $100 each. He said the Prominent Insurance Company is willing to pay $175 per share. The board of directors approved of the sale.

d. In November, the firm needed $12,000 cash to meet its payroll. Rather than borrow from a bank, John Stanton, the president of Stanton Department Store, said he would lend the company the money. On November 19, the company received a check for $12,000 from John Stanton. The company is to pay him back in one month with 10 percent interest.

Instructions: For each of the foregoing events, decide whether an asset, liability, or stockholders' equity account is to be recorded by Stanton. Specify the name of the account(s) that should be recorded. Explain your decision by reference to the definitions of assets, liabilities, and owners' equity.

C2-5

Paula Rivera, the chief financial officer of Lambert Toy Company, made the following decisions in Year 10:

a. Five years ago, one of the most popular toys sold by Lambert was the carrot doll, which was sold for $18.00. The cost to Lambert was $9.00. Because of its popularity, Lambert had purchased 5,000 of these dolls in Year 5. It sold 2,800 of them in Year 5. Suddenly in Year 6, the carrot doll lost its popularity. Although the retail price was dropped to $5 in Year 10, only 3 dolls were sold. At the end of Year 10, Lambert still has 2,100 of these dolls in storage. Paula decided that these dolls may become popular again in the future and so they should remain in the inventory count at their original cost of $9.00 each.

b. Because the amount of current assets was lower than usual at the end of the year, Paula decided to postpone the purchase of equipment which required a downpayment of $15,000.

By doing this, the total current assets will be higher on the December 31 balance sheet. The equipment will be purchased in February of the next year.

c. In late December, the company purchased $3,000 of badly needed office and store supplies on credit from Gould Supply Company. Paula was concerned about the large amount of liabilities on the balance sheet and so she called the manager of Gould Company and asked him not to send the bill to Lambert until January. Although the supplies were received, because the bill did not arrive the accounts payable was not recorded in December.

d. For its inventory count for ten of its products at the end of the year, Paula directed the accountant to increase the number by 100 for each of the ten items. She said that orders for the purchase of these products had been sent out recently to suppliers, and therefore they should be included in the physical count. Because of the increase in the size of the count, the total inventory at the end of the year rose by $13,000.

e. The president remarked to Paula that the building and land accounts were at values much lower than their current market values. He said the building is $80,000 more and the land is $60,000 more than the historical cost stated in the balance sheet. Paula said that these increases cannot be recorded because of accounting principles.

Instructions: Based on acceptable accounting practices, do you believe Paula's decisions were proper? Explain.

C2-6

Dan Freeman was helping his friend Diana Swanson with her accounting homework. She was puzzled about the balance sheet of Carson Company, the name of the company in the homework assignment. In his explanation of the balance sheet, Dan made the following remarks:

a. If the December 31, Year 10 balance sheet shows $50,000 cash, this means that Carson spent $50,000 during Year 10.

b. The amount of accounts receivable represents the amount customers owe Carson.

c. An asset is something Carson owns.

d. The accounts payable amount represents what Carson paid during the year because of purchases.

e. The double-entry principle means that whatever is purchased must be doubled in amount.

f. One of the limitations of the balance sheet is that not all assets and liabilities are on it.

Instructions: For each of Dan's remarks, specify whether you agree with him by writing "yes" or "no." Explain your answer.

C2-7

Refer to the four balance sheets in the appendix.

1. Current assets. Typical current assets listed on a balance sheet are: cash, receivables, and inventory.

a. Why do you suppose Delta Air Lines does not have inventory?

b. Why do you suppose Bank of America does not have receivables and inventory?

c. Why does Hewlett-Packard have two inventory accounts and GAP has only one?

d. Both Delta and Gap list "Prepaid expenses." What do you think these are?

2. Long-term assets.

a. Both Hewlett-Packard and Gap list "leasehold improvements." What do you think these are?

b. Accumulated depreciation is deducted. What is this?

c. Delta has an account called "Deferred income taxes." It is also listed under Current Assets. What do you suppose this is? (This will be discussed in Chapter 11.)

3. As you can see, the assets for Bank of America are quite different from the other companies. As best as you can, indicate what you think the following accounts are:

a. Interest-bearing deposit in banks

b. Federal funds sold, and securities purchased under resale agreements

c. Trading account assets

d. Held-to-maturity securities

e. Loans

4. Liabilities

a. Both Gap and Hewlett-Packard have Accounts payable and Notes payable. What are these?

b. Bank of America lists "Deposits in domestic offices" and "Deposits in foreign offices." What are these?

5. Stockholders' equity

a. What is preferred stock as opposed to common stock?

b. What is "Retained earnings?"

c. Gap, Delta, and Bank of America have "treasury stock," which is deducted. What do you think this is?

6. For 1996 only, compute the current ratio and the debt ratio for Gap, Hewlett-Packard, and Delta.

PROBLEMS

(see list of key answers at end of chapter)

P2-1

Paul Fagan is the sole proprietor of a small furniture store. He recently applied for a loan at the bank and was asked to submit a balance sheet. He prepared the following:

Fagan Furniture Store
Balance Sheet
For the Year Ended December 31, 1995

Assets		Liabilities and Equity	
Cash	$5,000	Accounts payable	$3,000
Store equipment (net)	20,000	Mortgage on home	67,000
Accounts receivable	30,000	Loan on delivery truck	12,000
Family home	185,000	Stockholder's equity	201,000
Merchandise inventory	25,000		
Delivery truck	18,000		
Total	$283,000	Total	$283,000

Additional information:

1. The delivery truck was purchased for $18,000 recently. Paul received a loan from the ABC Bank for $12,000 to finance the purchase of the truck. Because Paul has not fully paid for the truck, the bank has legal title to the truck.

2. The merchandise inventory includes $2,000 of items purchased on account by a customer, Raymond France, but the items have not yet been delivered to him.

3. Accounts payable include $1,000 for chairs ordered from the Lovett Chair Company. The order was recently sent to Lovett. The merchandise inventory includes the $1,000.

Instructions: Prepare a corrected balance sheet. Assets should be listed in proper order.

P2-2

Mike Chang owns a frozen yogurt shop called Mike's Frozen Treat. On April 1, Year 5, he had the following balance sheet accounts:

Cash	$ 9,000
Accounts payable	5,000
Bank loan payable	6,000
Inventory of food items	2,000
Equipment (net)	28,000
Furniture (net)	12,000
Chang, Capital	?

On April 2, the following events occurred:

a. Mike paid off some of his accounts payable, $1,200.

b. He purchased for cash some additional inventory food items, $300.

c. A salesman came by to encourage Mike to purchase a new machine. The cost of the machine is $600. Mike is interested and wants the salesman to return next week.

Instructions:

(1) Prepare a balance sheet for April 1, Year 5.

(2) Prepare a balance sheet at the end of the day, April 2.

(3) Is the amount in the capital account different on April 2? Explain.

P2-3

The actual balance sheet of Wal-Mart (in thousands) of a recent year shows the following items:

Cash	$ 13,014
Land	833,344
Receivables	305,070
Capital in excess of par value	415,586
Inventories	5,808,416
Accounts payable	2,651,315
Long-term debt	740,254
Other long-term liabilities	1,292,723
Common stock	114,228
Other current assets	288,275
Buildings and equipment (net)	2,890,808
Other long-term assets	1,249,988
Other current liabilities	1,339,099
Retained earnings	4,835,710

Instructions:

a. Prepare the balance sheet for Wal-Mart in proper form for the year ending January 31. The following classifications should be used: (1) current assets, (2) property, plant and equipment, (3) other long-term assets, (4) current liabilities, (5) long-term liabilities, (6) stockholders' equity.

b. Determine the amount of working capital. Calculate the current ratio. Based only on the current ratio, what would you conclude about the company's ability to pay its short-term debt?

c. Calculate the debt to equity ratio and the debt ratio. What do you think of the company's "leverage?"

P2-4

The actual balance sheet of Coca-Cola Enterprises, Inc. for a recent year shows the following balance sheet items (in millions):

Goodwill and other intangible assets	$4,193.3
Cash CA	64.1
Long-term debt LL	3,406.5
Accounts receivable (net) CA	375.3
Inventories CA	195.1
Land LA	171.7
Accounts payable CE	700.9
Common stock SE	140.7
Notes payable CE	684.5
Other long-term liabilities LL	442.1
Other current assets CA	71.8
Buildings and equipment (net) LA	1,450.7
Other long-term assets LA	83.2
Retained earnings	224.6
Investments LA	71.4
Capital in excess of par SE	1,077.3

Instructions:

a. Prepare the balance sheet for Coca-Cola in proper form as of December 31. Use the following classifications: Current assets, Investments, Property, plant and equipment, Intangible assets, Other assets, Current liabilities, Long-term liabilities, Stockholders' equity.

b. Determine the amount of working capital. Also calculate the current ratio. Based only on the current ratio, what would you conclude about the company's ability to pay its short-term debt?

c. Calculate the debt to equity ratio. Calculate the debt ratio. What do you think of the company's "leverage?"

d. What do you think the Goodwill account represents?

P2-5

Consider the information for the balance sheet for Layman Company at the end of Year 7.

Accounts receivable	$14,500	Cash	$ 8,000
Land	11,000	Merchandise inventory	5,000
Accounts payable	18,200	Investment in X Company	7,000
Equipment (net)	12,400	Building (net)	62,000
Bonds payable	50,000	Long term receivable	4,000
Capital stock	20,000	Notes payable	6,000
Wages payable	2,000	Capital in excess of par	8,000
Supplies	1,000	Taxes payable	2,000
Patents	13,000	Retained earnings	31,700

Instructions: (1) Prepare a classified balance sheet in proper form for Layman Company at the end of Year 7. (2) Calculate the current ratio. (3) Calculate the quick ratio. (4) Calculate the debt ratio. (5) Calculate the debt to equity ratio. (6) Based on the ratios, what are your conclusions about Layman's ability to pay its short-term debts? (7) Based on the ratios, what are your conclusions about the "leverage" of the company?

P2-6

Consider the condensed balance sheet of Kent Company:

Kent Company Balance Sheet July 31, Year 5			
Current assets	$60,000	Current liabilities	$40,000
Investments	20,000	Long-term liabilities	53,000
Property, plant, equipment (net)	87,000	Stockholders' equity	82,000
Other assets	8,000		
Total	$175,000	Total	$175,000

Instructions:

a. Based on the balance sheet, calculate the following (round off to nearest tenth):

(1). Current ratio

(2). Debt to equity ratio

(3). Debt ratio

b. For each <u>independent</u> event below, recalculate each of the above ratios:

(1). Kent borrows $30,000 from the bank, giving a 3-year note, payable at the end of 3 years.

(2). Kents pays accounts payable, $4,000.

P2-7

Almost all of the financial records of Halston Store were destroyed by the bookkeeper, who took all the cash on hand on June 30. From other records, the following information is derived:

1. Cash in the bank amounted to $7,850.

2. Cost of the merchandise on hand was $14,300.

3. Furniture and fixture are rented from Acme Furniture Store for $300 a month. The rental for June had not been paid.

4. A one-year fire insurance policy was purchased on May 1 for $1,200.

5. The amount due from customers was $3,570.

6. The amount owed to suppliers was $6,300.

7. Mr. Halston had originally invested $16,000 into the business. At the time of the theft, his total capital was $28,700.

Instructions:

a. Determine the amount that was stolen by the bookkeeper.

b. Prepare a balance sheet for Halston Store immediately after the theft.

P2-8

The following selected information for Year 3 are from the records of Kelsey Company and Marvin Company, which are in the same industry.

	Kelsey	Marvin
Cash	$41,000	$25,000
Accounts receivable	62,000	44,000
Accounts payable	76,000	30,000
Property, plant, equipment	320,000	200,000
Supplies inventory	5,000	7,000
Interest payable	6,000	8,000
Merchandise inventory	67,000	50,000
Salaries payable	22,000	15,000
Short-term investments	24,000	9,000
Long-term note payable	120,000	60,000
Stockholders' equity	295,000	222,000

Instructions:

a. Prepare the balance sheet for both companies.

b. Calculate the following for each company: current ratio, quick ratio, debt to equity ratio, and debt ratio.

c. Assume you are a possible creditor for each company. Based on the ratios, with which company would you prefer to do business? Explain.

P2-9

The following balance sheet was prepared improperly.

Melvine Company
Balance Sheet
December 31, Year 4

Assets

Current assets:

Cash	$ 35,000	
Capital in excess of par	18,000	
Marketable securities	17,000	
Merchandise inventory	62,000	
Accounts receivable	87,000	
Interest receivable	700	
Notes receivable	12,000	$194,700

Property, plant, and equipment:

Land	$ 20,000	
Building (net)	240,000	
Equipment (net)	66,000	$326,000

Intangible assets:

Land held for future use	$ 30,000	
Prepaid insurance	1,400	
Patents	15,000	
Interest payable	500	
Unearned revenue	800	$ 47,700
		$568,400

Liabilities and Stockholders' Equity

Current liabilities:

Accounts payable	$14,000	
Notes payable	25,000	
Salaries payable	5,000	
Prepaid rent	800	$ 44,800

Long-term liabilities:

Bonds payable (due in 10 years)		$130,000

Stockholders' equity:

Common stock	$240,000	
Retained earnings	153,600	$393,600
		$568,400

Instructions:

1. Prepare the balance sheet in proper form. Use the tear-out form in back of book.

2. Calculate the current ratio and the quick ratio.

3. Calculate the debt ratio and the debt to equity ratio.

KEY ANSWERS TO EXERCISES AND PROBLEMS

E2-2
  a. Liabilities = $9,000
  b. Assets = $181,000

E2-4
  Company X: Accounts payable $2,600

E2-5
  Total assets = $144,000

E2-7
  e. Total assets $1,913,000

E2-11
  Total assets $295,000

E2-12
  3. Total assets $467,000

E2-13

	1994
1. Current ratio	2.21
2. Quick ratio	1.46
3. Debt to equity ratio	29.9%
4. Debt ratio	23.0%

P2-1
  Total assets $97,000

P2-2
  (1). Total assets $51,000
  (2). Total assets $49,800

P2-3
  a. Total assets $11,388,915

P2-4
  a. Total assets $6,676.6

P2-5
  Total assets $137,900

P2-6
  b. Current ratio 2.25 to 1

P2-7
  b. Total assets $26,720

P2-8
  a. Kelsey: Total assets $519,000
  Marvin: Total assets $335,000

P2-9
  (1) Total assets $586,900

Chapter 3

The Income Statement

LEARNING OBJECTIVES

After studying this chapter, you should be able to:

• Understand some basic notions about income.

• Determine income.

• Define revenue.

• Understand what a sale is.

• Define expense.

• Recognize whether revenues and expenses exist in particular situations.

• Prepare an income statement.

• Appreciate the limitations of the income statement.

The SEC filed a complaint against F&C International, Inc., a manufacturer of flavorings and fragrances, accusing the company of a scheme to overstate revenues and operating income.[10] The SEC said the company fraudulently overstated its 1991 income by approximately $1 million. It understated its loss in 1992 by at least $3,833,000, or about 137 percent. To understand the charges, you must know something about the "income statement," which is the topic of this chapter.

One of the primary financial statements is the income statement. This statement shows how profitable a company is. As such, the "bottom line" is income or profit. These terms, "income" and "profit", come from economics. In economics, these concepts are not identical, but in accounting they are used interchangeably. Another expression used is "earnings."

INCOME

• Bearing Risk •

Running a business involves many risks. When you take a risk, you are taking a chance. The chance is that the outcome may not turn out well. Consider the possibilities. For example, when a company hires a new employee, it is taking a risk. The risk is that the employee may not perform well or may even cause harm to the firm. When a company buys a new machine, it is taking a risk. The machine may not operate as expected. When a company produces a product, it is taking a big risk. Will the product turn out well? Will the cost be reasonable? Will consumers purchase the product? When a company sells its product, it is taking a risk. Will customers be happy with the product? If something goes wrong with the product and people get hurt, the company will probably have a number of lawsuits on its hands. If the product is sold on credit, the risk is that the customer will not pay. Because practically every aspect of a business involves risk, the profit a company makes is said to be the reward or return for bearing risk.

• What Is Income? •

At the beginning of the month, suppose John had $2,000 which he decided to use to buy an old Honda from a friend. At the end of the month, his cousin offered to buy the Honda for $2,500. John noticed in the classified ads in the newspaper that similar Hondas were selling for the same price. Does the increase in value of his Honda constitute income or profit? It all depends on whom you ask. An economist would say "yes," and an accountant would say "no."

---

[10] SEC, *Accounting and Auditing Enforcement Release No 605*, 1994.

–Economic concept–

Fundamentally, income or profit represents how much "better off" economically a person or firm is between two points in time. In our example, the two points are the beginning of the month and the end of the month. In other words, it is how much wealthier a person or entity has become within a given period. An economist would say that John has become wealthier by $500, and therefore he has a profit of $500. Notice two details about how the profit was determined. First, the original amount invested of $2,000 is not part of income. Economists call the beginning amount invested "capital." This capital is the same as net assets or owners' equity (Assets less Liabilities). Second, the income is the *increase in value*, the $500. The capital of $2,000 had to be "maintained" before income could occur, which is the increase in value of the capital. This notion is often referred to as the "capital maintenance" view of income. Put another way, the way accountants see it, you cannot make a profit until you have first recovered your cost, the $2,000.

–Accounting concept–

In theory, accountants agree with the economist's view of income. The problem is that economists can philosophize about income without penalty, but accountants are the ones who actually have to calculate income for business firms and face the consequences of any errors.

Notice in our example that John could have sold the car to his cousin at the end of the month to realize the profit in cash, but he chose not to do so. For economists, it does not make any difference whether John actually sold his car at the end of the month. For accountants, it does. To make sure that income actually occurred and is not just an opinion, accountants insist on relevant evidence to support the "increase in value." The kind of evidence that persuades accountants that income has occurred is a "transaction." That is why accountants would insist that John sell the car at the end of the month before income is recognized. Accountants therefore have a *transactions* view of income.

–Business income–

If we say that the income for ABC Company for 1997 is $200,000, what does that mean? In accounting, the $200,000 represents two perceptions. First, based on economic theory, it is the amount by which ABC has increased its "wealth" in that year; that is to say, how much wealthier ABC has become between January 1 and December 31. Second, the $200,000 is a measure of the company's "performance." A company is in business to make a profit, and the income figure shows its performance toward that goal. If the profit is large, then the company is doing well; if it is small or negative, then the company is not doing well.

Income is an event, something that happens. Although it is represented by a specific sum of money, it represents the "increase in wealth" of the firm or the "performance" of the firm. Both notions denote events.

In Chapter 2, the definition of owners' equity contained the assertion that it represents a firm's obligation to convey the earnings to the owners. You can see therefore that owners' equity includes earnings or income. If Karen invested $4,000 in common stocks on March 1, and on March 31 sold the shares for $4,500, then her profit is $500 (ignoring broker's fees). Her "owner's equity" or capital on March 1 is $4,000 and on March 31 is $4,500. The $4,500 at the end of the period includes the profit. It is important to note that $4,500 is not her profit; the profit, as emphasized by economists, is the "increase in wealth," the $500. This is illustrated in **Figure 3.1.**

Figure 3.1

Capital, beginning	Capital, ending
$4,000	$4,500
	$500
	income

• Period of Time •

Notice that in our example of ABC Company we said that the income was for a period of time, from January 1 to December 31. In Chapter 2, we said that the balance sheet was true as of a moment in time, and that is why the balance sheet is for one day only. In contrast, the income statement is always for a period of time. Conventionally, the time period is for one month or 3 months or 6 months or a year. If you were told that the income of ABC was $200,000, it would make a difference if it were for one month or 3 months or 6 months or a year. Your impression of the firm would be quite different if the company earned $200,000 a month as opposed to $200,000 a year. Therefore, income must always be related to a time period.

• Determination of Income •

Based on accounting theory, there is a certain way income is to be calculated. It is based on certain transactions. These transactions result in two contrary flows that affect income, one positive and the other negative. For the positive flow, there are _revenues_ and _gains_. For the negative flow, there are _expenses_ and _losses_. If we subtract the negative flow from the positive flow, we will derive income as seen in **Figure 3.2** with assumed amounts.

Figure 3.2   Determining Income

Revenue	$100,000
Less Expenses	- 40,000
Add Gains	+ 1,000
Less Losses	-800
Income	$ 60,200

To illustrate, assume the following: On January 1, 1997, National Company has owners' equity or capital of $200,000. During the year, revenues amounted to $45,000 and expenses were $18,000. The ending balance is therefore $227,000 as seen in **Figure 3.3**. This illustrates what we have said about income, the conceptual view of income and the practical determination of it.

Figure 3.3

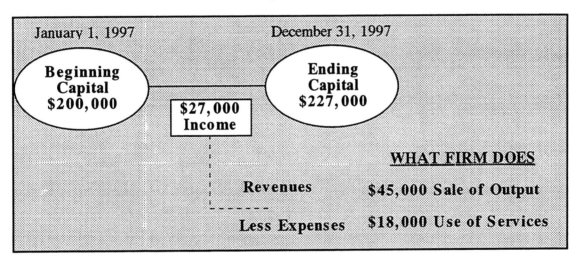

Income in this book is based on generally accepted accounting principles. It should not be confused with taxable income, which is prescribed according to tax laws.

Figure 3.4 shows the income statement of Apple Company for three years. Notice that Apple calls its income statement a statement of "operations." Net sales (revenues) is stated first, then expenses are deducted to derive income. We will return to Apple's income statement later.

Figure 3.4

Apple Computer Inc. Consolidated Statements of Operations (Dollars in millions)			
Three fiscal years ended September 26,	1997	1996	1995
Net sales	$ 7,081	$ 9,833	$11,062
Costs and expenses:			
Cost of sales	5,713	8,865	8,204
Research and development	485	604	614
Selling, general and administrative	1,286	1,568	1,583
Special charges:			
In-process research and development	375	–	–
Restructuring costs	217	179	(23)
Termination of license agreement	75	–	–
	8,151	11,216	10,378
Operating income (loss)	(1,070)	(1,383)	684
Interest and other income (expense), net	25	88	(10)
Income (loss) before provision (benefit) for income taxes	(1,045)	(1,295)	674
Provision (benefit) for income taxes	–	(479)	250
Net income (loss)	$(1,045)	$ (816)	$ 424

The rest of this chapter is a discussion of the practical aspects of determining income, which pertain to revenues (plus gains) and expenses (plus losses).

REVENUE

• Definition •

The following definition is given:

Revenue is the increase in the amount of assets (and sometimes a decrease in the amount of liabilities) of an entity because of production or sales of its product or service.[11]

---

[11] Cf. FASB, "Elements of Financial Statements," *Statement of Financial Accounting Concepts No. 6*, paragraph 78, 1985.

–An event–

Notice that revenue is a twofold activity or event. First, it is something the company does in the real world, which is to produce and/or sell its product or service. The company must *do something* to make revenue happen. Second, because of the production and/or sale, there is an increase in the amount of assets (or sometimes a decrease in the amount of liabilities).

To illustrate the concept, let us assume that George Mason invests $10,000 into a clothing store, which he names Georgie Clothes. During the first month, he sells $12,000 of clothes. There are various expenses he incurs as seen in **Figure 3.5**. His income is $4,500. It came about because of what Georgie Clothes did. Because income is created by business operations, that is why Apple Computer referred to its income statement as a statement of operations (**Figure 3.4**).

Figure 3.5

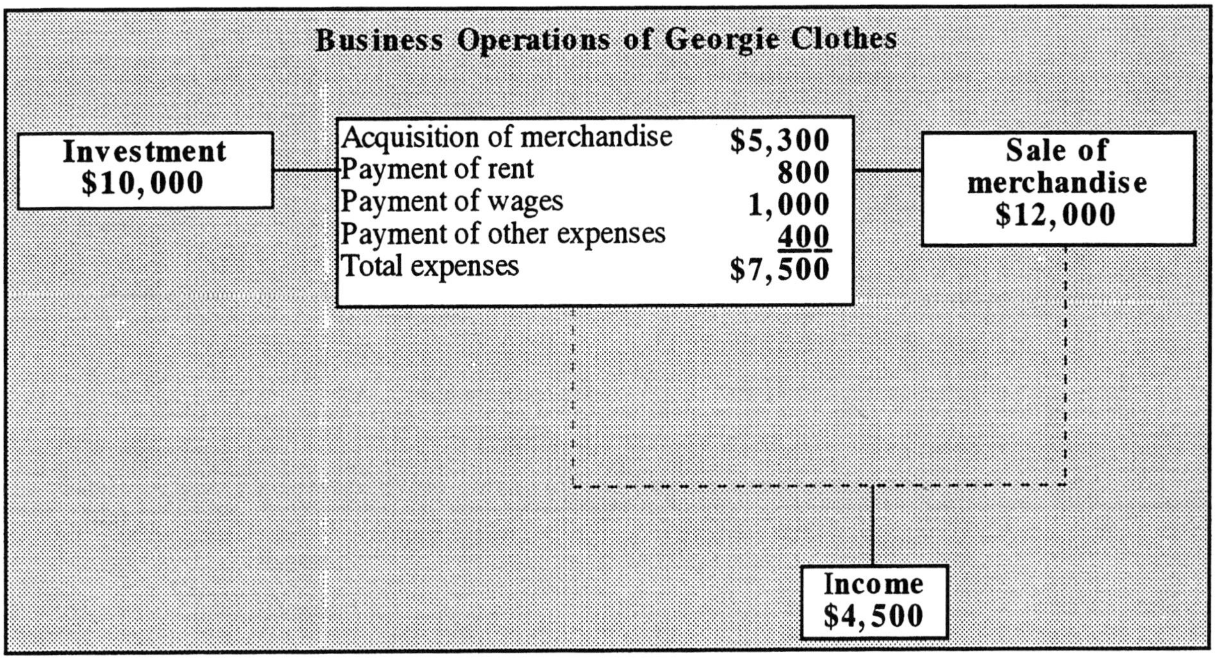

Our emphasis on activity or events is in contrast to the balance sheet definitions given in the previous chapter. There we defined assets, liabilities, and owners' equities as "objects" or things. Here, in keeping with the concept of income, we define revenue as an activity, an event, a happening, which involves the economic objects of assets and liabilities.

By selling, a firm receives assets, usually cash or a promise to pay cash (account receivable). Notice that the definition does not insist that cash be received. In a few cases, revenue is evidenced by a decrease in a liability. For example, a customer may have paid in advance (giving rise to a liability for the company) so that when the sale takes place the company will decrease its liability to the customer.

• What Is a Sale? •

The key element in revenues is for the firm to sell its output. How do we know when a sale has occurred? What must a firm do to have a sale? In answer to these questions, accountants have decided to follow the law. According to the law, if a firm sells a product, then a sale takes place when the product is **_delivered_** to the customer or the agent of the customer. When delivery is made, the "title" of ownership passes. If a firm sells a service, such as a law firm, then the sale takes place when the service is **_rendered_**.

In a footnote to its income statement for 1997, Apple Company makes the following statement:

Apple Computer Inc.

> **Revenue Recognition**
> The Company recognizes revenue at the time products are shipped.

–Use of common carrier–

Business operations are complex and so there will be times when the rule will not be easy to apply. For example, what if the buyer is a great distance away from the seller? Let's say that the seller is located in San Francisco and the buyer is in New York City. Obviously, it will be impractical for the company in San Francisco to have one of its trucks driven all the way to New York to deliver the product. The practice is to use a common carrier, a firm that is in business to deliver things. The common carrier wants to know which party is going to pay the freight charges when it makes the delivery. The law says the owner of the product should pay. The common carrier will issue a "bill of lading," on which will be specified the term, F.O.B., which means "free on board." For one party the delivery is free, and for the other it is not. The determination of which party pays is based on the specification of one of two points mentioned with the F.O.B.: shipping point or destination.

If the bill of lading reads: **_F.O.B. shipping point_**, this means that title to the goods passes at that point. In this case, the ownership of the goods is transferred to the buyer at the shipping point. The common carrier is acting as the agent of the buyer. The buyer pays for the freight charges.

If the bill of lading reads: **_F.O.B. destination_**, this means that title passes at that point. In this case, the ownership of the goods remains with the seller until the common carrier delivers them to the buyer at the point of destination. The common carrier is acting as the agent of the seller. The seller pays for the freight charges.

Accountants accept what the law says about when title passes. It depends on the F.O.B. stated on the bill of lading.

–Other complications about a sale–

Suppose a customer contracts with a furniture manufacturer to have some custom-made furniture built. Let's say that the design of the furniture is by the customer and can only be described as very unusual. The general rule of when a sale is made is that the company must deliver the product. But what if, before delivery, the customer changes his/her mind and decides that he/she doesn't want the furniture? Who else will want to buy the furniture which looks so unusual? The manufacturer will be left "holding the bag." Because of the loss the company will sustain, the law says that for custom-made products, the buyer is liable for the sale. He/she cannot back out of it. In fact, when the manufacturer starts to make the furniture, the buyer becomes obligated. Therefore, in accounting, we say that a company can record the total amount of the sale at the time there is "performance," that is when the company starts making the custom-made product.

What if a customer buys a TV set and asks that it be delivered at a later date because he will be out of town for a month. Although there is no delivery, the company can justifiably consider this to be a sale because the delayed delivery is due to the customer's convenience.

• Illustrations of Sales Revenue •

Let us apply the definition of revenue and the sales recognition rule to several cases to get a better understanding of them.

1. On March 1, Susan Smith purchased a coat for $200 in the ABC Clothing Store and charged it to her account. She took the coat with her. Is there sales revenue on March 1 for ABC?

ABC has sales revenue on March 1 of $200. The definition of revenue is met. First, there was an actual sale, because there was "delivery" of the product; the customer took the coat with her. Because of the sale, ABC charged her account, which means that total assets have increased because there is now an added amount to the asset, accounts receivable.

2. On March 10, Alan Albert purchased a suit for $350 in the ABC Clothing Store and paid for it in cash. Because the suit needed alterations, Albert was told to pick it up on March 20, which he did. Is there sales revenue on March 10 for ABC?

Technically, no sales revenue for ABC is to be recorded on March 10, because there was no sale. There was no sale, because there was no delivery of the product. The delivery did not take place until March 20. But what about the receipt of $350 on March 10? ABC received the money and gave nothing in return for it to Albert; therefore, strictly speaking, ABC owes the money to him until delivery of the suit. There is a liability on March 10, called "unearned revenue," not sales revenue.

For some business firms, they will actually record sales revenue on March 10, because it is convenient for their bookkeeping. By the time the income statement is issued at the end of the month on March 31, the transaction will be a sale because there will be delivery on March 20. However, in this book, we will abide by the rules strictly.

3. Marshall Company in Virginia purchased $2,000 of merchandise from Tom Company in Los Angeles. On April 5, Tom brought the merchandise to Railway Express, a common carrier, to have it delivered, F.O.B. shipping point. Is there sales revenue for Tom on April 5?

Tom has sales revenues on April 5, because the definition of revenue is met that day. There is a sale, because the goods were delivered F.O.B. shipping point. This means title passed to Marshall Company at the shipping point, which is the place where Railway Express received the merchandise. Railway Express is acting as the agent of the buyer.

4. Jim Reynolds is an auto mechanic and owns the Reynolds Auto Shop. On May 25, a customer brought his car in for repairs. The car was not fixed until June 3, at which time the customer paid the bill of $500. At the end of May, Reynolds estimated that the repairs up to that date amounted to $400 and therefore decided to record sales revenue of $400. How much sales revenue does Reynolds have on May 31?

Reynolds was incorrect to record $400 of sales revenue on May 31. A sale is made when the service is rendered, which means when the car is completely fixed. In some cases, when the total service rendered can be divided into logical, definable segments, a reasonable proportion can be recorded as revenue. But in this case, Reynolds must wait until the final action of the repair work, because a half fixed car is equivalent to not being fixed at all. He must wait until June 3 to record revenue.

• Exceptions to Sales Recognition Rule •

It is rarely possible to formulate one rule that is feasible for all business firms. The sales recognition rule which we have discussed and included in our definition of revenue is true for most firms, but there are three exceptions. Two are before the point of sale, and one after. This is illustrated in **Figure 3.6.**

Figure 3.6

During production	(end)	Sale	Collection

–Before sale–

For the two exceptions before the point of sale, this is where the word "production" in the definition of revenue enters. For some producers, accountants allow them to recognize revenue before the output is actually sold. First, for companies which have long-term construction contracts, such as building a bridge or an office building that will take more than a year, accountants will allow them to

120

record revenue _during production_. The method is called the "percentage of completion." By this method, the total revenue is allocated over a number of periods. For example, assume MMM Company has a $1,000,000 contract to build an office building which will take 3 years. In the first year, 40 percent of the work is completed, then MMM will recognize 40% x $1,000,000, or $400,000 as revenue.

Second, the other revenue recognition rule allowed before the point of sale is at the _end of production_. Only companies whose products are subsidized by the U.S. government can use this rule. Examples of these products are gold, silver, wheat, barley, and corn. The U.S. government stands ready to buy all the products if the company cannot sell them in the open market. Thus, the sale is a virtual certainty. Because of this, accountants will allow these companies to record as revenue all that has been produced, even if not yet sold.

–After sale-–

The third exception to the sales recognition rule is after the point of sale, which is when _cash is received._ This is a conservative principle. This rule should be employed when there is great uncertainty that a firm will be able to collect all the cash from a sale. In this case, accountants believe that revenue should not be recorded until the company receives the cash. For example, a refrigerator may be sold for $1,000 on an installment basis. If the credit rating of the customer is low, the company may decide not to record the total $1,000 as revenue at the time of sale, but to record revenue in increments only as each payment is received.

• Ethical Issues Relating to Sales •

At the beginning of this chapter, we mentioned the case of F&C International, which the SEC accused of overstating its revenues. Specifically, what the company did was to falsify invoice sales as occurring in one period when the goods were actually shipped to customers the next accounting period. Another practice was to prematurely ship goods to customers in order to record sales revenue.

The SEC also accused another company, Ciro Inc., a retailer of high-quality imitation jewelry and cultured pearls, of improperly recognizing revenue in three instances.[12] The first relates to the franchise business the company had established. The SEC charged that the chairman of the board and the president made $2.7 million in undisclosed payments to Ciro's franchisees to enable them to pay the franchise fees owed to the company. When the company received these payments, it recorded them as revenues.

---

[12] SEC, _Accounting and Auditing Enforcement Release No. 612_, 1994.

The SEC argued that these payments were additional investments, not revenues, and therefore the company should have recorded them as paid-in capital. Second, the SEC charged that the company improperly recorded revenue for rent concessions. Several of Ciro's landlords granted the company rent concessions whereby Ciro was not required to pay rent at the beginning of the lease. The company recorded these concessions as revenues, when they should have been considered a reduction of rental expense. Third, the SEC charged that the company recorded fictitious sales. In one instance, Ciro presumably made a sale to Femar, Inc., a sham company set up by the chairman of the board. The merchandise was never delivered.

EXPENSES

• Definition •

The following definition is given:

An expense is the decrease in the amount of assets (and sometimes increase in the amount of liabilities or owners' equity) of an entity due to the using up of services to create the current revenue.[13]

–An event–

Similar to the definition of revenue, notice that an expense is a twofold event or activity. First, a firm must "use up services." It does something to make expenses happen. Second, because of this using up of services, either the total amount of assets will decrease or total liabilities will increase. For example, say we have a company that has one employee who is paid $40 at the end of each day. As the company uses up the labor services of its employee each day for which it pays $40, we have an expense (the using up of the services) and a decrease in assets, the cash of $40.

–Using up of services–

A company is in business to make a profit. It does so by selling a product or service, which

---

[13] Vernon Kam, *Accounting Theory* (John Wiley, 1990), p. 277.

generates revenue. In this major activity of getting its output sold, a great deal of "services" are used up. For example, we need the services of sales people, of office workers, machines, buildings, and utilities.

Assets and expenses have one important similarity, both have to do with services or benefits. An asset can be seen as a bundle of future services. For example, a truck (an asset) will provide a bundle of trucking services. Let's say we have just purchased a truck that we believe will provide 100,000 miles of service for the total years we expect to keep the truck. As the services of the truck are used up each day (an event), this using-up of the services becomes an expense. Assume that on the first day of use, the truck was driven 500 miles. This means that 500 miles of service are used up, expired; this is the expense. For the remainder, the 99,500 miles, that continues on as an asset.

Not all services come from assets. For example, the using up of electricity is an expense, but the electric power company is not an asset of the firm.

–Typical expenses–

By convention, certain terms are used for different kinds of services used up. Listed in **Figure 3.7** are some typical expenses.

• Matching Principle •

In a company's quest to generate income, two types of activities are created: one that is positive and one that is negative. Revenues are a positive flow and expenses a negative flow. Accountants have decided that for the revenue that is recognized in a given period, the expenses that helped to create that revenue should be "matched" against it. Therefore, expenses are deducted from revenue to derive income.

It is not always easy to determine which expenses and what amounts are for a particular period. Professional judgment, conventions, and estimates are utilized to ascertain this.

Figure 3.7

Name of Expense	Service Used Up
Wages/salaries expense	Labor services
Depreciation expense	Service of equipment or buildings
Cost of goods sold	Merchandise inventory
Office supplies expense	Office supplies
Insurance expense	Insurance protection against fires, etc.
Freight out	Delivery services for goods shipped to customers
Interest expense	Money that has been borrowed
Income tax expense	Governmental services (e.g., protection from foreign invaders)
Property tax expense	Local government services, such as fire/police protection

For instance, in our previous example of the truck with 100,000 miles of future services, we had to make an estimate to derive this figure. When 500 miles were driven the first day, this means that 1/2 percent of the total became an expense. If the cost of the truck is $20,000, then depreciation expense for the first day is 1/2% x $20,000 = $100. The $100 expense is an estimate, because it is based on the 100,000 miles, which is an estimate.

–Estimates–

Many of the numbers on the financial statements are estimates. In its financial statements, Apple makes the following statement in a footnote which illustrates the point.

Apple Computer Company

> ## Accounting Estimates
> **The preparation of these consolidated financial statements in conformity with generally accepted accounting principles requires management to make estimates and assumptions that affect the amounts reported in these consolidated financial statements and accompanying notes. Actual results could differ materially from those estimates.**

• Illustrations of Expenses •

Let us apply our definition of expense to several cases to get a better understanding of it.

1. ABC Company uses its telephones constantly. On April 12, it received the March bill for $235 and paid it. What is the correct month to record the telephone expense of $235?

The telephone expense of $235 belongs to March, the month of use. The definition of expense states that it is the "using up" of the service that constitutes an expense, not the payment of it. Therefore, the telephone expense should be recognized at the end of March even though it has not been paid. On March 31, ABC did not know the amount of the telephone expense because the bill had not yet arrived. In most cases, it takes a couple of weeks or even months to prepare an income statement; therefore, by the time ABC issues the March income statement, the bill will have arrived. If not, it will have to make an estimate of the March telephone bill.

2. ABC Company borrowed $25,000 from the Continental Bank on May 1. The terms are that ABC will pay Continental the principal on August 1 with interest at 6 percent. Is there an expense to record for ABC on May 31?

There is interest expense for one month to record on May 31. The $25,000 received from the bank is an asset. Borrowing the $25,000 is not free. The definition of expense is met, because ABC used up one month of services, the use of the $25,000. Interest expense represents the cost of using borrowed money. When an interest rate is quoted, usually it represents the interest for one year. Therefore, in our case, the interest for one month is $125 (=$25,000 × 6% × 1/12). Actually, each day that passes there is interest expense. However, because of the inconvenience of recording this every day, accountants have decided to record it periodically.

3. ABC purchased a 12-month fire insurance policy from Universal Insurance Company on June 1 for $2,400. It paid in full on that day. On June 30, how much insurance expense does ABC have?

The insurance policy is an asset called "prepaid insurance." ABC should record one month of insurance expense, because by June 30 it has used up one month of fire insurance protection. This amounts to $200. The $2,400 paid does not represent the expense but the asset.

GAINS AND LOSSES

Besides revenues and expenses, there are also gains and losses on the income statement. Gains and losses occur when an asset or liability is disposed of and this is not considered part of the primary business of the firm. For example, the ABC Shoe Store may sell some of its old equipment. Selling equipment is not its major operation; selling shoes is. A gain or loss is determined as the difference between what is received and what is recorded as the value in the accounting books of the company. This is referred to as the "book value." For example, assume that National Company has land that it sells for $75,000, which it purchased 5 years ago for $40,000. The gain is calculated as follows:

$75,000 **amount received**
- 40,000 **book value**
$35,000 **gain on sale of land**

• Extraordinary Gain or Loss •

Some gains and losses are considered extraordinary and must be separated on the income statement. The reason is that users employ the information on the income statement as a basis for predictions. They need to know if a gain or loss can be expected to happen again.

A gain or loss is extraordinary if it is the result of an **_unusual_** event and this event is not likely to occur again in the near future. Examples are a loss due to a fire or a hurricane. However, not all casualty losses are extraordinary. For example, if a company has a building next to a river, and past experience indicates that it overflows causing flooding every 5 years, then the loss from the flooding is not extraordinary.

ILLUSTRATION OF INCOME STATEMENT

An income statement is presented in **Figure 3.8** for Daytona Company, a clothing store. The income statement shows a lot of details, which is desirable. However, some companies do not show many details, such as the income statement of Gap Inc. in the appendix.

Figure 3.8

	Daytona Company Income Statement			
(1)	For the Year Ended December 31, 1997			
	Sales revenue			$970,000
(2)	Less: Sales returns and allowances			19,000
	Net sales revenue			$951,000
(3)	Less: Cost of goods sold			387,000
(4)	**Gross profit**			$564,000
(5)	Less Operating expenses:			
	Selling expenses			
	Sales salaries and commissions	$ 54,000		
	Sales office salaries	38,000		
	Advertising expense	7,000		
	Freight out	2,000		
(6)	Depreciation on sales equipment	18,000	$119,000	
	Administrative expenses			
	Officers' salaries	$120,000		
	Office wages and salaries	44,000		
	Utilities expense	7,000		
	Insurance expense	9,000		
(6)	Depreciation of building	35,000		
(6)	Depreciation of office equipment	24,000		
	Office supplies expense	8,000		
	Miscellaneous expenses	2,000	$249,000	368,000
(7)	**Income from operations**			$196,000
(8)	Other items:			
	Interest expense			(2,000)
	Gain on sale of equipment			4,000
	Income before income taxes			$198,000
(9)	Income tax expense			82,000
	Income before extraordinary item			$116,000
(10)	Extraordinary item -- loss from hurricane			
	less applicable taxes			(35,000)
	Net income			$ 81,000

Notice the following on the income statement: (Numbers in left margin of income statement correspond with the numbers below.)

1. The date. A period of time, the calendar year 1997, is given. This means the income of $81,000 was earned for the year.

2. Sales returns and allowances. From sales revenue is deducted sales returns and allowances. This represents the goods returned by customers, and "allowances" given. An example of an allowance is a product that has a scratch on it and so the company gives a deduction from the original sales price.

3. Cost of goods sold. Sometimes this is called Cost of sales. This expense represents the cost to the company of the products that were sold in 1995. The company must sell the goods for a higher price than what they cost the company; otherwise, no profit will be made.

4. Gross profit. This profit figure is always the difference between net sale revenue and cost of goods sold. If the company is to make a "final" profit, gross profit must be large enough to cover all the other expenses of the company.

5. Operating expenses. These are the expenses to run the business. As seen on the income statement, they are divided between selling expenses and administrative expenses.

6. Depreciation expense. There is depreciation expense for the sales equipment, the building, and the office equipment. Depreciation represents the using up of the services of the particular long-term asset named. It is an expense that is sometimes controversial, because usually it does not represent a "current" figure. The dollar amount is an allocation of the original cost when the asset was purchased, which may have been 10 years ago. There are several methods to calculate depreciation, but the most common is the "straight line" method. Under this method, depreciation expense is determined by dividing the original cost (less any estimated salvage value) by the expected number of years of service. For example, if the cost of a machine is $10,000 and it is expected to be used 10 years, and a salvage value of $1,000 is anticipated at the end of 10 years, then depreciation expense each year is $900.

7. Income from operations. This is the income from the primary operations of the business. This is the amount that can be expected to recur in the future if conditions remain stable.

8. Other items. These are other expenses, or other income, or gains and losses that may have occurred. As shown, interest expense is placed here, because it is a "financial" expense, not an operating expense. It is the cost of using borrowed funds. The gain from selling equipment is put here also, because it came from a "peripheral" activity. The company is not in the business of selling equipment.

9. Income tax expense. This expense is conventionally separated. The amount is determined as a certain percentage of income before income taxes.

**10. Extraordinary item**. The loss sustained from a hurricane is placed in a separate category, because it is something that is not expected to recur in the foreseeable future.

**11. Discontinued operations.** This section has to do with the income made for the period of a line of product or segment of the company that has been dropped. Because this section does not appear often, we will not discuss it in this course.

**12. Comprehensive income.** Recently, the FASB decided that comprehensive income should be reported. Comprehensive income is based on the concept of economic income, where the change in wealth of the entity is emphasized even though a transaction may not have occurred. There are two ways comprehensive income may be reported. One is to include a special section at the end of the income statement. For example:

Net income	**$81,000**
Other comprehensive income:	
Unrealized gains on securities, net of tax	**5,000**
Comprehensive income	**86,000**

The other way is to show comprehensive income on a separate statement called "Statement of Comprehensive Income." The same information as mentioned above would be listed, beginning with net income.

Notice that there are various income figures before the final net income: gross profit, income from operations (or operating income), income before income taxes, and income before extraordinary item.

FINANCIAL RATIOS

The profitability of a company is a main concern of investors. The income statement shows how profitable a company is. To assess profitability, a number of "hidden" aspects can be revealed by ratios. In Chapter 15, we will present a more complete analysis of a firm. In this section we will discuss those ratios that directly involve the income statement and are important in assessing profitability.

• Gross Margin •

The gross margin is calculated as follows:

$$\frac{\text{Gross profit}}{\text{Net sales}}$$

Gross profit is net sales less cost of goods sold. This ratio shows how much "gross" profit is made on each sales dollar to help cover other expenses. For example, using the amounts in the income statement for Apple Company for 1995, 1996 and 1997 shown in **Figure 3.4**, we make the following calculations. First, we find the gross profit.

	1997	1996	1995
Net sales	$7,081	$9,833	$11,062
Cost of sales	5,713	8,865	8,204
Gross profit	$1,368	$ 968	$ 2,858

$2,858/$11,062 = 25.8% for 1995

$968/$9,833 = 9.8% for 1996

1,368/7,081 = 17.5% for 1997

You can see that the gross margin in 1996 declined, but in 1997 it rose. But the gross margin in 1997 is not as high as in 1995. In other words, for 1996, Apple was able to derive only $0.098 for every dollar of net sales as gross profit. It was not enough to cover all their other expenses and that is why they made a loss. The $0.175 cents for every dollaar of net sales in 1997 was still not sufficient for the company to make a profit.

• Profit Margin on Sales •

The profit margin on sales is calculated as follows:

$$\frac{\text{Net income}}{\text{Net sales}}$$

The ratio measures the amount of profit on each sales dollar. For example, using the amounts in the income statement of Apple Company illustrated in **Figure 3.4**, we calculate the ratio as follows:

For 1995: $424/$11,062 = 3.83%

For 1996: $(816)/$9,833 =(8.30%)

For 1997: $(1,045)/$7,081 =(14.8)%

The ratio indicates that for every $1.00 the company received, in 1995 it was able to squeeze $.038 as profit. This means also that $.962 was used to cover expenses. To determine whether this ratio is good or bad, one must compare it with those of past years and with other companies in the

129

same industry. In 1996 and 1997, the company made a loss. All the money received from sales revenue had to be used to cover expenses and there still was not enough. The company needed 8.3% percent more of sales revenue to cover all expenses and break even in 1996, and 14.8% in 1997. Obviously, Apple did not do well in 1996 and 1997.

• Rate of Return on Assets • $RO4$

Assets are used to generate profits. How effective is the company in using its assets to create profits? The rate of return on assets is an answer to that question. It is calculated as follows:

$$\frac{\textbf{Net income}}{\textbf{Average total assets}}$$

The net income figure is often adjusted, and this will be done in Chapter 15; however, for this chapter the unadjusted net income amount is sufficient for our purpose. Because the income figure is for a *period* of time, and the amount of total assets from the balance sheet is for a *moment* of time, to make it comparable to income we use the average for the period. The average is found as follows:

$$\textbf{Average total assets} = \frac{\textbf{Beginning balance of total assets + Ending balance of total assets}}{\textbf{2}}$$

For Apple, for 1997, the ratio is:

$$\frac{\$(1,045)}{\$5,364 + \$4,233/2}$$
$$= (21.8)\%$$

Because the income was negative in 1997 and 1996, we will calculate the ratio for 1995 also.

total assets at beginning of fiscal year 1995: $5,303
total assets at end of fiscal year 1995= $6,231

$$\frac{\text{net income} = \$424}{\text{average total assets} = 1/2\,(\$6,231 + \$5,303)}$$

$$\frac{\$424}{\$5,767}$$
$$= 7.4\%$$

This ratio indicates the profit rate for the company. For every $1.00 that was invested in the company in 1995, the company could earn $.074. To ascertain whether this rate is good or bad, one must compare it with the rates of previous years and with other firms in the same industry.

• Rate of Return on Stockholders' Equity •

The previous ratio is the profit rate for the company as a whole. But stockholders also want to know the return on their investment in the company. The rate of return on stockholders' equity is the ratio they tells stockholders what their return is. The calculation is as follows:

$$\frac{\text{Net income}}{\text{Average stockholders' equity}}$$

If there is preferred stock, some analysts would deduct preferred dividends to get the rate for common stockholders only. In this chapter, we will keep the calculation simple and assume no preferred stock.

For Apple, for 1997, the ratio is calculated as follows:

$$\frac{\$(1,045)}{\$2,058 + \$1,200/2} = (64.1)\%$$

For Apple, for 1995, the following was true:

Stockholders' equity at beginning of fiscal year 1995 = $2,383
Stockholders' equity at end of fiscal year 1995 = $2,901

$$\frac{\text{Rate of return on stockholders' equity} = 424}{1/2(\$2,383 + \$2,901)}$$

$$\frac{\$ 424}{\$2,642} = 16.0\%$$

To ascertain whether 16% is a good rate, one must compare it with the rates of previous years and with those of other companies in the same industry. Notice that the profit rate for the stockholders in 1995, 16.0% is much higher than the profit rate for the company as a whole, 7.4%. Why is this so? This is so, because Apple was "trading on the equity" successfully in 1995. We discussed this concept in Chapter 2. Apple was using borrowed money (the liabilities) and earning 7.4% on that amount. It was paying the creditors a rate of interest lower than that or nothing at all, and so the large "leftover" went to the stockholders. But trading on the equity involves a risk, and in 1996 and 1997, this showed up. The company made a loss, and the stockholders had to bear that loss.

• Earnings per Share •

Many investors like to see the earnings per share (EPS) of a company. As the name implies, it is the income of the company on a per common share basis. For example, the following is what Apple showed on its income statement:

Apple Computer Company

	1997	1996	1995
Earnings (loss) per common share	$(8.29)	$(6.59)	$ 3.45
Common shares used in the calculations of earnings(loss) per share (in thousands)	126,062	123,734	123,047

For 1997, the calculation was: $(1,045)/126.062 shares = $(8.29). To make the shares comparable to income (which is in millions), we used 126.062 shares.

Earnings per share should only be used in comparison with past years of the company. It is **not** sensible to compare it with other companies, because every company has a different number of shares. As you can see, 1995 was better than 1996 and 1997.

LIMITATIONS OF INCOME STATEMENT

The income statement shows how profitable a firm was for a given period based on the accepted rules of accounting. It is important to understand the rules on revenues, expenses, gains and losses so that you will not be misled.

• Conservatism •

As mentioned in Chapter 1, accountants believe in "conservatism." This means that for the positive flows, accountants have decided to be strict about recording them. There must be reliable evidence to support revenues and gains before they are recognized. Remember that sales revenue is based on *actual* transactions, mainly sales, made by a firm. For gains, the asset must be disposed of. What if the market value of some of the assets increased even though not sold? Because of conservatism, these increases are excluded from the income statement. For example, if a company has a building whose market value rose by $30,000 in 1995, this is not shown in the income statement, because accountants believe there must be an actual transaction engaged in by the company before a gain or revenue is recorded.

For the negative flows, of expenses and losses, accountants have decided not to be as strict as with revenues and gains. Although there still must be evidence to support expenses and losses, evidence that is weak is acceptable. For example, if another entity has filed a lawsuit against our company and we think we may lose the case, we should record the possible loss as though it had already occurred.

The position of conservatism then is that for something that is positive for a firm, recording it should be based on convincing evidence, while for something that is negative, recording it should still be based on evidence but the evidence need not be persuasive.

• Other Problems •

Despite conservatism, it may be that some expenses are not being recognized because accountants are unsure whether the definition of expense is met. For example, if in November a company promises its employees a Christmas bonus for doing a good job during the year, is there an expense in November? It is difficult to say. Based on what the company says, the bonus is due to services rendered throughout the year, but it will be paid in December. In November, 10 to 11 months of services by employees have already been rendered, and so theoretically there should be a bonus expense up till that point. But not everyone may have worked the whole year, and probably not everyone will get the same amount of bonus. Because of the complications of computing this, most likely the accountant will simply record the bonus expense in December when it is paid.

Some users are critical of the fact that depreciation expense, which usually is a large amount, is an "old" expense because it is an allocation of the cost of the assets which may have been purchased years ago.

Many judgments must be made in deciding whether expenses exist and what the amounts should be. For example, if a building is painted, is the expenditure an expense or should it be added to the cost of the building (an asset)?

• Ethical Issues •

Because judgments must be made about expenses, losses, gains, and revenues, manipulation of accounting methods is possible. If the managers of a company believe that income will be smaller than desired, which will give investors a poor impression of the company, they may decide to be more "liberal" about the recognition of revenues. Exchanges with customers that are not truly sales according to a strict interpretation of accounting principles may be recorded as revenue. For example, products that have been ordered by customers but not yet delivered may be recorded as revenue. Or expenditures that normally would be considered expenses may instead be "delayed" in their recognition as such. For example, new tires for a company's trucks are ordinarily considered an expense, but instead a company may decide that they should be added to the cost of the trucks (an asset). Because of these "creative" procedures, the income reported will be larger.

–Smoothing of income–

For some companies, if the managers believe that income will be too high, thus inviting criticisms about "excess profits," they will lower the amount of reported income by postponing recognition of some of the revenues and accelerating the recognition of some of the expenses. On the other hand, if income will be too low, they will try to increase the amount of reported earnings by finding accounting procedures to increase revenues and decrease expenses.

Terms such as "smoothing of income" and taking a "big bath" are common in financial circles. The first term means that a company wants income over the years to show a "smooth" picture rather than a volatile one. For example, compare the income trend of Hartford Company over 8 years with Mainline Company in **Figure 3.9**. The erratic income picture of Hartford makes many stockholders and creditors nervous.

Figure 3.9

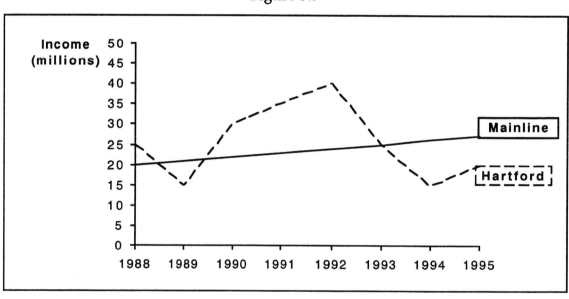

They prefer the smooth income picture of Mainline. Knowing what investors want, some managers will attempt to smooth income.

–Big bath–

A big bath means that if a company has a bad year, then it will record anticipated losses in that year, because the impression projected from its income statement is already poor and adding more negatives could not make things any worse. By doing this, the company is relieved of having to record significant losses in the future. For example, if the real estate investment a company holds has been declining in value for several years and the company anticipates selling it for a loss next year, it would record the total decline in value now.

SUMMARY OF KEY POINTS

The following key points were discussed in this chapter.

1. Bearing risk. Running a business involves many risks. Because practically every aspect of a business entails risk, the profit (income) a company makes is said to be the reward for bearing risk.

2. Income. Income creation is why firms are in business. Income depicts the "increase in wealth" of the entity. It belongs to the owners. It also shows the "performance" of the entity. It represents therefore an "event."

3. Time period. Income is always related to a period of time.

4. Determination of income. In accounting, income is the difference between the "positive" flows, which are revenues and gains, and the "negative" flows, which are expenses and losses.

5. Definition of revenue. Revenue is the increase in assets (and sometimes decrease in liabilities) due to the production or sale of an entity's products or services.

6. What is a sale? A sale occurs when the goods are delivered or the services rendered.

7. Exceptions. A few exceptions to the general revenue recognition principle concerning sales exist.

8. Definition of expense. An expense is the decrease in assets (and sometimes increase in liabilities) due to the using up of services by an entity to create the current revenue.

9. Matching. Accountants attempt to match expenses against revenue to derive income.

10. Gains and losses. These are due to "peripheral" activities of an entity as opposed to the primary operations. A few may be "extraordinary" if they are based on an event that is unusual in nature and is not likely to occur in the foreseeable future.

11. Composition of income statement. There is a specific format for the income statement. You should know how to put one together.

12. Financial ratios. The use of ratios is an important first step in asssessing the profitability of a company.

13. Limitations. The income statement has limitations. Accountants are at times unsure whether certain items meet the definitions of revenue and expense. Some disagree with the accounting rules for calculating income. Many judgments, conventions, and estimates must be made. Because of this, the income figure can be manipulated.

APPENDIX

The income statements of four actual companies are presented here: a retail company, Gap; a manufacturing company, Hewlett-Packard; a service company, Delta Air Lines; and a financial service company, Bank of America.

The Gap, Inc. and Subsidiaries
Consolidated Statements of Earnings

($000 except per share amounts)	Fifty-three Weeks Ended February 3, 1996	Fifty-two Weeks Ended January 28, 1995	Fifty-two Weeks Ended January 29, 1994
Net sales	$4,395,253	$3,722,940	$3,295,679
Costs of goods sold and occupancy expenses	2,821,455	2,350,996	2,121,789
Operating expenses	1,004,39	853,524	748,193
Net interest (income) expense	(15,797)	(10,902)	809
Earnings before income taxes	585,199	529,322	424,888
Income taxes	231,160	209,082	166,464
Net earnings	$ 354,039	$ 320,240	$ 258,424

Hewlett-Packard Company And Subsidiaries

Consolidated Statement Of Earnings

For the years ended October 31

In millions except per share amounts

	1996	1995	1994
Net revenue:			
Products	$33,114	$27,125	$21,380
Services	5,306	4,394	3,611
Total net revenue	38,420	31,519	24,991
Costs and expenses:			
Cost of products sold	22,013	17,069	13,012
Cost of services	3,486	2,945	2,478
Research and development	2,718	2,302	2,027
Selling, general and administrative	6,477	5,635	4,925
Total costs and expenses	34,694	27,951	22,442
Earnings from operations	3,726	3,568	2,549
Interest income and other, net	295	270	29
Interest expense	327	206	155
Earnings before taxes	3,694	3,632	2,423
Provision for taxes	1,108	1,199	824
Net earnings	$ 2,586	$ 2,433	$ 1,599

Delta Air Lines, Inc.

Consolidated Statements Of Operations

For the years ended June 30, 1996, 1995, and 1994

	1996	1995	1994
		(in millions)	
OPERATING REVENUES:			
Passenger	$ 11,616	$ 11,319	$ 11,269
Cargo	521	565	551
Other, net	318	310	257
Total operating revenues	12,455	12,194	12,077
OPERATING EXPENSES:			
Salaries and related costs	4,206	4,354	4,589
Aircraft fuel	1,464	1,370	1,411
Passenger commissions	1,042	1,195	1,255
Contracted services	704	556	457
Depreciation and amortization	634	622	678
Other selling expenses	594	618	614
Aircraft rent	555	671	732
Facilities and other rent	379	436	380
Aircraft maintenance materials and outside repairs.	376	430	418
Passenger service	368	443	522
Landing fees	248	266	261
Restructuring and other non-recurring charges	829	–	526
Other	593	572	681
Total operating expenses	11,992	11,533	12,524
OPERATING INCOME (LOSS)	463	661	(447)
OTHER INCOME (EXPENSE):			
Interest expense	(269)	(292)	(304)
Interest capitalized	26	30	33
Interest income	86	95	57
Miscellaneous income (expense), net	(30)	–	1
	(187)	(167)	(213)
INCOME (LOSS) BEFORE INCOME TAXES AND CUMULATIVE EFFECT OF ACCOUNTING CHANGES	276	494	660)
INCOME TAXES (PROVIDED) CREDITED, NET	(120)	(200)	251
INCOME (LOSS) BEFORE CUMULATIVE EFFECT OF ACCOUNTING CHANGES	156	294	(409)
CUMULATIVE EFFECT OF ACCOUNTING CHANGES, NET OF TAX	–	114	–
NET INCOME (LOSS)	156	408	(409)

Bank Of America

Consolidated Statement Of Operations

(in millions)	Year Ended December 31	
	1996	1995
INTEREST INCOME		
Loans, including fees	$13,363	$12,707
Interest-bearing deposits in banks	453	466
Federal funds sold	29	32
Securities purchased under resale agreements	653	618
Trading account assets	1,001	741
Available-for-sale and held-to-maturity securities	1,160	1,276
TOTAL INTEREST INCOME	16,659	15,840
INTEREST EXPENSE		
Deposits	5,359	4,923
Federal funds purchased	79	131
Securities sold under repurchase agreements	695	581
Other short-term borrowings	883	630
Long-term debt	1,023	1,067
Subordinated capital notes	33	46
TOTAL INTEREST EXPENSE	8,072	7,378
NET INTEREST INCOME	8,587	8,462
Provision for credit losses	885	440
NET INTEREST INCOME AFTER PROVISION FOR CREDIT LOSSES	7,702	8,022
NONINTEREST INCOME		
Deposit account fees	1,399	1,303
Credit card fees	355	315
Trust fees	229	300
Other fees and commissions	1,383	1,269
Trading income	630	527
Venture capital activities	427	337
Net gain on sales of assets	197	71
Net gain on sales of subsidiaries and operations	180	25
Gain on issuance of subsidiary's stock	147	–
Net gain on available-for-sale securities	61	34
Other income	404	365
TOTAL NONINTEREST INCOME	5,412	4,546

(continued)

139

The Income Statement

| | Year Ended December 31 ||
(in millions)	1996	1995
NONINTEREST EXPENSE		
Salaries	3,291	3,309
Employee benefits	773	718
Occupancy	757	738
Equipment	702	663
Amortization of intangibles	373	428
Communications	363	359
Professional services	344	313
Restructuring charges	280	–
Regulatory fees and related expenses	123	176
Other expense	1,335	1,297
TOTAL NONINTEREST EXPENSE	8,341	8,001
INCOME BEFORE INCOME TAXES	4,773	4,567
Provision for income taxes	1,900	1,903
NET INCOME	$2,873	$2,664

QUESTIONS

1. Concerning the concept of income, which of the following statements are true? If false, explain.

a. The main difference between the economic concept of income and the accounting concept of income is that economists insists on transactions to support income.

b. Income represents the change in the wealth of an entity.

c. Income is based on an event, an activity.

d. There must always be a period of time related to income.

e. Income is calculated as revenues and expenses minus gains and losses.

f. Income represents the performance of a business firm.

g. If Real Estate Company A has property that it purchased for $400,000 and sells the property for $500,000, its income is $500,000.

h. Income can never be negative.

2. Concerning the concept of revenue, which of the following statements are true? If false, explain.

a. Assets are never affected by revenue.

b. Revenue occurs because of something a firm does.

c. Revenue occurs only when cash is received.

d. Revenue is recorded only when there is a sale.

e. The difference between revenue and gain is that revenue pertains to a firm's major operations and a gain does not.

3. On the recognition of sales, which of the following statements are true? If false, explain.

a. A sale occurs when the product is delivered.

b. A sale of services occurs when the service is rendered.

c. "FOB destination" means that title to goods from seller to buyer is passed when the seller delivers the goods to the common carrier.

d. For "FOB shipping point," the common carrier is the agent of the buyer.

e. For a custom-made product, a sale is made when the product is delivered.

f. For most firms, the sales recognition rule should be used.

4. Concerning exceptions to the sales recognition rule, which of the following statements are true? If false, explain.

a. The exceptions are: (1) recognize revenue before production; (2) recognize revenue at the end of production; and (3) recognize revenue when goods are delivered.

b. The "percentage of completion" method allocates total revenue to a number of periods.

c. Only companies whose products are subsidized by the U.S. government can use the "end of production" rule.

d. The "cash received" rule should be used whenever a firm sells products on account.

5. On the concept of expenses, which of the following statements are true? If false, explain.

a. For an expense to be recorded, cash must be paid.

b. An expense denotes an event, something that happens.

c. The definition of expense includes the notion of using up of services.

d. The amount of an expense must sometimes be estimated.

e. Property tax expense is an expense because it is a penalty imposed on firms for doing business.

f. Depreciation expense represents the use of a fixed asset, such as a building.

g. The difference between an expense and a loss is that an expense helps to generate revenue while a loss does not.

h. A loss pertains to a firm's major operations.

6. Concerning the income statement,

a. What are extraordinary items?

b. What does "income from operations" mean?

c. What is an "operating" expense?

d. How is gross profit derived?

e. What is "cost of goods sold?"

f. Would interest income be placed in the "other items" section? Explain.

g. Would you expect to find accounts receivable in the income statement? Explain.

h. When "gain on sale of equipment" is in the income statement, is it stated net of income taxes? Explain.

7. On the limitations of the income statement, which of the following statements are true? Explain.

a. The increase in the market value of land is shown in the income statement.

b. Accountants sometimes disagree on whether an expense exists.

c. The amount for depreciation expense is often not a "current" cost.

d. Because accounting rules are very specific, manipulation of accounting methods is unlikely.

e. The term, "smoothing of income," refers to the practice of always reporting a large amount of income.

f. The term, "big bath," means that if a company has a large amount of income, then it can afford to record some losses.

8. Distinguish between revenues and cash receipts. Under what situation will they be the same?

9. Distinguish between expenses and cash payments. Under what situation will they be the same?

10. Is it possible for a company to have a large amount of income and yet have no cash? Explain.

11. On December 31, Year 2, Sinclair Company's balance sheet shows total assets of $98,000. On January 1, Year 2, the total assets amounted to $88,000. Does this mean that Sinclair made a profit of $10,000 for the year? Explain.

12. Indicate whether each of the following events gives rise to the recognition of revenue:

a. Sale of merchandise on account.

b. Receipt of cash because of money borrowed from a bank.

c. Receipt of cash from the sale of a company's own stock.

d. Recent shipment of merchandise to customer on terms of FOB destination.

e. Rendering of services by a dentist. No cash received.

f. Delivery of goods to common carrier to be shipped to customer, FOB shipping point.

g. Receipt of cash from sale of subscription to 12 issues of a magazine. No magazines delivered yet.

h. Collection of cash from accounts receivable.

13. Indicate whether each of the following events gives rise to the recognition of an expense:

a. Purchase of merchandise inventory from supplier. Cash paid.

b. Paid the rent on the office building for the past month.

c. Received services of employees for the week, but wages not yet paid.

d. Sold merchandise to customers.

e. Used equipment for the month. Equipment purchased 2 years ago with a useful life of 7 years.

f. Purchase of new battery for delivery truck.

14. Of the four sections of the income statement, (1) gross profit, (2) income from operations, (3) other items, and (4) extraordinary items, indicate in which section

the following items would be placed. Use the appropriate number for your response.

a. Depreciation expense.

b. Gain from sale of equipment.

c. Selling expense.

d. Loss from sale of delivery truck.

e. Uninsured loss due to destruction of building by a tornado.

f. Cost of goods sold.

g. Interest income from bonds held as an investment.

h. Interest expense on long-term bonds payable.

EXERCISES

(Refer to key answers at end of chapter)

E3-1

If you were to prepare an income statement, which of the following items would you not include in the statement:

Cost of goods sold	$40,000
Wages expense	10,000
Accounts payable	5,000
Sales revenues	88,000
Retained earnings	55,000
Supplies expense	4,000
Dividends paid	8,000
Interest expense	6,000

E3-2

Prepare the income statement for Headhunter Barber Shop for the 6 months ending June 30, Year 5. Consider the following information:

Revenues	$10,400
Telephone expense	80
Supplies on hand	220
Supplies expense	260
Equipment	2,000
Depreciation on equipment	100
Rent expense	1,800
Utilities expense	580
Miscellaneous expenses	40

E3-3

Below is a list of accounts. For each, specify whether it will be on the balance sheet or income statement.

Cash	$ 4,000
Sales revenue	32,000
Accounts payable	3,000
Common stock	14,000
Accounts receivable	8,000
Interest expense	1,000
Equipment	20,000
Depreciation expense	2,000
Interest payable	500
Retained earnings	12,000
Cost of goods sold	14,000
Accumulated depreciation	5,000
Prepaid insurance	2,500
Wages expense	13,000
Insurance expense	600
Gain on sale of land	5,000
Supplies expense	1,300

E3-4

Which of the following events of Mason Company would affect the income statement for July?

a. July 10, Mason paid its creditor, Atwood Company, $2,300.

b. July 12, Mason collected $4,000 on a customer's account for a sale made in June.

c. July 15, Sales of products were made, $12,000.

d. July 19, Mason received the utility bill for June, $430, and paid it.

e. July 27, Wages for July, $4,600, were paid.

f. July 30, Mason borrowed $10,000 from the bank.

g. July 30, Mason paid a dividend to its stockholders, $800.

E3-5

During September, the Wang Company engaged in the following selected transactions:

a. Paid $1,200 for a 1-year comprehensive insurance policy.

b. Purchased on account $920 for office supplies.

c. Purchased a machine for $800 cash.

d. Paid $920 for the office supplies mentioned in (b).

e. Paid wages to employees for the month, $2,700.

f. Paid the utilities bill for November, $134.

g. Mr. Wang, the owner, withdrew $300 for his use.

Which of the above transactions would expense be recorded? Explain.

E3-6

During October, the Wang Company engaged in the following selected transactions:

a. Sold $32,500 of goods to customers on account.

b. Collected $900 as advance payments from customers.

c. Collected $3,500 from accounts receivable.

d. Borrowed $6,000 from the bank.

e. Sold some securities of another company for $7,800. They had been purchased for $6,400.

f. Paid the utilities bill for October, $145.

g. Mr. Wang, the owner, invested $4,000 into the business.

What was the total amount of sales revenues for October?

E3-7

In February, Year 6, determine whether each of the specified events gives rise to an expense for Company X on the date of the event. Your answer should be one of the following: Expense, No Expense. If there is an expense, indicate the amount.

a. On February 1, Company X purchased for cash $10,000 of equipment.

b. On February 3, Company X purchased $500 of office supplies on account from Salvatore Supply Company.

c. On February 8, Company X paid the $500 owed to Salvatore.

d. On February 15, two new part-time employees began work. The wage rate is $12 an hour. Each worked 5 hours.

e. On February 28, a count showed that $430 of the office supplies purchased in February 3 remained.

E3-8

Myra Fong is considering purchasing the common stock of one of the two actual companies listed below. She has asked your help in compariing the two companies. Some of the information she obtained are as follows:

(dollars in thousands)	1994	1993	1992
Levi Strauss			
Net sales	$6,074,321	$5,892,479	$5,570,290
Net income	320,976	492,411	360,837
Change in accounting principle*	(236,517)		
Total assets	3,925,309	3,108,660	2,880,700
Total stockholders' equity	1,471,585	1,251,034	768,200
GAP			
Net sales	$3,722,940	$3,295,679	$2,960,409
Net income	320,240	258,424	210,701
Total assets	2,004,244	1,763,117	1,379,248
Total stockholders' equity	1,375,232	1,126,475	887,839

The change in principle was a special deduction, which reduced net income, due to Levi Strauss changing its accounting method for postretirement benefits (mainly medical benefits). This change was necessary to conform to a new accounting standard. Both companies only have common stock.

Instructions: Compute the following ratios for 1994 and 1993 for both companies:

(1) Profit margin on sales

(2) Rate of return on assets

(3) Rate of return on stockholders' equity

Based on the ratios, which company do you believe is more profitable? Explain.

E3-9

Consider the income statement of Apple Company in Figure 3.4. 1997 was not a good year for the company.

Instructions:

1. Was the amount of net sales similar to that of 1996 or 1995?
2. Calculate the gross profit for each of the 3 years.
3. Which of the 3 years has the largest amount of operating expenses?
4. What is the profit margin on sales for each of the 3 years?
5. Profit is made when sales are high and expenses are kept under control. Looking at the figures for 1997, why do you suppose a loss was made?

E3-10

Using the internet, find the income statement of Microsoft Company for 1997 (http://www.microsoft.com/msft/ar97/financial/income.htm). Get a printout of the income statement (use 80% scaling) and bring to class. At the bottom, click on the United Kingdom version and bring that income statement to class also.

Instructions: (for 1997)

1. Compute the gross margin.
2. Compute the profit margin on sales.
3. Would you say the company is profitable?
4. Look at the UK version of the income statement (remember that it is in British pounds).
a. What is "Turnover?"
b. Using the conversion rate specified by Microsoft, convert the profit in pounds (after the reconciliation) to U.S.dollars.

CASES

C3-1

Bob Jones, the new assistant controller of Leslie Company, disagreed with the way Susan Adams, the senior accountant, had accounted for some of the revenue transactions in December of Year 5. They disagreed on the following:

a. On December 31, the shipping department, located in Ohio, sent $25,000 of goods to the company's branch office in Illinois, to be delivered to customers in that area in a couple of days. Susan said sales revenue should be recorded in Year 5 because the goods were shipped in Year 5. Bob said the revenue is earned in Year 6.

b. Leslie Company received a check for $1,200 from a customer in full payment for its product to be shipped FOB destination. On December 31, the common carrier had possession of the goods. Susan said sales revenue should be recorded because the common carrier had the goods on December 31. Bob said the revenue was earned in Year 6.

c. In December, Jane Manion purchased the company's product for $800 and paid cash. However, because she was going to Europe, she asked Leslie to deliver the product in January, Year 6. Susan said sales revenue should be recorded because the sale was made. Bob said the revenue should not be recorded until January, Year 6.

d. On December 28, Lawrence Company, a new customer, sent in an order for $12,000 of goods to be purchased on account. On that day, the credit department of Leslie approved of the sale and a shipping order was sent to the shipping department. The goods are to be shipped FOB shipping point. Susan said sales revenues should be recorded because the shipping department had the goods. Bob disagreed.

Instructions: For each case, who is correct, Susan or Bob? Explain.

C3-2

Consider the following situations pertaining to Byron Company:

a. In a telephone marketing promotion, Byron obtained orders from new customers totaling

$12,000. The orders were all charged to the customers' VISA or MC accounts. As of January 31, none of the merchandise has been sent to the customers.

b. Byron is renting a new office building. The owner demanded that Byron pay for 3 months rent in the first month of each quarter, totaling $6,000. Byron made its first payment on January 31 for January, February, and March.

c. Laura Miller, one of the clerks, was absent on January 31 and therefore did not pick up her $1,550 paycheck for January.

d. Maria Fernandez purchased on account $500 of merchandise on January 15. On January 31, she called and said she wanted to return the merchandise. She was told that the company would gladly accept the return.

Instructions: For Byron Company, determine in each situation whether revenue or expense exists for the month of January. Explain.

C3-3

Income has been declining for Yarrow Company for the past three years. The president of the company recently hired Glen Stevens as the new controller and told him to do something about the sagging income. After looking over the books, Glen made the following recommendations:

a. He said the company has been too strict in their credit evaluation of new customers. Because of this, he said many sales had been lost. To increase sales revenue, he advised that the company sell on credit to all customers, except to those with the poorest credit rating.

b. So that income will increase, he advised that repairs and maintenance of the building and equipment be postponed, except for absolutely necessary repairs. Normally, the expense for repairs and maintenance is about $12,000 a year. Glen said only about $2,000 for essential repairs should be expended for the year. In this way, expense will decrease and therefore income will increase.

c. The land the company owns was purchased 10 years ago for $50,000. Glen hired a real estate appraiser who said the market value of the land is now $300,000. Glen recommended that the increase in value be recorded as a gain. He said the recording is justified because an outside party, the appraiser, has stated what the new value is. By recognizing the gain, income will be larger.

d. At the beginning of the year, Yarrow had purchased new tires and batteries for 5 of its large trucks at a total cost of $1,500. This had been recorded as an expense. Glen said the cost should instead be charged to the trucks. In this way, the $1,500 will not appear as an expense for the year, and therefore income will be larger.

Instructions: For each of Glen's suggestions, indicate whether you believe it is ethical. Explain.

C3-4

In late December, Year 7, the controller of Taylor Company, located in the midwest, informed the president that income would be very low that year. The president told the controller to do whatever was possible to increase income by manipulating accounting procedures. Consider the possibilities below:

a. A customer ordered a large amount of goods with a sales price of $24,000. The goods were in the shipping department of the company on December 31.

b. Some goods that were shipped to customers on the west coast had to be "tested" at Toledo's warehouse in Utah before final delivery. On December 31, $15,000 of goods were in the Utah warehouse being tested.

c. $5,000 of goods were shipped by train FOB destination to customers on the west coast on December 30.

d. Because of the holiday season, a number of employees were not present on December 31 to pick up their paychecks. The total amounted to $7,000.

e. The electricity bill for December did not arrive until January 10, Year 8. The amount, $850, was paid on January 13.

f. Expenditures for repairs and maintenance on Taylor's trucks and equipment for the year amounted to $9,400.

Instructions: What the president is asking the controller to do is questionable and probably unethical. Assume the controller has no concern for ethics and wants to please the president. For each situation above, what would you expect the controller to do and yet not raise the suspicions of the CPA who will audit the financial statements.

C3-5

Randy Morgan is the new accountant for Randolph Company, a manufacturer of small equipment. Some of the decisions he made in Year 5, which affected income, are as follows:

a. Randolph Company engaged an attorney to do some legal work for it in early December. Because the attorney had not yet sent his bill to the company by the end of the year, Randy said no expense for legal services should be recorded for Year 5.

b. A customer called to complain about the product he had received from Randolph. According to him, the product, which he had purchased on account for $950, was defective. Randolph offered to repair it, but the customer did not want the product anymore. He was told that his account would be credited, and that the product should be returned. As of December 31, the customer had not returned the product and so his account was not credited. Randy said this was proper.

c. A customer fell down the stairs in the Randolph building and had to be taken to the hospital. She later filed a lawsuit against the company, asking for $1,000,000. Randy consulted with an attorney who said it was too soon to predict the outcome. Randy said the company should be optimistic about winning the case, and therefore no recording about it should be made.

d. In May, Randolph signed a contract for $15,000 with Dale Company for Randolph to make a special machine according to specifications given by Dale. When the machine was finished in November, Dale refused delivery on the grounds that it no longer needed the machine. Randy said the company would continue to seek payment and therefore the total amount of $15,000 should be recorded as revenue.

e. Randolph gives a 1-year warranty on its product. It promises that within a year after the sale, if the product is defective, the company will repair the product without cost to the customer. In Year 5, 2,000 units of the product were sold. Of that total, 50 units were returned in Year 5 for repair. Randolph said that it would simply be a "wild guess" to figure out how many more units might be returned in Year 6 for repair and what the cost would be. Therefore, he said the company should wait until the units were actually returned and repaired to record any expense.

Instructions: Do you believe that Randy's decisions were proper? Explain.

C3-6

Toledo Company, a manufacturer of small appliances for the home, has had volatile earnings in the past 4 years. Marian Snyder, the controller of the company, was told to find ways to smooth the earnings picture. In December of Year 5, she estimated that Year 5 would have a small amount of income and Year 6 a very large amount. To smooth the income, she decided to do the following:

a. Toledo has several large contracts. Production for these contracts began in October of this year, Year 5, and delivery of the completed products is scheduled for Year 6. To smooth the income picture, Marian decided to adopt the "percentage of completion" method. By using this method, about 50 percent of the profit on these large contracts will be recognized in Year 5 and the other 50 percent in Year 6. If this method were not used, all of the income would be recognized in Year 6.

b. The ending inventory for Year 5 amounted to a cost of $210,000. Marian decided that because the inventory was supported by back orders, and it was simply a matter of shipping the goods to the customers, that the ending inventory should be recognized as revenue at the retail price of $440,000. This would conform with the "end of production" revenue principle.

c. Wong Company, a new customer, has a very large order. Toledo had insisted that Wong put down a deposit of $20,000. The products are expected to be shipped to Wong in early January, Year 6. Since the $20,000 was received in Year 5, Marian said the $20,000 should be considered as revenue in Year 5.

d. The payroll for December Year 5 is $43,000. So that income would be larger in Year 5, Marian ordered that employees not be paid until January 1, Year 6. She had the $43,000 recorded in January Year 6 as salaries and wages expense, because they were paid in January.

Instructions: For each of the foregoing cases, state whether you agree with Marian or not. Explain.

Case 3-7

In the actual cases that follow, the SEC charged the firms with improprieties. For each of the six cases below, determine what the improper conduct was.

1. To increase sales revenue for the year 1971, Mattel, Inc. instituted a program of "bill and hold." The program was one of billing customers for orders they had placed and recording them as sales revenue.

2. Mattel had a warehouse in Mexico that was destroyed by a fire in 1970. The insurance policy had a "business interruption" clause that provided up to $10 million for any revenues lost because of the destruction of the warehouse. Mattel recorded $10 million as a gain.

3. The auditor for Mattel, the CPA firm of Arthur Andersen, sent out letters to certain customers to confirm the amounts they owed Mattel. A number of customers said the amount Mattel said they owed the company was overstated. To provide documentary support of these "bill and hold" sales for the auditor, Mattel prepared bills of lading, which are used for the shipment of goods by a common carrier. These bills of lading were signed by an employee of the company for both Mattel and the common carrier. On checking the bills of lading, the auditors noticed that the words "bill and hold" were written on them. In its report, Arthur Andersen did not note anything improper.

4. The United States Surgical Corporation had a policy of recording sales revenue whenever it shipped goods to its sales people who were located throughout the country. The sales people worked on a commission basis. Each sales person kept an inventory of merchandise which was transported to clients. It was common practice for the company to send merchandise to the sales people without their asking for them.

5. In 1978, Charles Keating acquired Lincoln Savings and Loan Association, which was located in Arizona. In 1987, Lincoln loaned $19.6 million to E.C. Garcia & Co., a land development firm. Garcia was a close friend of Keating. In turn, Garcia loaned $3.5 million to Fernando Acosta, a friend of Garcia. Acosta owned Wescon, a mortgage real estate firm. After receiving the loan, Wescon purchased 1,000 acres of desert land owned by Lincoln for $14 million, twice the value established by appraisers. Acosta used the $3.5 million from Garcia as downpayment and signed a nonrecourse note for the balance. A nonrecourse note is where the person receiving the note accepts full responsibility for collection; there is no guarantee given for payment of the note. Lincoln recorded a profit of $11.1 million on the transaction. The business relationships are shown below. The profit was never realized, because Acosta never paid the nonrecourse note.

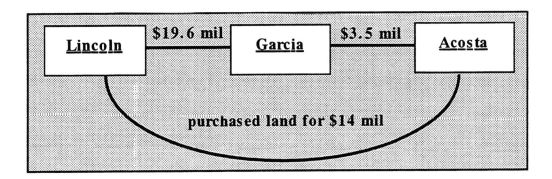

6. In 1985, Cardillo Travel, Inc. received $203,000 from United Airlines to shift from the American Airlines computer reservation system to the United Airlines computer reservation system. The amount was to cover expenses in making the change. It was to be paid back United Airlines if not used. Cardillo recorded the $203,000 as revenues earned.

C3-8

Refer to the income statements in the appendix.

1. Of the four companies, which one has the least informative income statement? Explain.

2. For Delta Air Lines, there was a loss in 1994. What was the main reason for the loss? As best you can, explain what you think happened.

3. For Bank of America, notice that its income comes from two sources: interest income and

noninterest income.

a. For the interest income, what is the largest source of income for the bank? What is the largest interest expense?

b. For the noninterest income, what is the largest source of income? What is the largest amount of noninterest expense?

4. Why do you suppose Hewlett-Packard has a large amount of expense for "research and development," and Gap has none?

5. For 1996, compute the profits margin on sales, and the rate of return on assets. (Refer to the balance sheets in the appendix of Chapter 2.)

C3-9

Consider the income statements of American Airlines presented on the next page. Answer the following questions:

1. What is the major source of operating revenue?
2. What is the largest expense?
3. Why did operating income increase by such a large amount in 1994 compared with 1993?
4. In the "other income (expense)" section, what is the largest expense?
5. Why did net earnings decrease in 1995 compared with 1994?
6. Compute the following ratios:
    a. Profit margin on sales for 1995 and 1994.
    b. Rate of return on assets for 1995.
Assets for 1995 totaled $17,629, and for 1994, $17,323.
    c. Rate of return on stockholders' equity for 1995.
Stockholders' equity for 1995 totaled $3,634, and for 1994, $3,233.
7. Based on the ratios you computed, what is your conclusion about the profitability of American Airlines?

American Airlines, Inc.
Consolidated Statement Of Operations
(in millions)

| | Year Ended December 31, | | |
	1995	1994	1993
REVENUES			
Airline Group:			
Passenger	$ 13,335	$ 12,826	$ 12,900
Cargo	668	648	637
Other	732	634	527
	14,735	14,108	14,064
Information Services Group	1,439	1,268	1,167
Less: Intergroup revenues	(564)	(539)	(494)
Total operating revenues	15,610	14,837	14,737
EXPENSES			
Wages, salaries and benefits	5,183	5,038	4,927
Aircraft fuel	1,565	1,556	1,818
Commissions to agents	1,236	1,273	1,393
Depreciation and amortization	1,138	1,138	1,115
Other rentals and landing fees	802	780	787
Food service	675	663	693
Aircraft rentals	604	620	639
Maintenance materials and repairs	494	438	542
Other operating expenses	2,460	2,143	2,259
Restructuring costs	485	276	–
Total operating expenses	14,642	13,925	14,173
OPERATING INCOME	968	912	564
OTHER INCOME (EXPENSE)			
Interest income	23	13	5
Interest expense	(557)	(457)	(408)
Interest capitalized	14	21	49
Miscellaneous - net	(55)	(47)	(136)
	(575)	(470)	(490)
Earnings before income taxes and extraordinary loss	393	442	74
Income tax provision	172	174	51
Earnings before extraordinary loss	221	268	23
Extraordinary loss, net of tax benefit	(13)	–	–
Net earnings	$ 208	$ 268	$ 23

PROBLEMS

(Refer to key answers at end of chapter)

P3-1

The following is a list of accounts for Newberry Company at the end of Year 12.

Cash	$12,000
Salaries expense	13,000
Salaries payable	1,000
Sales revenues	77,000
Cost of goods sold	43,000
Accounts payable	8,000
Accounts receivable	14,000
Advertising expense	2,000
Rent expense	8,000
Utilities expense	5,000
Retained earnings, January 1	9,000
Merchandise inventory	14,000

Instructions: Prepare an income statement for Newberry for the year.

P3-2

The following is a list of accounts for Roberts Company at the end of Year 14.

Retained earnings, January 1	$ 45,000
Cash	15,000
Sales revenues	170,000
Dividends paid	6,000
Gain on sale of equipment	8,000
Cost of goods sold	54,000
Wages and salaries expense	43,000
Depreciation expense	16,000
Merchandise inventory	42,000
Interest expense	3,000
Interest income	2,300
Rent expense	12,000
Wages and salaries payable	2,000
Income tax expense	15,000

Instructions: Prepare an income statement with proper classifications for Roberts Company for the year. Use the tear-out form at end of book.

P3-3

The following is a list of accounts for Carlton Company at the end of Year 6.

Sales revenue	$489,000
Buildings	300,000
Accumulated depreciation-buildings	42,000
Cash	54,000
Accounts payable	178,000
Salaries payable	25,000
Interest expense	9,000
Equipment	320,000
Accumulated depreciation-equipment	120,000
Interest payable	3,000
Cost of goods sold	189,000
Depreciation expense	34,000
Salaries expense	122,000
Utilities expense	21,000
Accounts receivable	180,000
Advertising expense	8,000
Merchandise inventory	260,000
Miscellaneous operating expenses	7,000
Supplies	21,000
Sales returns and allowances	6,000
Prepaid expense	24,000
Bonds payable	200,000
Retained earnings	371,000
Income tax expense	34,000
Land	300,000
Fire loss, less applicable tax effect	17,000
Long-term receivable	20,000
Common stock	500,000
Capital in excess of par	40,000

Instructions:

1. Prepare an income statemen for Year 6.

2. Prepare a balance sheet at the end of the year.

Use tear-out forms at end of book.

P3-4

For Dennis Corporation, a manufacturer of plastic kitchenware, determine the following on November 1:

a. The amount of sales revenue for the month of October, Year 5, based on the following information:

---

(1). Dennis sold (issued) its bonds with a face value of $100,000 for $102,000.

(2) Goods amounting to $87,000 were shipped FOB shipping point to customers. Of the total, only $35,000 was paid in cash by customers.

(3) Dennis received orders for $52,000 of goods during the last week of the month. It received $12,000 cash from customers as deposits on their orders. Dennis expects to ship the products the first week of November.

(4) One customer returned $1,300 of goods that had been shipped to him in October.

(5) Dennis sold for $36,000 its stock of Allen Company that it had purchased months before for $31,000.

b. *The amount of expenses for the month of October, Year 5, based on the following information:*

(6). Salaries of employees amounted to $12,000 for October.

(7) The utility bill for October was $880. It was not paid until November 15, because the bill did not arrive until then.

(8) Dennis sold some old equipment for $3,200. The carrying value was $4,000.

(9) Dennis had purchased a 12-month fire insurance policy on February 1, Year 5 for $2,400.

(10) Dennis has buildings and equipment which it had purchased several years ago. The accountant said that the depreciation expense on those assets was $12,000 a year.

P3-5

Consider the events that affected revenue for Excel Company, a manufacturer of paper products, for Year 5:

a. One of Excel's large customers, Mayberry Company, sent in an order in early December, Year 5 to purchase $23,000 of Product A. Due to a shortage of Product A in its inventory, Excel was not able to send it to Mayberry, but Excel is certain that the order will be filled by January, Year 6.

b. Products with a sales price of $90,000 were shipped FOB shipping point to Grossman Stores. As of December 31, Grossman has not received the goods.

c. Throughout the year, goods with a retail price of $134,000 were shipped to various customers. The customers were billed for the sales, but as of the end of the year only $112,000 cash has been collected.

d. Barney Company, a new customer, purchased $40,000 of products. Barney asked that it pay Excel in 4 equal installments. Because Barney's credit rating is very good, Excel agreed. By the end of the year, $10,000 cash was received by Excel.

e. The total inventory on December 31 of all its products amounted to $67,000. Excel is certain that it can sell all of them in Year 6 because of their popularity.

Instructions: For Year 5, determine the amount of revenue for Excel Company.

P3-6

Consider the following events that occurred for Abbey Company in Year 3:

a. Throughout the year, sales of its product were made amounting to $868,000. The cost of the products sold was $320,000.

b. An earthquake caused considerable damage to Abbey's building. The total cost of repairs was $450,000, of which the insurance company paid $420,000.

c. Some old equipment with a carrying value of $13,000 were sold for $15,000.

d. The corporate income tax rate for Abbey is 35 percent of income.

e. The following expenses were incurred during the year:

Advertising expense	$6,000
Depreciation on office building	$34,000
Depreciation on office equipment	$1,400
Sales salaries expense	$67,000
Officers salaries expense	$145,000
Insurance expense	$2,400
Utilities expense	$3,200
Interest expense	$900
Miscellaneous general expenses	$1,100
Freight paid for shipments to customers	$800

Instructions: (1) Prepare an income statement for Abbey Company for Year 3. (2) Calculate the gross margin and the profit margin on sales. (3) Assume the average amount of total assets for the year is $900,000. Calculate the rate of return on assets. (4) Assume the average amount of stockholders' equity is $750,000. Calculate the rate of return on stockholders' equity. (5) Assume Abbey has 12,000 common shares. Calculate the earnings per share.

P3-7

The actual income statement of a recent year for Paramount Communications Inc. shows the following items

	(in millions):
Cost of goods sold	$2,740
Selling, general and administrative expenses	1,129
Revenues	4,265
Other income (expense)	(7)
Interest and other investment income	122
Income tax expense	127
Interest expense	(114)
Extraordinary item	(9)

The company explains that the interest and other investment income of $122 is due mainly to its share of the income from affiliated companies (those companies in which Paramount owns from 20% to 50% of the stock). The company also explains that the extraordinary item resulted from the purchase back of some of its bonds.

Instructions:

(1) Prepare an income statement in correct form for Paramount.

(2) Calculate for the current year the gross margin, the profit margin on sales, rate of return on assets, and rate of return on stockholders' equity. Other pertinent figures are:

	(in millions)
Total assets at the beginning of current year	$6,640
Total assets at the end of current year	7,054
Total stockholders' equity at beginning of current year	3,895
Total stockholders' equity at end of current year	4,051
Total assets at the beginning of previous year	6,539
Total stockholders' equity at beginning of previous year	3,829

(3) For the previous year, revenues were $3,895 million, and the operating income was $158 million. Investment income was $134 million. There were no extraordinary items. Net income was $122 million. Based on the information provided and your calculations, indicate whether you believe Paramount did well for the current year. Explain.

P3-8

Consider the income statements of Company A and Company B which are in the same industry.

	Company A	Company B
Sales revenue	$120,000	$ 80,000
Sales returns and allowances	12,000	4,000
Net sales	108,000	76,000
Cost of goods sold	52,000	30,000
Gross profit	56,000	46,000
Operating expense	25,000	17,000
Income from operations	31,000	29,000
Other expenses	2,000	1,000
Income before income taxes	29,000	28,000
Income tax expense	8,700	8,400
Income before extraordinary item	20,300	19,600
Extraordinary item-fire loss	0	2,000
Net income	$ 20,300	$ 17,600

Instructions:

a. Compare the net sales of the two companies.

(1) Which company has the larger amount of sales?

(2) In proportion to sales, which company has the lesser returns and allowances?

b. Compare the gross profit.

In proportion to net sales, which company is paying less for its goods sold?

c. Compare the income from operations.

(1) What is the income from operations indicative of?

(2) In proportion to net sales, which company has the lesser amount of operating expenses?

d. The fire loss for Company B caused a decrease in income. If you were an investor trying to decide about Company B's future income, how would this loss affect your prediction?

e. Compute the profit margin on sales for each company.

f. Based solely on what is on the current income statement, what is your opinion about the profitability of each company?

g. For the company that is less profitable, what advice would you give the managers to improve the profitability of the company?

KEY ANSWERS TO CERTAIN EXERCISES AND PROBLEMS

E3-2

Income $7,540

E3-8

Levi Strauss 1993

Profit margin on sales 8.4%

Rate of return on assets 16.4%

Rate of return on stockholders equity 48.8%

P3-1

Income $6,000

P3-2

Net income $37,300

P3-3

Net income $42,000

Total assets $1,317,000

P3-6

Net income $167,830

P3-7

(1) Net income $261

Chapter 4

Accrual Accounting

LEARNING OBJECTIVES

After studying this chapter, you should be able to:

- Explain what accrual accounting is.
- Describe the statement of cash flows.
- Understand how the balance sheet and income statement relate to each other.
- Describe what an "account" is.
- Explain the meaning of "debit" and "credit."
- Record transactions.
- Identify activities as financing, investing, or operating.
- Record adjusting entries.

The SEC filed a complaint against the auditor of General Technologies Group Ltd., a company located in New York which designs, manufactures, assembles and sells electro-magnetic equipment.[14] One of the charges was that the auditor allowed the company to improperly record progress payments on its government contracts as sales. The SEC also filed a complaint against Bali Jewelry, Ltd., a New York company which manufactures and sells gold chains.[15] One charge was that the company failed to record at least $7 million in loan transactions. As you can see from these cases, certain transactions must be recorded and the recording must be done properly. In this chapter, you will learn how transactions are recorded, and the proper way to enter them. If these transactions are not properly recorded, a firm can get into trouble.

JUSTIFICATION FOR ACCRUAL ACCOUNTING

Of the many events that occur affecting an entity, accountants select only certain ones to record. This selection is based on generally accepted accounting principles (GAAP). In general, as discussed in previous chapters, accountants want to record all assets, liabilities, owners' equity, revenues, expenses, gains and losses. In this respect, accountants depend first on the *definitions* found in accounting theory. Second, accountants look to practical *recognition rules,* which are based on the desire for relevant and reliable information.

• Contrast with Cash Accounting •

The definitions we have discussed in Chapters 2 and 3 are based on *accrual accounting.* Accrual accounting is to be contrasted with cash accounting. In cash accounting, a transaction is recorded only if cash is involved. It is a very simple type of accounting. Accrual accounting is based on the objective of providing relevant information. Accountants have decided that cash information, although relevant, is very limited in helping users judge the profitability and financial position of a company. The focus of accrual accounting is on *important events* that affect a given entity, rather than simply on cash input and output. For instance, for a sale, under cash accounting a credit sale would not be recorded.

–Revenue–

Consider the following example: In January, ABC Company sold two units of its product, each with a sales value of $500, to two customers. Customer A paid $500 cash for the product, and

---

[14] SEC, *Accounting and Auditing Enforcement Release No. 552,* 1994.

[15] SEC, *Accounting and Auditing Enforcement Release No. 608,* 1994.

Customer B had the sale charged to her account. Customer B paid her account in February. The difference in accounting for ABC is as follows:

FOR JANUARY		
	Cash Accounting	Accrual Accounting
Sales revenue	$500	$1,000

Under accrual accounting, the sales revenue is $1,000, because the important event is making the sale, regardless of whether cash was received at that time or not. Under cash accounting, the important event is the receipt of cash rather than the sale.

FOR FEBRUARY		
	Cash Accounting	Accrual Accounting
Sales revenue	$500	0

In February, under cash accounting $500 would be recorded as sales revenue when Customer B paid. Under accrual accounting, the $500 in February is the collection of the receivable. According to the definition of "sale," a sale occurs when the product is delivered. GAAP is premised on accrual accounting.

–Expense–

To illustrate the difference between cash accounting and accrual accounting regarding expenses, suppose both Jane and Jim, employees of ABC Company, worked in February. Jane gets paid $2,000 at the end of each month, but because February was a short month, she was not actually paid until March 1. Jim gets paid $700 at the end of each week on Fridays. On February 28, he received his 4th paycheck for the month of February, giving him a total of $2,800. The difference in accounting for ABC is as follows:

FOR FEBRUARY		
	Cash Accounting	Accrual Accounting
Salaries and wages expense	$2,800	$4,800

Under cash accounting, only the actual amount paid in February for salaries and wages is an expense. Under accrual accounting, both amounts constitute the expense, because the focus is not when cash is paid but on when the services of the employees were *received* by the company.

–Accrual accounting and cash flow–

Eventually, accrual accounting is also based on cash receipts and payments, because everything must be cash in the end, otherwise it amounts to nothing. For example, if Customer B never paid her account, then the sales revenue of $1,000 under accrual accounting for January is not correct. If she never pays, then what really happened is that the firm gave her a product for "free." In such a case, the sales revenue under cash accounting, which shows only a sale to Customer A, is correct. What accrual accounting does is to adjust for the "leads" and "lags" of the cash flows. In other words, accrual accounting puts some of the revenues and expenses in a different time period, but eventually, in the end, both are basically the same.

To illustrate the point, consider the following simple example for Crowell Company:

Events in 1995:

Sold 5 units of product on account for a total of $5,000.

Of the amount sold on account, collected $3,000.

Purchased a machine for cash for $3,000. Expected useful life is 3 years.

Events in 1996:

Sold 5 units of product on account for a total of $5,000.

Of the amount sold on account in 1995, collected $1,000.

Of the amount sold on account in 1994, collected $2,000.

Expenses incurred were $2,000, of which $500 was paid in cash.

Events in 1997:

Sold 5 units of product on account for a total of $5,000.

Of the amount sold on account in 1996, collected $5,000.

Of the amount sold on account in 1995, collected $4,000.

Expenses incurred were $1,000, all of which were paid in cash.

Of the expenses incurred in 1995, paid $1,500.

Figure 4.1 summarizes the events in the determination of income for each of the 3 years and the 3-years combined under cash accounting and accrual accounting.

Figure 4.1

	1995		1996		1997		3-Years	
	Cash	Accrual	Cash	Accrual	Cash	Accrual	Cash	Accrual
Sales Revenue	$3,000	$5,000	$3,000	$5,000	$9,000	$5,000	$15,000	$15,000
Expenses	3,000	1,000	500	3,000	2,500	2,000	6,000	6,000
Income	$ 0	$4,000	$2,500	$2,000	$6,500	$3,000	$ 9,000	$ 9,000

Notice that in the end, for the three years combined, the total revenues and expenses are the or both cash accounting and accrual accounting. The difference is in the *timing* of the revenues and expenses. The definitions show why there is a timing difference.

> **Under cash accounting:**
> Revenue = Cash collected from customers
> Expense = Cash paid for services
>
> **Under accrual accounting**
> (which are the definitions presented in this book, but which we simplify here):
> Revenue = Sales to customers
> Expense = Use of services

As emphasized previously, accrual accounting focuses on the important events that occur, two of which are sales and use of services. The reason for accrual accounting is that accountants have concluded that information on cash inflow and outflow, although relevant, is limited. Users need information on a company's profitability and financial position. Information on profitability is on the income statement and information on financial position is on the balance sheet, and these are based on accrual accounting.

STATEMENT OF CASH FLOWS

The information on profitability and financial position, based on accrual accounting, is very important for users who must make decisions about their relationship with a firm. However, many investors also want to know the inflow and outflow of cash for a company. Creditors expect a company to pay them back in cash. Stockholders expect to receive cash dividends. Therefore, users of accounting information are interested in how much cash a company has. For this purpose, accountants have the Statement of Cash Flows. More details of this statement will be discussed in Chapter 14, but at this point we present an example of it in **Figure 4.2.**

• Cash Flow from Operations •

In the statement, the income of $41,000, which is on an accrual basis, must be converted to a cash basis, called "cash provided by operating activities." In Chapter 14, you will learn which accounts to select in the income statement and balance sheet to convert the accrual-based income to a cash basis. In our example of Lambert Company, cash income is greater than accrual income. By looking at the adjustments, you can ascertain why this is so. One reason is that depreciation expense of $10,000 was deducted to derive income, but because it is a noncash expense, it is added back to income to get the cash-based income. Accounts receivable decreased by $5,300. A decrease means that Lambert is collecting the cash from customers to whom it had previously sold merchandise on credit. This is added back to income because under cash accounting, the receipt of cash from customers is revenue.

Figure 4.2

Lambert Company	
Statement of Cash Flows	
For the Year Ended December 31, Year 7	
Cash flows from operating activities:	
Net income	$ 41,000
Adjustments to reconcile net income to net cash provided by operations:	
Depreciation expense	10,000
Decrease in accounts receivable	5,300
Cash provided by operating activities	56,300
Cash flows from investing activities:	
Purchase of equipment	(120,000)
Cash flows from financing activities:	
Dividends paid	$ (13,000)
Proceeds from bonds issued	150,000
Net cash provided by financing activities	137,000
Net increase in cash:	$ 73,300
Cash at beginning of year	3,000
Cash at end of year	$ 76,300

• Types of Activities •

All the activities that a firm may undertake, whether cash or noncash, can be placed into three categories: _**operating**_, _**investing**_, and _**financing**_. Notice that the statement of cash flows in **Figure 4.2** is divided into these three types of activities.

–Operating activities–

Basically, operating activities relate to the purpose of the firm, which is to make a profit, and so they pertain to revenues and expenses. They include payments for goods and services relating to the expenses. For example, for a manufacturing firm, operating activities might look like that illustrated in **Figure 4.3**.

Figure 4.3

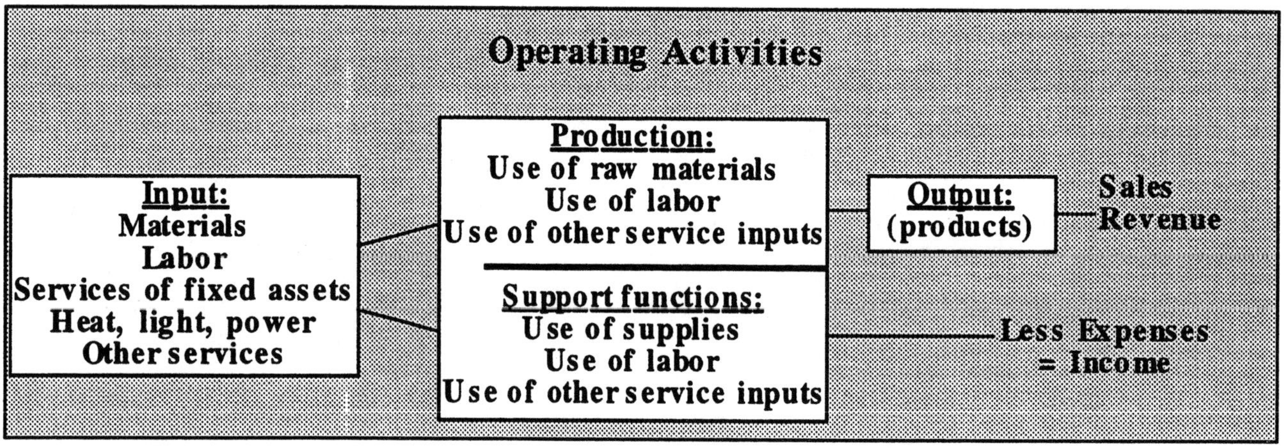

Operating Activities

| Input: Materials Labor Services of fixed assets Heat, light, power Other services | Production: Use of raw materials Use of labor Use of other service inputs Support functions: Use of supplies Use of labor Use of other service inputs | Output: (products) Sales Revenue Less Expenses = Income |

–Investing activities–

Investing activities pertain mainly to the acquisition and sale of long-term assets. They also include the purchase and sale of the securities of other entities, and loans to other entities.

–Financing activities–

These activities pertain to the raising of funds for a firm, such as the sale of the company's stocks and bonds. They also include the repayment of borrowed money and payment of dividends to stockholders. The activities are summarized in **Figure 4.4**.

Figure 4.4

Types of Activities

Operating activities:

Creating income (revenues and expenses)

Collecting cash from customers

Buying and paying for goods and services related to current assets

Investing activities:

Acquiring long-term assets

Selling long-term assets

Purchase and sale of securities of other entities

Financing activities:

Raising funds for the firm

Repaying any loans

Paying dividends

A logical flow of these activities is the following:

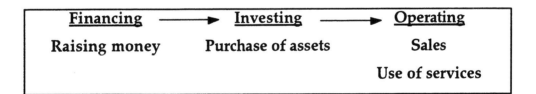

Financing	→	Investing	→	Operating
Raising money		Purchase of assets		Sales
				Use of services

The statement of cash flows reveals the cash inflow and outflow of a company in terms of these three major activities. These cash flows are not directly disclosed in the income statement and balance sheet. Essentially, the statement shows the sources of cash (where the cash came from) and the uses of cash (where the cash went). For Lambert Company, it received $56,300 from operating activities, it invested $120,000 in equipment which caused a cash outflow of that amount, and it received financing of a net amount of $137,000.

ACCOUNTING EQUATION

In Chapter 2, we discussed the accounting equation:

> **Assets = Liabilities + Owners' equity**

We explained that we are focusing on the total sum of the assets and looking at two characteristics of it. The first characteristic is the "physical," which, in effect, asks the question: What is the composition of the assets? We want to know the different kinds of assets, such as cash, accounts receivable, and equipment. The second characteristic is the "equity," which, in effect, asks the question: Who has a claim on the assets? As pointed out in Chapter 2, the relationship of these two characteristics to the accounting equation is as follows:

physical characteristic	equity characteristic
Assets	= Liabilities + Owners' equity

• Relationship between Balance Sheet and Income Statement •

The balance sheet follows the accounting equation. It shows as of a moment in time the assets, the liabilities and the owners' equity. Let's see how the balance sheet is directly related to the income statement.

In the previous chapter, in our definition of revenue we said that due to production or sale, the effect is an increase in the amount of assets or decrease in the amount of liabilities. For an expense, due to the using up of services, the effect is the opposite for revenue: a decrease in assets or increase in liabilities. This is illustrated in **Figure 4.5**.

Figure 4.5

Effect on Accounting Equation	
Revenue =	increase in assets or decrease in liabilities and increase in owners' equity
Expense =	decrease in assets or increase in liabilities and decrease in owners' equity

For example, assume that ABC Company on March 1 has the balances as shown in **Figure 4.6**. On March 2, ABC sells some of its products for $500 cash. The cost of the products sold is $300,which as we mentioned in Chapter 3, is an expense called cost of goods sold. The effects are shown in **Figure 4.6**.

Figure 4.6

	Assets	=	Liabilities	+	Owners' equity
March 1 balance	$100,000	=	$40,000	+	$60,000
March 2 revenue	500	=			+ 500
March 2 expense	- 300	=			- 300
Totals	$100,200		$40,000		$60,200

Notice that the revenue is an increase in assets (the cash), and the expense is a decrease in assets (the merchandise inventory). Notice also that both the revenue and expense affect owners' equity. The reason is that revenue and expense are part of income, and income belongs to the owners.

• Debit-Credit Form •

Because of the "double-entry" principle discussed in Chapter 2, there is always a "double" effect on the accounting equation for each transaction as can be seen in our example in **Figure 4.6**. We are consistently keeping track of the total assets in terms of the *two characteristics* previously mentioned. As shown in **Figure 4.6**, for revenue there is an increase in assets and also an increase in owners' equity. For expense, there is a decrease in assets and also a decrease in owners' equity. At all times, the equation is in balance.

–The account–

Each item on the balance sheet and income statement, such as cash and sales revenue, is called an "account" in accounting. An account is the accounting representation of a particular object (balance sheet item) or event (income statement item) where its increases, decreases, and balances are maintained. Instead of the terms, increases and decreases, by convention accountants use the expressions, "debit" and "credit." The reason for these terms is that historically the first book in accounting was published in Italy in the 15th century, and this terminology was used in that book. We can picture the account as having a left side and a right side as in a "T." **Figure 4.7** illustrates the rule regarding debits and credits for balance sheet accounts:

Figure 4.7

Asset		=	Liability		+	Owners' equity	
increase	decrease		decrease	increase		decrease	increase
debit	credit		debit	credit		debit	credit

Notice that for every account the left side is the "debit" and the right side is the "credit." But notice that whether the debit stands for an increase or decrease depends on what kind of account it is. For an asset, the debit is always an increase and the credit a decrease. Because the liabilities and owners' equity are on the opposite side of the accounting equation, their arithmetical sign is also the opposite. For a liability and owners' equity account, a debit is a decrease and a credit is an increase. **Figure 4.8** illustrates the rule regarding debits and credits for income statement accounts.

Figure 4.8

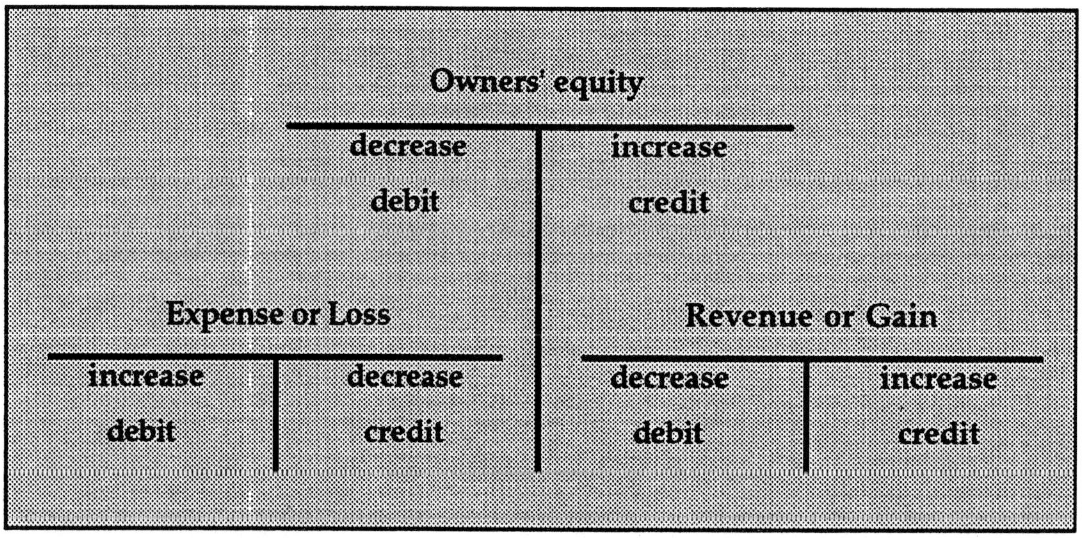

Income statement accounts are actually part of owners' equity. They are separated, because users want the detailed information about revenues, gains, expenses, and losses. In Chapter 3, we said that revenues and gains are the "positive" flows, and expenses and losses are the "negative" flows in the determination of income. If revenues and gains were put directly into owners' equity, they would be a credit, because owners' equity would increase. If expenses and losses were put directly into owners' equity, then they would be a debit, because owners' equity would decrease. Therefore, as you see in **Figure 4.8**, an increase in revenue is a credit, and an increase in expense is a debit.

As a help to remember the correspondence of debits and credits and increases and decreases in _income statement accounts_, keep in mind that they are actually owners' equity accounts, and must therefore be in consonance with the increase/decrease in owners' equity. When you debit an expense account, in effect you are increasing the "negative" flow in the determination of income.

RECORDING TRANSACTIONS

In Chapter 1, we illustrated the accounting system as shown in **Figure 4.9**. In Chapters 2 and 3, we discussed the financial statements, the balance sheet and the income statement, and in this chapter, the statement of cash flows.

Figure 4.9

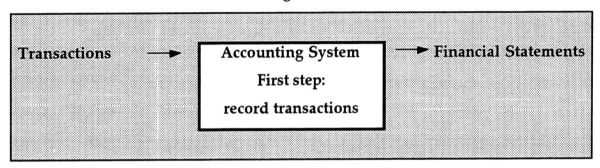

As you can see in **Figure 4.9**, the financial statements are the end products of the accounting system. Now we want to take a step back and see what is done in the "accounting box." What do accountants do to derive the financial statements? The first step in the process is to record *transactions*.

• Decision to Record •

All transactions are events. They involve an exchange of some sort. Each transaction involves accounting *elements*, such as asset, liability, owner's equity, revenue, gain, expense, or loss. As we saw in Chapter 2, the ending balances of all the assets, liabilities and owner's equity are placed in the balance sheet. As discussed in Chapter 3, the total amounts for an accounting period of the revenues, expenses, gains and losses are placed in the income statement. This is illustrated in **Figure 4.10**.

Figure 4.10

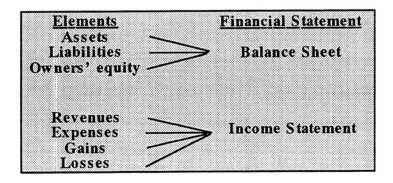

In recording a transaction, the accountant must decide what elements to record. The accountant must ask, "What elements are involved in the transaction?" As mentined above, an element is an asset, or a liability, an owner's equity, revenue, expense, gain or loss. To answer the question, the accountant must refer to the definitions. These definitions were discussed in Chapters 2 and 3. Then the accountant must ascertain whether the element is measurable. That is, can a dollar amount be determined without undue subjectivity? This decision process is illustrated in **Figure 4.11**.

Figure 4.11   Decision to Record

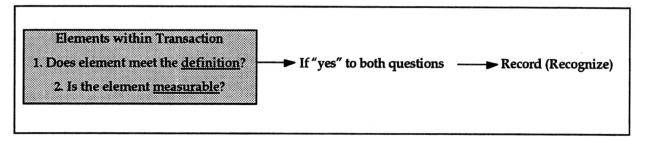

• Journal and Ledger •

Transactions are recorded as they _occur_ in a book called the _journal._ Because of this, the journal is sometimes referred to as the book of original entry. As noted in Chapter 1, what is considered pertinent depends on GAAP. Later, the information in the journal is transferred (in accounting, this is called "posting") to another book called the _ledger,_ which lists all the accounts in a convenient order. In this book, we will use a T to illustrate an account in the ledger. This is illustrated in **Figure 4.12**.

Figure 4.12

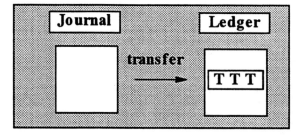

When people refer to the "accounting books," these are the books they mean. Today, except for very small business firms, the journal and ledger are not actually books with pages, but may be on a computer disk. However, for classroom purposes, it is convenient to think of them as actual books.

• Increases and Decreases •

What accountants record is a representation of the actual transactions of a firm. In every transaction, there is an exchange, a _receiving_ and a _giving_ of something of value. Accountants capture this receiving and giving in the entries they make. In recording the transactions, accountants use the double-entry format discussed previously, which is denoted by the accounting equation, Assets = Liabilities + Owners' Equity. Every recorded transaction affects the accounting equation. In effect, what accountants do is to keep track of the increases and decreases of assets, liabilities, and owners' equity.

–Debits and credits–

Recall the rule illustrated in **Figure 4.7**. We summarize it in a different format in **Figure 4.13**. As seen in **Figure 4.13**, the normal balance in the accounts is what would be positive (increase). For example, the normal balance of an asset is a debit balance.

Figure 4.13

Account Type	Increase	Decrease	Normal Balance
Assets	Debit	Credit	Debit
Liabilities	Credit	Debit	Credit
Owners' Equity	Credit	Debit	Credit
Revenues and Gains	Credit	Debit	Credit
Expenses and Losses	Debit	Credit	Debit

–Misinterpretation of debits and credits–

You must not be confused concerning the usage of debits and credits because of your dealings with retail stores. If you have a credit balance in your account at a department store, this means you have overpaid your account and therefore you owe the store nothing; in fact, the store owes you. Whether a debit or credit is "good" or "bad" depends on where you stand. For the store, your account is the asset, account receivable. A debit in that account means that you, the customer, owes the store (good for the store); a credit, means that the store owes you (bad for the store but good for you). Therefore, the store uses the terms, debits and credits, based on the amounts in its accounts receivable in its dealings with you, the customer.

• Example of Journal Entry •

To illustrate the recording of a journal entry, assume that on June 8, ABC Company purchased office supplies from Taylor Supply Company for cash for $2,000. The transaction would be recorded in the journal as follows:

Date	Transaction recorded	Debit	Credit
June 8	Office Supplies	2,000	
	Cash		2,000
	(Purchased supplies for the office from Taylor.)		

Notice the following:

1. The date of the transaction is specified.

2. In the transaction, there is an increase in office supplies for ABC, and therefore the asset account, Office Supplies, is debited. The account that is debited is always recorded first.

3. To receive the supplies, ABC had to give cash. Thus, the cash account must be credited, because it decreased. The account to be credited, Cash, is recorded after the debit. It is indented to distinguish it from the debit. The amount of the credit is also in a different column.

4. Next is the explanation. This explains in words what happened.

Remember that what accountants are trying to do is to "capture" certain parts of reality so that there is an "accounting" of what actually happened. It is like a painter who is painting a picture of an apple. His painting is a representation of the real thing, the apple; he is trying to depict in his own way what is reality. Likewise, a real transaction for a company occurs. The accountant records the transaction in a certain form to depict this reality. The journal entry is this depiction. For example, the preceding entry tells a story of what happened -- the company purchased (received) office equipment and paid $2,000 for it.

ADJUSTING ENTRIES

• External and Internal Transactions •

The transactions we have referred to are "external" transactions. These are "visible" events in which a firm is dealing with an "external" entity. They are recorded in the journal as they happen. Examples of such transactions are the following:

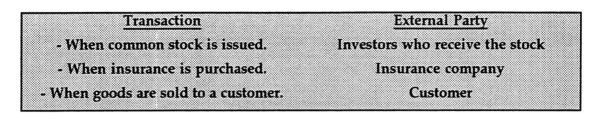

Transaction	External Party
- When common stock is issued.	Investors who receive the stock
- When insurance is purchased.	Insurance company
- When goods are sold to a customer.	Customer

For an external transaction, it is recorded on the day that it occurs. The exchange with the other party prompts its recording. However, based on accounting theory, other events exist that should be recorded even though no direct participation of an external party is involved in the particular event. There may have been an external party in an earlier transaction, but not for the present one. These transactions exist by virtue of accounting theory. They are "internal" transactions and when recorded are called "adjusting entries." **Figure 4.14** shows that both kinds of transactions are recorded.

Figure 4.14

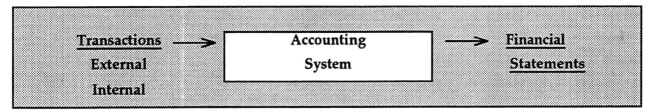

Transactions ⟶ Accounting System ⟶ Financial Statements
External
Internal

–When recorded–

For the sake of convenience, adjusting entries are recorded at the *end of the accounting period.* An accounting period is one where at the end, financial statements will be prepared. If financial statements are prepared monthly, then the accounting period is one month; if financial statements are prepared quarterly, then the accounting period is a quarter (every 3 months).

• Kinds of Adjustments •

There are four kinds of adjustments that must be made at the end of the accounting period. Two involve revenue (accrued revenue and unearned revenue), and two involve expenses (accrued expense and prepaid expense).

–Need for adjustment–

If there is need for adjustment, then there must be something that isn't right that needs "fixing." What is the problem? The problem is that certain balances in the financial statements are not properly stated. This is brought about because of the use of accrual accounting as opposed to cash-basis accounting. It is an issue of *timing.* We want to record revenues and expenses in the proper period, rather than when cash is received or paid.

–Effect on revenue–

If you remember, based on accrual accounting, for almost all firms, revenue is recognized when a firm makes a _sale_ of its output. One problem arises when cash is received from customers _before_ the sale, and so the revenue needs to be recognized in the current period when the sale is actually made. The other problem arises when revenue is earned in the current period but is not recorded; the cash will be received in a _future_ period. This is illustrated in **Figure 4.15**.

–Effect on expense–

If you remember, based on accrual accounting, an expense is incurred when a firm **uses up** services. One problem arises when the firm pays for services in advance, and so there is need to record the expense in the current period when the service is actually used. The other problem arises when a service is used in the current period but is not recorded, and so the adjustment is to record the expense. The expense will be paid in the future.

Figure 4.15   Revenue

Prior Time	End of Current Period	Future Time
Cash received from customer in advance of sale (external transaction)	→ (adjustment needed to record revenue; called "unearned revenue" adjustment)	
	Revenue earned but not recorded (adjustment needed to record revenue; called "accrued revenue") →	Cash received (external transaction)

An example of this type of accrual, where an expense is debited and a liability is credited, can be seen on the _1997_ balance sheet of Apple Company in **Figure 2.2**, and shown again below.

Apple Computer Company	
Current liabilities:	
Accrued compensation and employee benefits	99
Accrued marketing and distribution	278
Accrued warranty and related costs	128
Accrued restructuring costs	180

The accruals which affect expense is illustrated in **Figure 4.16**.

• Example of Four Types of Adjustments •

We will discuss the four basic types of adjustments next.

–Accrued revenue–

Something that accrues is something that grows; it gets larger over time. The implication is that the growth is silent and has not been recorded in the current period. Accrued revenue then is revenue that is growing over time in a quiet way.

Figure 4.16   Expense

Prior Time	End of Current Period	Future Time
Cash paid in advance for services →	(adjustment needed to record expense; called "prepaid expense" adjustment)	
	Expense incurred but not recorded → (adjustment needed to record expense; called "accrued expense")	Cash paid (external transaction)

It keeps growing until the cash is received. It is revenue by definition, but because it is not an "external" transaction, it may be overlooked unless one makes a point of noting it. At the end of the accounting period, the accountant must examine the books and make sure that this revenue is recorded.

To illustrate, we will assume the following transactions for Richmond Company. On April 20, one of Richmond's good customers, Lemon Company, was short on cash and so Richmond loaned Lemon $5,000. The terms are that the principal will be paid in 30 days with interest at 20 percent. The external transaction is recorded as follows:

External transaction recorded by Richmond:		
April 20	Notes Receivable	5,000
	Cash	5,000
	Loan to Lemon Company payable in 30 days at 20% interest.	

At the end of the accounting period, April 30, there is an accrued revenue, which is the interest revenue on the $5,000 loan to Lemon Company on April 20. The definition of revenue is met, because Richmond has rendered a service to Lemon, the use of its $5,000 for 10 days. The agreement mentions a 20 percent interest rate. When the interest rate is not specifically stated for a given period, such as 15% per month, then it is assumed that the rate is for a year, which is true in our example. Therefore, the interest for 10 days is $27.78 (= $5,000 × 20% × 10/360 days). Conventionally, in calculating interest in terms of days, 360 days are used. What we have said is illustrated in **Figure 4.17**.

Figure 4.17

					April						
20	21	22	23	24	25	26	27	28	29	30	
↓										↓	

$5000 given to Lemon for 30 days

end of period 10 days of interest earned, $27.78

The adjusting entry is:

Adjusting entry recorded by Richmond:		
April 30	Interest Receivable	27.78
	Interest Revenue	27.78
	To record accrued interest on $5,000 loan	
	to Lemon at 20% for 10 days.	

The interest receivable represents the expectation of cash. It is a promise to pay Richmond received by Richmond. The interest revenue was earned in April, because Richmond gave a service to Lemon, the use of its $5,000.

–Unearned revenue–

When a company receives cash from a customer and has not given anything to the customer, then there is unearned revenue (a liability). On the day it receives the cash, the company owes something to the customer.

To illustrate, assume that Richmond decides that one of its trucks is not needed in its operations. Therefore, on April 15, it signs an agreement with Atlas Company for Atlas to rent the truck for $400 a month. Richmond demands and receives 3 months of advance rent, $1,200. The external transaction would be recorded as follows:

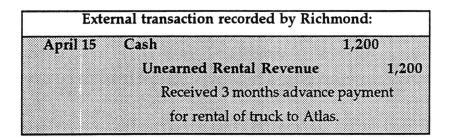

In the ledger, we see the following:

Unearned Rental Revenue (liability)
|1,200 April 15

On April 15, there is unearned revenue for Richmond because Atlas has not yet used the truck; therefore, there is a liability (unearned rental revenue). Richmond received cash and gave its promise to provide rental services.

On April 30, Atlas has used the truck for 2 weeks. For Richmond, the definition of revenue is met, because it has rendered a service, the use of its truck, for 2 weeks.

Figure 4.18

April															
15	16	17	18	19	20	21	22	23	24	25	26	27	28	29	30
↓															↓
$1200 received for 3												end of period			
months rent												2 weeks rent earned $200			

Therefore, an adjustment of the unearned revenue must be made; namely, a transfer to revenue of $200, which is 1/2 of a month's rent. What we have said is illustrated in **Figure 4.18**.

The following adjusting entry is made:

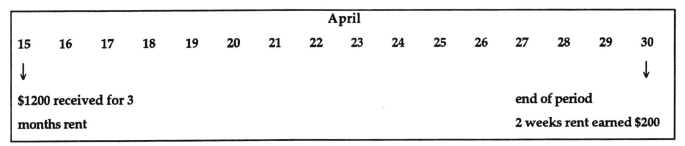

In the ledger, we see the following:

Unearned Rental Revenue

April 30	<u>200</u>	1,200	April 15
		1,000	balance

–Accrued expense–

As mentioned for accrued revenue, the term "accrued" means that something is growing and no recording of the growth has been made. Accrued expense keeps growing until paid. Two examples of accrued expenses are discussed next.

1. Accrued interest. Assume that on April 5 Richmond borrows $7,000 from the National Bank. The terms are that the principal is payable in 60 days, and that interest is due at the end of 60 days at 7 percent. The external transaction is recorded as follows:

External transaction recorded by Richmond:		
April 5	Cash	7,000
	Note Payable	7,000
	Received loan from National Bank payable	
	in 60 days at 7% interest.	

Each day, interest expense is accruing, growing. It grows until it is paid. On April 30, there is accrued interest expense on the $7,000 loan, because Richmond has used a service, the use of the $7,000 for 25 days. The interest rate is 7 percent; therefore, for 25 days the amount of interest is $34.03 (= $7,000 × 7% × 25/360).

The situation is illustrated in **Figure 4.19.**

Figure 4.19

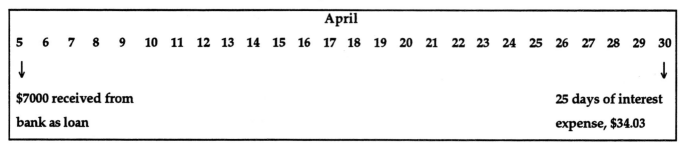

The adjusting entry is:

Adjusting entry recorded by Richmond:		
April 30	Interest Expense	34.03
	Interest Payable	34.03
	To record interest on $7,000 loan	
	from bank at 7% for 25 days.	

2. *Bad debts.* Assume that Richmond had a total of $40,000 credit sales in the month of April. Unfortunately, based on past experience it always turns out that some customers will not pay what they owe the company. Bad debts is an accrued expense, but it grows only in relation to credit sales and accounts receivable. If there were no credit sales and accounts receivable, it would not exist.

On April 30, the end of the accounting period for Richmond, the company is not able to identify the particular customers who will not pay, but based on past experience it knows that about 2 percent of credit sales is "uncollectible." Therefore, as an adjusting entry, the company makes an estimate of the amount of "bad debts" expense, which in this case is 2 percent x $40,000 or $800. The following adjusting entry will be recorded:

Bad Debts Expense	800	
Allowance for Uncollectible Accounts		800

The allowance account is called a "contra valuation" account and will be shown as a deduction from accounts receivable in the balance sheet.

–Prepaid expense–

Prepaid expense is an asset; it represents a bundle of future services that has already been paid for. As the asset is used, that part that has been used up becomes an expense. In our example of Richmond Company, we will demonstrate three cases of a prepaid expense.

1. *Depreciation.* Assume that Richmond purchased two trucks on April 1 for $16,000 each. The following external transaction is recorded:

External transaction recorded by Richmond:		
April 1	Trucks	32,000
	Cash	32,000
	Purchase of two trucks which have	
	a useful life of 5 years.	

The trucks are assets for Richmond, and as they are used the used-up portion becomes an expense, called depreciation expense. The definition of expense is met, because Richmond has used the trucks for one month. The cost of each truck is $16,000 with an estimated salvage value at the end of 5 years of $3,000. Depreciation expense is calculated as follows:

$32,000 Cost of 2 trucks

\- 6,000 Salvage value

$26,000 Amount to depreciate

$26,000/5 years = $5,200 a year

$5,200/12 months = $433 a month

The situation is illustrated in **Figure 4.20**.

Figure 4.20

April																
1	2	3	4	5	6	7	8	9	10	11	12	13	14	15	16	17
				18	19	20	21	22	23	24	25	26	27	28	29	30

↓   ↓

trucks purchased for $32,000   end of period

used trucks for 1 month,

depreciation, $433

The recording of depreciation expense, which is an adjusting entry, for the two trucks would be as follows:

Adjusting entry recorded by Richmond:		
April 30	Depreciation Expense - Trucks 433	
	Accumulated Depreciation	433
	To record depreciation on trucks for one month.	

The accumulated depreciation account is a "contra valuation" account and will be shown as a deduction from the Trucks account in the balance sheet.

2. Amortization. Something similar to depreciation is the "amortization" of an intangible asset. Assume that on April 1, Richmond purchased a patent for $42,000. A patent has a legal life of 17 years from the date the patent was granted. A company, however, may decide that its useful economic life is shorter. Assme that the patent has a useful life of 10 years.

External transaction recorded by Richmond:		
April 1	Patent	42,000
	Cash	42,000
	Purchased patent	

The amount of the amortization is calculated as follows:

$42,000/10 years   = $4,200 a year
$4,200/12 months =$350 a month

Adjusting entry recorded by Richmond:		
April 30	Amortization Expense 350	
	Patent	350
	To record the monthly amortization of	
	the patent.	

Notice that the term is "amortization" rather than depreciation for the expense. Also notice that the asset, Patent, is credited directly and is not put into a contra account as is the case with depreciation.

3. _Insurance expense._ For the third example of prepaid expense, assume that on April 1 Richmond also purchased a 12-month casualty insurance policy from All Risk Insurance Company for $2,400 cash. The external transaction is recorded as follows:

External transaction recorded by Richmond:		
April 1	Prepaid Insurance	2,400	
	Cash		2,400
	Purchase of 12-month casualty insurance policy.		

At the time of purchase, the insurance policy is an asset embodying 12 months of casualty insurance protection. Conventionally, it is named "prepaid insurance." If the insurance was not fully paid for at the time of purchase, the term "unexpired insurance" can be used. As time passes, a portion becomes an expense because the insurance protection expires. By April 30, one month of insurance protection has been used up; therefore, the following adjusting entry is recorded:

Adjusting entry recorded by Richmond:		
April 30	Insurance Expense	200	
	Prepaid Insurance		200
	To record the expiration of one month of casualty insurance protection.		

In the ledger, we see the following:

Prepaid Insurance

April 1   2,400 | 200   April 30

balance 2,200

• Effect on Financial Statements •

The adjusting entries that Richmond Company recorded on April 30 are summarized in **Figure 4.21**. If adjustments are not made, the financial statements will be incorrect. Consider what the effect would be on the balance sheet and income if Richmond Company had not recorded the adjusting entries. See **Figure 4.21**.

Figure 4.21

ADJUSTING ENTRIES:			Assets	Liabilities	Income
				Effect If Not Recorded:	
				Understated= U	
				Overstated= O	
Interest Receivable	$ 27.78		U		
Interest Revenue		$ 27.78			U
Unearned Rental Revenue	200			O	
Rental Revenue		200			U
Interest Expense	34.03				O
Interest Payable		34.03		U	
Bad Debts Expense	800				O
Allowance for Uncollectible Accounts		800	O		
Depreciation Expense-Trucks	433				O
Accumulated Depreciation		433	O		
Amortization Expense	350				O
Patent		350	O		
Insurance Expense	200				O
Prepaid Insurance		200	O		

• Summary •

How do we identify what needs to be adjusted? As the foregoing discussion points out, there are four types of adjustments. They all affect income. Two pertain to revenue and two relate to expenses. **Figure 4.22** provides a summary explanation.

Figure 4.22

Revenue	Expense
Accrued revenue This is revenue that has not yet been recorded in the current period but exists by definition. The passage of time is relevant.	**Accrued expense** This is expense that has not yet been recorded in the current period but exists by definition. The passage of time is relevant.
Unearned revenue (liability) This account has already been recorded in an external transaction. Adjustment is to transfer an amount from unearned revenue to earned revenue as the product is delivered or service rendered.	**Prepaid expense (asset)** This account has already been recorded in an external transaction. Adjustment is to transfer an amount from the asset to expense as the services of the asset expire.

COMPREHENSIVE ILLUSTRATION

So that you will have a better understanding of how transactions are recorded, we will present the following example case for Mangold Company for the month of April and show the journal entry for each transaction and the effect on the accounting equation. Remember that all transactions can be categorized as either operating, investing, or financing.

• Financing Activities •

–Issuance of stock–

On April 1, Mangold Company received $50,000 from investors. It issued 5,000 of common stock to them.

April 1	Cash	50,000	
	Common Stock		50,000
	Issued 5,000 shares of common stock to investors.		

As discussed previously, because accountants use the double-entry principle, the accounting equation is affected by every transaction. Every transaction causes either an increase or a decrease in assets, liabilities, or owners' equity (including revenues-gains, expenses-losses). Whatever is recorded, the accounting equation must always be in balance. What is increasing or decreasing in transactions is recorded from the point of view of the firm.

In this case, Cash is debited because it is an asset and it increased. Common stock is credited because it is owners' equity and it also increased.

The effect on the accounting equation is as follows:

$$\text{Assets} = \text{Liabilities} + \text{Stockholders' equity}$$
$$+ \$50,000 = + \$50,000$$

What we have said can be summarized as follows:

Other Parties	What Mangold received (debit)	What Mangold gave (credit)
Investors	Cash (increase)	Common stock (increase)

–Borrowing money–

On April 5, Mangold borrowed $7,000 from National Bank. The terms were 60 days, 6 percent interest payable at the end of 60 days.

April 5	Cash	7,000	
	Notes Payable		7,000
	Borrowed cash from the bank for 60 days, 6%.		

Cash is debited because it is an asset and it increased. A note is given, representing the liability, Notes Payable. It is credited because the liability increased.

The effect on the accounting equation is as follows:

$$\textbf{Assets} \quad = \quad \textbf{Liabilities} \quad + \textbf{Stockholders' equity}$$
$$+ \ \$7,000 \quad = \quad + \ \$7,000$$

What we have said can be summarized as follows:

Other Party	What Mangold received		What Mangold gave	
		(debit)		(credit)
National Bank	Cash	(increase)	Mangold's promise to pay (represented by Notes Payable)	(increase)

–Adjusting entry–

The note above has accrued interest for 25 days. Mangold will not pay the interest until May 5. But at the end of April, 25 days of interest expense must be recorded.

| April 30 | Interest Expense | 29 | |
| | Interest Payable | | 29 |

$$6\% \ \text{x} \ \$7,000 \ = \ \$420 \ \text{a year interest}$$
$$25/360 \ \text{x} \ \$420 \ = \ \$29 \ \text{for 25 days}$$

For short periods of time, it is common to calculate interest based on 360 days for the year.

• Investing Activities •

–Purchase of trucks–

On April 15, Mangold purchased for cash two trucks for $16,000 each from Midwest Company. The trucks are expected to be used for 5 years. The estimated salvage value is $3,000 each.

April 15	Delivery Equipment	32,000	
	Cash		32,000
	Purchased two trucks from Midwest Company.		
	Expected useful life is 5 years.		

The delivery equipment is debited because it is an asset and it increased. The cash is credited because it is an asset and it decreased.

The effect on the accounting equation is as follows:

$$\textbf{Assets} \quad = \quad \textbf{Liabilities} + \textbf{Stockholders' equity}$$

$$+ \ \$32,000$$

$$- \ \$32,000$$

What we have said can be summarized as follows:

~~Other Party~~	What Mangold received (debit)		What Mangold gave (credit)	
Midwest Company	Delivery equipment	(increase)	Cash	(decrease)

–Adjusting entry–

The trucks must be depreciated at the end of the accounting period to denote their use. The calculation of depreciation is:

$$\$32,000 \quad \text{cost}$$
$$\underline{6,000} \quad \text{less salvage value}$$
$$\underline{26,000} \quad \text{amount to depreciate}$$
$$\$26,000/5 \text{ years} \ = \$5,200 \text{ depreciation a year}$$
$$5,200/12 \text{ months} \ = \$433 \text{ a month or } \$216 \text{ for } 1/2 \text{ month}$$

| April 30 | Depreciation Expense | 216 | |
| | Accumulated Depreciation | | 216 |

• Operating Activities •

–Purchase of inventory–

On April 16, Mangold purchased $11,000 of merchandise inventory on account from Bush Company. The purchase of inventory is considered an operating activity because the merchandise is to be sold to earn revenues.

April 16	Merchandise Inventory	11,000	
	Accounts Payable		11,000
	Purchased inventory on account from Bush		
	Company.		

Merchandise inventory is debited because it is an asset and it increased. Mangold owes Bush, and so a liability, Accounts Payable, is credited to show the increase in the liability.

The difference between accounts payable and notes payable is that the accounts payable is an informal promise to pay, while the notes payable is evidenced by a formally signed note. Usually, in transactions between firms in which credit is granted, there is a certain amount of trust or faith in the other party, and so no formal note is demanded. Banks, however, normally require a signed note. Sometimes with a new customer or when the amount involved is very large, a business firm may ask for a signed note.

The effect on the accounting equation is as follows:

$$\text{Assets} = \text{Liabilities} + \text{Stockholders' equity}$$
$$+\ \$11,000 = +\ \$11,000$$

What we have said can be summarized as follows:

Other Party	What Mangold received (debit)	What Mangold gave (credit)
Bush Company	Merchandise (increase)	Mangold's promise to pay (represented by Accounts Payable) (increase)

–Sales to customers–

On April 17, Mangold sold to customers for $15,000 merchandise that had cost $7,000. Some of the customers paid cash, $1,200, and the others charged their accounts.

April 17	Cash	1,200	
	Accounts Receivable	13,800	
	Sales Revenue		15,000
	Sold merchandise for cash and on account.		
April 17	Cost of Goods Sold	7,000	
	Merchandise Inventory		7,000
	To record the cost of merchandise sold.		

When a sale is made, there is a twofold transaction. One is the sale to the customer at the sales price, and the other is the giving of the merchandise stated at cost. The first transaction shows that Mangold received cash and the customers' promise to pay Mangold, accounts receivable. Both are assets and are debited to show the increase in these accounts. The credit shows the increase in sales revenue.

The second entry shows that Mangold incurred an expense, the "use" of the merchandise, Cost of Goods Sold, in this transaction. It is debited because the expense has increased. Merchandise inventory, an asset, is credited to show the decrease in the asset, since Mangold had to give the merchandise to make the sale.

The effect on the accounting equation is as follows:

$$\text{Assets} = \text{Liabilities} + \text{Stockholders' equity}$$
$$+\ \$1,200$$
$$+\ \$13,800 = +\ \$15,000 \text{ (revenue)}$$
$$-\ \$7,000 = -\ \$7,000 \text{ (expense)}$$

What we have said can be summarized as follows:

Other Parties	What Mangold received		What Mangold gave	
		(debit)		(credit)
Customers	Cash	(increase)	Sales	(increase)
	Customers promise to pay (represented by Accounts Receivable)	(increase)		
Customers	Use of merchandise (represented by Cost of Goods Sold)	(increase)	Merchandise	(decrease)

–Sales returns–

On April 20, some of the customers who had purchased merchandise on account returned their goods. The original sales price was $400.

April 20	Sales Returns and Allowances	400	
	Accounts Receivable		400
	Merchandise returned by customers.		

Sales returns and allowances is a "contra" sales revenue account. It is not an expense, but an amount that is to be subtracted from sales revenue. Because the customers have returned the merchandise, Accounts Receivable, the asset, is credited to show the decrease.

The effect on the accounting equation is as follows:

$$\text{Assets} = \text{Liabilities} + \text{Stockholders' equity}$$
$$-\$400 = (-\$400)$$

What we have said can be summarized as follows:

Other Parties	What Mangold received		What Mangold gave back	
		(debit)		(credit)
Customers	Returned merchandise)	(increase)	Customers promise to pay (Accounts Receivable)	(decrease)

–Payment of liability–

On April 24, Mangold paid Bush Company $11,000 for the amount owed for the purchase of merchandise inventory on April 16. Because the payment of this liability is for inventory, it is considered an operating activity. If the payment had been for a loan, it would be a financing activity.

April 24	Accounts Payable	11,000	
	Cash		11,000
	Paid Bush Company for inventory purchased April 12.		

Mangold's liability, accounts payable, is decreased and so it is debited. The liability decreased because it was paid, and so Cash, an asset, is credited to show the decrease in the cash account.

The effect on the accounting equation is as follows:

$$\text{Assets} = \text{Liabilities} + \text{Stockholders' equity}$$
$$-\$11,000 = -\$11,000$$

What we have said can be summarized as follows:

Other Party	What Mangold received back (debit)		What Mangold gave (credit)	
Bush Company	Mangold's promise to pay (Accounts Payable)	(decrease)	Cash	(decrease)

–Collection of cash–

On April 29, Mangold collected $2,000 from customers for sales made to them on account on April 17.

April 29	Cash	2,000	
	Accounts Receivable		2,000
	Received cash from customers in payment of their accounts.		

Mangold debited cash to show the increase in cash. The reason for the increase in cash is that some of its customers are paying off their debt to Mangold. Accounts receivable is credited for the decrease to show that the customers no longer owe Mangold.

The effect on the accounting equation is as follows:

Assets = Liabilities + Stockholders' equity
+ $2,000
- $2,000

What we have said can be summarized as follows:

Other Parties	What Mangold received (debit)	What Mangold gave back (credit)
Customers	Cash (increase)	Customers promise to pay (decrease) (represented by Accounts Receivable)

–Utilities expense–

On April 30, Mangold received a bill from the Skyline Utility Company for $200 for April and paid it.

April 30	Utility Expense	200	
	Cash		200
	Paid utility bill.		

Mangold used up utility services and therefore it has an expense. Utility Expense is debited to show the increase in the expense account. To receive the utility service, Mangold had to pay cash. Therefore, the cash account, an asset, is credited to show the decrease in cash.

The effect on the accounting equation is as follows:

Assets = Liabilities + Stockholders' equity
- $ 200 =   - $ 200 (expense)

What we have said can be summarized as follows:

Other Party	What Mangold received (debit)	What Mangold gave (credit)
Skyline Utility Co.	Utility service (increase)	Cash (increase) decrease

–Salaries expense–

On April 30, Mangold paid its salaried employees, $4,000.

April 30	Salaries expense	4,000	
	Cash		4,000
	Paid the salaries for April.		

Mangold used up the labor services of its employees, and therefore has an expense. Salaries expense is debited to show the increase in the expense. Cash was paid the employees for their services, and so the cash account, an asset, is credited to show the decrease in cash.

The effect on the accounting equation is as follows:

$$\text{Assets} = \text{Liabilities} + \text{Stockholders' equity}$$
$$-\$4,000 = -\$4,000 \text{ (expense)}$$

What we have said can be summarized as follows:

Other Parties	What Mangold received		What Mangold gave	
		(debit)		(credit)
Employees	Labor services (represented by salaries expense)	(increase)	Cash	(decrease)

• Summarizing the Information •

If we wanted to know the balance in each account, the journal would be a difficult place to see this. The _ledger_, which is a book of accounts, presents in the order of the balance sheet and income statement this information. The data in the journal are transferred to the ledger. This is what accountants call "posting." We will illustrate the ledger with T-accounts for Mangold Company. The assumption is that Mangold began operations this year in April, and therefore there are no beginning balances.

Cash					Accounts Receivable				Merchandise Inventory			
Apr1	50,000	32,000	Apr10	Apr17	13,800	400	Apr20	Apr16	11,000	7,000	Apr17
5	7,000	11,000	24			2,000	29				
14	1,200	200	30		13,800	2,400		bal.	4,000		
29	2,000	4,000	30								
	60,200	47,200		bal.	11,400						
bal.	13,000										

Delivery Equipment				Accum. Depreciation				Accounts Payable		
Apr15	32,000				216	Apr30	Apr24	11,000	11,000	Apr16
									0 bal.	

Notes Payable			Interest Payable			Common Stock		
	7,000	Apr 5		29	Apr30		50,000	Apr1

Sales Revenue			Sales Returns			Cost of Goods Sold		
	15,000	Apr17	Apr20	400		Apr17	7,000	

Depreciation Expense			Utilities Expense			Salaries Expense		
Apr30	216		Apr30	200		Apr30	4,000	

Interest Expense		
Apr30	29	

The ledger is a record of the increases, decreases, and balances of each account. From the ledger, we can pick up the ending balances of each account and place them in a statement called the "trial balance." The trial balance for Mangold is shown in **Figure 4.23**.

Mangold Company
Trial Balance
April 30, 1995

	debit	credit
Cash	$13,000	
Accounts Receivable	11,400	
Merchandise Inventory	4,000	
Delivery Equipment	32,000	
Accumulated Depreciation		$ 216
Notes Payable		7,000
Interest Payable		29
Common Stock		50,000
Sales Revenue		15,000
Sales Returns and Allowances	400	
Cost of Goods Sold	7,000	
Depreciation Expense	216	
Utilities Expense	200	
Salaries Expense	4,000	
Interest Expense	29	
Totals	$72,245	$72,245

The statement is called a "trial" balance, because it is like a "trial run" in preparing the financial statements. In the accounting process, mistakes can easily be made. If the trial balance does not balance, then the accountant knows that there is an error or several errors. Even if the statement is in balance, there may still be errors. When the trial balance does not balance, two typical errors are the following:

1. In transferring the information from the journal to the ledger (posting), an incorrect figure was used or placed on the wrong side.

2. An error was made in adding or subtracting.

From the trial balance, the amounts for the financial statements can be picked up.

SUMMARY OF KEY POINTS

To appreciate the information in the financial statements, one must understand the theory, the

SUMMARY OF KEY POINTS

To appreciate the information in the financial statements, one must understand the theory, the difficulties, the limitations, and the ethical issues involved. **Figure 4.24** illustrates the concepts we have discussed in the first four chapters in relation to the accounting system.

Figure 4.24

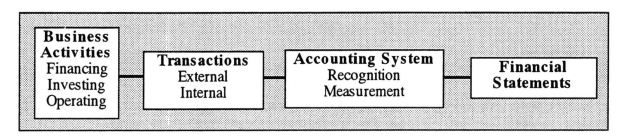

As seen in **Figure 4.24**, the activities a firm engages in can be categorized as financing, investing, and operating. These activities are the basis for the external and internal transactions that are *recognized* by the accounting system. Recognition has to do with what will be recorded. For example, the accountant must decide that a sale has been made and therefore should be recorded. Transactions are recorded according to the double-entry principle.

Measurement, which has to do with placing dollar amounts to pertinent items, is also involved in the recording process. Within the accounting system, there are choices to be made regarding procedures, values and estimates, which give rise to ethical questions. Proper accounting conforms with GAAP. The final outcome is the financial statements, which contain the information desired by users.

The following key points were discussed in this chapter:

1. Risk of recording transactions incorrectly. At the beginning of the chapter, we saw that the SEC filed complaints against some companies for incorrectly recording certain transactions. The SEC sees itself as the "watchdog" for investors. Incorrect accounting information will mislead investors. Therefore, companies must be careful about how they record transactions, or the SEC will get after them or stockholders and creditors may file a lawsuit against them.

2. Relationship between balance sheet and income statement. The two statements are related, because both are based on the accounting equation and the double-entry principle. The balance sheet shows the balances of assets, liabilities, and owners' equity as of a moment in time. The income statement shows the *changes* in these items as they relate to the definitions of revenues, expenses, gains and losses.

3. Accrual accounting. Generally accepted accounting principles are based on accrual accounting, which is to be contrasted with cash accounting. Accrual accounting focuses on important events that affect the company as opposed to simply the cash inflow and outflow.

4. Statement of cash flows. The statement shows for the given period the sources of cash (where it came from) and the uses of cash (where it went).

5. Debit and credit. The terms, debit and credit, come from the Latin/Italian, because double-entry accounting began in Italy in the late 13th century. The terms relate to the notions of increase and decrease. For an asset, a debit is an increase; for a liability or owners' equity, a debit is a decrease.

6. Account. An account is the accounting representation of an economic object (such as an asset, liability, or owners' equity) or event (revenue, expense, gain, or loss). Increases, decreases and balances are kept track of in the account.

7. Transactions. Transactions are recorded in the journal, and later the information is transferred to the ledger. Accountants use the debit-credit form. A transaction can be identified as one involving a financing, or investing or operating activity.

8. External and internal transactions. External transactions involve directly an external party and are "visible" events. Internal transactions arise mainly because of accounting theory. Adjusting entries are for internal transactions.

9. Recording of adjusting entries. Adjusting entries are recorded

at the end of the accounting period.

10. Four types of adjusting entries. Four kinds of adjustments, all affecting income, exist. They are accrued revenue, unearned revenue, accrued expense, and prepaid expense.

a. Accrued revenue and accrued expense. The notion is that revenue or expense has grown over time. This growth is unseen and is based on accounting theory. They must be recorded because the definitions of revenue and expense are met.

b. Unearned revenue and prepaid expense. An external entry was recorded when cash was involved. In the case of unearned revenue, the company receives cash from a customer but gives nothing for it and therefore owes the customer. When services have been provided, then the adjusting entry is to transfer the amount earned from the liability to revenue. In the case of prepaid expense, the company pays for an asset but has not used it. When it does use the asset, then the adjusting entry is to record the used portion of the asset as an expense.

11. Trial balance. The information in the ledger is conventionally placed in the trial balance before financial statements are prepared.

12. The whole accounting process. This chapter gives a general view of the whole accounting process where the end-product is the financial statements. This involves a step by step process called the "accounting cycle." For those interested in the details of the accounting cycle, this is discussed in the appendix.

APPENDIX

• The Accounting Cycle •

What accountants do for a business firm involves a step-by-step process called the "accounting cycle." We have already discussed parts of it. Listed below are the steps of the accounting cycle:

During the accounting period:

1. Record the external transactions in the journal as they occur.

2. Post the entries in the journal to the ledger.

At the end of the accounting period:

3. Prepare the unadjusted trial balance.

4. Record the adjusting entries in the journal and post to the ledger.

5. Prepare an adjusted trial balance.

6. Prepare the financial statements.

7. Record the closing entries in the journal and post to the ledger.

8. Prepare a post-closing trial balance.

So far, we have illustrated all the steps except Steps 2, 7, and 8. Because we are taking a user's approach, we have not emphasized these bookkeeping details. However, for those interested in the details of Steps 2, 7, and 8, we will discuss these steps next to give you an understanding of them.

• Posting •

Regarding Step 2, we have not said much about "posting," except to say that the information from the journal is transferred to the ledger. In this book, we have used T-accounts for the ledger, rather than actual pages. To be more precise on how posting is done, we present the following illustration of the journal and ledger.

General Journal				page 3
Date	AccountTitle	Ref.	Debit	Credit
1997 June 2	Cash	101	60,000	
	Notes Payable	205		60,000
	To record loan from Nolan Bank.			

Ledger					
Cash				**Account No. 101**	
Date	**Explanation**	**Ref.**	**Debit**	**Credit**	**Balance**
1997					
June 1	balance				20,000
2	loan	J3	60,000		80,000
Notes Payable				**Account No. 205**	
Date	**Explanation**	**Ref.**	**Debit**	**Credit**	**Balance**
1997					
June 1	balance				10,000
2	Nolan Bank	J3		60,000	70,000

As we post an entry from the journal to the ledger, the "reference" column is pertinent. Notice that as the information is transferred, the account number in the ledger is placed in the reference column in the journal. In this case, cash is account number 101, and notes payable is account number 205. For the ledger, the page number of the journal is listed. In this case, "J" means the journal, and "3" means page 3.

• Closing Entries •

Step 7 is for closing entries. We mentioned that income statement accounts (revenues, expenses, gains, and losses) are actually owners' equity accounts. Because users want the specific details of income, we separate these "temporarily." Once we find what we want, which is income, then we "close" the temporary accounts and transfer the income into owners' equity. To illustrate, let us record the closing entries for Yang Associates.

1997				
Oct. 31	Service Revenue		7,600	
	Rental Revenue		1,000	
	Income Summary			8,600
	To close the revenue accounts to Income Summary.			
Oct. 31	Income Summary		7,250	
	Advertising Expense			300
	Wages Expense			6,000
	Depreciation Expense -building			233
	Depreciation Expense -equipment			350
	Supplies Expense			300
	Interest Expense			67
	To close the expense accounts to Income Summary.			
Oct. 31	Income Summary		1,350	
	Yang, Capital			1,350
	To close the Income Summary to the capital account.			

Notice that revenue accounts (and gains if any) are closed first into a special account, Income Summary. Next the expense accounts (and losses if any) are closed in the Income Summary. Last, the Income Summary, which now has the amount of income, is closed, and the income is transferred into the capital account. If Yang Associates had been a corporation, instead of the capital account, we would have closed the amount into Retained Earnings. Notice also, that once an account is closed, the balance in that account is _zero_. For example, let us look at the Rental Revenue account after the closing entry, where Rental Revenue is debited.

	Rental Revenue			
(closing)	Oct 31	1,000	1,000	Oct 31
			0	balance

This means that after the closing process, all income statement accounts are _zero._ In other words, at the beginning of each accounting period, there is a fresh start for all income statement accounts. This is not true for balance sheet accounts, such as Cash and Accounts Receivable. Balance sheet accounts are never closed; their balances are forwarded.

The post-closing trial balance, Step 8, is essentially the same as the adjusted trial balance, except that all income statement accounts are not in it because they have been closed, that is, balanced to zero.

QUESTIONS

1. Concerning revenues and expenses,

a. How do they relate to the accounting equation?

b. For revenue, what is the effect on owners' equity?

c. For expense, what is the effect on owners` equity?

2. For the following, specify whether the account should be debited or credited.

a. Increase in asset.

b. Increase in liability.

c. Decrease in asset.

d. Increase in owners' equity.

e. Decrease in liability.

f. Decrease in owners' equity.

g. Increase in revenue.

h. Increase in expense.

3. For the statement of cash flows,

a. What are the three main categories?

b. What is its purpose?

c. Explain what "cash from operating activities" is.

4. The statement of cash flows is connected to the balance sheet and income statement. For the following information in the statement of cash flows, indicate to what financial statement it can be traced. Your answer should be either balance sheet or income statement.

a. Net income

b. Increase in accounts payable

c. Purchase of equipment

d. Decrease in salaries payable

e. Depreciation expense

f. Proceeds from bonds issued

g. Decrease in supplies

h. Issuance of common stock

5. What is a journal? What is a ledger?

6. In comparing accrual accounting with cash accounting,

a. What is accrual accounting?

b. What is cash accounting?

c. If ABC Company sold on account $500 of goods to Customer X in January, and collected the $500 in February,

> *1. under accrual accounting what month should sales revenue be recorded?*
> *2. under cash accounting what month should sales revenue be recorded?*

d. If Employee X worked for ABC Company in February but actually got paid for it in March, under cash accounting is there any wages expense in February for ABC for Employee X?

7. ABC Company purchased a 12-month fire insurance policy for $1,200 cash on January 1, Year 5.

a. Under accrual accounting, what is the amount of the insurance expense in March, Year 5?

b. Under cash accounting, what is the amount of the insurance expense in March, Year 5?

c. Under accrual accounting, what is the total amount of insurance expense for Year 5?

d. Under cash accounting, what is the total amount of insurance expense for Year 5?

8. Concerning the relationship of increases and decreases and debits and credits, for each of the following entries state what is increased and what is decreased.

a. Merchandise Inventory 500
Accounting Payable 500

b. Accounting Receivable 400
Sales Revenue 400

c. Supplies Expense 100
Supplies 100

d. Cash 900

Common Stock 900

e. Equipment 1,000

Cash 1,000

9. Give one example of each of the following activities:

a. Financing

b. Investing

c. Operating

10. Concerning external transactions,

a. When are external transactions recorded?

b. Where are they recorded?

c. Give an example of an external transaction and identify the external party.

d. What is the difference between an external and an internal transaction?

11. Regarding adjusting entries,

a. When are they recorded?

b. Why are they recorded?

c. What is an "accounting period?"

d. Name the four types of adjustments that are made.

e. Explain why the cash account is never part of an adjusting entry.

12. Concerning accrued revenue,

a. What is meant by the term "accrued?"

b. Why must it be recorded as an adjusting entry?

c. If the accrued revenue is interest revenue, present the typical adjusting entry.

d. Explain why you debited and credited the particular accounts in c.

13. Concerning unearned revenue,

a. When is the receipt of cash by a firm "unearned?"

b. Why is the unearned revenue account a liability?

c. If the unearned revenue pertains to rental revenue, present the typical adjusting entry.

d. Explain why you debited and credited the particular accounts in c.

14. Concerning accrued expense,

a. Why must it be recorded as an adjusting entry?

b. If the accrued expense is interest expense, present the typical adjusting entry.

c. Explain why you debited and credited the particular accounts in b.

15. Concerning prepaid expense,

a. Why is the payment of cash by a firm considered a "prepayment?"

b. Why is the prepaid expense account an asset?

c. If the prepaid expense relates to fire insurance, present the typical adjusting entry.

d. Explain why you debited and credited the particular accounts in c.

16. If employees of a company are paid $5,000 a week for working Monday to Friday, what adjusting entry must be made at the end of the accounting period if it ends on a Tuesday?

17. If $500 of accrued expenses are not recorded at the end of Year 3, explain the effect on:

(1) the income of Year 3, (2) the balance sheet of Year 3. Assume that the $500 is paid in Year 4, explain the effect on (3) the income of Year 4, (4) the balance sheet of Year 4.

18. The following information on interest for Year 3 for Ramsey Company is shown below:

Interest paid in Year 2 applicable to Year 3	$ 200
Interest expense accrued the previous year but paid in the current year	134
Total interest paid during the current year	432
Interest accrued at the end of the year	144
Interest paid in advance as of December 31	87

What is the proper amount of interest expense for the year?

• Based on Appendix: •

19. Why are revenue and expense accounts closed at the end of the accounting period?

20. After the closing of the books, what accounts will have a zero balance? What accounts will have their balances forwarded?

21. The following are steps of the accounting cycle. Put them in proper order.

a. Post entries in journal to ledger.

b. Record closing entries in journal and post to ledger.

c. Record external transactions in journal.

d. Prepare unadjusted trial balance.

e. Prepare the financial statements.

f. Prepare post-closing trial balance.

g. Prepare adjusted trial balance.

h. Record adjusting entries in journal and post to ledger.

22. Concerning the accounting cycle,

a. After closing entries are made, what would you expect the balance in the following accounts to be? Your answer should be positive, negative, or zero.

1.Sales revenue

2. Salaries expense

3. Accumulated depreciation

4. Interest receivable

b. Where does the information in the ledger come from?

c. What information do you need to record the following as adjusting entries?

1. Depreciation expense

2. Salaries payable

3. Rent receivable

EXERCISES

E4-1

For each of the following events for Grandview Company, specifiy whether it is a financing, investing, or operating activity.

a. Sold merchandise to customers.

b. Purchased equipment.

c. Borrowed money from the bank.

d. Purchased on account merchandise inventory.

e. Sold shares of Grandview common stock.

f. Sold the equipment purchased in (b).

g. Paid wages expense.

h. Paid dividends to stockholders.

i. Paid for utilities.

j. Purchased supplies.

k. Paid the supplier for merchadise purchased in (d).

E4.2

In a statement of cash flows, the following three types of activities are found: operating, investing, and financing. For each event below, indicate under which of the three activities it falls:

a. Dividends paid e. Increase in salaries payable

b. Depreciation expense. f. Sale of land

c. Proceeds from bonds issued g. Decrease in accounts receivable

d. Purchase of equipment h. Issuance of common stock

E4-3

For the table below, for each of the following transactions, fill out the information. For type of activity, your answer should be: financing, investing, or operating. For effect on income, your answer should be: increase, decrease, or no effect. For effect on cash flow, your answer should be: inflow, outflow, or no effect. The inflow or outflow of cash may be in the future. An example is provided.

Transaction	Type of Activity	Effect on Income	Effect on Cash Flow
1. Sale of merchandise for cash.	*Operating*	*Increase*	*Inflow*
2. Purchase of merchandise on credit.			
3. Purchase of equipment for cash.			
4. Payment of dividends.			
5. Sale of equipment for cash for gain.			
6. Use of labor services.			
7. Use of equipment.			
8. Borrowing money from bank.			
9. Purchase of building for cash.			
10. Sale of company's common stock.			

E4-4

For a given year, on which financial statement (balance sheet, income statement, statement of cash flows), would you find the following information?

a. Amount owed to creditors.

b. Salaries expense for the year.

c. Total accounts receivable.

d. Cash paid for equipment purchased.

e. Total sales revenues.

f. Total amount of merchandise inventory.

g. Increase in the amount of merchandise inventory.

h. Retained earnings balance.

i. Total stockholders' equity.

j. Total operating expenses.

k. Decrease in accounts receivable.

l. Proceeds from issuance of common stock.

m. Proceeds from sale of office building.

E4-5

In June, Lakeland Company sold $435,000 of merchandise. It collected $255,000 in cash from these sales. It also collected $347,000 cash from sales made in prior months. For the table below, for each question mark, specify the amount.

	Cash Inflow in June	Cash Inflow in Future	SalesRevenue for June
Cash from June sales	?	?	?
Cash from prior sales	?		
Total cash received in June	?		

E4-6

In June, Lakeland Company paid $134,000 in wages. Of this total, $42,000 were for labor services received in May. In addition to the $134,000 total, wages of $38,000 represent labor services received in June but will be paid in July. For the table below, for each question mark, specify the amount.

	Cash Outflow in June	Cash Outflow in Future	Wages Expense for June
Cash paid for June wages	?	?	?
Cash paid for prior wages	?		
Total cash paid in June	?		

E4-7

From its income statement based on accrual accounting for Year 5, the following information is available for Spartan Company:

Sales revenue		$87,000
Less Expenses:		
Depreciation	$22,000	
Other	12,000	34,000
Net income		$53,000

From the balance sheets of Years 4 and 5, the following information is derived:

	End of Year 4	End of Year 5
Accounts receivable	$65,000	$62,000

Assuming all other items were on a cash basis, (1) How much cash was collected from customers in Year 5? (2) How much cash was paid for expenses in Year 5? (3) What was the "cash income" for Year 5?

E4-8

For each of the following, indicate whether it should be a debit or credit.

	Debit	Credit
1. To increase a liability account		
2. To decrease an asset account		
3. To increase an expense account		
4. To decrease a liability account		
5. To increase a revenue account		
6. To increase an asset account		
7. To decrease an owners' equity account		
8. To decrease an expense account		
9. To increase an owners' equity account		
10. To decrease a revenue account		

E4-9

For each of the following, state whether the change is accomplished by a debit or credit.

1. Increase in accounts receivable.
2. Decrease in cash.
3. Decrease in wages expense.
4. Increase in accounts payable.
5. Increase in capital stock.
6. Increase in supplies expense.
7. Decrease in bonds payable.
8. Increase in dividends paid.
9. Increase in sales revenues.
10. Decrease in interest income.

E4-10

For each of the following transactions, indicate the <u>account name</u> of the asset involved and whether the amount is an <u>increase</u> or <u>decrease.</u>

1. Borrowed $3,000 from the bank.

2. Performed services for a customer and billed his account for $500.

3. Purchased supplies on account, $400.

4. Collected the $500 from the customer mentioned above.

5. Issued common stock to acquire equipment, $5,000.

6. Paid the bank the $3,000 principal (see 1) and also $100 for interest.

7. Paid wages for the month, $1,200.

E4-11

Consider the following events:

1. Purchased merchandise inventory on credit (Accounts Payable).

2. Purchased supplies for cash (Supplies).

3. Used some of the supplies (Supplies Expense).

4. Sold common stock for cash (Common Stock).

5. Paid the creditor for the merchandise purchased in (1) (Accounts Payable).

6. Borrowed money from the bank (Notes Payable).

7. Sold merchandise to customers (Sales Revenue).

8. Paid wages to employees (Wages Expense).

9. Purchased equipment for cash (Cash).

10. Sold merchandise to customers on account (Accounts Receivable).

Instructions:

(1) indicate whether the account specified in parentheses is debited or credited and why.

(2) Indicate whether the event is a financing, investing or operating activity.

E4-12

Describe one transaction that will result in the following:

1. A debit to an asset and a credit to a liability.

2. A debit to an asset and a credit to owners' equity.

3. A debit to an asset and a credit to an asset.

4. A credit to an asset and a debit to a liability.

5. A debit to owners' equity and a credit to an asset.

E4-13

For each of the following accounts, indicate whether normally the balance is debit or credit.

1. Cash	6. Common stock
2. Accounts receivable	7. Sales revenue
3. Merchandise inventory	8. Wages expense
4. Equipment	9. Bonds payable
5. Accounts payable	10. Retained earnings

E4-14

For each account that follows, give a reason for the account being (a) debited and (b) credited.

1. Cash	6. Merchandise inventory
2. Accounts receivable	7. Interest receivable
3. Notes payable	8. Rent expense
4. Equipment	9. Service revenue
5. Common stock	10. Accounts payable

E4-15

For each of the following transactions, for the account mentioned, indicate whether the account will be increased or decreased as a result of the transaction.

Transaction	Account	Increase or Decrease
1. Equipment is sold.	Cash	
2. Borrowed cash from bank.	Notes Payable	
3. Sold merchandise to customers	Accounts Receivable	
4. Sold merchandise to customers	Merchandise Inventory	
5. Wages for month are paid	Cash	
6. Purchase of merchandise	Accounts Payable	
7. Purchase of fire insurance policy	Prepaid Insurance Expense	
8. Use of equipment	Depreciation Expense	
9. Services of employees received	Wages Expense	

E4-16

Indicate the <u>immediate</u> effect of the error described below on the ccounting element specified. Use the following responses for your answer:

Overstated

Understated

No effect

1. Error: Did not record services rendered to a customer.

a. Net income
b. Total revenues
c. Total expenses

d. Total assets
e. Total liabilities
f. Total owners' equity

2. Error: A machine was purchased and this was debited to expense.

a. Net income
b. Total revenues
c. Total expenses

d. Total assets
e. Total liabilities
f. Total owners' equity

E4-17

For Leroy Company, the total assets and liabilities for Year 4 are as follows:

	January 1	December 31
Assets	$75,000	$110,000
Liabilities	27,000	32,000

Determine the amount of net income or loss for Year 4 based on each of the following assumptions. Each is independent of the others.

1. The company paid $10,000 dividends during the year.
2. The company issued additional capital stock, $5,000.
3. The company paid $12,000 dividends and issued $6,000 of additional capital stock.

E4-18

> *Consider the following activities of Benson Company:*

a. Sale of merchandise on account.

b. Cash sale of merchandise.

c. A competitor is about to sell a new product.

d. Purchase on account by Benson of supplies.

e. Purchase on account of merchandise for resale by Benson.

f. Collection of cash by Benson when customer paid his account (see a).

g. Benson decides to buy equipment next month.

h. Benson paid a supplier for the amount owed (see d.)

i. Paid wages and salaries.

j. Cash received from bank for amount borrowed.

k. Use of employee services. Employees not yet paid.

l. Sale of Benson's common stock.

m. Cash purchase by Benson of merchandise for resale.

n. Sale of Benson's bonds.

o. Payment of rent on building.

Instructions:

(1) For each of the foregoing activities, indicate whether it would be recorded under accrual accounting. Your answer should be yes or no.

(2) For each of the foregoing activities, indicate whether it would be recorded under cash accounting. Your answer should be yes or no.

E4-19

> *The effects of transactions on different categories of the balance sheet are listed below from a to k.*

	Current Assets	Long-term Assets	Current Liabilities	Long-term Liabilities	Stockholders' Equity
a.	+				+
b.	+		+		
c.	+	−			
d.	+			+	
e.	−	+			
f.	−			−	
g.	−		−		
h.	−				−
I.		+	+		
j.		+			+
k.	+,−				

Below are listed some typical transactions. For each transaction, identify the effect on the balance sheet as indicated above by listing the letter shown. For example, for the following transaction:

Purchased equipment on account.   (The answer is I)

1. Purchased merchandise inventory on account.

2. Sold capital stock for cash.

3. Purchased equipment for cash.

4. Purchased merchandise inventory for cash.

5. Borrowed money from bank for 6 months.

6. Paid salaries expense.

7. Paid accounts payable.

8. Sold bonds for cash.

9. Sold goods to customers on account.

10. Issued capital stock to acquire land.

11. Sold goods to customers for cash.

12. Paid dividends to stockholders.

E4-20

For each of the following transactions, indicate the effect on the accounting equation (A=Assets, L=Liabilities, O=Owners' Equity) of both Lambert Company and Duncan Company. For an increase, use +; for a decrease, use -; for no effect, use 0.

	Lambert			Duncan		
	A	L	O	A	L	O

1. Lambert purchases supplies from Duncan for $3,000 on account.

2. Duncan purchases $4,000 of equipment from Lambert for cash.

3. Lambert returns to Duncan $300 of defective supplies.

4. Lambert purchases $5,000 of stock from Duncan.

5. Duncan receives $2,700 payment from Lambert.

6. Lambert signs a contract to construct special equipment for Duncan for $5,500.

E4-21

The Sun Company was organized on June 1. Record its transactions in T-accounts for Cash, Supplies, Equipment, Building, Accounts Payable, and Common Stock. Use the tear-out form at end of book.

June 1 Issued common stock for $20,000 cash.

    5 Purchased equipment on account for $3,000.

  11 Paid $2,000 owed on the equipment.

  17 Purchased supplies, $500, paying $100 cash with the balance on account.

  27 Paid $400 owed for the supplies.

  30 Issued $50,000 of common stock in exchange for a building.

E4-22

The Frank Company was organized on May 1. Record the following transactions in T-accounts. Use the tear-out form at end of book.

May 1 Issued common stock for $25,000 cash.

    1 Purchased equipment on account, $16,000.

  10 Purchased merchandise inventory on account, $10,000.

  12 Gave a note to the bank for money borrowed, $2,000.

  24 Paid $16,000 on the amount owed for the equipment.

  28 Paid $10,000 for the amount owed for the merchandise inventory.

  30 Paid $1,000 for wages.

E4-23

Carson Clothing Company rents its store from Lawson Corporation. Lawson insists that rents be paid in advance in quarterly installments. On April 1, Year 5, Carson paid $3,000 for the April, May, June rents. It prepares monthly financial statements.

	April	May	June	Total for 3-mo.
Rental Expense	?	?	?	?
Month when cash paid	?	?	?	?

Instructions:

(1) For Carson, for the table above, indicate the amount for each question mark.

(2) What adjusting entry would Carson record on April 30?

E4-24

Milton Company prepares monthly financial statements. On April 1, Year 6, it paid $24,000 for a bond issued by National Company. The bond pays an annual interest of 8%, payable each quarter. The first quarterly payment will be received on June 30.

	April	May	June	Total for 3-mo.
Interest revenue	?	?	?	?
Cash interest received	?	?	?	?

Instructions:

(1) For the table above, indicate the amount for each question mark.

(2) What adjusting entry will Milton record on April 30?

E4-25

Leroy Company prepares monthly financial statements. In April 1996, it insisted that a new customer pay in advance for merchandise he had ordered. The customer paid $4,000. In May, the merchandise was delivered in the customer.

Accrual Accounting

	April	May	Total for 2-mo.
Sales revenue	?	?	?
Cash received	?	?	?

Instructions:

(1) For the table above, for the information given, indicate the amount for each question mark.

(2) What adjusting entry will Leroy record on May 31?

E4-26

Before year-end adjustments were made, the balance sheet categories for Norton Company showed the following:

Current assets	$124,000
Long-term investments	40,000
Property, plant and equipment	540,000
Intangible assets	20,000
Total	$724,000
Current liabilities	$ 64,000
Long-term liabilities	150,000
Stockholders' equity	510,000
Total	$724,000

Adjustments were made for the following:

1. Interest payable was accrued, $475.
2. Depreciation expense, $3,500.
3. Rent expected from tenant but not received, $800.
4. Office supplies used, $1,200.
5. Delivery of product to customer who had paid in advance, $560.
6. Wages accrued, $600.

Show what the balances are for the balance sheet categories (e.g., current assets) after all the proper adjusting entries have been made.

E4-27

The accounts on the balance sheet of Ray Company affected by adjustments at the end of Year 5 are shown below.

	December 31, Year 5	
	Before	After
Interest receivable	$ 500	$ 700
Prepaid insurance	2,400	1,200
Accumulated depreciation	4,000	5,000
Wages payable	0	900
Unearned revenue	2,000	1,400

Before the adjusting entries were made, the net income was $18,000. What is the amount of income after the adjustments are made?

E4-28

Determine the correct amount for the following cases for the month of September, Year 4:

a. On September 1, the supplies inventory had a balance of $500. During the month, $300 of supplies were purchased. At the end of the month, a physical count of the supplies shows that $250 of supplies are left. What is the amount of the supplies expense for September?

b. On August 31, the accrued wages expense amounted to $400. On September 3, $1,000 of wages were paid, including the $400 accrued in August. On September 10, 17, and 24, payment for wages was $1,000 for each week. On September 30, accrued wages amounted to $800. What is the total wages expense for September?

c. On March 1, Year 4, $25,000 of equipment was purchased. The estimated useful life is 8 years. The salvage value at the end of 8 years was estimated at $1,000. What is the depreciation expense on the equipment for September?

E4-29

E4-29

In each of the independent cases, prepare the adjusting entry:

	Present Balance	Required Balance
1. Prepaid insurance	$2,000	$1,600
2. Supplies expense	400	500
3. Unearned revenue	700	400
4. Taxes payable	200	700
5. Depreciation expense	200	400
6. Insurance expense	600	700
7. Rent revenue	400	800
8. Interest expense	900	1,200

E4-30

The accountant for Lawrence Company failed to record certain adjusting entries at the end of the month, April 30, Year 8. The errors were as follows:

1. Did not record accrued wages.

2. Did not adjust the supplies account to reflect the use of supplies for the month.

3. Did not record depreciation expense.

4. Did not adjust the unearned revenue account to reflect the amount earned for the month.

5. Did not record accrued interest revenue.

For each of the errors, state what the effect is on the following:

a. Revenues for April

b. Expenses for April

c. Income for April

d. Assets, April 30.

e. Liabilities, April 30.

f. Ending balance of retained earnings, April 30, Year 8

Your answer for each error for each item should be overstated, understated, or no effect.

EXERCISES BASED ON APPENDIX:

E4-31

Lance Company's trial balance is shown below.

Lance Company		
Trial Balance		
March 31, Year 3		
Cash	$ 4,200	
Accounts receivable	300	
Merchandise inventory	5,000	
Equipment (net)	42,000	
Accounts payable		$14,000
Capital stock		30,000
Sales revenue		13,200
Cost of goods sold	3,200	
Rent expense	400	
Salaries expense	1,200	
Miscellaneous expenses	900	-----
	$57,200	$57,200

Record the closing entries.

E4-32

Consider the following accounts:

Depreciation expense

Cash

Interest expense

Accounts receivable

Accumulated depreciation

Sales revenue

Salaries expense

Salaries payable

Which of the accounts

a. Are called temporary, nominal accounts?

b. Will appear in the post-closing trial balance?

c. Are closed into Retained Earnings?

CASES

C4-1

Mark Larkin owns a small clothing store. The following transactions occurred in Year 4. Some occurred in Year 5 if so stated.

1. Sales of merchandise	
Sales on a cash basis	$22,000
Credit sales	9,000
Cash collected from credit sales	8,400
2. Purchase of equipment on account	15,000
The equipment was purchased on October 1, Year 4 with a useful life of 5 years. The amount was paid on January 15, Year 5.	
3. Purchase of merchandise	9,000
Merchandise was purchased on account throughout the year. Of the total purchased, $4,000 was paid for by the end of the year.	
4. Expenses	
Cost of goods sold (The retail price is 200% of the cost of the merchandise sold.)	
Wages paid	15,000
Utilities expense paid for 11 months	1,350
Utilities expense for December paid in January, Year 5	125
Rent expense paid for 11 months	5,500
December rent paid in January, Year 5	500
Miscellaneous expenses paid	1,240

Mark wants to borrow $6,000 from the bank and submitted the following cash-basis income statement to the bank.

Larkin Clothing Store		
Income Statement		
For Year Ended December 31, Year 4		
Sales revenues		$30,400
Cost of goods sold		$4,000
Gross profit		$26,400
Less expenses:		
Wages	$15,000	
Utilities	1,350	
Rent	5,500	
Miscellaneous	1,240	
Total		23,090
Net income		$ 3,310

Instructions:

a. Prepare the income statement on an accrual basis for Year 4.

b. Compare the two income statements. What items are different?

c. If you were the banker, would you lend Mark the $6,000? Explain.

d. In your opinion which income statement tells the "truer" story?

C4-2

Kevin Young and Carla Monson were recently hired by Kenwood Company to work in its accounting department. Kenwood's financial statements must be approved by a CPA. Kevin and Carla disagree on how the following transactions should be recorded:

a. On February 15, Year 6, Kenwood purchased a machine at a total cost of $5,700. It put down $1,500 and agreed to pay the balance in 4 equal monthly installments beginning April 15.

Kevin said the entry to record the transaction on February 15 should be:

Machinery and equipment	5,700	
Cash		1,500
Accounts Payable		4,200

Carla disagreed. She said the proper entry should be:

Machinery and equipment	1,500	
Cash		1,500

She said each time Kenwood makes a payment, then the amount should be added to the machinery and equipment account.

b. On June 19, The Laura Burch Store ordered 1,000 units of product from Kenwood for a total of $4,300. The goods were delivered to the store, and an invoice sent on June 23 specifying that payment was due in 30 days. As of June 30, no payment had been received from Laura Burch.

Kevin said the following entry should be made on June 23:

Accounts Receivable	4,300	
Sales Revenue		4,300

Carla disagreed. She said no entry should be made until Laura Burch pays for the goods. She said the sale is not made until the cash is received. Without the cash, there is no revenue.

c. On September 24, Kenwood ordered and received from National Supply Company $1,200 of supplies. It sent a check to pay for the supplies on October 4.

Kevin said the following entries should be made:

Sep 24	Supplies	1,200	
	Accounts Payable		1,200
Oct 4	Accounts Payable	1,200	
	Cash		1,200

Carla disagreed. She said the proper accounting is as follows:

Sept 24	no entry	----	
Oct 4	Supplies	1,200	
	Cash		1,200

d. Kenwood hires 10 part-time workers who are paid weekly, on Fridays. They work from Monday to Friday. Daily wages for the 10 employees amount to $350. December 31, Year 6 fell on Wednesday.

Kevin said that despite the fact that wages for the week had not been paid, the following entry should be made on December 31:

Wages Expense	1,050	
Wages Payable		1,050

Carla disagreed. She said it was a waste of time to record the entry, because in a couple of days the week's wages would be recorded. She said there is no expense until it is paid for.

Instructions:

1. For each case, do you agree with Kevin or Carla? Present an explanation for each.
2. On the annual balance sheet, state what the differences would be between Kevin's and Carla's methods.
3. On the annual income statement, state what the difference would be between Kevin's and Carla's methods.
4. If you were a stockholder of Kenwood, which method would you prefer, Kevin's or Carla's? Explain.

C4-3

Consider the following cases from the files of the SEC:

1. Corporate Capital Resources, Inc. (CCR) showed on its 1988 balance sheet an investment of $4,404,500 in Night & Day Power Technologies. CCR documents reveal that in August 1988 the two companies entered into an agreement whereby Night & Day would issue common stock to CCR upon completion of an internal reorganization. On December 12, 1988, the president of Night & Day wrote to CCR indicating that he would transfer the shares of stock "upon execution of the written agreements." No exchange of shares or cash occurred. Should CCR have recorded the investment in Night & Day? Explain. (Based on Accounting and Auditing Enforcement Release No. 551)

2. The CPA for General Tech (GT) sent a letter to one of the creditors of GT to confirm the $3,084 amount owed. The creditor wrote back stating that the amount owed by GT was not $3,084 but $97,412. He had a promissory note from GT to support his claim. At this point, what should the CPA do? If a recording should be made, what should the entry be? (Based on AAER No. 552)

3. Fidelity Medical, Inc. entered into agreements with certain equipment brokers who agreed to warehouse the medical equipment Fidelity manufactured pending sale of the equipment. The brokers would receive a 5 percent fee if and when the equipment was sold. Fidelity shipped

equipment (cost $400,000, sales price $700,000) to these warehouses. What entry should Fidelity make in its books when the equipment was shipped? Explain. (Based on AAER No. 558)

4. In 1986, ZZZZBest Co., Inc. (Z Best) purchased equipment from The Generator Corporation. According to Z Best, the amount of the purchase was $1.97 million. One of the officers of Z Best, Maurice Rind, was the owner of The Generator Corporation. He received $720,000 from Z Best for arranging the transaction. Appraisers say the equipment was worth only $580,000. If you were the CPA for Z Best, what would you do? If you believe an entry should be recorded, present that entry. (Based on AAER No. 559)

5. Care-Med Centers, Inc. loaned money to Thermosonics, Inc. for $270,000. The loan is long overdue. What should Care-Med do? If you believe an entry should be made, what is that entry? (Based on AAER No.564)

C4-4

Consider the following adjusting entries:

a.	Rent expense	100	
	Rent payable		100
b.	Depreciation expense	200	
	Accumulated depreciation		200
c.	Insurance expense	300	
	Prepaid insurance		300
d.	Unearned service revenue	200	
	Service revenue		200
e.	Interest receivable	100	
	Interest revenue		100
f.	Bad debts expense	300	
	Allowance for uncollectible accounts		300
g.	Interest expense	120	
	Interest payable		120
h.	Amortization expense	300	
	Patents		300

Instructions:

1. State the adjusting-entry classification for each of the foregoing entries The classifications are: accrued revenue, unearned revenue, accrued expense, and prepaid expense.

2. Give a brief explanation of each adjusting entry.

C4-5

The following correct annual adjusting entries were made by Fong Enterprises on December 31:

1.	Insurance Expense	1,200	
	Prepaid Insurance		1,200
2.	Depreciation Expense	3,000	
	Accumulated Depreciation- Equipment		3,000
3.	Unearned Rental Revenue	4,000	
	Rental Revenue		4,000
4.	Interest Expense	450	
	Interest Payable		450
5.	Rental Receivable	600	
	Rental Revenue		600
6.	Wages Expense	520	
	Wages Payable		520

Instructions:

1. For each adjusting entry, indicate the circumstance that makes it necessary to record it.
2. For each entry, indicate when the cash received or paid took place or will take place.

C4-6

Consider the following cases from the files of the SEC:

1. Cable Applications, Inc. failed to make its income tax payments. It received a number of notices from the IRS stating the penalties and interest due. By the end of 1989, Cable owed $1,300,000 in taxes, and $340,100 in interest and penalties. The financial statement did not show the $340,100. Do you agree with Cable that no recording was necessary for the interest and penalties? Explain. If you disagree, what entry do you believe should be recorded? (Based on Accounting and Auditing Enforcement Release No.553)

2. National Medical Enterprises, Inc.(NME), a psychiatric and substance abuse facility, engaged in the following practices in order to collect insurance payments of its insured patients: delayed patient discharges, made unnecessary hospital admissions, falsified patient medical charts to create the appearance of diagnoses, falsified patient medical charts to justify billing

for services that were not provided. Obviously, these practices exposed the company to substantial risk of criminal prosecution as well as civil and criminal fines. In November 1990 and September 1991, NME learned that certain state regulatory agencies were conducting an investigation of its practices. What entry should the firm have recorded when it learned of the investigation? Explain. (Based on AAER No. 573)

3. The president of Programming and Systems, Inc. in 1990 directed the bookkeepers to record false entries to increase revenues and decrease expenses so that income was substantially overstated. He had negotiated an employment contract with the company for 1990 which gave him a bonus of 5 percent of income in excess of $1.5 million. The reported 1990 income was $5.1 million. Actually, the company sustained a loss of $790,000. Because of the overstatement, the president received a bonus of $180,000. If you were the CPA for the company, what would you do? What entry or entries would you make? Explain. (Based on AAER No. 584)

C4-7

Don Freeman and Jack Carter are partners in a hardware store. Jack said he would take care of the accounting books since he had taken a course in accounting in college. Profits are distributed each month on the basis of the ratio of their capital account balances. For the past year, Don has had a feeling that his share of the profits is smaller than it should be. He hired Carol Outberg, a private investigator who specializes in fraud detection. Carol has a CPA certificate, and once worked for a CPA firm and taught accounting at the local college. Don had Carol hired as a part-time cashier. During the week she was there, this is what Carol discovered:

1. One of Don's acquaintances, Fred Hopper, had purchased $285 of tools and charged his account. After 7 months of trying to collect, Jack gave up. He said Fred was a "bad debt." He reduced Don's account, D.Freeman, Capital, for the amount with the explanation that Fred was Don's customer.

2. A new counter was purchased for $1,500. Jack charged the amount as Store Expenses.
3. One customer, Dale Lottig, wanted to buy a lawnmower which the store did not carry. Jack said he would order it for him, but that Dale would have to pay a deposit ahead of time. Dale put down $100 as a deposit. Jack did not record anything, because he said the sale had not yet been made, not until the lawnmower arrived.

4. A customer who had purchased tools for $65 cash returned them. Jack noted that Don had made the sale, and so charged Don's account, D.Freeman, Capital for the return.

5. Jack was successful in negotiating a loan of $3,000 with the bank. Jack recorded the receipt of the cash and credited his account, J.Carter, Capital. When the interest of $150 was due and paid, he recorded Interest Expense.

Instructions: For each situation listed, do you believe Jack acted properly? Explain.

PROBLEMS

P4-1

John Cummins was unable to find a job after graduating from college. As a temporary measure, he decided to sell T-shirts at a flea market in the city he lives in.

For the first month, the following transactions occurred:

a. He purchased 500 T-shirts from a wholesaler for $3.00 each. He paid cash. —cash decrease

b. At a T-shirt printshop, he had the T-shirts printed with the name and picture of the city. The cost was $500, which he promised to pay the following month. accounts payable

c. He paid $100 for the month to have a stall in the flea market. — rent expense

d. He sold 250 T-shirts for $8.00 each. He received $1,600 cash. The customers who owed the balance, friends and relatives of his, said they would pay him later.

For the second month, the following transactions occurred:

a. He paid $100 for the month to have a stall in the flea market. — rent expense

b. He sold the rest of the T-shirts, 250, for $8.00 each and collected cash on all of them.

c. He collected the cash from his friends and relatives who had purchased the T-shirts the previous month but not paid him.

d. He paid the print-shop owner $500. — cash

Instructions:

1. Prepare two separate income statements for John, one for the first month and one for the second month, on an accrual-accounting basis. Use tear-out form at end of book.

2. Prepare two separate income statements for John, one for the first month and one for the second month, on a cash basis. Use tear-out form at end of book.

3. What is the total income for the two-month period on an accrual-accounting basis?

4. What is the total income for the two-month period on a cash basis?

P4-2

Consider the following information for Berry Company for Year 4:

Net income	$50,000
Decrease in accounts receivable	5,000
Purchase of equipment for cash	12,000
Dividends paid	4,500
Depreciation expense	9,000
Proceeds from bonds issued	10,000
Increase in inventory	2,000
Proceeds from sale of building	65,000

Instructions: Prepare a statement of cash flows for Berry. The statement should have the three categories of activities: operating, investing, financing.

P4-3

The following transactions occurred in the month of October for Charles Store:

a. Sold merchandise for $500 on account. The cost of the merchandise was $250.

b. Paid the rent on the store, $1,440.

c. Received a bill from Layman Supply Company for office supplies, $350.

d. Paid travel expenses incurred by an employee, $155.

e. Paid the bill from Layman Supply Company.

f. Paid salaries for the first half of October, $3,000.

g. Sold merchandise for $1,400 on account. The cost of the merchandise was $700.

h. Collected $600 from customers on their accounts.

i. Invested $1,000 in marketable securities.

j. Paid miscellaneous expenses, $40.

k. Purchased equipment for $1,700 on account.

l. Purchased a 1-year fire insurance policy, $2,400 cash.

Instructions: Record the transactions for the month of October in the journal. No explanations are needed.

P4-4

Lang Company was organized in September of Year 1. The Year 1 transactions are listed below.

a. Issued 420 shares of common stock for cash, $50,000. The par value of the stock is $100 each.

b. Purchased equipment on account, $8,000.

c. Purchased merchandise inventory on account, $32,000.

d. Sold merchandise to customers on account, $60,000. The cost of the merchandise was $30,000.

e. Purchased municipal bonds as a long-term investment, $5,300.

f. Collected cash from customers on their accounts, $24,000.

g. Paid for the equipment previously purchased (see b), $8,000.

h. Paid rent for the year, $4,000.

i. Paid salaries, $9,000.

j. Received $300 interest from the bond investment.

k. Paid $200 dividends to stockholders.

Instructions: Record the entries in the journal. No explanations are needed.

P4-5

Consider the following entries recorded by Terry Company in May:

1. Accounts Receivable	8,700	
Sales Revenue		8,700
2. Wages Expense	4,200	
Cash		4,200
3. Cash	9,500	
Sales Revenue		9,500
4. Cost of Goods Sold	8,400	
Merchandise Inventory		8,400
5. Equipment	22,000	
Cash		10,000
Accounts Payable		12,000
6. Merchandise Inventory	6,000	
Accounts Payable		6,000
7. Rent Expense	1,500	
Cash		1,500
8. Cash	6,000	
Accounts Receivable		6,000
9. Accounts Payable	5,400	
Cash		5,400
10. Cash	15,000	
Common Stock		15,000
11. Miscellaneous Expenses	2,300	
Cash		2,300

Instructions:

a. For each entry, explain what the transaction is.

b. If the company had $2,000 cash at the beginning of May, what is the amount of cash at the end of the month? Show your calculations.

c. On an accrual basis, what is the amount of income for May? Show your calculations.

P4-6

Gladys Alstrom is the newly hired accountant for Reba Shoe Store. For the events described below, she made the following entries:

```
a. Borrowed $5,000 from the Windsor Bank.
                        Cash                          5,000
                            Accounts Payable                    5,000
b. Sold on credit $230 of shoes to Joan Biggs.
                        Sales Revenue                   230
                            Accounts Payable                      230
c. Purchased equipment for $1,200 cash.
                            Equipment               1,200
                            Cash                                  1,200
d. Sold to customers for cash $340 of shoes.
                        Shoes Inventory                 340
                            Cash                                    340
e. Paid the monthly rent, $500.
                        Cash                            500
                            Rent Expense                          500
f. Purchased on credit 50 pairs of shoes from Taylor Shoe Company for $2,100.
                            Shoes Inventory             2,100
                            Accounts Receivable                 2,100
g. Collected $230 from Joan Biggs (see b).
                        Cash                            230
                            Sales Revenue                         230
h. Signed agreement with Luther Company to purchase a machine for $900.
                            Equipment                   900
                            Cash                                    900
```

Instructions: For each of the events, state whether you agree with the entry Gladys made. If you disagree, present the entry you would make. Be ready to defend your decision.

P4-7

Barney Lowe owns a clothing store. In March, the following events occurred:

1. Sold $13,000 of merchandise. Of the total, $9,000 was sold for cash and $4,000 was sold on credit.

2. The cost of the merchandise sold was $5,200. However, Barney has only paid $3,600 to the supplier. He still owes the balance.

3. Collected $4,200 from customers who had purchased merchandise in February on account.

4. Wages to employees are paid weekly each Saturday for the past 6 days. The store is closed on Sundays. During the month, the following payments to employees were made on Saturdays:

March 5	$618
March 12	800
March 19	800
March 26	820

The next payday was April 2 for $800.

5. No rent was paid in March because Barney had paid for it in advance in February. The amount was $1,100.

6. The $515 utilities bill for February arrived in March and was paid. The March bill did not arrive until early April. The amount is $485 and has not yet been paid.

7. Other expenses pertaining to March amounted to $890. Of that total, only $420 was paid by March 31.

Instructions: On an accrual basis, prepare an income statement for the month of March for Barney's store.

P4-8

Frank Jordan opened an auto repair shop this year and called it "Frank's Auto Shop." Because his is a small operation, he felt that cash basis accounting would be sufficient. At the end of the year, his accountant prepared the following financial statements:

Frank's Auto Shop
Balance Sheet
December 31, Year 1

Cash	$ 6,000		
Supplies	1,300		
Equipment (net)	31,000	Jordan, Capital	$38,300
Total	$38,300	Total	$38,300

Frank's Auto Shop
Income Statement
For Year Ended December 31, Year 1

Service revenue		$76,500
Supplies expense	$ 9,000	
Wages expense	12,000	
Rent expense	7,700	
Utilities expense	2,400	
Miscellaneous expenses	800	31,900
Income		$44,600

Additional information:

a. At the end of the year, a few customers owed the auto shop a total of $3,700. This amount was not included in revenue.

b. Supplies of $870 were purchased and received. Because the supplies have not been paid by December 31, the supplies were not recorded.

c. One part-time worker is employed. The last 4 days of his wages in December amounting to $200 had not been paid and not recorded.

d. The rent for December, $700, has not been paid, and therefore not recorded.

e. The utility bill for December for $230 arrived in January Year 2 and so was paid in January and recorded at that time.

f. Frank withdrew $20,000 cash, which was recorded.

Instructions: Present a balance sheet and income statement on an accrual basis. Use the form in the back of the book.

P4-9

The income statement shown below is incorrect because year-end adjustments had not been made.

Carney Company
Income Statement
For the Year Ended December 31, Year 6

Service revenues		$125,000
Less expenses:		
Salaries expense	$45,000	
Utilities expense	4,500	
Income tax expense	3,200	
Miscellaneous expense	1,200	53,900
Income		$ 71,100

The assets and liabilities before and after year-end adjustments are shown below:

	Before	After
Assets		
Cash	$11,000	$11,000
Marketable securities	17,000	17,000
Interest receivable	0	400
Supplies inventory	3,000	2,300
Prepaid rent	4,000	3,000
Equipment	30,000	30,000
Accumulated depreciation	(5,000)	(6,000)
Liabilities		
Accounts payable	$ 5,000	$ 5,000
Salaries payable	0	2,000
Unearned revenue	900	700
Income taxes payable	0	550

Instructions: Prepare a corrected income statement.

P4-10

The unadjusted trial balance of Henry Company on December 31, Year 5 is as follows:

Henry Company Trial Balance December 31, Year 5		
Cash	$62,000	
Accounts receivable	120,000	
Merchandise inventory	315,000	
Prepaid insurance	2,000	
Prepaid rent	1,200	
Furniture and fixtures	230,000	
Allowance for uncollectible accounts		$ 8,000
Accumulated depreciation on furniture and fixtures		125,000
Accounts payable		140,000
Common stock		290,000
Retained earnings, January 1, Year 5		97,000
Sales revenue		250,200
Cost of goods sold	90,000	
Wages expense	40,000	
Miscellaneous expenses	50,000	
	$910,200	$910,200

The accountant has determined that the following expenses pertain to the month of December:

Rent expense	$1,200
Insurance expense	200
Depreciation expense	2,300
Wages expense (not yet paid)	3,000
Bad debts expense	4,000

Instructions:

1. Record the adjusting entries.

2. Prepare the balance sheet and income statement (Use tear-out forms in back of book.)

P4-11

Consider the following events at the end of Year 3 for Fong Company:

a. Wages earned by employees during the last week of December amounted to $600. The amount was paid in January of Year 4.

b. Received a bill on December 29 from Pacific Utility Company for $357 for December. The bill was paid in January, Year 4.

c. Borrowed $3,000 from Atlas Bank on December 1. Interest is to be paid when the loan is paid, which is due February 1. The interest rate is 7 percent per year.

Instructions:

1.. Based on the information given, prepare the adjusting entries at the end of Year 3 for Fong Company.

2. Record the following entries in Year 4:

(a) On January 2, Fong paid the wages for the last week of December and the first two days of January, a total of $1,000.

(b) On January 6, Fong paid the utility bill specified above.

(c) On February 1, Fong paid Atlas Bank the amount borrowed plus interest.

P4-12

In reviewing the records of Lang Company, you discover the following errors:

For Year 3, the reported income was $8,500. The following were not recorded:

1. Accrued revenues of $600 were not recorded at the end of the year.

2. Accrued expenses of $350 were not recorded at the end of the year.

3. Revenue of $120 should have been considered unearned at the end of the year.

For Year 4, the reported income was $6,800. The following were not recorded:

4. Accrued revenues of $145 were not recorded at the end of the year.

5. Accrued expenses of $440 were not recorded at the end of the year.

6. Of the total expenses, $200 should have been considered a prepaid expense at the end of the year.

Instructions: Determine the correct income for Year 3 and Year 4.

P4-13

Consider the following transactions for Smith Company in its first year of operations.

1. Mr. Smith invests $15,000 into the business.
2. The company purchases furniture and fixtures for $10,000 cash.
3. The company purchases on credit $5,000 of merchandise from Tell Company.
4. Sales of $10,000 are made to customers on credit. The cost of the goods sold is $2,000.
5. The company purchases a 3-year fire insurance policy for $3,600 on July 1.
6. Cash of $5,000 is received from collections of accounts receivables.
7. The company pays its clerks $4,000 for salaries.
8. A customer submits $200 as deposit for merchandise he orders.
9. The company pays Tell Company $5,000 (see 3).
10. The company pays $1,000 for utilities.

At the end of the year, the following adjustments are to be made:

1. Depreciation for one year on the furniture and fixtures. The life of the furniture and fixtures is estimated at 10 years (see 2 above).
2. Adjustment of the fire insurance coverage (see 5 above).
3. Salaries payable for the last three days of the year is $400.
4. Bad debts expense is estimated to be 1 percent of sales.

Instructions:

(a). Record the external transactions in the journal. Explanations are not necessary.

(b) Record the adjusting entries at the end of the year, including the explanations.

PROBLEMS BASED ON APPENDIX:

P4-14

The following chart of accounts, with each account numbered, is used by Tracy Company.

Assets

1 Cash

4 Accounts receivable

6 Prepaid insurance

10 Equipment

11 Allowance for uncollectibles

12 Accumulated depreciation

Liabilities

21 Accounts payable

23 Notes payable

25 Salaries payable

Revenue

40 Service revenue

Expenses

50 Salaries expense

52 Depreciation expense

53 Rent expense

54 Miscellaneous expense

Stockholders' equity

30 Common stock

31 Capital in excess of par

32 Retained Earnings

33 Dividends paid

The transactions for July are noted below:

Year 4, July 1 Issued 500 shares of common stock, par value $100, for $55,000.

1 Purchased equipment for $40,000 for $20,000 cash. The balance is due in 60 days. The useful life of the equipment is 5 years.

15 Provided services to various customers for $8,000 on account. Uncollectibles are estimated to be 1 percent of sales.

16 Paid $130 for miscellaneous expenses.

20 Paid a dividend to stockholders, $100.

31 Paid salaries, $3,000.

31 Paid rent for the month, $800.

Instructions:

1. Record the external transactions in the journal.

2. Post the entries from the journal to the ledger. Use T- accounts for the ledger accounts. Use page 1 of journal for external transactions.

3. Prepare the unadjusted trial balance.

4. Record any necessary adjusting entries in the journal and post to the ledger. Use page 2 in the journal for adjusting entries.

5. Prepare the adjusted trial balance.

6. Prepare the balance sheet and the income statement.

7. Record the closing entries in the journal and post to the ledger. Use page 3 of the journal for closing entries.

8. Prepare a post-closing trial balance.

KEY ANSWERS TO EXERCISES AND PROBLEMS

E4-11
1. Accounts payable credited
Operating activity

E4-20

	Lambert			Duncan		
	A	L	O	A	L	O
1.	+	+		+		+
				−		−

E4-26
adjusted current assets $123,600
adjusted current liabilities $64,515

E4-27
Income after adjustments $15,700

E4-28
a. Supplies used in September $550

P4-1
1. For first month, income $900
For second month, income 900

P4-2
Net increase in cash $120,500

P4-7
Income $1,754

P4-8
Income $47,170

P4-9
Net income $66,450

P4-10
Income $59,500
Total assets $589,500

P4-12
Income for Year 3 $8,630

P4-14
(3) Unadjusted Trial Balance, total debits $83,000
(5) Adjusted Trial Balance, total debits $83,747

Chapter 5

Cash

LEARNING OBJECTIVES

After studying this chapter, you should be able to:

• Understand what the term "cash" represents in the ledger and on the Balance Sheet.

• Recognize the difference between internal and external sources (uses) of cash.

• Explain the concept of internal control.

• Describe the process of the bank reconciliation.

• Identify the need for cash management.

In the preceding chapters we have provided an overview of accounting information, emphasizing the financial statements that present that information, and the accrual accounting process by which we generate those statements. In this and the following chapters we examine in detail the elements that make up those statements. You saw in Chapter 2 that the Balance Sheet begins with a list of assets, and the list of assets begins with cash, the most liquid asset.

THE NEED TO SAFEGUARD CASH

To understand the need for a careful study of cash and the need for both the ability to control cash and the accuracy of reporting cash, let us begin with an example. Suppose a group of people who worked for a pharmacy, which happened to be a corporation, got together and decided to divert cash from the cash registers to their own pockets. They did this by falsifying sales records and using the cash to pay themselves, including officers, directors, other employees, and even the accountant. The accountant willingly went along, even falsifying the cash and sales records in the financial statements and signing off on these seriously misstated documents.

Suppose this went on for five years before they were caught. What impact might that have on the firm?

First, the firm might fall into a serious cash flow problem. With a material amount of cash diverted, the firm would be using inventory (and incurring both inventory and sales costs) but not generating either the sales or the actual cash receipts expected to cover all their costs.

Second, the corporation's financial statements are materially misstated for both cash and sales revenue. This will affect the balance sheet by showing a much lower total for both current assets and total assets than the firm should have. The income statement will show lower income than expected, and also a lower gross margin and lower profit ratio than expected. These misstatements can have a variety of adverse effects on both the firm and the external users of the statements. For example, a creditor is less likely to continue credit to a firm showing lower income, lower gross margin and less cash flow than expected. A customer or potential investor may be reluctant to deal with this firm. An investor will see the stock price drop, and may even receive a lower dividend than usual if cash flow is a problem for the firm.

Third, sales misstated for five years will carry serious consequences for the firm with the Internal Revenue Service. Moreover, it is probable that the people who diverted (stole) the cash from the pharmacy to begin with are not reporting this as income on their tax returns.

You may think this scenario is farfetched. Perhaps, but these are precisely the facts from a 1994 case brought by the Securities Exchange Commission against Ronald G. Sherry, CPA for Accuhealth,

Inc. and a variety of officers of the corporation.[16] Sherry, without admitting guilt, submitted an Offer of Settlement. In their judgment against him the SEC has permanently barred him from practicing accounting.

Cash is simultaneously one of the easiest assets for which to account and one of the most difficult assets for which to account. The notion that it is easy stems from the valuation and recognition of cash transactions. That is, if one must record a cash transaction it is easy to identify the point in time when that transaction occurs, and it is equally easy to determine whether and by how much the cash balance is increasing or decreasing because of the cash receipt or payment.

One difficulty in accounting for cash lies in the nature of cash. To shed light on this issue, first we need to define cash. Second, we discuss the *safeguarding* of cash, which is intrinsically related to the accounting for cash.[17] Another difficulty is the overall *management* of cash apart from just the safeguarding function; that is, a firm does not want to be caught short of cash, but too much cash on hand can also be problematic. Too much cash on hand is cash that should be used productively elsewhere. Thus, the third major issue in this chapter concerns cash management.

WHAT COMPRISES CASH?

To a business entity, the term *cash* denotes not only coin and currency on hand, but all funds immediately available to pay bills. Thus, the balance of a checking account, or a savings account if the firm draws on it regularly, or any other source from which the firm intends to make payments, will be considered cash. This is in contrast to funds which are set aside or *restricted* for a specific use. Such restricted cash is usually classified as an *investment,* and may be either short or long term, such as a sinking fund. See **Figure 5.1**.

Figure 5.1   Funds Classified as Cash or Investments

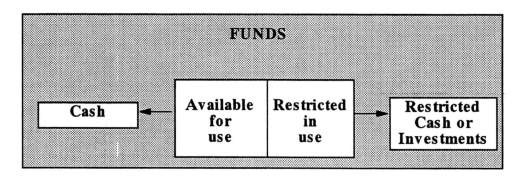

---

[16] See SEC Release No. 32514.

[17] One of the responsibilities of a good accounting system is to safeguard the assets as well as keep records regarding their acquisition, use and disposal.

In accounting, a firm's INTENT is an important consideration in indentifying the elements of cash. So, a savings account is classified as cash if the firm intends to make payments from savings, but is classified as an *investment* if the firm intends to hold the account untouched so it can accrue (accumulate) interest.

Checks that the firm has received from another party, money orders, cashiers' checks and certified checks are also considered cash. You may wonder if postage stamps are part of cash. The answer is NO. They are more appropriately classified as supplies or prepaid items.

VALUATION OF CASH TRANSACTIONS

Cash transactions are easy to identify because cash is either being paid out or received at some point in time. NO adjusting entries (which typically adjust for things that occurred *over a period* of time) include cash as one of the elements of the transaction. Recall from Chapter 4 that adjusting entries are for "internal" transactions, while all cash transactions are "external."

Since all transactions are measured in terms of money, the dollar value associated with a cash transaction simply equals the amount of cash being exchanged. For example, if on February 3 a firm buys a piece of equipment with a $14,000 list price but is required to pay only $12,000 in cash, then the change in the cash account is only a $12,000 decrease. (As you will see in Chapter 10, the value of the equipment thus also becomes $12,000, the amount given up to obtain the equipment.) The journal entry looks like this:

| Feb. 3 | Equipment | 12,000 | |
| | Cash | | 12,000 |

In fact, cash transactions are the easiest to analyze and journalize, since you know that one of the debits or credits must be made to the Cash account. If a firm is receiving cash, then one debits Cash, since receiving cash increases it. Likewise, the payment of cash will be reported as a credit to Cash, since paying cash decreases it.

The other account(s) involved in the transaction depend on the nature of the transaction. As you learned in Chapter 4, firms may receive cash either from *operating sources* or *operations*, or from *investing* and *financing activities*. Firms may also use cash in operations, investing and financing activities.

OPERATING, INVESTING AND FINANCING SOURCES AND USES OF CASH

As you are aware, cash is a very important asset to a firm, because it is necessary to pay bills, purchase other assets and pay off debts. However, in order to use cash, first a firm must obtain cash. Keeping a good balance between the cash one receives and the cash one needs to use is termed **cash** *management*, and is discussed in more detail later in this chapter. First, however, we wish to focus on the *sources* and *uses* of cash within a firm. As mentioned in the preceding paragraph, these sources and uses may be described as either operating, investing or financing activities.

Figure 5.2 outlines the basic idea of the internal vs. external sources and uses of cash. Each element is then discussed in the text. Users of accounting information prefer that a company be able to generate internally the cash needed to pay expenses and short-term debts.

Figure 5.2   Sources and Uses of Cash

```
SOURCES FROM OPERATING ACTIVITIES
        – Cash sales of goods
    – Collections on Accounts Receivables

    USES IN OPERATING ACTIVITIES
– Cash purchases of inventory and other services
– Cash payments to suppliers on Accounts Payable

SOURCES FROM INVESTING AND FINANCING ACTIVITIES
        – Sale of long term assets
            – Issue of stock
             – Borrowings

USES IN INVESTING AND FINANCING ACTIVITIES
        – Purchase of long term assets
            – Repayment of loans
            – Payment of dividends
        – Repurchase of a firm's own stock
```

• Cash Provided by Operations •

The nature of a business entity is usually to sell a product or service. Any cash sale, or the subsequent collection on a credit sale, is considered an operating activity providing a source of cash. That is, a firm's *major business operations* provide the operational sources of cash.

As an example, suppose Company A manufactures and sells a product, and Company B buys that product to resell as a merchandising firm. On April 9, Company A sells some product to Company B for $4,000. The transaction, as it would appear on Company A's books, is:

For Company A:

April 9	Cash	4,000	
	Sales Revenue		4,000
	To record sale to Company B.		

As you see, this transaction increases Company A's cash by $4,000 and at the same time increases the revenue for the period by $4,000.[18]

Were this a credit sale on April 9, the subsequent collection of $4,000 by Company A on Company B's account would have been the source of cash, and would still be considered internal, since it involves the major business operations of Company A. For example:

April 9	Accounts Receivable	4,000	
	Sales Revenue		4,000
	To record the sale on account of inventory		
	to Company B.		
April 20	Cash	4,000	
	Accounts Receivable		4,000
	To record the collection from Company B.		

• Cash Used in Operating Activities •

As the sales function generates a source of cash from operations, some uses of cash arise also from major business operations of the firm. Purchase of inventory, of raw materials, payment of wages

---

[18] Of course, there will also be a cost of goods sold, so the net profit from the sale will be less than $4,000.

and salaries, payment of utilities, purchase of business insurance, and payment of other cash operating costs are all considered uses of cash in operating activities.[19]

Like the sales transaction, purchases of inventory or raw materials may be made on credit. In that case, the use of the cash occurs when the Account Payable is reduced. However, the use is still considered an operating activity, since it involves the major business operations of the firm.

As an example, recall the April 9 purchase of inventory by Company B from Company A. Company B's books will reflect the purchase of inventory with a simultaneous decrease in cash:

For Company B:

April 9	Merchandise Inventory	4,000	
	Cash		4,000
	To record purchase of inventory from Company A.		

Were this a credit purchase, the cash would be used at the time Company B paid its account to Company A. For example:

April 9	Merchandise Inventory	4,000	
	Accounts Payable		4,000
	To record purchase of inventory from Company A.		
April 20	Accounts Payable	4,000	
	Cash		4,000
	To record payment to Company A.		

Note that with the same transaction one firm (Company A) may have a source of cash, while another firm (Company B) may make use of cash.

---

[19]Remember, however, that not all operating costs become cash costs. For example, depreciation of fixed assets is a common noncash operating cost.

• Sources of Cash from Investing and Financing Activities •

Besides from operating activities, a firm may get cash from investing activities when it sells assets other than inventory, including investments, fixed assets, and intangibles such as patent rights. These sales may occur because a firm needs cash, or because the firm no longer has use for those assets.

For example, N.E. Company may sell its bond investment because they need the cash to cover payroll and quarterly tax payments. However, N.E. Company may sell an old piece of equipment because they no longer use it, or want to replace it with a newer machine. These sales provide sources of cash to N.E. Company, regardless of the subsequent use of the cash received.

A firm may also engage in financing activities which include both borrowings (**_debt_** financing) and issue of capital stock (**_equity_** financing.) Those activities represent sources of cash apart from sales of inventory or other assets. Suppose Company A needs extra cash, and borrows $60,000 from the bank on June 12. The journal entry for this would be:

June 12	Cash	60,000	
	Notes Payable		60,000

Suppose Company B also needs extra cash, but does not want to borrow money.[20] Assuming Company B is a corporation, Company B may issue additional capital stock for its cash. If the market price is $12 per share, the stock has no par value, and they issue 5,000 shares, they will also receive $60,000 in cash:

June 12	Cash	60,000	
	Capital Stock		60,000
	To record the issue of 5,000 shares of		
	no-par capital stock.		

These are both sources of cash from financing activities.

---

[20]The choice between additional debt and equity financing is very complicated, and involves (among other things) a choice between paying back interest or dividends, which are external uses of cash. This topic is usually studied in finance.

• Uses of Cash in Investing and Financing Activities •

In the preceding example, N.E. Company sold assets and used some of the cash for payroll. You recall that the payroll function is an operating activity, since it pays for operating costs. However, they also wish to buy a new piece of equipment. This will be an investing activity. The purchase of long term assets is considered a use of cash for investing.

Also, as financing can be a source of cash, financing activities may be a cash _use_ when debts are repaid, dividends are paid to stockholders, and stock is repurchased by the issuing firm. The specific accounting procedures for these types of transactions will be discussed in more detail in Chapters 11, 12, and 13.

CASH MANAGEMENT AND CONTROL

Given the importance of having cash available for a firm's current needs, a system that accurately _reports_ the ready amount of cash, that _safeguards_ cash from misuse, theft and embezzlement and that effectively _manages_ cash inflows and outflows can be vital to a firm. For example, consider the large cash flow amounts of Apple Computer Company for 1997 as shown in **Figure 5.3.** The challenge to the managers was to control the $7,841 million of cash flowing into the company, and the $8,163 million flowing out of the company.

In this chapter, we will discuss the control procedures a company should follow, and the possible consequences if they are not followed.

• Internal Control •

The methods used to safeguard cash are colletively referred to as the control of cash, or _internal control_. These methods vary based on both the industry and size of the firm. For example, controls for cash in the banking industry will be somewhat different from controls for cash in the mining industry, since the uses and availability requirements of cash vary widely in those two industries. Also, a small store run by the owner will need fewer controls over cash than will a large corporation with multiple administrative sites.

The larger the firm or the more cash required on the premises, the more likely a firm will have an elaborate security system. Consider the small store run by the owner. This store will probably have a safe, with the combination known by the owner and perhaps one or two trusted employees in case of emergency. The store may also have an alarm system to foil burglary and robbery attempts.

A bank has a much more complex system for safeguarding cash, including a vault that often needs two employees to open the door, and armed guards as well as an alarm system to help deter robbers.

Figure 5.3   Apple Computer Company

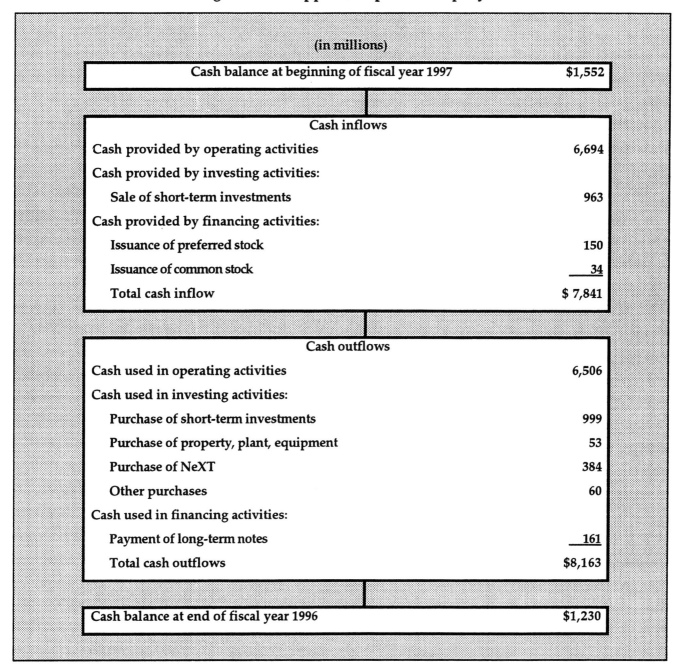

(in millions)

Cash balance at beginning of fiscal year 1997	$1,552

Cash inflows	
Cash provided by operating activities	6,694
Cash provided by investing activities:	
Sale of short-term investments	963
Cash provided by financing activities:	
Issuance of preferred stock	150
Issuance of common stock	34
Total cash inflow	$ 7,841

Cash outflows	
Cash used in operating activities	6,506
Cash used in investing activities:	
Purchase of short-term investments	999
Purchase of property, plant, equipment	53
Purchase of NeXT	384
Other purchases	60
Cash used in financing activities:	
Payment of long-term notes	161
Total cash outflows	$8,163

Cash balance at end of fiscal year 1996	$1,230

• The Need for Cash Controls •

Now you may be thinking, "Why is it only cash that we are concerned about, when a burglar or robber could take other assets as well?" The answer is that while thieves often do take other assets, cash is both easy to transport and has the specific problem that ownership is difficult to establish.

Consider this experiment. Throw a dollar bill on the floor. When someone tries to pick it up and carry it away, try to prove that this dollar belongs to you. Does it have your name, address or photograph on it? If it has your fingerprints on it, it also contains the prints of many other people who handled it before you did.

Given the difficulty of establishing ownership, cash must be protected not only from external but also from internal manipulation. Hence, most firms do not keep large amounts of cash on hand. Instead, every day (and sometimes more than once a day) cash is taken to the bank and deposited in the firm's account(s). The firm also keeps a checking account for most cash payments, and often requires receipts of cash at least by mail to be paid by check.

Try the cash experiment again, but this time throw a check for $1.00 made out to cash on the floor. This time it is easy to establish ownership; the check will have your name, address, phone number, signature, and in some cases even a fingerprint I.D. on it.

• Some Consequences of Poor Internal Controls •

–Burglary and robbery–

If a firm keeps large amounts of cash on hand which could be kept in the bank and used through a checking account, then the firm is prone to large losses in the case of burglary or robbery. This is the reason you may see signs on convenience stores or taxicabs claiming less than $20 is held in cash. The store clerks and cab drivers make several bank deposits per day to avoid holding large sums which may be lost in a robbery.

–Internal theft and embezzlement–

Clerks and other employees in retail stores have many chances to steal cash. So do employees who handle cash in any business. Without an internal control system, employees could take money out of cash registers. They could ring up sales for less than the actual sales value, and pocket the difference between what the customer gives them and what the cash register tape reports as the sales revenue. They could steal cash received in envelopes from customers who pay by mail. They could write checks to themselves on the firm's account.

In a more elaborate scheme, an employee could set up a fake supplier (prepare fake invoices with a fake business name reflecting purchases the firm never really made) and write checks on the firm to pay off debts to this "supplier". The employee will then pocket the cash, and the cash will not be missed because there are invoices to "prove" the purchases are real. This and even more complex plots work when employees have access to both the books and the cash, or have sole access to one or the other.

–Fraud–

Fraud is a deliberate misrepresentation by one party to gain something, usually unlawfully, from another party. Firms may be defrauded by other firms or by individuals who act as credit customers or as debtors to the firm, claiming to have more assets than they actually do. When the firm tries to collect, they find the customer or borrower cannot pay, and does not have the assets to cover the loss. Also, a customer who knowingly pays a firm with a bad check (one for which the customer does not have enough cash in the bank) is committing fraud against the firm.

Banks are frequently victims of fraud. The most common type of bank fraud occurs when an individual opens a new account with a bad check, withdraws the cash before the check clears, and does not put any money in the account to offset the withdrawal.

Sometimes individuals or firms write checks on an account before they deposit enough money to cover the check, though they know the cash will be there by the time the check clears. Carrying this further, individuals or firms will write checks back and forth between two or more of their own accounts to cover these balances, such that the balance in each account builds up when much less money actually exists. This is known as *kiting*. Check kiting usually occurs either by an employee internally to cover embezzlement by that employee, or by management to generate the illusion of additional funds. Kiting will be discussed in more detail in the section on cash management.

Given the above consequences of poor internal controls, the following are some of the most common elements of cash control that OUGHT TO be used within a firm. (The controls a firm actually uses depend on its size, business, and the diligence of the management in safeguarding cash.)

• Safeguarding Cash Receipts •

–Receipts by mail–

When cash payments arrive by mail at a firm with a large enough number of employees, two people or more should open the mail together. That way, unless they are in collusion, they will watch each other so it is less likely that one will pocket the incoming cash or checks. As mentioned above, most firms now require that customers make payments in the form of a check to further safeguard the receipts, so that ownership of the receipt is clearly established. While opening the mail, these two or more employees should keep a record of what has arrived for the day. These records are forwarded to the accounting department, where a clerk journalizes the day's receipts.

Meanwhile, the cash itself is transferred to a clerk who prepares deposit slips. The cash and deposit slips are taken by courier to the bank, and the bank prepares a deposit receipt. Finally, the deposit receipt will be checked against the accounting department journal entries either then or during the **_bank reconciliation_** (discussed later in this chapter.)[21] That way the deposit records can be compared with the accounting records, all prepared by different people. This is illustrated in **Figure 5.4**. Such a delegation of tasks is called **_separation of duties_**, and is essential to a strong system of cash control. If one person prepared all the records that person could pocket some receipts and fake the records.

Figure 5.4

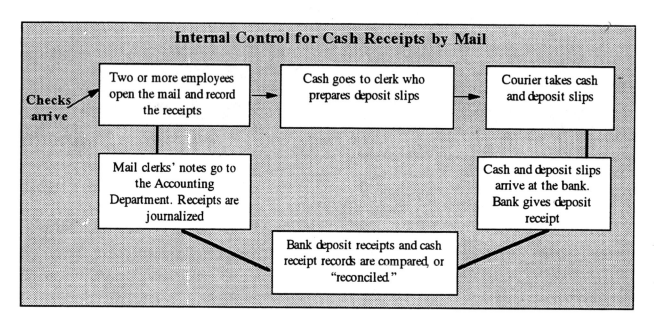

Separation of duties in its basic form means that the people who handle cash are not the same people who keep the accounting records relating to cash. This reduces the possibility that someone inside the firm will be able to take cash from the firm or have the firm write checks to that person without authorization. In the case of cash receipts, the people who handle incoming cash either by mail or at a cash register should not be the people who record the receipt of cash in the journal. Likewise, those preparing the checks for cash payments ought not record the payments in the journal and ledger.

–Cash register receipts–

When cash in the form of coin, currency or checks arrives in the firm through a cash register system, the checker or cashier (the person operating the register and receiving the cash) will create a receipt for the customer. The firm keeps copies of the receipts. At the end of each business day the cash in the registers is counted, usually by someone other than the checker, and compared to the totalled

---

[21] Customers may now also pay with direct transfers between the customer and firm account. These transactions require less complex control procedures within the firm.

receipts. This prevents theft directly from the cash registers or as customers pay for goods. To prevent checkers from ringing up amounts less than the customer is about to remit, some firms advise the customers to check their receipts.[22] Other firms hire security people to randomly spot check the checkers, or to pose as customers.

The cash from the registers should be deposited in the bank daily by an employee who should not have access to the accounting books, and the total of the day's sales and cash receipts are recorded in the books by an accountant or bookkeeper. Separating these duties keeps the person making the deposits from pocketing cash on the way to the bank.

• Safeguarding Cash Payments •

For most cash payments, the firm uses a checking account. Payments must be *__authorized__* before they are made, so that one can trace each cash disbursement to a legitimate purpose. This will prevent employees from requesting payments to themselves, and it will also keep external parties such as suppliers from requesting payment for the same item more than once.

As **Figure 5.5** illustrates, if the firm is large enough, one person should submit a written request for each payment by filling out a *__voucher__* or some other *__source document__*.[23] A separate person will authorize the payment, another will prepare the check, a fourth will sign the check, and a fifth person will make the necessary accounting notation (journal entry) that a transaction has occurred. Involving so many people for one payment will keep employees from writing checks to themselves as they prepare other payments.

---

[22]Sometimes this is done subtly. For example, you may have been in a store that claims that if you (the customer) do not get a receipt for your purchase, or if the receipt is incorrect, you will receive either a discount on your purchase or free goods. This promotion encourages customers to check their own receipts, and provides some additional cash control for the firm.

[23]Source documents are any receipt or paperwork that can independently verify the details of a transaction. Some examples are bank deposit slips, sales receipts and purchase orders.

Figure 5.5

Cash Payment Safeguards

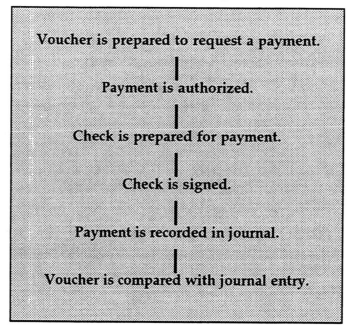

Voucher is prepared to request a payment.

Payment is authorized.

Check is prepared for payment.

Check is signed.

Payment is recorded in journal.

Voucher is compared with journal entry.

Later, a sixth person may compare the original voucher to the accounting records to be sure the payment was properly authorized, the correct amount was paid, and the correct amount was recorded in the books. Some firms even require that each check be signed by two different people to be sure that all check disbursements are legitimate authorized payments.

• The Bank Reconciliation •

Another aspect of cash control is making sure that the bank records, which reflect deposits into, payments from and the balance of the firm's checking account(s) confirm the accounting records. That is, every month when the firm receives its bank statement, it needs to reconcile the listed activities and balance with the activities and balance reflected in the ledger account labelled "Cash". This is done through a standard procedure called the ***bank reconciliation***.

–Balancing your checkbook–

If you have a checking account, you have probably done something similar to a bank reconciliation using the check register in your checkbook in place of a ledger account. You look through the bank statement at the checks that have cleared (been paid out by the bank.) Any checks the bank has not yet cleared are called ***outstanding checks***. You also confirm that the deposits you recorded have been received and recorded by the bank. Any deposits you made that do not yet appear on the bank statement are called ***deposits in transit***.

Deposits in transit usually occur because of a timing difference between your records and the bank's records. This happens less frequently now in the age of wire transfers and direct deposits, but if you mail deposits to the bank there is a delay between the time you record them and the bank receives them. Also, if you carry deposits to the bank after a certain time of day (which varies from bank to bank) the deposit is not recorded in your account until the next business day.

Aside from these two differences, there may be things the bank has done to your account that you were not aware of until you received the bank statement. For example, the bank may have paid interest into your account, or charged a service fee for any number of things. A debtor, customer, or your parents may even have made a payment directly into your account without your prior knowledge. This is also the time to look for _errors_ in both your checkbook and the bank statement. The bank is not likely to make an error, but it does happen occasionally. For example, the bank may pay the wrong rate of interest on your account, may charge a service fee for a service you did not use that month, or may even fail to charge a fee that it should have.

In the books it is unlikely that you have left out any cash transactions, but it is easy to make a transcription error while writing the amount of a check or deposit, or to make a subtraction or addition error. (Yes, even WITH a calculator.)

Another adjustment you may need to make when you balance your checkbook is that for an _NSF check_. Here NSF stands for _"non sufficient funds."_ These are checks you receive from someone else, deposit in your account and record in your books as cash received, but which cannot clear the sender's bank because the sender does not have sufficient funds in the sender's own account. Thus, when the bank notifies you of the problem, you need to adjust your books to reflect that this was not a cash receipt after all.

–The firm and the bank reconciliation–

All these reconciliations and adjustments from bank records to book records hold for firms as well as for you. When a firm receives the bank statement it makes the same comparisons as described in the preceeding section. Further, any actions the bank has taken that have not yet been reported in the ledger account (such as interest payments or collections of cash directly from customers) need to be journalized and posted to the ledger. Since the ledger account reflects all the firm's cash and not just that in the bank, one must also adjust for cash on hand as a reconciling item for a firm.

There are several different formats for a bank reconciliation, but the easiest is the "Bank and Books to Corrected Balances" format, because it highlights the entries necessary in the books following the reconciliation procedure.

–Corrected cash balance per bank–

The objective of the corrected balance approach is to determine the cash balance that the bank would have had for the firm if: (1) the bank had all the relevant information, and (2) the bank had made no errors. GrouCo's cash (ledger) account balance on May 31 is $48,678, including $300 of coin and currency on hand. The firm receives a bank statement for May, illustrated in **Figure 5.6**. Given the objective for the corrected balance approach, GrouCo will study the bank statement from this perspective: What does the bank NOT know that affects GrouCo's balance? It will then work toward the goal of finding the corrected cash balance per the bank statement.

The bank statement shows four checks cleared, but with two out of sequence, indicating some outstanding checks. The employee preparing the bank reconciliation would investigate by examining the check register to find the amounts not yet paid by the bank that have already been recorded as reductionsin the cash account. Assume that the employee finds the following: Checks written by the company, but not yet paid by the bank:

Check #4046 $323

Check #4048 $503

The employee would then subtract these from the bank balance. The employee would also check to see if GrouCo has recorded any deposits that the bank has not yet received. Assume the **Figure 5.6** employee finds a deposit in transit on May 31 of $5,124. The bank is unaware of this deposit in transit, so this amount will be added to the bank balance.

Also, since the bank is not aware of the firm's $300 cash on hand, the employee will add the $300 to the bank's total. Finally, assume that GrauCo maintains a $2,500 minimum monthly balance, and so is supposed to receive the safe deposit box rental free. Then the erroneous service charge of $10 will be corrected by adding it back to the bank balance. This is illustrated in **Figure 5.7**.

Figure 5.6   The Bank Statement

Weazelpod National Bank 1844 Weazelpod Road Weazelville, OH 55555	
GROUCO Interest Checking Account #33344555	
Beginning balance, May 199z	$44,228
Ending balance, May 199z	46,990
Interest earned this period	230
Checking Summary – Payments	

DATE	CHECK NUMBER	AMOUNT
May 3	4044	$1,223
May 7	4045*	700
May 22	4047*	2,450
May 29	4049	821

* indicates a break in check sequence

Account Summary – Deposits		
May 2	ATM Deposit	$5,046
May 14	Direct Deposit From Customer	3,200

Fees And Other Transactions		
May 9	NSF Check From Fred Futz	$500
May 9	NSF Check Fee	10
May 31	Monthly Safe Deposit Box Rental	10

Figure 5.7   Reconciliation of Bank Balance and Book Balance to Corrected Balance

Balance per bank statement	$46,990
Add: Deposit in transit	5,124
Bank fee, charged in error	10
Cash on hand	300
	$52,424
Less: Outstanding checks	
#4046	323
#4048	503
Corrected cash balance	$51,598
Cash balance per books	$48,678
Add: Interest earned from bank	230
Payment from customer	3,200
	$52,108
Less: NSF check from Futz	500
Bank fee on NSF check	10
Corrected cash balance	$51,598

–Corrected cash balance per books–

The balance in the ledger, called the cash balance per books, is also reconciled to the corrected cash balance. The objective here is to determine the cash balance the company would show in its books if: (1) the firm had all the relevant information, and (2) the firm made no errors.

Again the firm employee will scan the bank statement, this time for items noted by the bank but which the firm has not yet recorded in its own books. The check payments and the ATM deposit are all recorded by the firm, but the interest earned, the direct deposit from the customer, and the NSF check and its related fee are not yet recorded by GrauCo.[24] The "Book to Corrected Balance" reconciliation will add in the interest and direct deposit to the book cash, and will subtract the NSF check and any fees from the books. **Figure 5.8** shows these calculations. You can now see that the corrected book balance equals the corrected bank balance.

---

[24] Most banks will notify customers of NSF checks as they occur rather than passing the information on to the customer for the first time on the bank statement.

–Journal entries–

We are not quite finished. Since the foregoing book calculations represent real transactio hat have occurred but are not yet recorded in the books, they now require journal entries:

May 31	Cash	230	
	Interest revenue		230
	To record the interestreceived in May.		
	Cash	3,200	
	Accounts Receivable		3,200
	To record payment of customer account.		
	Accounts Receivable	500	
	Cash		500
	To reinstate Futz account after payment using an NSF check.		
	Bank Fees	10	
	Cash		10
	To record the fee charged for Futz NSF check.		

These journal entries are easy to identify and prepare. They represent each line in the "per books" column of the bank reconciliation. Since each transaction deals with an adjustment to the cash account, all the lines labelled "Add" are debited to the Cash account, and all lines labelled "Less" are credited to Cash. The bank reconciliation and journal entries have the twofold purpose of checking for errors (by the bank as well as the bookkeepers) and keeping the cash account balance current.

It is important for a firm to be aware of the balance in the Cash account. Too little cash may mean lost investment opportunities, or the inability to pay debts. However, too much cash on hand means the firm is not making productive use of cash. Keeping this balance between too little and too much cash is called cash management.

CASH MANAGEMENT

• The Problem of Insufficient Funds •

–Cash flow and insolvency–

If a firm has too little cash on hand, or *insufficient funds*, many problems may arise. Serious problems include the inability to pay off even long term debts. This is called *insolvency*.

Insolvent firms may either reorganize or simply cease to exist. In the case of reorganization, accountants treat the reorganized firm as a new entity, separate from the old firm. Sometimes other firms will buy out the insolvent firm. In that case the old firm is absorbed by the new firm and is again treated as a separate entity.

Cash flow problems may be less serious than those causing insolvency. Examples include the inability to pay short term obligations quickly, the inability to borrow additional money, or missing a good investment opportunity because cash is not currently available.

If a firm cannot pay short term obligations on time, such as meeting a payroll deadline, paying back short term borrowings, or paying taxes due, it may resort to *short term financing*, or borrowing money for short periods of time. This is particularly true if the firm expects to have incoming cash in the future. Some firms simply pay late, angering the employees, creditors, suppliers, or whomever expects to receive the cash. Besides jeopardizing their reputation, they may be charged with late fees, fines, and penalties from their delayed payments, which indicates that they may have been better off borrowing additional funds and paying interest.

Firms that must forego investment opportunities because they do not have available cash do not incur real (accounting) costs, but they do lose the chance to earn some additional revenues or profits. In economics (and in accounting) a foregone revenue or profit is called an *opportunity cost.* Opportunity costs are not recorded in the accounting books. However, it is easy to see that the additional revenues or profits would have made the firm better off.

Of course, no one can know with certainty what cash they may need in the future. Some firms simply pay things as they have the cash available without regard to any planning. However, many firms find it much more practical to plan ahead for future needs, and try then to have the necessary cash available.

• The Problem of Excess Funds •

One would think that a large amount of excess cash on hand is good to have. However, if a firm has excess cash on hand, it needs to put that cash to productive use, otherwise the firm is missing opportunities to generate more revenues. If excess cash is always available, the firm may consider expanding or making long term investments of some sort.

–Possible uses of excess cash–

Expansion yields the opportunity to earn additional operating revenues, though the firm will also incur additional expenses. Budgeting for expansion, based on forecasts of expanded sales territories, product quantities or product lines, will give the firm some idea whether expansion is an appropriate action with the excess funds.

Investment is also risky, but the amount of risk depends on the investment and the economy. For example, investing in real property (land and buildings) in California in the early 1980's was an excellent way to earn profits, because property values were increasing tremendously. However, investing in real property in Texas would probably have resulted in losses.

Long term bonds have the assurance of regular interest payments, and many stock investments regularly pay a dividend. Even the simple act of buying a certificate of deposit or putting extra cash in a savings or money market (interest bearing) checking account is more productive than letting the cash sit idle in a "regular" checking account.[25]

Some firms hesitate to put idle cash to work because they believe the cash excess to be temporary. However, there are still places to invest cash in the short term that will be more beneficial than letting the cash sit idle. Choosing the right property or stock to purchase may yield a short term gain. The choice or decision about how to invest in the short term is usually left to a financial adviser either within the investing firm or with an external brokerage firm.

For example, suppose Boing Company (manufacturer of coils and springs) has $40,000 of idle cash, but expects to need the cash for purchase of new inventory and payment of taxes within three months. Boing's financial analyst Wilt Waltman suggests that Boing buy 10,000 shares of Gloopy's Ketchup stock, currently selling for $3.75 per share. Two months later the stock price has risen to $4.25, and Boing decides to sell the stock. Boing has thus earned $5,000 on this investment (excluding any brokerage fees.) This indeed is a more productive use for the $40,000 than just leaving it in the checking account for two months, which at current interest rates will yield about $100. A more detailed look at a firm's investment opportunities and alternatives will be provided in Chapter 9.

---

[25] Regular checking accounts bear no interest or less interest than money market checking acounts.

• Budgeting for Financial Control •

Budgeting is a financial tool of management to control all aspects of operations. The budget can be seen as management's "game plan" for the coming year. The budget includes specific goals for revenues and expenses (operating budget), for acquisition of long-term assets (capital budget), and for cash flows (cash budget). The cash budget is usually a topic explored more thoroughly in managerial accounting, but because of its pertinence to cash management let us briefly look into this question.

–Cash budget–

Figure 5.8 provides a simple example of a cash budget for the coming four quarters. As you can see, the main categories are the _sources_ and _uses_ of cash. The firm will begin with operating activities, then plan on any desired or necessary investing activities, and finally on any desired or necessary financing activities.

Figure 5.8   Cash Budget

	QUARTER 1	QUARTER 2	QUARTER 3	QUARTER 4
SOURCES OF CASH:				
Beginning Cash Balance	$ 50,000	$ 87,000	$114,000	$ 3,550
Cash Collections On Sales	290,000	310,000	328,000	347,000
Other Cash Collections	12,000	12,000	12,000	12,000
TOTAL CASH AVAILABLE	$352,000	$409,000	$454,000	$362,550
USES OF CASH:				
Payments For Inventory Purchases	$140,000	$170,000	$185,000	$183,000
Salaries	100,000	100,000	100,000	100,000
Purchase Of Equipment			170,000	
Quarterly Taxes	25,000	25,000	25,000	25,000
TOTAL DISBURSEMENTS	$265,000	$295,000	$480,000	$308,000
CASH EXCESS (DEFICIENCY):	$ 87,000	$114,000	$(26,000)	$ 54,550
FINANCING:				
Borrowings			$ 30,000	
Repayment				$(30,000)
Interest			(450)	(450)
ENDING CASH BALANCE	$87,000	$114,000	$ 3,550	$ 24,100

–Estimating sources of cash–

The budgeting process usually begins by estimating expected sales revenue. This is known as a *sales forecast*. This is the first thing estimated because, sincethe firm's main objective is to sell a product or service, all its activities will revolve about the sales function and will depend on the level of sales the firm expects.

The sales forecast would usually be divided into quarters or months; the firm may even prepare a weekly sales forecast. After the sales forecast has been prepared, the firm would examine its past patterns of sales to see approximately what percentage of these were cash sales versus credit sales. They would also look at past patterns of collections on Accounts Receivable. Given this information, the firm would prepare a schedule of cash collections on sales. This, plus any additional information on planned cash collections such as interest or dividends to be received from investments, planned long term borrowings or stock issues, or incidental revenues such as property rental for a firm whose major business is not rentals, will compose theestimated sources of cash for the coming year. Again this will be divided into quarterly, monthly or weekly sums.

–Estimating uses of cash–

Next, the firm would look at the costs expected for the year. Given the estimated level of sales, they could forecast related costs based again on past experience. These costs would include supplies, materials, and inventory costs, labor costs, marketing costs and general administrative costs. Again they would use past experience to prepare a schedule of *cash disburesements* based on these incurred costs. They would then combine this with other expected cash payments such as payment of dividends, payment of interest and principal on debt, expected purchase of long term assets, or payment of taxes. All these payments would comprise the uses of cash for the year, broken into the needs by month or by week.

–Analysis of cash budget–

Analyzing the cash budget will alert the firm to potential cash shortfalls, and allow them to plan and organize cash flows more carefully. For example, they may rearrange priorities in paying short term obligations, such as paying taxes before paying the suppliers, or paying salaries before buying that new delivery truck. They may try ways to increase or hasten the collection of receivables, and they may even plan for short term borrowings. In the preceding example you can see that plans for short term debt and its repayment were even included at the bottom of the budget.

Whatever they decide, the budget prepares the planners for some potential problems and makes it much less likely that they will be unpleasantly surprised. Moreover, the budget will also alert them if they can expect to have a large cash excess for the year or in any particular period.

–Apple Company–

For its first 5 years, from 1976 to 1981, Apple did not have a budget.[26] How much cash was coming in or going out was not really known. Fortunately, in those early years when the company was making large amounts of sales, there were no adverse effects. It was not until 1982 that a budget was made. However, because of the inexperience of the personnel, there was no logical plan in putting the budget together in which sales estimates were based on production estimates. After John Scully became president in 1983, it took him a while to learn what was going on. He was able to increase profits in 1985 simply by improving the budgetary process.

• Ethical Issues and Fraud •

Earlier in this chapter we discussed some ways in which a firm may be defrauded. However, sometimes firms with insufficient funds, or those that simply want to use extra cash to earn additional investment income, may themselves resort to fraud.

–Checks written on insufficient balance–

In its simplest form a firm may write checks on insufficiently funded accounts if the firm believes it will be depositing cash before those checks clear. While this does not sound fraudulent, because the firm does intend to pay, it is at least certainly in violation of accounting principles if not unethical. After all, as probable as it is that the firm will have the cash before the checks clear, nothing about the future is ever certain. Expected receipts may be delayed or even lost,[27] and then the firm's checks will not clear. Conservatism in accounting warns us not to recognize increases in assets until they materialize, so the firm should not have anticipated the receipt of cash, even if it later occurred without incident.

–Kiting–

Using a system of writing checks back and forth among its own banks (kiting) allows a firm to give the illusion that it has more cash than really exists. This is done by the firm either to inflate cash balances and make the firm's Balance Sheet appear stronger, or to allow the firm to use this "phantom" cash to pay debts, earn additional bank interest, or purchase other investments.

---

[26] Robert Cringely, *Accidental Empires* (Addison-Wesley, 1992), pp.200-201.

[27] There are actual cases of mailed payments delayed, sent to the wrong bank or firm, or even stolen or lost in disasters such as fires, train wrecks, and helicopter crashes.

In a simplified example, pick two banks, A and B, that credit your account for deposits before the deposit checks clear. Suppose you open a bank account in Bank A with $100 cash. Now, open an account in Bank B by writing a $200 check from Bank A. Before the $200 check is processed by Bank B, write a $300 check to Bank A from Bank B. At this point (assuming no checks have cleared or bounced twice,) using $100 in cash you have generated an account in Bank A with a $400 balance, and an account in Bank B with a $200 balance. You could then report cash of $600 on your Balance Sheet, when only $100 actually exists. Look at **Figure 5.9** for an illustration of this simple example.

Figure 5.9   Check Kiting Scheme

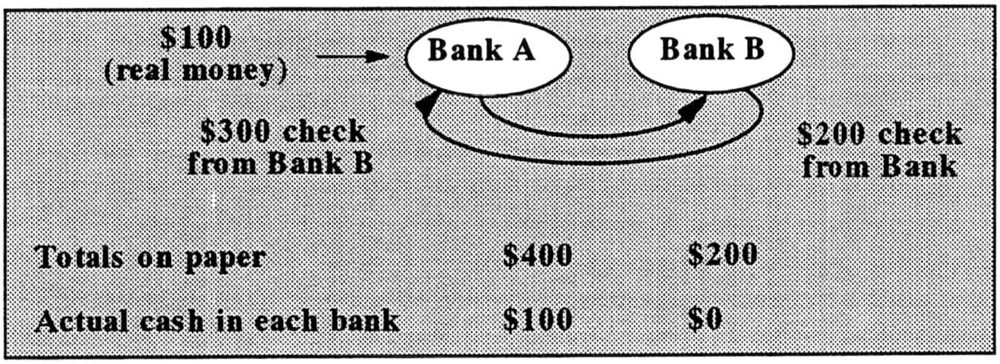

It is also possible then to withdraw some of the cash as long as you keep writing checks back and forth. That is, suppose the first ($200) check bounces. By then you have written another check, perhaps for $500, to cover the second check. You perhaps wish to use the cash withdrawn for personal items, to repay debts, or to invest elsewhere. If you do this last, you may earn a healthy investment income and still be able to repay the principal before you are caught. Of course, these actions are illegal and not sanctioned by this book's authors.

–Actual cases–

In a real life example, the brokerage firm E.F. Hutton engaged in a large and lengthy check kiting scheme from 1979 to 1982, which involved several hundred banks all over the United States. One of the key components of their plan was that checks to and from out of town banks would take several days to clear. However, when detected this scheme led to Hutton's downfall in 1985.

In another example, Edward Halloran and Harold Madden, using two firms and two major New York banks, each with many branches, managed to kite 15,000 checks with a total value of $9.2 billion between their two firms. Of this money they then withdrew $23 million for personal use. Besides the total sum involved, what makes this case so astounding is that, when caught, they repaid the money and claimed it was just an unauthorized loan, since they were already rich and so always had the capital to pay it back.[28]

One of the responsibilities of the auditor is to assure users of financial statements that reported asset balances are *reliable*. However, with a clever check kiting scheme it may be difficult to detect inflated cash balances on the financial statements. In the Hutton example the auditors detected irregularities in the firm's cash accounts, for the firm did not attempt to conceal the overdrafts on the books caused by the kiting scheme. However, because of the complexity of the scheme, it took the auditors some time to figure out what Hutton was doing. If a firm engaged in check kiting also falsified the accounting books, this form of fraud might take years for an auditor to detect.

This section souunds very exciting, but remember that check kiting is fraudulent and illegal. It is not an acceptable method for generating funds or planning for cash shortages in accounting.

• Cash and the Balance Sheet •

Cash on the balance sheet reflects only the amount available at a specific point in time. Without looking at other accounts such as the payables and receivables, one cannot say whether the cash balance is sufficient, or whether it is being managed wisely. Analysis of the balance sheet includes comparing ratios of items, and not just looking at one item or the change in that item from one period to the next. Even the change in Cash from the prior period is not enough of an indicator of the firm's efficient use of cash.

Cash may also be overstated on the balance sheet for several reasons. First, one may delay some payments near the end of the year to keep the cash balance from decreasing. Second, some NSF checks your firm received may not have gone through the clearing process yet, so you do not yet know they are bad. Third, as discussed earlier, one may fraudulently increase the cash balance by kiting checks.

In sum, if you see a large balance in Cash on the balance sheet, it really tells you nothing about the firm. That cash may be used up quickly to pay debts, it may be used to expand the business, or it may even sit idle when it could be used to generate investment income. It is only one element of the many-faceted financial statements, and must be treated as part but not all of the information about a firm's financial health.

[28] Ed Cony and Stanley Penn, *"Tale of a Kite,"* The Wall Street Journal, August 11, 1986.

SUMMARY OF KEY POINTS

The following key points were discussed in this chapter:

1. Risks of holding cash. Running a business is a risky undertaking, and holding cash is one of the risks one must take. A firm must have enough cash at all times to pay for debts when they fall due (such as paying employees). But having cash involves the risk of having it stolen or misappropriated. Not having enough is undesirable, but having too much in the Cash account is also undesirable.

2. The accounting defintion of cash. Cash includes all coin, currency, checks, money orders and accounts from which payments are made.

3. Recording cash transactions. Cash transactions are relatively easy to record. It is clear to see when they occur, the amount involved, and whether cash is increasing and should be debited or is decreasing and should be credited.

4. Sources and uses of cash from operations. Sources of cash from operations are those activities that relate both to earnings and to the receipt of cash, such as sales and collections on accounts receivable. Uses of cash from operations are those uses that relate to income, such as payment of operating expenses, payment for inventory and supplies, and payment of interest.

5. Sources and uses of cash for investing activities. Sources of cash for investing is usually from sale of noninventory assets. Cash used for investing typically is used to purchase long term assets.

6. Sources and uses of cash for financing activities. Sources of cash from financing activities include borrowings and issue of stock. Financing uses of cash include paying dividends and paying off the principal on the borrowings. Interest payments are considered part of operations, since they are expenses.

7. Internal control. The strategy of safeguarding Cash falls under the heading of "internal control." Safeguarding cash is usually done through physical controls such as checking accounts and safes, and through other controls such as separation of duties for employees.

8. The Bank Reconciliation. This is one aspect of internal control which reconciles the cash amount recorded in the firm's books with the amount recorded in the bank's records for the firm.

9. Petty cash. This is a small amount of cash handy in the firm, subject to less administrative control than the general cash account. It is usually held for emergencies or when very small amounts of coin or currency are required.

10. Cash management. When a firm receives and uses cash, it is in the firm's interest to plan for the receipt and payments carefully. Insufficient funds may lead to serious problems. However, a large excess of cash also indicates inefficient management, for that excess could be put to productive use.

11. Ethical issues. Firms and cash managers must be aware of several ethical issues involving payment of funds before they exist, and of artificially increasing cash balances through check kiting. Be aware that not only is this unethical, but it is also illegal.

12. Balance sheet presentation of cash. The cash balance on the Balance Sheet merely reflects the amount the firm has at a specific point in time. It is not entirely indicative of the firm's ability to manage cash effectively.

APPENDIX

• Special Journals •

The journal entries shown in this chapter assume the use of only a General Journal, one in which all transactions may be recorded. However, many firms streamline the recording of cash transactions because they may be dealing with many, even hundreds, of the same type of transaction each day. Consider a place like Bob's Burgers or Cleo's Clothing, where many cash sales transactions may occur daily, or where many receivables may be collected each week.

These firms, and in fact all firms, may use special *cash receipt* and *cash disbursement* journals to speed the recording of cash transactions. The cash receipts journal will omit the debit to Cash for each transaction, since it is implied by the name of the journal. Likewise, the cash disbursements journal omits the credit to the Cash account for each transaction.

If you have a checking account, your checkbook serves in a sense as a cash disbursements journal. For each check you write (cash disbursement transaction) you record the date, the check number as a reference, the name of the party whom you are paying, and the amount paid. You may also write an explanation for the transaction. It is understood that all these notations are disbursements of cash, and you may even keep a running balance of your cash account in the checkbook. Back before debit cards (ATM cards) these balances were even fairly accurate.[29] To maintain accurate balances, to keep cash safe from theft and embezzlement, and to keep cash in productive use, firms use the tools of cash management and cash control.

---

[29] I do not mean to imply that the use of debit cards leads to incorrect account balances. I just know from personal experience how easy it is to forget to note ATM transactions in one's checkbook.

QUESTIONS

1. What items are specifically included in Cash?

2. Why is cash classified as a current asset?

3. How are cash transactions valued? How is this reported on the financial statements?

4. Define internal control and give an example.

5. What are some consequences of poor internal control?

6. Define "separation of duties."

7. Explain the difference between sources of cash from operations, and from investing and financing activities.

8. Discuss some ways in which cash can be used for operations, for investing and for financing activities.

9. Why should the person who receives cash in a firm not be the same person who makes the journal entry for receipt of cash in the books?

10. What is the purpose of the Petty Cash account?

11. What is the purpose of the Bank Reconciliation?

12. What is an NSF check, and how does it affect cash?

13. Why is having excess cash on hand considered problematic?

14. Define the terms "deposits in transit" and "outstanding checks."

15. Why must extra care be taken to safeguard cash?

16. What problems may be caused by insufficient funds?

17. What is insolvency?

18. What is kiting? Is it unethical? Is it illegal?

19. How may the Cash balance on the Balance Sheet be misleading?

20. Describe a scenario in which an employee may steal cash from a firm, and describe a solution to the problem.

21. Why would a firm prepare a cash budget? How is it set up?

22. What is a sales forecast?

23. Why are excess funds considered a problem?

EXERCISES

(See key answers at end of chapter)

E5-1

Which of the following items are classified as Cash?

a. a checking account

b. a cashier's check received from a customer

c. an IOU written by a customer

d. a quarter in the petty cash box

e. a two year certificate of deposit

E5-2

Which of the following items are classified as Cash?

a. a savings account on which checks are written

b. a money order from an investor

c. a refundable deposit paid to the utility company

d. receipts for credit sales (from use of store's own credit card)

e. a check received from a customer that is postdated

E5-3

Suppose you are looking at the cash balance on the Balance Sheet and you see the number $5,933,458. What does this represent? What would you expect it does not include?

E5-4

Journalize the following cash transactions. Omit the dates, but include explanations.

a. Issue 4,000 shares of no par stock for $20 per share.

b. Borrow $40,000 from the bank.

c. Sell 60 items for $3 each for cash.

d. Collect $500 from a customer for a prior credit sale.

e. Buy $200 of inventory for cash.

f. Pay sales clerks' wages. They earn $20 per hour and have worked 470 hours.

g. Pay $400 interest on the loan from part b.

E5-5

Refer to Exercise 4. Which of those transactions reflect investing and financing activities? Which reflect operating activities?

E5-6

For each transaction below, state whether it is an investing source of cash, an investing use of cash, or neither. If it is neither, explain why.

a. Purchase of equipment

b. Sale of long term investment in bonds

c. Payment of interest on a loan

d. Purchase of inventory

e. Use of supplies

f. Sale of a trademark

E5-7

For each transaction below, state whether it is a financing source of cash, a financing use of cash, or neither. If it is neither, explain why.

a. Purchase of equipment

b. Payment of principal on a loan

c. Payment of interest on a loan

d. Purchase of bonds

e. Issue of capital stock

f. Payment of dividend

E5-8

For each transaction below, state whether it is a source of cash from operations, a use of cash from operations, or neither. If it is neither, explain why.

a. Sale of equipment

b. Payment of principal on a loan

c. Payment of interest on a loan

d. Sale of inventory

e. Use of supplies

f. Payment of dividend on stock

E5-9

Suppose you are examining quarterly Balance Sheets for Bailbale Company. You see that cash for the first, second and third quarters remains around $400,000, but cash reported at the end of the fiscal year is $6,700,000. Explain what might cause this big jump in cash, and what you would look for to verify your explanation, assuming:

a. You thought the cash increase arose honestly.

b. You thought the cash increase arose fraudulently.

E5-10

Below is a bank reconciliation for Glorm Co. Fill in the missing amount, and explain what might have caused it.

Glorm Company					
Bank Reconciliation					
Balance per bank		$4,908	Balance per books		$5,331
Add: Deposits in transit		?	Add: Interest earned		40
Less: Outstanding checks			Less: NSF Check	$590	
#3900	$312		Fees	25	615
#3912	240	552			
Corrected bank balance		$4,756	Corrected book balance		$4,756

E5-11

Refer to Exercise 10. Prepare the journal entries for that bank reconciliation.

E5-12

Weereel Inc. has just received its bank statement, showing a balance in the bank of $420,400. The bank statement shows interest added to Weereel's account in the amount of $4,000, and shows a $200 fee charged to Weereel. Weereel discovers in comparing the bank statement with its records that it has deposits in transit totalling $20,000, and outstanding checks totalling $30,000. Weereel also finds an error in the books in which a cash sale for $5,000 was accidentally recorded as a credit sale. Weereel's cash account balance is $401,600 before a bank reconciliation; prepare the bank reconciliation to find the corrected cash balance.

E5-13

count more

D.deFoe, Inc. has hired six employees: Ann, Bob, Carla, David, Ellen and Fong. They all have identical skills. D.deFoe sells sandwiches as a cash only business. Using the concepts of internal control, assign cash collection and recording duties to the other five employees, assuming Ann works as the cashier. Write your answer out as a memo from the sales manager to the company president.

E5-14

Gorg Whendell, is the controller for Whoops Company, whose fiscal year end is December 31. On December 27 the firm sold some goods and received a check for $5,000 from a customer who, being afraid the check would not clear before his next payday, postdated the check as January 5 of the following year. Gorg wants to record this check as an account receivable. The firm's owner and president wants Gorg to record the check as cash, because he is sure it will clear soon. Is there an ethical dilemma here, and who is correct?

E5-15

Moof Inc. has forecast sales revenue for the coming year as $40,000. They expect to collect 98% of this in cash. They would like to buy a new machine; the machine currently costs $18,000. Its cost will increase to $25,000 after the end of the coming year. Their cash expenses typically average 60% of total sales revenue.

a. Can Moof budget to purchase the machine in the coming year?

b. If Moof's sales revenue and costs both increase by 10% over the estimates above in the coming year, can they buy the machine?

c. If Moof does not buy in the coming year, and sales revenue and costs increase by 10% each year, will they be able to buy the machine in the following year?

E5-16

Wilbur Company has found itself with $200,000 of excess cash on January 1, 199x. If they invest the cash in $200,000 of bonds, they will earn 5%. If they invest the entire amount in 4,000 shares of Voobly stock, they will receive $1 per share in dividends each quarter, but the stock price is expected to drop to $40 per share by the end of the year. Which investment will give Wilbur more total income by December 31, assuming they would cash in the bonds or sell the stock on December 31?

CASES

C5-1

Silly Industries is a mail order business. Sally Silly, the owner, has four employees. Two employees take care of cash receipts. They open the mail orders, record any cash arriving, take the deposits to the bank, and forward the order forms to Sally, who ships all the goods herself. The other two employees pay all the bills and record all payments in the books. They are authorized to sign checks. Discuss the internal control problems that may arise in Silly Industries.

C5-2

Wilson Wilson, owner of Wilsonworld, does not believe in cash planning. "Budgeting is boring," says Wilson. "I'd rather just pay things as they come due." Wilsonworld's suppliers offer a 5% discount if customers pay in cash. Wilsonworld never takes advantage of this, always buying on credit and paying late. "I don't need the discount," says Wilson. "I always have enough cash to pay eventually, and I'd just have to borrow money to pay on time."

Comment on Wilson's view of cash management and on the effect his attitude might have on his suppliers.

C5-3

Kate Brown is the controller at Zestril, Inc. They manufacture farming machinery. Zestril's business is seasonal, and they frequently find themselves short of cash in the late winter and spring, but with an excess of cash in the late summer and fall. Kate Brown thinks that if they use the excess cash in the summer for short term investments and projects, they will have less need to borrow to cover the late winter and spring payments. The owner is afraid to invest the excess summer cash, fearing that they will be caught even shorter in the winter.

Discuss the ways in which short term summer investments may benefit Zestril. Write your answer as a supporting memo for Kate Brown to the owner.

C5-4

Wendell Wiff is the cash manager for TofuDog, a vegetarian fast food restaurant. Mr. Tofu, the supplier, is requesting payment on a $4,000 bill from a credit purchase by TofuDog made six months ago. TofuDog is having cash problems; however, Wendell expects his firm to receive a $7,000 tax refund by direct deposit into their Big Bank account by October 10. On October 1 Wendell decides to write a check for $4,000 from TofuDog's Big Bank account to TofuDog's Little Bank account in another state. The Little Bank credits deposits immediately, but out of state checks take 12 working days to clear. Wendell then writes a check on October 1 on the Little Bank to Mr. Tofu.

Are Wendell's actions unethical? Are they fraudulent? Are they illegal? Is Wendell kiting checks? Discuss this.

C5-5

(This case does not have a specific solution. It asks for your opinion to stimulate discussion.) John Gilmore owns John's Pizza Parlor. On June 1, his business has $3,000 in the cash account. John is considering purchasing at the end of the month some new tables and chairs for the pizza parlor. The cost would be $5,000.

He estimates that in June the following revenues and expenses would occur:

For June	
Cash received from sales of pizza and other food items	$8,000
Wages and salaries to employees	3,000
Utilities	600
Food items used	2,240
Other supplies used	500
Rent to be paid in June	900

The wages, salaries, utilities and rent are all paid in cash when due. Of the food items used, half is already on hand and paid for and the other half must be purchased for cash. Of the supplies used, all are on hand and already paid for.

The seller of the tables and chairs, National Company, has offered John a financing plan as follows: $2,000 down and the balance of $3,000 due on August 31 with an additional charge of $300.

John does not want to pay the additional charge and is considering paying the *full $5,000 in cash on June 30. His only external source of funds is to borrow from the bank up to $1,000 for one month at 10 percent annual interest.*

He asks your advice on what he should do.

Instructions:

1. Determine if on June 30 John will have enough to pay in full the $5,000, assuming that his estimates are correct.

2. You look at the sales record for the past 12 months and find that the range of cash sales for a month is from $6,000 to $8,000. If June proves to be a low sales month, how much net cash will John have on June 30?

3. One of John's food suppliers has informed him that *in July* a special 4th of July discount of 40 percent will be given on any cash purchases from July 1 to July 3. John determined that for the amount of perishable items he needs he could save $500 if he took advantage of the special discount. This means that he will have to pay in cash $750.

Considering the purchase of the tables and chairs on June 30 and the special discount offer by the supplier, what would you advise John to do? List his alternatives and decide which is the best. Assume that his original estimates for June are correct.

C5-6

Grand Merchant Corporation has the following bank reconciliation. Examine it and discuss what you would investigate to see why the "Corrected Cash Balance" for the bank does not match that of the books.

Grand Merchant Corporation			
Bank Reconciliation			
Balance per bank	$437,000	Balance per books	$441,900
Add: Deposits in transit	52,300	Add: Interest earned	4,312
Less: Outstanding checks	(22,000)	Less: Service fees	(92)
Corrected cash balance	$467,300	Corrected cash balance	$446,120

C5-7

Mr. Flippy's Pancake Wagon is a small restaurant which has found itself with $500,000 in excess cash on July 1, 199z. Mr. Flippy's fiscal year ends on December 31, after which they will need the cash to pay for new supplies. However, for the coming six months, they have several options for this $500,000. They could:

A. keep the cash in the bank. The current annual interest rate is 1.2%.

B. invest in $500,000 of bonds. The annual interest rate on the bond issue is 6%, and the bonds would be redeemed on December 31.

C. use $400,000 to buy 20,000 shares of stock. The stock pays $0.50 per share in dividends every six months. The price of the stock is expected to be $22 per share on December 31, when Mr. Flippy would sell it. The other $100,000 would remain in the bank at 1.2% interest.

D. use the $500,000 to expand the business. Mr. Flippy expects that expansion will earn a 10% return on the investment; however, they would not get any cash from this return until the following July.

Answer the following questions about Mr. Flippy's choices:

a. Which option has the least risk?

b. Which option is most likely to earn the most money?

c. Why would option D be unwise despite its return?

d. What considerations do you need to make in choosing an option?

d. (This asks for an opinion and has no correct answer) Which option would you advise Mr. Flippy to take? Why?

PROBLEMS

(See key answers at end of chapter)

P5-1

Fiona Dooley of Dooley Co. has received the following items during her sales transactions today:

a. a check for $40

b. a money order for $100

c. an IOU for $50

d. $20 in currency

e. a painting of Elvis worth $120

Dooley's cash balance at the beginning of the day was $2,230. Assuming Dooley makes no payments during the day, what is her cash balance at the end of the day?

P5-2

Marvin Moy Imports has $5,678 of cash on hand at the end of the day in the cash registers. They also have checks totalling $56,770. This total includes a postdated check for $1,000 that cannot be cashed until next week. They have rung up $78,233 in credit sales on this day.

Marvin's firm has a checking account with a balance of $690,500. Marvin himself has a checking account with a balance of $4,877 and a $10,000 certificate of deposit.

If Marvin prepared a Balance Sheet for Marvin Moy Imports dated today, what would be the balance in the Cash account? (Assume all amounts above are material.)

P5-3

How will each of the following transactions affect cash from operations, from investing or from financing activities:

a. Issue of $20,000 of no par common stock.

b. Sale of a plot of land for $250,000. The land had a historical cost of $125,000, and was being held as an investment.

c. Sale of $390 of inventory for $460 in cash.

d. Borrowing $20,000 from the bank.

e. Receipt of $300 interest on an investment in bonds.

f. Receipt of $450 on a customer's account receivable.

P5-4

How will each of the following transactions affect cash from operations, from investing or from financing activities:

a. Cash purchase of inventory for $3,000.

b. Payment of $200 interest on a borrowing.

c. Payment of a $1,000 cash dividend to stockholders.

d. Purchase of new equipment for $76,000.

e. Payment of monthly salaries, $500,000.

f. Payment to a supplier of an account payable, $900.

P5-5

For each transaction below, state whether it is an investing source of cash, an investing use of cash, or neither. If it is neither, explain why.

a. Sale of land held as an investment

b. Issue of bonds

c. Payment of dividends

d. Sale of inventory

e. Purchase of a building

f. Purchase of supplies

P5-6

For each transaction below, state whether it is a financing source of cash, a financing use of cash, or neither. If it is neither, explain why.

a. Taking out of a loan

b. Issue of long term bonds

c. Payment of interest on a loan

d. Payment of dividends on stock

e. Purchase of stock investment

f. Receipt of cash on a customer account

P5-7

For each transaction below, state whether it is a source of cash from operations, a use of cash from operations, or neither. If it is neither, explain why.

a. Sale of stock investment

b. Payment of dividends

c. Payment of a supplier account payable

d. Purchase of supplies on account

e. Use of prepaid insurance

f. Payment of wages accrued

P5-8

Glamma Corp. has just received its March bank statement. The balance per bank is $32,300. The bank statement shows March interest of $3,100, and a collection of $500 on a customer account for Glamma made directly into the bank account. There is also a $30 service charge for this collection.

A review of Glamma's books shows a cash balance at the end of March of $25,630. There are deposits in transit totalling $7,000, and outstanding checks totalling $10,100. Glamma Corp. detects no errors either on the books or in the bank statement.

Prepare a bank reconciliation to find the corrected cash balance in March for Glamma. Use the tear-out form in back of book.

P5-9

Measle Company has just received its October bank statement. The balance per bank is $105,270. The bank statement shows October interest of $100, and a collection of $520 on a customer account for Measle made directly into the bank account. There is also a $440 NSF check about which Measle had not been notified before the bank statement arrived. The bank charged Measle $120 for the NSF check. The bank also erroneously charged Measle $40 for dropping below the minimum required average *daily balance of $1,500.*

A review of Measle's books shows a cash balance at the end of October of $99,440. There are deposits in transit totalling $1,400, and outstanding checks totalling $7,570. Measle Corp. also finds a $154 cash receipt misrecorded as $514. -36°

Prepare a bank reconciliation to find the corrected cash balance in October for Measle. Use tear-out form in back of book.

P5-10

Wingnut Co. has just received the bank statement for June. The ending balance in the bank is $89,700. The statement shows interest of $74 paid to Wingnut in June, and a payment of $900 directly to their account by a customer who is paying on a prior credit sale. The firm, in reviewing the statement, notices $360 in outstanding checks and a deposit in transit of $5,600. They also discover that a cash collection of $462 on a customer account has erroneously been recorded as $426 in the books.

a. Find the corrected cash balance.

b. Find the balance in the cash account before the bank reconciliation.

c. Prepare any necessary journal entries associated with this bank reconciliaiton.

P5-11

Hairball Corporation's CEO, Ima Katt, thinks someone has been stealing cash from the firm. They currently have $46,588 in cash on hand from today's sales. This cash has been counted, but cash sales were recorded in the journal and ledger based on sales receipts.

Hairball has just received the monthly bank statement. Ima prepares a bank reconciliation using this additional information:

The balance per bank for the end of the month is $929,300. The bank has paid $774 in interest this month to Hairball Corp. Hairball recorded and deposited a check from G. Goober for $670, but G. Goober has insufficient funds and the check did not clear. The bank charged Hairball $10 for the NSF check, and charged $14 to print a new order of checks.

Hairball finds a deposit in transit of $14,553 and finds three outstanding checks: #4566 for $45, #4578 for $356, and #4579 for $20,800. Hairball's balance per books before the reconciliation is $975,290.

a. What is the corrected cash balance for Hairball Corp.?

b. Is Hairball missing a substantial amount of cash?

P5-12

Refer to Problem 11. How could Ima Katt safeguard the cash on hand against theft?

P5-13

Loonerai Inc. is preparing its quarterly cash budget, to see if they will need short term financing, since their business is cyclical. Loonerai expects to sell $50,000 of goods each month over the quarter, and expects to collect 90% of the cash for all sales in the quarter. They have $4,000 of cash at the beginning of the quarter. If they expect to spend $142,000 in cash over the quarter, will they need to borrow money?

P5-14

Izmuz Brothers has been collecting $1,300,000 in cash on sales and miscellaneous revenues every year for the past five years. Their cash expenditures five years ago (in 1996) were $900,000. The expenditures have been growing by 10% every year, and they expect this trend to continue.

a. In what year did/will Izmuz Brothers' cash payments exceed their cash collections?

b. Will this trend lead to insolvency? Why or why not?

P5-15

Clara Corp. has $20,000 in excess cash that it will not need for four months. They are considering purchasing stocks for $20 per share. They will not earn dividends on this investment, but they expect the stock price to rise between $1 and $6 per share over the next four months. If they do not invest in the stock, they will leave the money in the bank, earning 3% per year.

a. Which investment is riskier?

b. What would you consider before advising Clara what to do?

c. (opinion question - no correct answer) What would you do? Why?

WRITING EXERCISES

W5-1

In essay format, describe the internal controls you would need to implement for the cash receipts at a movie theater. Consider both physical and accounting controls.

W5-2

Discuss the effect you think a firm with insufficient funds would have on the owners, employees, creditors and customers of that firm.

W5-3

By looking at financial statements in the library or on the Internet, compare the year end cash balance of a bank with that of a merchandising or manufacturing firm. Discuss whether you think the two balances are comprised of different things, given the definition of cash, and what those different components might be.

KEY ANSWERS TO CERTAIN EXERCISES AND PROBLEMS

E5-12

Corrected cash balance $410,400

E5-15

a. Cash excess $15,200

P5-2

Cash reported on balance sheet $751,948

P5-8

Corrected cash balance $29,200

P5-9

Corrected cash balance $99,140

P5-11

a. Corrected cash balance $969,240

Chapter 6

Receivables

LEARNING OBJECTIVES

After studying this chapter, you should be able to:

• Understand the accounting definition of receivables.

• Differentiate between Accounts and Notes Receivable.

• Explain how various discounts affect the valuation of trade receivables.

• Account for bad debts and overdue notes and their effect on the valuation of receivables.

• Describe the concept of interest.

Smith Investigations was founded by John Smith in 1981. It was a public company that primarily provided investigative services. Its main source of revenue was billings from investigative work, and its major asset was Accounts Receivable. Though it was a growing firm, Smith reported larger and larger losses each year until in 1985 its founder decided to change the way revenues were reported. Rather than billing (to record accounts receivable) and reporting revenues when investigations were complete, Smith began to bill and recognize revenues as work was done on each investigation. Moreover, rather than billing for actual work, the firm president would pick a target revenue for each quarter, and the employees would then bill and recognize revenue for work to meet that target.

Using this scheme, Smith managed to record over $45 million of false revenues over the next three years. In spite of the large revenues and receivables, Smith continued to have a cash flow problem and was generally unable to collect a large proportion of the reported receivables. So, what happened to Smith? Smith went bankrupt in 1989, and because of its improper revenue recognition practices and its intentional misstatement of financial position, many of its officers are now serving prison terms for fraud.[30]

What then was the impact of the fraudulent accounts receivable? To understand this, first we must understand what *receivables* are supposed to represent.

TYPES OF RECEIVABLES

This chapter discusses the concept of and the accounting for various receivables. Receivables, as the name implies, refer to a firm's future collections of cash[31] which have been promised by a customer, debtor, or other party in some transaction with the firm. Most receivables are short term, expected to be collected within the longer of one year or operating cycle. These receivables are classified as *current assets*. Receivables expected to be collected after more than one year are usually classified as *intangible* or *other assets* if they do not bear interest, and as *investments* if they do bear interest. Note the placement of receivables on the sample partial Balance Sheet in **Figure 6.1**.

Why, you may wonder, are receivables considered assets, since they only represent promises of future cash? The answer is twofold. First, they do represent promises of future cash, and so provide *future economic benefits* to the firm. Recall that the FASB specifically defines an asset as something that provides future economic benefits.

---

[30]From SEC file #3-8340, 1994 SEC LEXIS 3332. The names have been changed, but the facts are consistent with the case.

[31]Although most receivables are expected to be collected in cash, a firm may also reduce its receivables by receiving some other asset, or in turn by having a liability reduced.

Second while they are promises and therefore intangible, they may still be borrowed against or even sold for cash. In this way they also may provide future economic benefits to a firm.

Figure 6.1   Placement of Receivables on the Balance Sheet

ASSETS	
Current assets	
Cash	$70,000
Investment in trading securities	3,000
Notes receivable	14,000
Accounts receivable (net)	150,000
Interest receivable	1,700
Inventory	340,300
Prepaid assets	20,000
Total current assets	$ 599,000
Long term investments	
Notes receivable (long term)	33,000
Investment in available for sale securities	200,000
Investment in held to maturity bonds	250,000
Investment in stocks - equity method	140,000
Property plant and equipment	
Plant and equipment (net)	800,000
Natural resources (net)	60,000
Intangibles and other assets	
Patents, copyrights, etc., net of amortization	2,000
Long term accounts receivable	12,000
Total assets	$2,096,000

To a user of financial information, two important points about receivables are type and collectibility. Just because a firm reports a receivable on the Balance Sheet does not mean that the receivable is *guaranteed* collectible.

While receivables may arise for any number of reasons, the most common receivables are *Accounts Receivable*, *Notes Receivable* and *Interest Receivable*. "Accounts Receivable" is sometimes used as the general term for all receivables, but it specifically refers to those receivables arising from *sales on credit* (also called *credit sales* or *sales on account*) to customers.

Notes receivable may arise from simple sales transactions, but since they bear interest they also may indicate lending money or the financing of a sale. Interest receivable is thus related to notes receivable. If the note receivable has not been collected by the end of a firm's fiscal year, the interest not yet collected on the note is recorded as an asset separate from the note itself. Interest receivable may also arise from long term lending such as the purchase of bonds. Refer to Chapter 5 to review the concept of interest receivable and how it arises.

In the remainder of this chapter we concentrate our discussion on Accounts Receivable (as customer accounts) and Notes Receivable. For a user, the important issue is the *valuation* or *collectibility* of the receivables on the Balance Sheet. We will discuss accounting for and reporting these receivables so that you will have an understanding of their valuation and collectibility.

ACCOUNTS RECEIVABLE

As mentioned above, accounts receivable usually arise from credit sales transactions. Accounts receivable are "promises" by customers to pay the company (seller) a certain sum of money. The promise is not evidenced by a formally written note but usually by a sales slip. Collectibility is not certain. Although the company may ask that a customer pay within 30 days or 60 days or some other time period, the customer may choose to delay payment.

This unpaid account may become interest bearing after the specified collection date passes.[32] This is discussed further in the "Notes Receivable" section. If the account (or note) remains unpaid for a long time, the seller may either give up trying to collect it and *write off* the account (remove it from the books and take a loss,) or sell it to a collection agency.

Accounts Receivable (abbreviated A/R) are usually classified as current assets, since the intent is to have customers pay as soon as possible. The Accounts Receivable account that we discuss in this book is the general account, which is really a summary of all the individual customer accounts. On the

---

[32]You have probably heard advertisements where the seller offers credit terms and says, "90 days same as cash" or some similar phrase. This means that, to the seller, the unpaid bill is an account receivable for 90 days, after which it becomes an interest bearing (note) receivable.

balance sheet there is no desire to disclose the individual customer accounts since users of financial information are either not interested in this information or are probably interested for the wrong reasons. That is, the firm has reasons to maintain the confidentiality of the individual customer accounts.

To understand the valuation or collectibility issue, let us begin by examining how accounts receivable are originally recorded in the books as they arise from sales to customers on account.

• Recording Accounts Receivable in the Books •

Suppose that A Firm sells merchandise for $600 to Another Firm on September 16. Another Firm agrees to pay A Firm later, and does not have to pay interest over time on the amount unpaid. The journal entry in A Firm's books for such a sale would be:

Sept. 16	Accounts Receivable	600	
	Sales Revenue		600
	To record a credit sale to Another Firm.		

As expected, the asset account is debited at the time of the sale for the amount of money that the firm expects to collect from the customer later. If A Firm expects to collect the entire amount, then $600 will be reported on the Balance Sheet of A Firm.

• Credit Card Sales •

It is important to note that a credit sale is not the same type of transaction as a sale for which a firm accepts a *major (bank) credit card* such as Visa or Discover. In a credit sale, the seller carries the customer account, which is a receivable directly from the customer. Sales using major credit cards are paid for by the credit card firm within days of the sale, and the credit card company carries the customer account.

When a firm accepts a bank credit card for a sale, it treats the transaction as a cash sale. The reason is that the firm gets guaranteed rapid payment from the credit card company. However, the credit card company also charges a fee for the transaction, so the amount of cash the seller receives is less than the sales price. This fee, typically from 3% to 6% of the transaction total, is given in exchange for the guarantee of payment to the seller, even if the buyer later refuses to pay the credit card company.

Suppose A Firm sells an item to N. E. Customer for $400 on September 17. N. E. Customer presents a credit card (VISA, Discover, etc.) and the credit card company charges a 4% fee to A Firm for the transaction. Then A Firm will record the sale as a cash sale less the fee to the credit card company:

Sept. 17	Cash	384	
	Charge Card Fees	16	
	Sales Revenue		400
	To record a credit card sale to N.E. Customer.		

The charge card fee will be reported on the Income Statement. The firm is willing to pay this fee for a guaranteed cash payment, and also because more and more individuals are now using credit cards to buy services and merchandise. Firms that do not accept any credit cards may even lose customers, so they are again willing to pay the fee. The point of this discussion however is that, unlike credit sales, bank credit card transactions <u>do not</u> create receivables to the seller. Thus, on such credit card sales, there is no valuation problem; the value of the sale is the cash received plus the fee remitted to the credit card company.

Note that some firms carry their own credit cards, such as Sears, Macy's and Exxon. These are not bank credit cards, and transactions on these cards are treated as accounts receivable to the firm. Such accounts usually become notes receivable (interest bearing) if the balance is not paid by the cardholder within 30 days of the billing cycle.

• Discounts •

We have seen that credit sales create accounts receivable from customers, but credit card sales do not. Firms are willing to pay credit card company fees in order to generate more sales; they are also willing to give *discounts* directly to customers on some items in order to generate more sales.

Firms are willing to pay credit card company fees in order to collect cash quickly from customer sales. Firms are also willing to give discounts on credit sales directly to customers to entice them to pay quickly. Discounts affect the valuation of receivables, and for this reason we want to discuss some common types of discounts.

–Trade discounts–

A trade discount is any discount on the regular or *list price* of an item, when the discount is given BEFORE the sales transaction occurs. Stores advertising a "sale" (e.g. the Memorial Day Sale at Macy's) are offering a form of trade discount. For example, if Your Firm usually sells a particular item for $500, but this week only it is marked down to a special price of $459, then Your Firm has offered a trade discount on this item. Because the special price is offered before the sale transaction occurs, your firm expects to collect $459 on each cash or credit sale of this item made this week.

Quantity discounts are another form of trade discount. Suppose Your Firm sells inventory items for a price of $10 each, but gives a 3% discount on orders of over 10,000 items. If A Customer buys 11,000 items on credit on September 18, then A Customer will receive the discount, and will owe Your Firm only $106,700, and not $110,000. The journal entry will appear so on Your Firm's books:

Sept. 18	Accounts Receivable	106,700	
	Sales Revenue		106,700
	To record sale of 11,000 items on account to		
	A. Customer with a 3% trade discount.		

To reiterate, the point is that with a trade discount on a credit sale, the receivable is valued at the amount the seller _**expects to collect**_ from the buyer, regardless of the merchandise list price or historical cost.

–Sales discounts–

One case in which it is difficult to determine the correct value for the receivable is that of the sales discount. Unlike the trade discount just illustrated, the sales discount is offered for credit sales only, and is offered for a specified period <u>after</u> the point of sale (sales transaction.) At the point of sale the seller does not know whether the customer will take the discount. Whether the sales discount is taken is determined by the customer's willingness to pay quickly on credit sales.

For sales discounts, the seller offers something called _**credit terms**_ or _**terms of payment.**_ If the buyer pays within a specified number of days following the sale, the buyer will received a specified discount. Otherwise the buyer must pay the full amount. The terms are usually written like this:

2/10/n30

–or–

5/15/EOM

The first number in each of those examples represents the discount being offered. The seller will take 2% off the total selling price in the first example, and 5% in the second. The discount may be any amount the seller wishes to offer.

The second number, after the first slash, represents the discount period measured in days. In the first example the buyer will receive the 2% discount if the buyer pays within ten days of the sale. In the second case the buyer has 15 days to take the 5% discount. This period is also set by the seller, and may be any number of days. However, since the point of the discount is to entice customers to pay in the cash quickly, it is usually a small number such as ten or fifteen.

The last sequence of letters and numbers following the second slash reminds the customer that even without paying in the discount period, the seller would like prompt payment. n30 means that if the discount is not taken, the gross amount is due within 30 days of the sale. EOM means the gross amount is due by the end of the month.

–Reporting receivables–

Offering a sales discount will affect the value of the receivable, for the customer may pay the lesser amount, or may not. Because of its uncertain nature, receivables from transactions offering sales discounts may be reported either at the total possible amount receivable (the *gross* amount) or the discounted amount (the *net* amount.) That is, if A Company makes a $500 credit sale to Another Company and offers credit terms of 3/12/n60, A Company may report the receivable as either $500 or $485.

–Case of Apple Company–

In 1976, when Steve Jobs and Steve Wozniak started Apple Computer Company, Jobs asked Kierulff Electronic Company in Palo Alto for a line of credit. Apple was given credit for $20,000 on 30 days net. Jobs said they didn't know what the terms meant.[33] But he soon learned that it meant no interest would accrue for 30 days. A line of credit is not the same as a sales discount, but is more like a loan. This experience started the policy for the company of taking advantage of the maximum amount of grace time and then paying the bill just before the 30-day limit ended.

• Accounting for Bad Debts •

An important problem in valuing accounts receivable is that the selling firm can never be certain whether all its customers will pay off their accounts. However, the accounts receivable are recorded as if the seller assumes all the cash will be collected. Left unadjusted, this violates the conservatism principle which maintains that assets not be overstated. One would *not* want users of the balance sheet to assume all accounts receivable are *guaranteed* collectible. Also, failing to record bad debts expense in the period the sales revenue was generated would violate the matching principle.

To solve the conservatism and matching problems, one of the adjusting entries prepared every period records a value in an account called Allowance for Bad Debts (or Allowance for Doubtful Accounts, or Allowance for Uncollectibles.) This allowance account is an *estimate* of the portion of the Accounts Receivable ending balance that the firm feels will not ever be collected from customers.

---

[33] Jeffrey Young, pp.94-95.

The end of year adjustment is an estimate because at that point in time the firm is not yet certain which customers will default on their payments, or by how much. All the firm knows is that there is some probability, usually calculated based on past experience, that not all the accounts receivable will be collected. If a firm knows that a particular account will not be collected, it does not include this information in the estimate of bad debts. Instead the firm *writes off* the customer's account. That means the firm removes the customer's receivable from the books. The year end estimated bad debts are calculated and netted against the *remaining* receivables, using the allowance account as explained below.

The Allowance for Bad Debts is a *contra asset* account. It has a credit balance, but is not included with liabilities and equities on the Balance Sheet. Rather, it is found in the asset section, but as a *reduction* to assets. Specifically, it is subtracted in the current asset section of the balance sheet from the Accounts Receivable account, and the net amount is shown as the amount expected to be collected from customers. For example, in its 1997 balance sheet, Apple Computer Company showed the following:

Apple Computer Company	
Accounts receivable	$1,134,000,000
Less: Allowance for doubtful accounts	99,000,000
Accounts receivable (net)	$1,035,000,000

The Allowance account is a permanent account, and must be adjusted periodically to reflect the current estimate of uncollectible accounts. In other words, how did we determine that the balance in the Allowance account should be $2,000 at the end of this year?

There are two basic ways to adjust the Allowance account. In one method the emphasis is on calculating the *bad debt expense* for the period. The other method emphasizes the *allowance* itself and its relationship to Accounts Receivable. Let us call the first method the income statement method, and the second the balance sheet method.

–Income statement method–

This method focuses on the "correct" amount of *bad debt expense* to record each period on the Income Statement. It accords with the matching principle because it matches the bad debt expense with the period in which the sales that might generate bad debts were made.

The bad debt expense estimation is very simple. Based primarily on past experience, a firm will estimate some percentage of that period's credit sales[34] to be *uncollectible*. The amount estimated will be added (on the credit side of the account) to any previous balance in the Allowance for Bad Debts.

To illustrate, suppose Us, Inc. has $100,000 of credit sales this period and a year end (debit) balance in Accounts Receivable of $40,000. Us, Inc. uses the Income Statement method for reporting bad debts. Suppose from past experience they estimate that about 2% of credit sales will not be collected:

$100,000   credit sales
x 2%
$ 2,000   estimated bad debt expense for
          this period's credit sales

Us, Inc. will record the year end estimated bad debts with this adjusting entry:

December 31	Bad Debt Expense	2,000	
	Allowance for Bad Debts		2,000
	To record the adjusting entry matching the expense of bad debts with sales revenue for the year.		

Notice that the expense for the year is $2,000 and that the ending balance in the allowance is increased (credited) by $2,000. If Allowance for Bad Debts contained a credit balance of $1,200 before the adjusting entry, it would now have an ending balance of $3,200 ($1,200 + $2,000.)

Allowance for Bad Debts

	1,200 beginning balance
	2,000 adjusting entry
	3,200 ending balance

Net (expected collectible) *Accounts Receivable* would be reported on the balance sheet thus:

---

[34]While using credit sales is considered more correct, many firms do not distinguish between credit and cash sales on the books. Thus, estimating a percentage of total sales is often the more expedient calculation.

US Inc.	
Accounts receivable	$40,000
Less: Allowance for bad debts	3,200
Accounts receivable (net)	$36,800

At this moment you might be picturing the Allowance for Bad Debts increasing every year until it is a huge number, possibly bigger than the Accounts Receivable balance! Why does that not happen? Because the allowance account is also reduced every year by entries on the debit side. These entries are made whenever a bad debt from a customer becomes reality. That is, the adjusting entry for each year's bad debt expense is an _estimate_, and when bad debts actually occur and the uncollectible amount is _written off_ (removed) from Accounts Receivable (no point in keeping a bad debt on the books,) then in that journal entry one also removes the same amount from the allowance account. Why? Because if the bad debt is no longer listed as a receivable, then the contra asset showing that customer's account is probably a bad debt should no longer appear on the books.

To illustrate, suppose Us, Inc. decides at some point that Customer A will not pay on a $320 account. Then Us, Inc. will write off this customer account so:

December 31	Allowance for Bad Debts	320	
	Accounts Receivable - Customer A		2,000
	To write off an uncollectible account from		
	customer A.		

You must remember that a writeoff is _not_ a year end adjustment. The estimation of the bad debt provides the adjusting entry for a total the firm believes uncollectible; the writeoff occurs whenever the firm is fairly certain it will not collect a specific account.

–The balance sheet method–

A firm using the balance sheet method rather than the income statement method would still use past experience to determine a bad debt estimate. This time, however, the firm would estimate the _percentage of the ending balance of accounts receivable that is uncollectible,_ rather than a percentage of sales. The estimate may be based on a single percentage of the receivables ending balance (the Composite Receivables method,) or the firm may estimate different percentages for different groups of receivables, depending on how long these accounts have remained on the books (the Aging of Receivables method.) Either way, the number calculated represents the amount that should appear in the contra account, Allowance for Bad Debts.

If the allowance account has a balance left over from a prior period, the allowance must be adjusted _to_ this new figure, and _not by_ this new figure as was done in the income statement method. The reason is that while the income statement method focuses on the "correct" amount of bad debt expense for the period (matching,) the balance sheet method concentrates on the "correct" amount of net receivables to report on the balance sheet. That is, the emphasis in this method is on reporting the correct amount of receivables expected to be collected (conservatism.)

Assume that Them, Inc. has the same ending balances before adjusting entries in Sales, Accounts Receivable, and Allowance for Bad Debts as Us, Inc. did in the previous example:

Credit Sales	**$100,000**	**(credit)**
Accounts Receivable	**40,000**	**(debit)**
Allowance for Bad Debts	**1,200**	**(credit)**

Suppose that, based on past patterns, Them estimates uncollectibles as 5% of the composite[35] balance of accounts receivable:

$40,000   in Accounts Receivable
x 5%
$ 2,000   of bad debts

This time the $2,000 represents the amount of receivables that will probably be uncollectible, and not the expense for the period. The adjusting entry should be in an amount that makes the ending balance of the allowance equal to $2,000. Since the allowance already has a credit balance of $1,200, Them Inc. needs to credit only an _additional $800_ to the allowance.

Allowance for Bad Debts

	1,200 beginning balance
	800 adjusting entry needed
	2,000 desired ending balance

---

[35] "Composite" means all the accounts receivable still on the books, regardless of age. Some firms prefer to break receivables down by age (number of days outstanding) and calculate a separate estimate for each age group, since the older the receivable, the less likely one is to collect. This is called the Aging of Accounts Receivable.

December 31	Bad Debt Expense	800
	Allowance for Bad Debts	2,000
	To record the adjusting entry that	
	corrects the allowance account to reflect	
	5% of the current accounts receivable.	

In this case the expense for the year is only $800. The ending balance in the allowance is $2,000 as calculated ($1,200 + $800.) Net Accounts Receivable will be reported on the balance sheet for Them, Inc. as $38,000, as shown at the beginning of this section.

–Comparison of the two methods–

Figure 6.2 shows how sales, bad debt expense, the allowance for bad debts, and net receivables will be reported for Us, Inc. and Them, Inc.

Figure 6.2

Accounts	Us, Inc. (Income Statement Method)	Them, Inc. (Balance Sheet Method)
Sales	$100,000	$100,000
Bad debt expense	2,000	800
Accounts receivable	$40,000	$40,000
Allowance for bad debts	3,200	2,000
Net receivable	$36,800	$38,000

Notice in **Figure 6.2** that by using the income statement method, Us, Inc. reports the "correct" amount of bad debt expense, but the net receivables are not the amount Us, Inc. expects to be collectible. So, while the income statement is fairly accurate, the balance sheet is "incorrect." However, Them, Inc. in using the balance sheet approach reports the amount of net receivables they expect to collect, while the bad debt expense on the income statement will be "incorrect" with respect to the sales figure.

Which method a firm chooses depends on which financial statement the firm wishes to highlight. However, since users are aware of both methods and the advantages and failings of each, the choice of method will not mislead an informed user.

• Writing off Normal and Abnormal Bad Debts •

–Ordinary bad debts–

When a bad debt actually occurs, the treatment is the same for both the income statement and balance sheet methods. When a customer is identified as a bad debt, the customer's account receivable is removed from the books. The related amount in the Allowance for Bad Debts is also removed such that the balance in the allowance decreases. No adjustment to income is made at this time; the bad debt expense has already been recorded in the prior period.

Suppose on January 25 Us, Inc. finds that So Zilch, a customer who owes $400, is not able to pay at all because of bankruptcy. Then Us, Inc. will make this entry:

January 25	Allowance for Bad Debts	400	
	Accounts Receivable		400
	To record the uncollectibility of So		
	Zilch's customer account.		

–Abnormal bad debt losses–

The accrual accounting adjusting entry for bad debts above is based on "normal" or ordinary bad debts that a firm may incur annually. If, however, a firm realizes a bad debt that is *abnormal*, such as an unusually large bad debt due to the bankruptcy of a major customer, the firm will *write this off directly* as a *loss*. If So Zilch were a major customer with a large account to be written off, the journal entry for this abnormal bad debt would look so:

January 25	Loss on Customer Account	40,000	
	Accounts Receivable		40,000
	To record the uncollectibility of So		
	Zilch's customer account.		

• Receivables and Financial Statement Analysis •

The main risk with respect to receivables is their collectibility. Creditors as well as stockholders want to know how "good" the amount of receivable is on the balance sheet. Since the receivables are related to sales revenue, the most common way of assessing a firm's receivables is to relate it to the sales figure by calculating a ratio called the Accounts Receivable Turnover.

Receivables

–Accounts receivable turnover–

The ratio measures how often an average amount of receivables turns over (become collected) each year. The formula for the ratio is:

$$\text{Accounts Receivable Turnover} \quad = \quad \frac{\text{Net Sales Revenue}}{\text{Average Net Accounts Receivable}}$$

In theory, the numerator should be *net credit sales* for the period. However, most firms do not report credit sales on their financial statements as a separate item from total or cash sales. Moreover, if a firm's ratio of cash to credit sales is fairly constant, including cash sales in the numerator will not significantly affect the results when comparing a series of ratios. *Net* means that sales discounts, returns and allowances are deducted from sales revenue.

The denominator is *average net accounts receivable,* which again in theory should be a weighted average. However, since users of financial statements generally know only the ending balance, and by looking at the prior year's balance sheet know the current year's beginning balance, this average is simply the sum of the beginning and ending receivables balances divided by two. In the denominator the word *net* refers to accounts receivable less the allowance for bad debts.

For Apple Company, for 1997, the pertinent information for the turnover is as follows:

	(in millions)
Net sales revenue	$7,081
Net accounts receivable, beginning	1,496
Net accounts receivable, ending	1,035

$$\text{Accounts Receivable Turnover} \quad = \quad \frac{\$7,081}{\dfrac{(\$1,496 + \$1,035)}{2}} \quad = 5.6 \text{ times}$$

The turnover is 5.6 times. In other words, in 1997 an average amount of receivables turned over (became collected) 5.6 times.

–Days in accounts receivable–

The example above implies that it takes 65 days (=365/5.6) on average to collect on a customer account. This calculation, 365 over the receivables turnover, is called days in accounts receivable. Whether 65 days is good or bad depends on Apple's credit policy. In general, one would like to collect on customer accounts as quickly as possible, generally within 30 days. If Apple's policy is 30 days, then 65 days is a long time (and is bad.) If its credit policy is 60 days, then 65 days is reasonable.

While Apple would like to collect quickly on its customer accounts, a <u>very</u> short collection period may also be bad. For example, if the days in receivables is only 10 days, this may mean the company is too strict with its credit policy, and is losing sales because of the strict policy.

As you can see, the turnover ratio and the days in receivables give much more information to the user than simply the knowledge that the net receivables at year end are $1,035. By calculating and analyzing these ratios you can make a couple of inferences. One is that Apple may need a better collection policy. Second, there may be old receivables that ought to be written off but have not. By looking at a series of these ratios over several years (or comparing the ratios of several firms in the same industry) one can make useful inferences as a potential investor, creditor, or customer of Apple.

For example, a trend over time will tell whether Apple's collecting ability has gotten better or worse. If it has worsened, this may put off creditors. By comparing with other firms in the industry a user can tell whether 65 days is really out of line for Apple. If similar firms exhibit a similar ratio, then it isn't so bad after all.

–Errors and ratios–

If accounts receivable are misreported, then the turnover and days in receivables will also be misreported and thus useless as decision tools. For example, suppose the net Accounts Receivable ending balance for Apple were misreported as $800 instead of $1,035. This could have happened because of a recording error, an intentional misstatement, or an erroneous or intentional miscalculation of this period's allowance for bad debts. Given this incorrect ending balance, the turnover ratio would be 6.2 instead of 5.6, and days in receivables becomes 365/6.2 = 59 days, instead of 65 days. Correct valuation of receivables is important to anyone trying to analyze this financial information for any kind of decision.

–Cash basis accounting and accounts receivable–

Many creditors and business analysts, for evaluation purposes, wish to determine revenues on a *cash basis*. Why? Because sometimes cash flow information is more relevant to a decision than accrual earnings information. For example, a potential creditor may be more concerned that a firm generates enough cash to pay interest and repay a loan than what it reports as earnings each period.

Recall that according to generally accepted accounting principles revenues are reported on the *accrual basis.* To determine cash revenues on a cash basis you must remember that receivables reported in the current period represent revenues for which the cash has not yet arrived. Thus, if the balance in Accounts Receivable has increased over the year, this increase represents an increase in accrual revenues, but not revenues on a cash basis.

If you *subtract* the increase in A/R from the period's accrual revenues reported on the Income Statement, you will have the period's cash-basis revenues. For example, suppose Wingnut Company

Receivables

has $100,000 of accrual revenue reported on the Income Statement for 1997. Assume that Accounts Receivable increased by $4,000 from the beginning to the end of 1997.

Figure 6.3   Determining cash-basis revenue

Accrual revenue on Income Statement	$100,000
Less: Increase in Accounts Receivable	4,000
Cash-basis revenue	$ 96,000
or	
Accrual revenue on Income Statement	$100,000
Add: Decrease in Accounts Receivable	16,000
Cash-basis revenue	$116,000

If the A/R balance had decreased by $16,000, you must <u>add back</u> the decrease to the accrual revenues to get cash revenues. **Figure 6.3** illustrates the calculations.

–Receivables and sales–

You may already have deduced from this discussion that Accounts Receivable and the Allowance for Bad Debts, while themselves Balance Sheet accounts, are related to the Income Statement through the revenue account Sales Revenue and the expense account Bad Debt Expense, respectively. Sales Revenue, however, typically includes cash as well as credit sales. The Sales Revenue account measures the revenue over a period in time, and is a temporary account.

Accounts Receivable is a permanent account that increases for credit sales, but also decreases as cash is collected. Also, some firms use the generic title "Accounts Receivable" to represent all non-interest bearing receivables, and not just those from customers. So, while both Sales Revenue and Accounts Receivable will increase for credit sales, and while they are related, remember when you are analyzing a firm's financial information that they represent very different concepts on the financial statements.

However, another way that receivables relate to the Income Statement is through bad debt expense. If a firm uses the Balance Sheet method to find bad debts and receivables are misstated, then the bad debt expense is misstated, and the net income is affected by this error. Look for example at the sample income statements in **Figure 6.4**.

Figure 6.4   Bad Debt Expense and Net Income

	Correct A/R	Overstated A/R	Understated A/R
	$40,000	$45,000	$35,000
Sales revenue	$100,000	$100,000	$100,000
Cost of goods sold	50,000	50,000	50,000
Gross margin	$ 50,000	$ 50,000	$ 50,000
Less: Bad debt expense			
(5%x$40,000 - $1,200)	800		
(5%x$45,000 - $1,200)		1,050	
(5%x$35,000 - $1,200)			550
Other expenses*	30,000	30,000	30,000
Net income	$ 19,200	$ 18,950	$ 19,450

*Other expenses are assumed to be $30,000

Here we assume sales revenue is $100,000 and Cost of Goods Sold is $50,000, and that this firm uses the balance sheet method of valuing bad debts. Assume that the correct value of Accounts Receivable is $40,000, that bad debts are reported as 5% of the receivables, and that the allowance account already has a credit balance of $1,200. Then we assume that Accounts Receivable is overstated by $5,000, then understated by $5,000: Notice that the misstatement of receivables by $5,000 will misstate the income by $250 (or 5% of $5,000) which can be significant.

If this firm had used the income statement method, the bad debt expense would not be misstated because they would base the expense on percentage of sales. However, if the bad debts themselves are misestimated, then the income statement will again be incorrect. Thus, valuation of the receivables _and_ the related bad debts is very important.

• Ethical Issues and Accounts Receivable •

There are several ways that a firm can build up _(window dress)_ its balance sheet by manipulating or misrepresenting the accounts receivable.

–Misreporting credit sales–

Firms may try to overreport accounts receivable (or underreport them) by recording credit sales at an inappropriate time. Recall from Chapter 3 that there is a specific point in time (called _point of sale_) at which revenue should be reported. If a firm chooses to report credit sales after this point in time, for example waiting until cash is collected on the sale, the firm will underreport receivables and may report the revenue in the wrong period. Under most circumstances this violates generally accepted accounting principles. There is one exception: reporting on credit *installment sales* may be put off until cash is collected, but even then the receivable should be recorded at point of sale although the revenue is deferred.

Overreporting accounts receivable is more common than underreporting them. This occurs when credit sales are recognized before they should be.

–Channel stuffing–

It is a fairly common trick for manufacturers who ship their products to distributors or dealers for retail sales to overreport accounts receivable. The manufacturers will record their total shipments as credit sales and as increases in accounts receivable although they know the distributers will return any unsold merchandise without having to pay for that merchandise. This practice is called *trade loading* or *channel stuffing*. Book publishers and computer software firms may engage in channel stuffing, since they also sell through distributors. While this violates GAAP, it is also somewhat difficult to detect by simply reading the financial records and thus may be misleading to users. As an example, suppose CompuNerd, Inc., a software firm, sells $1,600,000 of software products to its distributor for $2,000,000, knowing the demand for the software is not that great. Moreover, the distributor is able to only sell half the goods and plans to return the other half. How would this affect CompuNerd's reported assets and income? **Figure 6.5** illustrates this.

Figure 6.5   CompuNerd Assets and Income With and Without Channel Stuffing

	with channel stuffing	without channel stuffing
PARTIAL BALANCE SHEET		
Accounts receivable	$2,000,000	$1,000,000
Inventory		
($3,000,000-$1,600,000)	1,400,000	
($3,000,000- $800,000)		2,200,000
Net effect on assets	$3,400,000	$3,200,000
INCOME STATEMENT		
Sales	$2,000,000	$1,000,000
Cost of goods sold	1,600,000	800,000
Gross margin	$ 400,000	$ 200,000
Other expenses*	100,000	100,000
Income	$ 300,000	$ 100,000
*Assume other expenses are $100,000.		

Assume for this example that before the sale to its distributor, CompuNerd had $3,000,000 of software in inventory. Clearly, while the channel stuffing uses more inventory than the actual sales, it also creates a higher receivable. Also, although cost of goods sold is higher as more product is shipped to the distributor, sales revenue is also proportionally higher. Thus, channel stuffing overstates both the balance sheet and the income statement.

–Misestimating bad debts–

Net collectibility of receivables and as a consequence net income may be under or overreported by the deliberate misestimation of bad debts. If a firm believes, for example, that 10% of the receivables are uncollectible, but calculates only 5% uncollectible in the adjusting entry, then both the receivables and the income will be overstated for the period.

As an example, suppose Gloomy Corp. has gross accounts receivable for the period totalling $450,000. If past experience indicates that 10% of these receivables will probably be uncollectible, then the allowance for bad debts (assuming the Balance Sheet method) should be $45,000 (10% of $450,000.) However, if Gloomy misestimates bad debts as only 5%, then the allowance will be only $22,500. If the allowance had a beginning balance of $10,000, then the two different estimates would yield in one case a $35,000 expense ($45,000 - $10,000), and in the other a $12,500 expense ($22,500 - $10,000). **Figure 6.6** illustrates the effect this will have on total assets; clearly the understated allowance will overstate both current and total assets. This figure also shows the effect on the income statement of Gloomy Corporation.

For this example assume Gloomy has total sales of $1,000,000, Cost of Goods Sold of $400,000, and other expenses excluding bad debts of $300,000.Note that income is overstated if the bad debt estimate is understated (underestimated.)

Under the income statement approach, the misstatement of bad debts will affect both the balance sheet and income statement; here, however, the expense will be calculated as a precentage of sales.

–Actual case–

According to an article in *the Wall Street Journal*, Sears Roebuck managed its earnings through bad debts to make itself look good.[36] When the new chief executive officer took over in 1993, a "big bath" (see Chapter 3) was put into effect which increased the Allowance for Bad Debts account by a substantial amount.

---

[36] *Wall Street Journal*, November 4, 1996.

Figure 6.6 Effect of Understated Bad Debts for Gloomy Corporation

	correct bad debt estimate	underestimated bad debts
PARTIAL BALANCE SHEET		
Accounts receivable	$ 450,000	$ 450,000
Less: Allowance for bad debts	45,000	22,500
Net amount of accounts receivable	$ 405,000	$ 427,500
included in both current and total		
assets		
INCOME STATEMENT		
Sales	$1,000,000	$1,000,000
Cost of goods sold	400,000	400,000
Gross margin	$ 600,000	$ 600,000
Bad debt expense	35,000	12,500
Other expenses	300,000	300,000
Net income	$ 265,000	$ 287,500

Because of this, the earnings picture for the next few years showed greatly improved results. This was done by use of the balance sheet approach. How did it work? To illustrate, let's assume the following.

Balance that should be in the Allowance account:

Year 10	5% of Accounts Receivable of $100,000	=	$5,000
Year 11	5 1/2% of Accounts Receivable of $110,000	=	6,050
Year 12	6% of Accounts Receivable of $120,000	=	7,200

Write offs turn out to be exactly as estimated:

Year 10	$5,000
Year 11	6,050
Year 12	7,200

What the company should have done is illustrated in **Figure 6.7**. Let's say that in Year 10, because of a desire to implement a "big bath," $10,000 is put into the Allowance account instead of

$5,000. In order to increase income, the company decides in Year 11 to record only $3,500 of bad debts expense, and in Year 12, only $4,750.

Figure 6.7

(should have done) Allowance for Bad Debts			
		$5,000	bad debts Yr 10
Yr 10 writeoff $5,000			
		$6,050	bad debts Yr 11
Yr 11 writeoff $6,050			
		$7,200	bad debts Yr 12
Yr 12 writeoff $7,200			

For Year 11, The company could record only $3,500 (instead of $6,050) of bad debts expense, because there was a $5,000 beginning balance to help cover the $6,050 of actual writeoffs. The company did not use up all the $5,000 because it wanted to have a balance for Year 12 so that a lesser amount of bad debts could be recorded for that year. In Year 12, only $4,750 of bad debts expense (instead of $7,200) was recorded, because there was a $2,450 beginning balance. What the company did do is seen in **Figure 6.8**

Figure 6.8

(did do) Allowance for Bad Debts			
		$10,000	bad debts Yr 10
Yr 10 writeoff $5,000			
		5,000	balance
Yr 11 writeoff $6,050		3,500	bad debts Yr 11
		2,450	balance
Yr 12 writeoff $7,200		4,750	bad debts Yr 12

• Discussion of Opening Scenario •

Now that you are more familiar with the concept of receivables and the effects bad debts can have on both the balance sheet and income statement, let us return to the case of Smith Company. In reporting a fraudulent amount of Accounts Receivable they misled investors, creditors and other users of their financial statements. Not only were these receivables based on revenues Smith had not yet earned (they had not yet provided the service for which they were billing) but in carrying these large receivables on the books Smith apparently was not writing off major bad debts. Thus, receivables and income were both grossly overstated, and Smith appeared a healthy and growing firm while still cash poor.

While one would expect Smith's auditors to notice something suspicious about this firm, the auditors gave Smith **_unqualified_** (faultless) reports on their financial statements in all the years until Smith declared bankruptcy.

We are now ready to move from Accounts Receivable to a discussion on another kind of receivable.

NOTES RECEIVABLE

The most important difference between accounts receivable and notes receivable is that notes receivable are evidenced by formally written notes that bear interest. The interest rate is always specified or stated at the beginning of the note's term.

Notes receivable always have a specified _life_ and **_payment date,_** called the **_maturity date_**. Consider, for example, a 90 day note for $400 bearing a 5% interest rate. The note is due after 90 days, and interest accrues over the 90 days at a rate of 5% per **_year_**, which is 1.25% over the 90 days (5% x 90/360,) or about 0.4166% per month (5% x 30/360 or 5% x 1/12.) If the note requires monthly interest payments by the maker, you as the holder of the receivable will receive $1.66 ($400 x 0.4166%) each month, and will receive the $400 principal with the final interest payment. If the note requires that all interest be repaid with the principal after 90 days, you will receive $5 (400 x 1.25%) at the end of three months (or 90 days) along with the $400 principal. These terms and the notion of interest will be explored later in this chapter. First let us discuss the notes themselves in more detail.

• How Notes Receivable Arise •

One question you may have is how a note receivable may arise from transactions.

–Credit sales–

Credit sales that require customers to pay interest on their account balances generate notes receivable. Why might some firms require customers to sign a note when others do not? It depends on the relationship the firm has with the customer, and on the risk the firm is willing to take. When a firm allows a customer to take goods or receive services before payment is made, the firm risks losing the merchandise or service to a customer who refuses to pay. To ensure legal enforceability of the debt, the company may demand a formally written note be given. For taking greater risks, the firm is compensated by the interest it will receive on the note. This is a typical situation for sales of expensive merchandise such as furniture or cars, when the customer usually makes monthly payments that include interest, and the seller does its own financing.

Firms that believe their customers are generally reliable, or, firms that sell less expensive items may sell to customers on account (Accounts Receivable) rather than for a note, since they are incurring less risk.

–Overdue accounts–

While accounts receivable have somewhat unenforceable due dates, one way to encourage timely customer payments on accounts receivable is to convert them into interest bearing notes receivable after a specified time period. That is, the customer need not pay interest if they pay the account within a certain number of days, but after that period has elapsed, interest starts to accrue. If you have a credit card, you are familiar with such an exchange from the customer's point of view. Purchases paid for within the month are free from interest, but if you fail to pay within the month the credit card company starts charging interest on the unpaid purchases.

Note that the receivable is to the credit card company, and not to the seller of the goods you purchased with the credit card. It was shown earlier in this chapter that the credit card transaction is a cash transaction to the seller. However, you still owe the credit card company until you pay your monthly bill, and to them this is an account receivable or note receivable, depending on whether interest is accruing.

Other firms that sell on account may convert an account receivable into a note receivable either because it has been outstanding for a long time, or according to a specific schedule. For long overdue accounts the seller may write them off, pass them to a collection agency, or notify the customer that the customer has a certain amount of time left in which the customer may delay payment, but that the account is now accruing interest.

For accounts that convert after a specific period as with the credit card company, here is the accounting from the seller's point of view. Suppose N.E. Industries sells merchandise to B Late on account for $400 on January 2, with the agreement that the customer does not need to pay interest for the first 60 days the account is due. If B Late has still not paid the account by March 2, the account receivable will become a note receivable for N.E. Industries:

January 2	Accounts Receivable	400	
	Sales		400
	To record credit sale after 60 days		
	interest accrues.		
March 2	Notes Receivable	400	
	Accounts Receivable		400
	To record reclassification of B Late's		
	account as interest bearing.		

–Loans–

Notes receivable also arise when the firm has a short term or long term lending arrangement such that for each note there is one amount loaned to one external entity who will pay interest over some period of time and eventually repay the amount of the loan (at the maturity date.) We will discuss short term receivables in this context; accounting for long term notes receivable is similar to accounting for bond investments, and first requires a discussion of the concept of discounted cash flows.

• Short Term Notes and Lending Money •

Suppose Whatta Firm offers to lend $20,000 to any employee who wants to buy a house. Suppose the term of the loan is one year, and the interest rate is 6%. The journal entry for a loan to Jan Smith on July 12 would be:

July 12	Notes Receivable	20,000	
	Cash		20,000
	To record one year 6% loan to Jan Smith.		

If the term were six months and the interest rate 8%, or the term were 45 days and the interest rate 12%, or the term were 120 days and the interest rate 9%, the journal entry would look the same. In other words, the Note Receivable is recorded at the amount due, called the *principal*. The interest is considered a separate element, unrelated to this transaction for accounting purposes.

• What is Interest? •

–Ordinary interest–

As you probably already know, *interest* is an amount one usually pays in excess of the principal in a loan or financing arrangement. The purpose of interest is to allow the lender to earn a *profit* on the transaction. Otherwise, there would be no economic incentive for the lender to let someone else use the lender's money. Also, as discussed in the section on sales for notes receivable, the interest is the lender's reward (called the _return_) for bearing risk in the lending or sale transaction.

The amount of interest is stated as a percentage of the amount of the loan. The amount of the loan is called the _principal_ or _face value_ of the loan. Stated interest rates are ordinarily _annual_ rates, regardless of the term of the loan. Thus, if lenders are currently offering money for 120 days at 9%, they mean that a one year loan would pay 9% interest. This works out to about 3% for the 120 days. You calculate this by simply taking the 9% and multiplying by 120, then dividing by 360 or 365. (Accountants often round the number of days in a year from 365 to 360 to make calculations easier. This also makes calculations using the number of days per year more consistent with calculations using the number of months per year. For example, 120 days is roughly four months, so 9% times 4/12 is also 3%.) Thus, the total interest on $1,000 for 120 days at 9% is $1,000 x (9% x 120/360) = $30.

Frequently for short term notes receivable the interest is all paid at the end of the term of the loan. However, it may be paid monthly, or at any other intervals set by contract between the borrower and lender. If the note discussed above had monthly interest payments, each month's payment would be $1,000 x (9% x 30/360) or $1,000 x (9% x 1/12) = $7.50. (Note that $7.50 is also one-fourth of $30, and $30 was the amount we determined to be the full interest for four months in the preceding paragraph.)

–Imputed interest–

In the discussions of notes receivable, we have so far assumed that the interest rates reflected in the terms of the notes are reasonable. Sometimes, however, a firm will offer a loan or financing of a sale at a rate significantly lower than the current market rate.

Look back at the discussion of the loan from Whatta Firm to Jan Smith. This was a $20,000 loan for one year at 6% interest, used to aid Jan's house buying efforts. If 6% is the current market rate of interest (the rate Jan would get from any other finance company for a house loan) as it is currently, then this note bears ordinary interest. However, if the current market rate for home loans is 12%, then Whatta Firm is grossly undercharging Jan. Presumably Whatta Firm's motivation is to help its own employees, thereby boosting morale and employee loyalty. However, for accounting purposes one assumes, since the market rate is 12% and Whatta Firm would be foolish to charge less, that part of the $20,000 loaned must actually be interest as well. This notion of interest hidden in the loan's stated value is called "imputed interest."

A calculation of imputed interest may also be required for notes exchanged for goods or services rather that for cash, and is required for notes that do not specifically state any interest rate.

• Recording Ordinary Interest •

As already explained, the interest earned and accrued on notes is recorded separately from the note which generates the interest. For example, here are the journal entries for the making of the $1,000 120-day 9% note on May 1, and the first monthly receipt of interest:

On July 1, August 1, and September 1, the company will make the same entry as on June 1 for the receipt of interest.

May 1	Note Receivable	1,000	
	Cash		1,000
	To record a loan to Some Body for 120 days at 9% interest.		
June 1	Cash	7.50	
	Interest Revenue		7.50
	To record the first interest payment from Some Body for the 5/1 loan.		

On September 1 also, when the customer pays the company the note, the following entry will be made:

Sept 1	Cash	1,000	
	Note Receivable		1,000

• Collectibility of Notes Receivable •

To this point you may have noticed that we are treating notes receivable as if the cash will always be received. That is, the Notes Receivable account does not typically have a contra account like Allowance for Bad Debts. This is primarily because notes receivable are not a large proportion of most firms' assets, and secondarily since notes carry a specific life and maturity date, it is usually clear whether the note is overdue at any point in time. Notes not yet due are considered collectible, and any interest that has accrued is reported as a separate collectible account.

As a user of financial information you must not be misled by the statement of notes receivable at face value if there is no allowance for bad debts. You must be aware that the collectibility of any receivable is not guaranteed. This is particularly important for investors and creditors, since notes receivable may constitute a material amount of a firm's assets. The problem in estimating collectibility for the user is that you have no way to determine what type of transaction (sales, lending, etc.) arose to create the receivable, so you do not know whether the note was made to mitigate risk of defaulting customer or defaulting borrower, or simply to earn some income on a loan to a sound borrower.

The problem in estimating collectibility for the firm reporting notes receivable depends on why the receivable arose. For example, in the franchise business in the 1960's, collectibility of receivables from franchisees depended on how the business did, which had little to do with the nature of the debtor. Collectibility became an issue because many franchisees failed in their business, and therefore the franchisor was unable to collect on the notes. If the note receivable arises from sales to questionable customers, determining collectibility is based on very different factors.

OTHER ISSUES ABOUT RECEIVABLES

• Borrowing Against Receivables •

While receivables represent *future* collections of cash, collecting on them immediately if you are short of cash is not always practical. For example, if a note receivable has a 120 day life, you cannot require payment sooner than 120 days from when the note was made. You also cannot force customers to pay their accounts at once, though you may tempt them by offering a sales discount.

–Assignment–

Sometimes firms short of cash may use receivables to generate cash in ways other than collecting on them. Since Accounts Receivable and Notes Receivable are assets, they can be used as collateral for loans, or borrowed against. This is very common with Accounts Receivable and is known as *assigning* the accounts.

A firm may assign *general accounts,* which means they simply borrow against the balance of total Accounts Receivable. If this happens, a firm must disclose the fact in a footnote in the financial statements.

A firm may assign *specific accounts,* which means they borrow against specific customer accounts. This requires reclassification of the accounts borrowed against from Accounts Receivable to Assigned Accounts Receivable. If Needscash, Inc. borrows $30,000 at the bank against the customer Frank Furter's $40,000 account on September 19, Needscash will make these journal entries:

Sept. 19	Cash	30,000	
	Notes Payable		30,000
	To record the borrowing at x% interest		
	for xxx days.		
Sept. 19	Assigned Accounts Receivable	40,000	
	Accounts Receivable		40,000
	To reclassify Frank Furter's customer		
	account, borrowed against on 9/19.		

Thus, if you see a line on a balance sheet that reads "Assigned Accounts Receivable" you will know that these receivables have simply been used to back a loan, but are still receivable to the firm.

• Selling Accounts Receivable •

Another way to generate cash by using receivables without collecting on them immediately is to *sell* them.

–Factoring–

Selling an Account Receivable such that the buyer (called the factor) charges a fee and collects directly from the customer is known as factoring the account. This is illustrated in **Figure 6.9**.

Figure 6.9

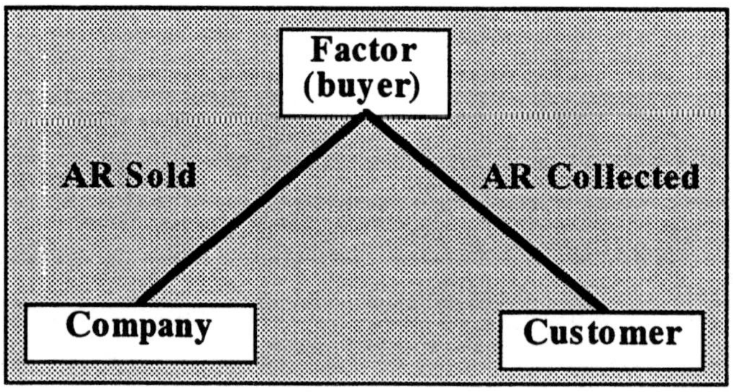

Generally when an account is factored the seller must pay the buyer a small percentage of the balance, which gives the buyer the economic incentive to purchase the receivable. The buyer sometimes also holds back part of the money due the seller as protection in case the account receivable is uncollectible by the factor. The fee and the amount held back (called Due From Factor, and treated as a receivable by the seller) are usually taken out of the amount of cash that the factor remits to the buyer, rather than paid through separate transactions. For example, if Needscash, Inc. factors a $40,000

330

account at the bank, the bank charges a 3% fee, and the bank decides to hold back payment of 10%, then Needscash will receive $34,800. $1,200 will be reported as the fee to the factor, and will appear on the income statement as a financial expense. $4,000 will be reported as Due From Factor until the customer pays the receivable to the bank. Then the bank passes along this $4,000 to Needscash.

Cash	34,800	
Fee to Factor	1,200	
Due from Factor	4,000	
Accounts Receivable		40,000

• Discounting Notes Receivable •

Selling a *note* is called *discounting* the Note Receivable. It is similar to factoring an account receivable in that the buyer charges a fee. However, this fee is usually an interest rate based on the amount of time the buyer must hold the note. Another difference comes from the fact that here the seller is actually selling the *maturity value* (principal plus interest) to the buyer rather than selling just the principal or face value. Thus, the seller could in fact sell this asset for less cash than it is worth, and realize a gain on the sale.

• Financial Statement Disclosures and Receivables •

One generally finds little additional disclosure on the balance sheet regarding the Accounts Receivable. You may, in fact, simply find the *net* balance on the face of the balance sheet, stated as:

Accounts Receivable, net $38,000

The term "net" here is understood to mean net of the Allowance for Bad Debts.

For Notes Receivable a firm may disclose in footnote the *terms* (life and interest rates,) though those are more important for the borrower than the lender. Also, if a large amount, the *past due* notes are classified separately and thus the fact that they are past due is clearly disclosed.

One must be careful when analyzing the receivables on the balance sheet to remember the following: first, just because something is reported as a receivable does not mean the firm is guaranteed to receive it. Next, while some provision for uncollectibility is made through the Allowance for Bad Debts, bear in mind that this allowance is only an estimate. The correct amount could be more or less than the estimate.

Finally, if a receivable is assigned, factored or discounted, the creditor or buyer is not guaranteed payment by the customer. Thus, the borrowing or selling firm may be liable for the payment to the creditor or buyer if the customer does not pay. This will depend on the specific arrangements made in the borrowing or selling transaction, and should be disclosed in the financial statement notes.

SUMMARY OF KEY POINTS

The following key points were discussed in this chapter:

1. Risk of having receivables. Receivables arise because the company extends credit to customers. The big risk for the firm is the collectibility of the receivables, that is, the possibility that customers will not pay.

2. The accounting definition of receivables. Receivables are assets that a firm will collect upon, usually in cash, in the future.

3. Valuing Accounts Receivable. Accounts receivable are valued at the amount one is expecting to collect in the future from the transaction that generated the receivable. They generally arise from sales to customers on credit.

4. How sales discounts affect receivables value. Credit sales which offer discounts may be recorded at the gross amount expected or the net amount expected. While the net amount better suits accounting theory, the gross amount is used much more in practice.

5. Accounts Receivable and Bad Debts. Since accounts receivable are not guaranteed collectible, firms estimate the amount uncollectible each period and call these bad debts.

6. Bad Debt Expense and the income statement method. The Income Statement method estimates the bad debt expense a firm has for a specific period as a percentage of the period's sales, and records this to match the sales revenue generated that period. The credit entry goes to the Allowance for Bad Debts.

7. Allowance for Bad Debts and the balance sheet method. The balance sheet method estimates what proportion of the current Accounts Receivable may be uncollectible, and records this as the Allowance for Bad Debts balance by adjusting the allowance account TO that number. The debit entry goes to Bad Debt Expense.

8. Ethical issues and Accounts Receivable. Accounts receivable can be manipulated by reporting credit sales either too soon or in the period after they should have been reported. They may also be overreported by misestimating bad debts, or by delaying writeoffs of uncollectible customer accounts until a future period. These are all considered unethical if not illegal misrepresentations of accounts receivable.

9. How Notes Receivable arise. Notes receivable may arise from many kinds of transactions including sale of inventory, exchanging an account receivable for a note receivable, or lending money.

10. Notes receivable and interest. Notes receivable bear interest, which means the firm will receive more cash than is stated as the face value of the note. The interest will be recorded in separate accounts from the note. Interest accrued will be "Interest Receivable," and interest received will be debited to cash. The interest earned for the period will be credited to "Interest Revenue."

11. Calculation of interest. Interest rates are usually stated as the annual rate, and need to be adjusted for the time period over which interest has accrued or been paid. The adjustment is usually made as a fraction of days or months per year, such as 120/360 or 4/12 for a 120 day (4 month) note.

12. Collectibility of Notes Receivable. Notes receivable are reported as if they are all collectible prior to their maturity dates. However, users of financial statements must be aware that collectibility is not guaranteed. If the maturity date passes without payment on the note, these receivables are reclassified as Past Due Notes Receivable and are reported separately from other notes receivable.

13. Borrowing against and selling receivables. For firms that want their cash sooner, both accounts and notes receivable may be borrowed against or sold. However, this does not guarantee the creditor or buyer that the customer will pay on the account or note receivable.

QUESTIONS

1. Explain in your own words what the term "receivable" means.

2. Is the following statement true or false? Explain your answer. "When receivables are listed as assets on the Balance Sheet, this implies they are guaranteed collectible."

3. How do accounts receivable arise?

4. How do trade accounts receivable differ from other accounts receivable?

5. Why are credit card sales not accounted for as receivables to the seller?

6. How do trade discounts differ from sales discounts? Explain in terms of collectibility of the sale amount.

7. What is the purpose of offering a sales discount?

8. What are bad debts? Why must they be estimated at the end of the year?

9. Explain why estimating bad debts based on sales differs from estimating bad debts based on accounts receivable. Discuss the reasons, not the accounting entries or calculations. What are the two methods called?

10. What does writing off a bad debt entail? How do writeoffs of normal bad debts differ from writeoffs of abnormal bad debts? Why?

11. What other transactions affect the Allowance for Bad Debts besides the year end adjustment?

12. Why is the end of year balance in accounts receivable different from the end of year total credit sales?

13. Explain how the Accounts Receivable Turnover Ratio is calculated, and how it may be used.

14. If you used cash basis accounting rather than accrual accounting, what would happen to the accounts receivable account?

15. Discuss ways that accounts receivable can be deliberately misstated. Discuss similar ways that accounts receivable can be accidentally misstated.

16. Explain how accounts receivable and notes receivable differ.

17. Discuss how notes receivable may arise.

18. Define these terms: interest rate, maturity date, accrued interest.

19. Explain why a firm would sell accounts receivable or notes receivable.

20. Discuss the financial statement disclosures required for: accounts receivable, notes receivable.

21. How do ordinary interest and imputed interest differ?

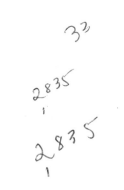

EXERCISES

E6-1

Determine the amount to record in accounts receivable for each of these situations:

a. You sell $400 of merchandise for $900 on account.

b. You normally sell widgets for $10 each. However, if a customer buys in quantities over 100, you give a 10% discount. You sell one customer 500 widgets on account.

c. You normally sell widgets for $10 each. However, if a customer buys in quantities over 100, you give a 10% discount. You sell one customer 500 widgets for cash.

d. You normally sell gidgets for $59 each. This week you are having a special on gidgets, selling them for $45 each. A customer buys two gidgets on account.

e. You normally sell gidgets for $59 each. This week you are having a special on gidgets, selling them for $45 each. A customer buys two gidgets using a major credit card.

f. You sell merchandise on account for $900 with credit terms 3/12,n45. Gross method used.

E6-2

Zeno's Files sells office furniture and equipment. Their total sales this year are $900,000. The balance in accounts receivable at year end is $56,700. What amount would they charge to bad debt expense this year assuming:

a. Bad debts are calculated as 1% of sales.

b. Bad debts are calculated as 1% of credit sales. Credit sales are ypically 80% of total sales.

c. Bad debts are calculated as 5% of accounts receivable, and there is no balance in the Allowance for Bad Debts before the adjusting entry.

d. Bad debts are calculated as 5% of accounts receivable, and there is a $500 credit balance in the Allowance for Bad Debts before the adjusting entry.

e. Bad debts are calculated as 5% of accounts receivable, and there is a $500 <u>debit</u> balance in the Allowance for Bad Debts before the adjusting entry.

f. Bad debts are calculated as 5% of accounts receivable, and there is a $1,000 credit balance in the Allowance for Bad Debts before the adjusting entry.

E6-3

Refer to Exercise #2, parts a and d. Discuss the different roles bad debt expense and the allowance account take in the two methods, what the methods are called, and why.

E6-4

The Balance Sheet of Lunei Corp. shows net receivables for 1996 of $50,000, and net receivables for 1995 of $68,000. Net sales on the 1996 Income Statement are reported as $404,500.

a. Calculate the accounts receivable turnover for Lunei Corp. for 1996.

b. Assume the 1995 receivables turnover was 10 times. Comment.

c. Assume the industry average accounts receivable turnover is eight times. Comment.

E6-5

N. Zane Company has $500,000 of sales this period. Accounts receivable has increased from $40,000 at the beginning of the period to $47,000 at the end of the period. How much cash revenue would N. Zane report if they were trying to determine cash revenue for the period?

E6-6

How would the following transactions affect the Notes Receivable account, and by what dollar amount, if any?

a. Sale of merchandise on account for $300.

b. Sale of merchandise for $330, requiring the buyer to sign a 6% 120 day note.

c. Collection of $600 on a customer account.

d. Accrual of one month (30 days) of interest on the note in part b.

e. Reclassification of a $450 account receivable as a 5%, six month note.

f. Receipt of the face value plus all the interest for 120 days on the note in part b.

E6-7

How would the following transactions affect the Notes Receivable account, and by what dollar amount, if any?

a. Sale of merchandise on account for $1,000, requiring the buyer to sign an 8% 90 day note.

b. Sale of merchandise for $380 for which the customer uses a major credit card.

c. Collection of a $600 note receivable plus 30 days of interest at 12%.

d. Accrual of one month (30 days) of interest on the note in part a.

e. The loan of $550 to an employee for 120 days at 7%.

f. Receipt of the face value plus all the interest for 120 days on the note in part e.

E6-8

The following transactions refer to Loner Company. Tell which transaction will affect cash, interest revenue, or interest receivable, whether those accounts will increase or decrease, and by what amount.

a. Loner lends $2,000 to another firm for 90 days at 6% interest on November 1.

b. Loner prepares the adjusting entry for the interest on the loan in part a on December 31.

c. Loner receives the face value of the loan plus the 90 days of interest for the loan in part a on February 1.

E6-9

Factotum Inc. has an account receivables balance of $500,000. What happens to their balance of accounts receivable in each of these situations?

a. Factotum assigns general accounts receivable for a $30,000 loan.

b. Factotum assigns a customer account with a balance of $14,566 for a $10,000 loan.

c. Factotum factors a $30,000 customer receivable, receiving $20,000 in cash. Factotum treats this as a sale.

d. Factotum factors a $27,000 customer receivable, receiving $20,000 in cash. Factotum treats this as a borrowing.

E6-10

Needscash Co. needs cash. Explain to Needscash how factoring accounts receivable and discounting notes receivable can generate cash. Discuss the risks involved with respect to the seller's relationship to the buyer of the receivables and the collectibility of the receivables for the buyer.

CASES

C6-1

Byron Books Corp. sells books to individuals, libraries, and other bookstores. Byron Books generally makes half its sales for credit, one fourth for cash and the other fourth on major credit cards. For the credit sales they offer 2% discounts if the buyer pays within five days, and they use the gross method to record these discounts. Approximately ten percent of the credit buyers take the discount. The credit card company charges 3% of the total sale for each transaction. If Byron Books sells $400,000 of books in one month for $600,000 BEFORE any discounts or credit card fees:

1. How will this affect the following accounts: Sales, Sales Discounts, Cash, Accounts Receivable?
2. What TOTAL effect will the sales have on the Income Statement and Balance Sheet of Byron Books?

C6-2

Newtie Gee Enterprises sells entertainment packages to travel agencies, typically on credit. Newtie Gee has been using the Balance Sheet method to report bad debts since 1995. In 1995 their ending balance in Accounts Receivable was $688,000. There was no allowance for bad debts at the beginning of 1995. They estimated bad debts as 5% of receivables that year.

In 1996 Newtie Gee's end of year receivables balance was $1,223,000. During 1996 Newtie Gee wrote off $67,400 of bad debts, and again estimated future bad debts to be 5% of year end (1996) receivables.

In 1997 Newtie Gee's end of year receivables balance was $1,674,000. They had written off $189,000 of bad debts that year, and sales that year were $1,800,000. Newtie Gee is afraid to show another large bad debt expense since they are trying to issue new stock and generate loans to expand the business.

They decide in that year to estimate bad debts using the income statement method rather than using receivables to estimate bad debts. They figure that five percent of sales would give about the same answer as five percent of gross receivables.

Instructions:

1. What does the relationship between 1997 sales and the increase in receivables for 1997 tell you about Newtie Gee's collection policy or customer base? (Hint: You may want to calculate the receivables turnover.)

2. Explain why changing methods of bad debt estimation will make Newtie Gee look better. Include in the explanation a discussion of the relative merits of each method.

3. Discuss the ethical problems in this scenario, including the effect that changing methods will have on users of financial statements.

C6-3

Armando Fragrances, Inc. sells expensive colognes and perfumes. They have a select clientele, but demand either cash or a note receivable for all sales. Armando Fragrances is currently holding a $10,000 120 day note with an interest rate of 12% from a client; the note was made 30 days ago. Armando's year end is in 15 days, but all the interest from the note will be received at the maturity date of the note. Armando Fragrances is trying to decide whether to hold the note to maturity or to discount (sell) the note today for the cash. Armando has already determined that if they discount the note at the bank they will receive $10,250 and have a $100 gain on the transaction. Given that the note is on the books at its face value, $10,000, determine:

1. the effect on the year end Income Statement and Balance Sheet of the sale of the note, and

2. the effect on the year end Income Statement and Balance Sheet of the decision to keep the note.

In the above discussion be sure to mention the specific accounts affected and the overall change in the income and total assets, liabilities and equities between now and year end that these alternatives would cause.

C6-4

Ned Neddles Inc. is a manufacturing firm that makes and sells needles. Ned Neddles usually sells needles by the case to merchandising firms on credit, but always with credit terms 4/12, n60. The undiscounted price of a case of needles is $40. Ned Neddles uses the net method to record sales discounts, which is a method that assumes the discount will be taken. The accounts receivable turnover for Ned Neddles has been about four times per year over the last four years.

341

Ned Neddles has a new manager in the finance division, Norm Nidile. Norm Nidile thinks Ned Neddles should sell cases of needles for $38.40 without credit terms, and should convert all the customer receivables to notes receivable if they are not paid within 60 days. Norm Nidile has suggested that the interest rate on these notes be 5%.

Norm Nidile believes these changes will increase the receivables turnover and generate a higher cash flow for Ned Neddles without affecting sales.

Instructions:

1. Determine the effect on receivables turnover these changes would have if Ned Neddles's total sales this year are expected to be 1,000,000 cases of needles.
2. Discuss how reclassifying the receivables as notes receivable affects the turnover. Is this really making a difference to the firm?
3. Is Ned Neddles really going to increase cash income by making these changes?
4. Do you think Norm Nidile is correct in thinking the change in policy will not hurt customer relations or sales? Would your answer be different if Ned Neddles's turnover were seven rather than four times?

C6-5

Go to the library, and look up the most recent financial statements of any two firms you find interesting. These statements should have at least two years of financial information. Compare the sizes of the firms by comparing both total assets and total sales. Look then at the most recent net accounts receivable for each firm. Calculate the accounts receivable turnover for each firm.

Discuss:

1. The comparison of the turnovers,– and–
2. How calculating a ratio makes the comparison of financial information from different size firms more comparable.

C6-6

(1) Discuss two scenarios in which you might find Notes Receivable on the Balance Sheet.

(2) For the following accounts, discuss a scenario in which they are classified as short term and long term assets:

a. Accounts receivable

b. Notes receivable

c. Interest receivable

PROBLEMS

P6-1

Which of the following will be included in the "accounts receivable" reported on the Balance Sheet?

a. a customer account with a balance of $30,000

b. a customer account with a balance of $45,000, which is 90 days overdue

c. a customer account with a balance of $37,000, that is overdue and has become an interest bearing account

d. a loan to a customer for 4% interest

P6-2

Which of the following will be included in the "notes receivable" reported on the Balance Sheet?

a. a customer account with a balance of $30,000

b. a customer account with a balance of $45,000, which is 90 days overdue

c. a customer account with a balance of $37,000, that is overdue and has become an interest bearing account

d. a loan to a customer for 4% interest

P6-3

Classify each of the following receivables as current asset, investment or other asset:

a. accounts receivable

b. note receivable due in 30 days

c. interest receivable

d. rent receivable

e. account receivable expected to be collected in 18 months

P6-4

Classify each of the following receivables as current asset, investment or other asset:

a. accounts receivable due in 180 days

b. note receivable due in two years

c. interest receivable on long term note

d. 30 day note receivable overdue

e. account receivable expected to be collected in 18 months

P6-5

What is the value of accounts receivable after the following transactions?

a. Sale of goods for $40,000 on account

b. Sale of goods for $15,000 on a major credit card

c. Sale of goods for $36,000 on account, less a 10% trade discount

d. Collection of $20,000 on a customer account

P6-6

What is the value of accounts receivable after the following transactions?

a. Sale of goods for $30,000 on account, <u>after</u> a quantity discount

b. Sale of goods for $23,000 for an interest bearing note

c. Collection of $12,000 note receivable

d. Sale of goods for $55,000 on account, less a 10% trade discount

P6-7

Wendel Wiif, owner of and accountant for TakeaWiif, a perfume manufacturer, sells to deparment stores on credit. The current balance in Accounts Receivable is $45,000. The Allowance for Bad Debts has a $3,000 credit balance BEFORE adjusting entries, and the sales for the period total $135,000.

Find net receivables and bad debt expense for the period for each of these independent assumptions:

a. Wendel estimates bad debts as 1% of total sales.

b. Wendel estimates bad debts as 15% of the Accounts Receivable balance.

c. Wendel estimates bad debts as 10% of the Accounts Receivable balance.

Bernie Gliz, owner of and accountant for GlizWear, a clothing manufacturer, sells to deparment stores on credit. The current balance in Accounts Receivable is $93,000. The Allowance for Bad Debts has a $1,500 credit balance before adjusting entries, and the sales for the period total $678,000.

Find net receivables and bad debt expense for the period for each of these independent assumptions:

a. Bernie estimates bad debts as 1.5% of total sales.

b. Bernie estimates bad debts as 15% of the Accounts Receivable balance.

c. Bernie estimates bad debts as 10% of the Accounts Receivable balance.

P6-9

Christopher Grackle's is an exclusive department store which carries its own non-interest bearing credit line. They have a total in A/R at the end of the year of $500,000. Their bad debt Allowance contains a DEBIT balance of $3,200. Assume bad debts are typically estimated at 6% of accounts receivable. Find the year end net receivables and bad debt expense for Grackle.

P6-10

Assume that your year end balance in Accounts Receivable is $40,000, and your sales for the year total $500,000. Describe the effect that each of these independent situations would have on the Income Statement. Use the tear-out form in back of book.

a. You write off a $500 bad debt. *debit Allowance $500 Crediting AR.*

b. You write off a $5,500 abnormal bad debt. *= Extra expense/lost.*

c. You estimate bad debts at year end to be 3% of Sales.

d. You estimate bad debts at year end to be 3% of Accounts Receivable. Before the estimation the Allowance account has a credit balance of $200.

e. You estimate bad debts at year end to be 3% of Accounts Receivable. Before the estimation the Allowance account has a credit balance of $1,500.

f. You estimate bad debts at year end to be 3% of Accounts Receivable. Before the estimation the Allowance account has a <u>debit</u> balance of $200.

P6-11

Assume that your year end balance in Accounts Receivable is $70,000, and your sales for the year total $660,000. Describe the effect that each of these independent situations would have on the Balance Sheet. Use the tear-out form in back of book.

a. You write off a $200 bad debt.

b. You write off a $9,500 abnormal bad debt.

c. You estimate bad debts at year end to be 10% of Sales.

d. You estimate bad debts at year end to be 2% of Accounts Receivable. Before the estimation the Allowance account has a credit balance of $900.

e. You estimate bad debts at year end to be 2% of Accounts Receivable. Before the estimation the Allowance account has a credit balance of $1,500.

f. You estimate bad debts at year end to be 2% of Accounts Receivable. Before the estimation the Allowance account has a debit balance of $200.

P6-12

Suppose Wilsonworld has a total of $700,000 in A/R, which INCLUDES the account of F.X.Penny totalling $93,000. How would each of the following transactions affect Wilsonworld's accounts receivable and other receivables?

a. Wilsonworld takes out a bank loan for $40,000, assigning general A/R.

b. Wilsonworld takes out a bank loan for $80,000, assigning the Penney A/R.

c. Wilsonworld reclassifies the Penney accounts as notes receivable. The maturity date is in 120 days, and the interest rate is 7%.

d. Wilsonworld collects the Penney note plus interest after 120 days.

e. Wilsonworld pays off both bank loans plus $160 interest.

P6-13

Weenee Company has a $300,000 account receivable from Rice Enterprises, a customer. Discuss how writing this off as a bad debt will affect Weenee's Balance Sheet and Income Statement if:

a. this is an ordinary bad debt

b. this is an abnormal bad debt

P6-14

Dooley Corp. has an account receivable balance of $470,000 and an allowance for bad debts of $4,700 on December 1, 199x. Their fiscal year end is December 31. On December 10 they write off an ordinary bad debt of $3,000 and an abnormal bad debt of $89,000. At year end they calculate the bad debt allowance as 2% of Accounts Receivable.

a. What is the year end balance in Accounts Receivable?

b. What is the bad debt expense for the year?

c. Are there any other effects of the above transactions on the Income Statement?

P6-15

Greegey Co. has an account receivable balance of $566,000 and an allowance for bad debts of $6,700 on December 1, 199x. Their fiscal year end is December 31. On December 12 they write off an ordinary bad debt of $6,000 and reclassify an account receivable of $23,000 as a note receivable. On December 24 they write off an abnormal bad debt of $104,000. At year end they calculate the bad debt allowance as 5% of Accounts Receivable.

a. What is the year end balance in Accounts Receivable?

b. What is the bad debt expense for the year?

c. Are there any other effects of the above transactions on the Income Statement?

P6-16

Romvegy Inc. has an account receivable balance of $876,000 and an allowance for bad debts of $14,400 on December 1, 199x. Their fiscal year end is December 31. On December 5 they write off an ordinary bad debt of $7,500 and assign general accounts receivable for a $30,000 bank loan. On December 9 they reclassify an account receivable of $20,000 as a note receivable. On December 24 they write off an abnormal bad debt of $200,000. At year end they calculate the bad debt allowance as 5% of Accounts Receivable.

a. What is the year end balance in Accounts Receivable?

b. What is the bad debt expense for the year?

c. Are there any other effects of the above transactions on the Income Statement?

P6-17

Discuss a scenario in which the following accounts may have arisen on the Balance Sheet of Dork, Inc. How does EACH account relate to the other two?

Accounts Receivable	$500,000 (debit)
Allowance for Bad Debts	4,000 (credit)
Liability on Factored Accounts Receivable	100,000 (credit)

P6-18

Discuss a scenario in which the following accounts may have arisen on the Balance Sheet of Bork, Inc. How does EACH account relate to the other two?

Notes Receivable	$500,000 (debit)
Discount on Notes Receivable	4,000 (debit)
Liability on Discounted Notes Receivable	100,000 (credit)

P6-19

Howard Wobbly, manufacturer of wobbly bobblies, ships his products to distributors and recognizes the sales at the time of shipment. Howard Wobbly has recognized $6,000,000 of sales revenue this period. Typically, the distributors manage to dispose of 80% of the goods, but Howard Wobbly has made no provision for returns from this year's sales to distributors in his financial records.

a. Is there an ethical issue in Howard Wobbly's behavior? Are any accounting principles being violated?

b. How will Howard's recordkeeping affect the financial statements?

c. How do you think his recordkeeping will affect <u>users</u> of financial statements?

P6-20

<u>Before</u> the year end adjustments, Wiffle Co. had $56,000 in Accounts Receivable, a credit balance of $400 in the Allowance for Bad Debts, Notes Receivable with a face value of $10,000, and a Note Receivable Past Due of $5,050. Bad debts for the period are typically estimated as 1% of Accounts Receivable. Notes receivable that

are not past due are almost always collectible, and the note has been accruing interest over the past month at the annual rate of 6%.

a. What is the total value of all the GROSS receivables after adjusting entries that would appear on Wiffle's Balance Sheet?

b. Of this total, how much should a user of the financial information assume is really collectible?

c. How will the adjustments affect the Income Statement?

P6-21

Before the year end adjustments, Woffle Co. had $109,000 in Accounts Receivable, a *debit* balance of $200 in the Allowance for Bad Debts, Notes Receivable with a face value of $50,000, and an Assigned Account Receivable of $7,000. Bad debts for the period are typically estimated as 1% of unassigned Accounts Receivable. Notes receivable that are not past due are almost always collectible, and the note has been accruing interest over the past two months at an annual rate of 6%. As they are making the adjusting entries, Woffle also decided to write off an abnormal bad debt of $9,000.

a. What is the total value of all the GROSS receivables after adjusting entries and writeoffs that would appear on Woffle's Balance Sheet?

b. Of this total, how much should a user of the financial information assume is really collectible?

c. How will the adjustments and writeoff affect the Income Statement?

P6-22

Beaswz Co. has $500,000 of sales this period, and net Accounts Receivable at fiscal year end of $40,000. Their beginning balance in Accounts Receviable for the year was $46,200. Find:

a. the accounts receivable turnover

b. the days in accounts receivable

P6-23

6900

Worle Corp. has total sales revenue this period of $690,000. Their Accounts Receivable balance at year end is $33,000 and at the beginning of the period was $28,000. They estimate bad debts as 1% of accounts receivable. Find:

a. bad debt expense for the period

b. the accounts receivable turnover

c. the days in accounts receivable

d. an interpretation of your answer to part c, assuming average days in receivables for the industry is 20.

P6-24

Giggle Enterprises has total sales revenue this period of $455,000. Their Accounts Receivable balance at year end is $99,000 and at the beginning of the period was $86,000. They estimate bad debts as 1% of sales revenue. Find:

a. bad debt expense for the period

b. the accounts receivable turnover

c. the days in accounts receivable

d. an interpretation of your answer to part c, assuming average days in receivables for the industry is 30.

WRITING EXERCISES

W6-1

Igor Poe, Inc., is a firm that sells equipment. They have a machine for sale for $40,000. ZXC Company plans to buy the equipment on December 1, 1998. Igor Poe will either sell the equipment on account, which if unpaid becomes an interest bearing account (note) after 30 days, or will sell the equipment on an interest bearing note. The interest rate on the unpaid account is 18%, while the rate on the note is 10%. Either way, ZXC plans to pay on January 15, 1999.

Discuss the advantages and disadvantages both from a financial point of view (what Igor Poe would receive) and an accounting point of view (the recording and reporting of the transactions) of the two sales plans.

W6-2

Assume you are the Controller for a furniture retail store, and you must decide whether to use the Balance Sheet method or Income Statement method for recording bad debts. Write a memo to the CEO of your firm stating which method you have chosen, and why. Discuss both the advantages of the method you prefer and the disadvantages of the method you did not choose.

(There is no correct answer for this assignment; either method is acceptable. You will be graded on your arguement, not your choice.)

W6-3

Using the Internet or the library, look up the financial statements of any firm that you would expect to have "Sales Revenue" and "Accounts Receivable." Calculate the most current accounts receivable turnover, and discuss what this number might mean given the type of business the firm does.

KEY ANSWERS TO CERTAIN EXERCISES AND PROBLEMS

E6-2

a. Bad debts expense $90,000
e. Bad debts expense $3,335

P6-5

Accounts Receivable $52,400

P6-6

Accounts Receivable $79,500

P6-7

a. Net Accounts Receivable $40,650
c. Net Accounts Receivable $40,500

P6-8

a. Net Accounts Receivable $81,330
b. Net Accounts Receivable $79,050

P6-10

b. Income reduced by $5,500.
c. Income reduced by $15,000.

P6-11

c. Net accounts receivable reduced by $66,000.
e. Net accounts receivable increased by $100.

P6-14

a. Accounts receivable $378,000
b. Bad debts expense $5,860

P6-16

a. Accounts receivable $648,500
b. Bad debts expense $25,525

P6-20

a. Gross receivables $71,100
c. Decrease in income $110

Chapter 7

Inventory

LEARNING OBJECTIVES

After studying this chapter, you should be able to:

• Understand the accounting definition of inventory.

• Differentiate between inventory and noninventory costs.

• Explain how various types of firms account for inventory costs.

• Understand the meaning of cost flows and how they differ from physical flows of goods.

• Account for inventories at the end of the year and understand how this accounting affects both the Income Statement and the Balance Sheet.

• Perceive the effects of inventory errors and fraud on the financial statements.

• Describe internal control measures to protect inventory from damage and theft.

She walked into the warehouse like she was walking into a mess. She knew that there was something wrong, so she was there to recount all the units left in the warehouse. Things seemed strange. They were trying to fool her, but she's smart, so the company couldn't fool her.

The firm that she was auditing had inventory in one place, and every time she counted it they would move it to another space. Then they'd bring her in again, pretending it was new, so she would count the identical units over and over. She knew that they were trying to fool her, but the company just couldn't fool her.

She started to get suspicious when she noticed the product mix at every inventory site seemed to be equally fixed. The number of units at each site was also unusually close. She went back unannounced to a warehouse and found that it was almost empty. The firm she had been auditing was trying to fraudulently report more inventory than they actually had.

What difference would this make to users of financial statements? Remember that for a firm that sells products (rather than services) the inventory is one of the largest amounts on the asset side of the balance sheet. If one overstates the amount of inventory owned at the end of the year, this would inflate the assets on the balance sheet. It would also artificially inflate the income statement, as you will see later in this chapter.

We will explore both the physical and valuation aspects of inventory, including internal control and accounting for ending inventory and cost of goods sold. To help sort out all these aspects of inventory, **Figure 7.1** illustrates the relationship of the topics to be covered in this chapter.

Figure 7.1 Relationship of Inventory Topics

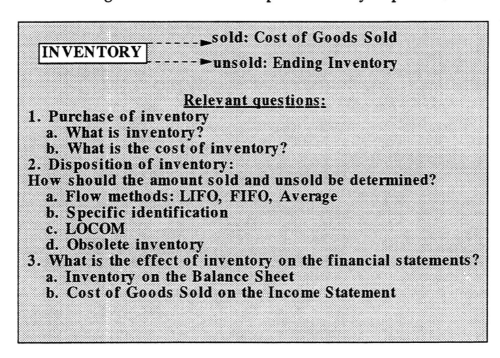

PURCHASE OF INVENTORY

• Definition •

Inventory is defined as goods or merchandise over which a firm has control, and which the firm intends to use to generate sales revenue. To be included as inventory an item need not be physically present in the firm; it need only be controlled by the firm.

Inventory is a current asset. It is an asset because it provides future economic benefits to the firm in the form of sales revenue (less cost of sales.) It is current because, under most circumstances, a firm wants to sell the inventory as quickly as possible. For example, grocery stores, clothing stores, electronics stores and even car dealerships try to sell as much as possible as fast as possible. Placement of inventory on the balance sheet is illustrated in **Figure 7.2.**

Figure 7.2   Placement of Inventory on the Balance Sheet

ASSETS	
Current assets	
Cash	$ 70,000
Investment in trading securities	3,000
Notes receivable	14,000
Accounts receivable (net)	150,000
Interest receivable	1,700
Inventory	340,300
Prepaid assets	20,000
Total current assets	$ 599,000
Long term investments	
Notes receivable (long term)	33,000
Investment in available for sale securities	200,000
Investment in held to maturity bonds	250,000
Investment in stocks - equity method	140,000
Property plant and equipment	
Plant and equipment (net)	800,000
Natural resources (net)	60,000
Intangibles and other assets	
Patents, copyrights, etc., net of amortization	2,000
Long term accounts receivable	12,000
Total assets	$2,096,000

• Inventory For Different Types of Firms •

–Manufacturing firms–

A manufacturer produces its own salable inventory, called Finished Goods Inventory. Manufacturing firms also have Materials Inventories of raw materials for future use in the manufacturing process, and inventories of goods started but not yet finished called Work in Process. For example, notice how Apple Computer Company shows its inventories in its 1997 balance sheet:

Apple Computer Company
Inventories:

Purchased parts	141
Work in process	51
Finished goods	281

Instead of Materials Inventory, Apple has Purchased Parts Inventory.

–Merchandising firms–

Retail firms, such as Wal-Mart or Macy's, buy goods from manufacturers (or from other merchandising firms) and sell them to their customers. This is the inventory on which we will concentrate in this chapter.

–Service firms–

Service firms do not have merchandise inventory, since their function is to sell services such as accounting, legal aid or health care.

–Supplies–

Most firms carry supplies, which are sometimes referred to as supplies inventory. Supplies are often accounted for as a prepaid asset. Supplies are debited in the dollar value purchased, then at the end of the period an adjustment to expense is made for the amount of supplies used up.

In this chapter we deal with _**merchandise inventory**_ rather than supplies inventory. The physical difference is that merchandise is sold to customers to provide revenues, while supplies are used internally to aid in the operations of the business. For example, cleaning solutions used by custodians or sales slips, paper clips, pens and order forms are all supplies that may be used by any type of firm. When we refer to inventory in this chapter, we are referring to merchandise rather than supplies.

• Inventory Costs •

Be aware that the specific expense labelled "Cost of Goods Sold" refers to the *cost of inventory* as the inventory is sold (and delivered to the customer) to generate sales revenue. <u>Any</u> other cost or expense is considered *noninventory*. However, inventory costs do not consist only of the purchase price of inventory for a merchandising firm. The accounting rule for determining the cost of inventory is:

All expenditures to acquire the inventory, to bring it to the place of business, and to put it in saleable condition are costs of the inventory.

For a manufacturing firm the cost of inventory includes all costs of manufacturing the product, including materials, labor and what is called *overhead*. Overhead is comprised of all factory costs other than materials and labor, such as factory rent or property taxes, factory utilities, and depreciation on the factory and the factory equipment. This topic is covered more comprehensively in managerial accounting. In this chapter our examples will arise from transactions of a merchandising firm.

–Examples of determining cost–

Let us look at two examples in applying the rule on determining the cost of inventory.

1. Suppose Albright Company buys 1,000 units of Product A for a cost of $10,000. It pays $800 to have them shipped to its warehouse. In order to sell the product, each unit has to be put in a special paper box that cost $.50 each. What is the cost of the 1,000 units of inventory?

The cost would be calculated as follows:

Purchase price	$10,000
Shipping cost (called freight-in)	800
Special box (1000 units x $.50)	500
Cost of inventory	$11,300

2. Suppose Baker Company buys 200 units of Product B, a special motor, for a cost of $120,000 from Allison Company. Allison agrees to pay the shipping cost of $900. Baker purchases a 1-month all-risks insurance policy on the 200 units for $300. The units are shipped on March 1 and arrive at Baker Company on March 14. The units have to be inspected by one of the employees before they can be sold to ensure that they are in salable condition. The inspector takes 2 hours. His pay is $20 an hour. What is the cost of the 200 units of inventory for Baker?

The cost would be calculated as follows:

Purchase price	$120,000
All-risks insurance for 2 weeks	150
Inspection cost	<u>40</u>
Cost of inventory	<u>$120,190</u>

The shipping cost is not part of the inventory cost, because it will be paid by Allison Company. The insurance is an inventory cost only while the product is in transit. It is considered a cost to bring the units to the place of business. Once the units arrive, the insurance is an ordinary expense. The inspection cost is necessary to put the units in saleable condition.

Figure 7.3 summarizes what we have said about inventory costs.

Figure 7.3   Inventory Costs for Merchandising Firm

Purchase price (net of discounts)	Include
Shipping costs	Include
Insurance in-transit	Include
Inspection of product	Include
Container for product	Include

• Physical Aspects of Inventory •

As with all assets, inventory is initially recorded in the accounting books at its dollar value, which is usually its historical cost. However, because inventory is a large portion of a merchandising or manufacturing firm's current assets and its cost becomes a large portion of that firm's expense, it is important to <u>verify</u> the values in the accounts by periodically *physically counting* the inventory on hand, and then determining the correct value of that inventory. For this reason it is important to understand what is counted and what is excluded from end-of-period inventory valuation.

–Goods in transit–

As mentioned above, control over the inventory, often represented by legal ownership or title to the goods, establishes who records merchandise as theirs at any point in time. If Company A orders goods from Company B and the goods are shipped *f.o.b. shipping point,* then the goods are reported as inventory to Company A as soon as they are in transit, because by law A takes title to the goods. However, if Company A sends goods f.o.b. shipping point to a *customer*, the goods belong to the customer as soon as they are in transit, and therefore Company A *excludes* them from its inventory.

(Technically, for f.o.b. shipping point, title transfers when the common carrier receives the goods from the sender.)

Antithetically, if Company A orders goods from Company B and they are shipped _f.o.b._ _destination,_ they do not become property of Company A until they reach Company A, which is their destination. Thus, while in transit they are still the property of, and recorded as inventory by, Company B. Likewise if the firm sends goods f.o.b. destination to a customer, those goods are counted as inventory by Company A while still in transit. They are only removed from Company A's books when they physically reach the customer. (Techically, for goods shipped f.o.b. destination, title transfers when the common carrier hands over the goods to the buyer.)

The implications of when title passes from buyer to seller affect not only the accounting records but also the liability of damage or loss to inventory in transit. In other words, goods shipped f.o.b. destination to a customer that are lost in transit must be replaced by the firm. However, if the goods had been shipped f.o.b. shipping point, the customer would absorb the loss.

–Goods on the premises–

Most goods physically located on a firm's property are owned by the firm, and thus are counted as the firm's inventory. However, goods physically located on the firm's property are only counted as inventory if the firm controls the goods. Thus, goods in a store _on consignment_ are not counted as the store's inventory.

Consignment goods are those with a special agreement that the store act as the _agent_ for the seller of the goods; the seller is not related to the store. The store holds the goods, collects the sales revenue in cash for the seller, and passes the cash along to the seller (usually for a fee,) but is never legally the owner of the goods.

As an example, think of the newspaper you might see in a grocery store. Usually the newspaper publisher has an agreement with the store that the store sell the papers for the publisher without actually buying the papers themselves. The store collects money for all newspapers sold, then remits the money (less a fee for the service of selling the papers) to the publisher. The store is the agent and the publisher controls the papers, which are on consignment at the store. When counting inventory, the store _excludes_ the papers. The publisher _includes_ the papers even though they are not physically in the publisher's possession.

The point again is that if you want to count inventory for a firm, you must be aware of what qualifies as countable inventory. This is summarized above in **Figure 7.4**. If you read a Balance Sheet, the value given for inventory should correspond to the historical cost of the merchandise over which the firm has control at that point in time.

Figure 7.4   Goods To Include/Exclude From Physical Count

Goods physically present; firm has legal title to goods	Include
Goods not physically present[37]; firm has legal title to goods	Include
Goods physically present; firm does not have legal title to goods[2]	Exclude
Goods not present; firm has no legal title to goods	Exclude

VALUATION OF INVENTORY

Much more complex than the topic of physical count is the issue of *valuation* of inventory. That is, when a person counts inventory items, that person must then have a way to figure out the **cost** of those items, given that inventory may be purchased several times a year, and that inventory may be left over from a prior year, and that the purchase price (historical cost) of inventory may be different for every purchase date. Valuation of inventory is also referred to as "costing" of the inventory.

• Physical Flow of Merchandise •

When you buy inventory in batches (as happens in real life) you must store the inventory until you use it. If you store it in a way that the last things you bought are the first ones you take out to sell, this is called the *Last In, First Out* flow. Last In, First Out, also commonly referred to by the acronym *LIFO* in accounting, is a typical physical flow pattern for goods that do not spoil or change with age. For example, if you sell identical picture frames you may stack them so that the last ones on the stack are the first the customer picks up.

If you store inventory in a way that allows you to take out the first items stored before any other items, you call this *First In, First Out* or *FIFO*. FIFO physical flows are common for products that may spoil or change over time. Milk, bread and bananas are typical of products that physically use the FIFO flow. If you store inventory so that you take random sections of goods out for each purchase, as would happen if you sold sand and kept it in one pile, you are using an *average* flow. These three flows are illustrated in **Figure 7.5**.

---

[37]   Goods may be in transit or on consignment at another location.

Figure 7.5   Cost Flow Assumptions for Inventory

Here are five inventory items: A, B, C, D and E. Assume they have been purchased in alphabetical order, and that you are about to sell two of the five.		
unsold	sold	cost flow assumption
A,B,C	D,E	LIFO assumes the last items purchased are the first to be sold.
C,D,E	A,B	FIFO assumes the first items purchased are the first to be sold.
A,C,E	B/D	AVERAGE assumes that items are sold in random order.

If you sell *specific* items, as happens at a car dealership or in an antique store, you use *specific identification*. But how do these physical flows relate to accounting for inventory?

• Cost Flows of Merchandise •

The accounting or *cost flow* of inventory can also be LIFO, FIFO, average or specific identification. You must remember that these are *assumptions* and do not necessarily mean that the physical flow is the same as the cost flow. LIFO, FIFO and average are more common than specific identification, so we will discuss them first.

To illustrate, suppose the following:

100 chairs purchased on January 1 for $40 each

100 chairs purchased on January 25 for $43 each

–Last in, first out cost flow–

The cost flow LIFO assumes that the costs of the last things you purchased are the first things you expense when you sell goods. If you sell 12 chairs on January 31, then:

Cost of Goods Sold will be $516 (=12 chairs x $43)

This is so, because you assume that the last chairs into the warehouse are the first sold.

You also have a remaining inventory valued at $7,784 (100 chairs x $40 plus 88 chairs x $43,) which assumes the first things you purchased are still in inventory. The remaining inventory in any period is referred to as the *ending inventory* of the period.

-First in, first out cost flow-

The cost flow FIFO is the opposite of LIFO. If in the above example you assume that the first things in are the first out, then:

Cost of goods sold for 12 chairs will be $480 (=12 chairs x $40)

Your ending inventory is now valued at $7,820, which is 88 chairs x $40 plus 100 chairs x $43. The last things you purchased are still in inventory at the end of the period.

-Average cost flow-

The average cost flow is exactly as it sounds. You assume an average of all goods in inventory are sold, and so you expense an average cost for each sale. Using the example above, if you buy 100 chairs for $4,000 in total and another 100 chairs for $4,300 in total, then you have 200 chairs in the warehouse at a total cost of $8,300. That means the average cost of one chair is $41.50 ($8,300/200). Therefore,

Cost of goods sold is $498 (=12 chairs x $41.50).

You also have 188 chairs left at an average unit cost of $41.50, so ending inventory for January will be reported as $7,802.

-Comparison of the three methods-

Remember that the cost flows _do not have to match the physical flows_ as long as you use one method consistently. For example, you could sell milk at a grocery store and use the physical flow of first in first out, but the LIFO cost flow. As long as you consistently use LIFO every year for every set of financial statements, you will end up with the same _overall_ set of inventory costs as you would have if you matched the cost flow to the physical (FIFO) flow.

Figure 7.6   Cost of Goods Sold Comparison for LIFO, FIFO and Average Cost Flows

Inventory Method Used	LIFO	FIFO	AVERAGE
Period One Cost Of Goods Sold*	$516	$480	$498
Period Two Cost Of Goods Sold	5,064[1]	4,896[2]	4,980[3]
Period Three Cost Of Goods Sold	2,720[4]	2,924[5]	2,822[6]
Total COGS For Three Periods	$8,300	$8,300	$8,300

*Calculated in the text above.

[1] (88 chairs x $43) + (32 chairs x $40) [2] (88 chairs x $40) + (32 chairs x $43)

[3] 120 chairs x $41.50 [4] 68 chairs x $40 [5] 68 chairs x $43 [6] 68 chairs x $41.50

Refer to the previous example in which you assume you have purchased 100 chairs for $40 each and another 100 chairs for $43 each. Suppose in three consecutive accounting periods you sell 12 chairs, 120 chairs, and 68 chairs respectively (totalling 200.) **Figure 7.6** contains a chart comparing the costs of goods sold for the LIFO, FIFO and average methods in the three periods.

Although the cost of goods sold varies by accounting method in each period in this example, you see in **Figure 7.6** that over the three periods if you sell all 200 chairs you have a total cost of goods sold of $8,300 regardless of the method you choose per period.

–Specific identification–

Most firms use LIFO, FIFO or average to find the cost of goods sold and thus also to find the dollar value of ending inventory. However, for firms that sell large or easily distinguishable products such as cars, antiques or original artwork, it is possible to identify specific products that are sold and thus specific costs of the goods sold as well as specific costs of those items in ending inventory. While cost flows need not match physical flows of goods, it is not practical to use the specific identification cost flow unless you plan to physically specifically identify the goods you sell and those still in ending inventory, since you need to keep track of each item purchased in this method.

As an example, refer to **Figure 7.7**. Suppose you own an antique store.

Figure 7.7   Example of Specific Identification

	SOLD			SOLD
BED	CLOCK	MIRROR	MIRROR	DESK
$400	$70	$33	$1	$125

Ending inventory = $400+$33+$1 = $434
Cost of Goods Sold = $70 + $125 = $195

You purchase an antique bed for $400, an antique clock for $70, an antique mirror for $33, another antique mirror at a garage sale for $1, and an antique desk for $125. It is quite obvious if you sell the clock that cost of goods sold is $70, and the cost of the remaining (ending) inventory is $559. If you sell both the clock and the desk your cost of goods sold is $195 ($70 + $125) and ending inventory is $434. You are specifically identifying both the items sold and the items left in the store.

• Lower of Cost or Market Valuation •

One aspect of inventory valuation which we have not yet discussed is the valuation method called "Lower of Cost or Market." This is the proper method of valuation of inventory when there is evidence that market value is less than cost.

Lower of Cost or Market refers to the conservative practice of reporting inventory in the financial statements at market value when their sales (market) value falls below historical cost, and this decline is not temporary. Otherwise, of course, inventory must be reported at historical cost. Lower of Cost or Market is usually referred to by the acronyms LOCOM or LCM.

Why is LOCOM allowed? It follows conservatism. Typically a firm buys inventory to sell for a profit; that is, selling or market price will be set higher than historical cost. However, some items become obsolete so quickly or drop in price permanently before they can be sold. If the firm knows it will have a loss on the sale of goods, and if the amount is *estimable*, as it will be if both cost and market values are known, then as with all losses this loss should be recorded now rather than waiting until the goods are sold.

–Disclosure–

When LOCOM is used, this must be disclosed on the balance sheet or in a footnote to the balance sheet, usually by a statement such as "Inventory is valued at market, which is below cost." Otherwise, the balance sheet or footnotes should clearly state that inventory is reported at cost. Consider, for example, how Apple Computer Company disclosed in a footnote the information in its 1997 balance sheet as shown below.

Apple Computer Company

> **–Inventories–**
>
> Inventories are stated at the lower of cost (first-in, first-out) or market. If the cost of the inventories exceeds their market value, provisions are made currently for the difference between cost and the market value.

–Calculation–

How does LOCOM work? After counting and valuing ending inventory at cost, using FIFO, LIFO, average or specific identification, one then finds the *designated market value* of the ending inventory. The designated market value is essentially the sales value, but the FASB has imposed a floor and ceiling on this value so that it cannot be easily manipulated.

Once the designated market value is found, it is compared to inventory cost. This can be done by groups of inventory (for example, comparing cost and market for chairs, and separately comparing cost and market for tables) or can be done for the whole set of inventory (comparing cost and market of furniture.) If cost is below market value, then inventory is reported at cost and no adjustment to the accounting books is necessary. However, if market is below cost, then a loss must be recorded in the books, and the balance in the Inventory account is *written down* (decreased) to market value.

As an example, suppose you count chairs and tables, and value them using LIFO. Suppose the ending cost of chairs this period is $4,300, and the ending inventory of tables using LIFO is $6,698. Assume that you find the designated market values of chairs and tables, respectively, to be $5,778 and $6,300. If you value the two types of inventory separately, then chairs will appear on the balance sheet at $4,300. Tables will be written down by a journal entry so that they will be valued on the balance sheet at $6,300. The loss of $398 ($6,698 - $6,300) will be reported on the income statement for this period. Refer to **Figure 7.8** for a summary of this example.

If you see the phrase "lower of cost or market" or the phrase "valued at market, which is below cost" on a balance sheet, you should understand what it means whether you are an investor, creditor, customer, employee, government agent, or just a person reading the financial report.

Figure 7.8   Lower of Cost or Market Example

Inventory Item	Ending Inventory At Historical Cost	Ending Inventory At Designated Market Value	Locom Value Reported On Balance Sheet	Loss On Income Statement
chairs	$4,300	5,778	$4,300	$ 0
tables	6,698	6,300	6,300	398
	$10,998		$10,600	$398

• Verifying the Ending Inventory •

In all these examples we have assumed that we are keeping records of what we buy and sell, and that our records are correct, so that when we calculate the value of ending inventory it corresponds with what we actually have in stock. However, in "real life" it is possible to make recording errors and to lose inventory through *normal spoilage* and *loss* or through *theft*. It may also be the case that a firm keeps track of items purchased but not those sold. This is known as *periodic* inventory valuation. Thus, internal control for inventory requires a physical count of ending inventory be made to verify the numbers in the accounting records.

–Periodic inventory valuation–

When a firm uses the periodic method of valuation, the ending inventory from the previous period is considered the beginning inventory of the current period. Inventory purchases in dollars are recorded for the current period in a special account called *Purchases*, but when inventory is sold the journal entry including the debit to Cost of Goods Sold and credit to Inventory is <u>not</u> made at the time of sale. (Of course, the debit to Cash or Receivables and credit to Sales Revenue are still made.)

Why might a firm not record decreases in inventory at the point of each sale? Consider a firm that sells a high volume of small and varied goods, such as a grocery store. Imagine the paperwork involved (in a world with no computers) if the sales clerk were required to keep track of <u>each</u> item sold to every customer in a checkout line. Of course, with modern technology such as computers and bar code scanners, now grocery stores can keep track at least of the items sold each day and the number of items left in stock, if not the actual costs.

Nevertheless, some firms that sell goods still prefer to use the periodic method. Since the goods being sold are not being tracked, the firm (or its employees) must physically count the number of items left in stock at the end of an accounting period, and then attach a dollar value to those goods as described in the section on LIFO, FIFO, average and specific identification. After ending inventory is valued, cost of goods sold can be calculated using the formula:

> **Beginning inventory**
> **+ Net Purchases**
> **= Goods Available for Sale**
> **– Ending Inventory**
> **= Cost of Goods Sold**

where beginning and ending inventories are valued at historical cost, and net purchases are the dollars both spent and owed on inventory *purchases* this period, less purchase returns, discounts and allowances.[38]

The calculation for cost of goods sold and ending inventory is made at the end of the period They are recorded as an ***adjusting entry.***

---

[38] Purchase returns are returns of unwanted or unsatisfactory goods to the supplier. Purchase discounts are amounts taken off the price of the purchase at the time of payment, and purchase allowances are reductions in price for faulty or impaired goods.

Inventory

–Perpetual inventory valuation–

In this method a firm will constantly or <u>perpetually</u> keep track not only of purchases but also of what is sold at least in units if not in dollars. Thus, at the end of the period the firm has a record of cost of goods sold for the period and an idea of what should be in ending inventory. However, as mentioned earlier, a physical count of ending units is still required to verify the records. In this method, if the ending inventory count does not match the ending inventory on the books, the difference is dealt with as a loss (or gain) on the income statement, rather than as part of Cost of Goods Sold.

–Comparison–

Remember that the difference between the periodic method and the perpetual is that for the periodic method the inventory account is left untouched during the year until the end of the year, even though purchases and sales are made during the year. It is only *periodically*, at the end of the period, that the correct amount of inventory is actually recorded. In contrast, the perpetual method keeps track of the inflows (purchases) and outflows (sales) *perpetually*, so that at all times during the year the correct amount of inventory is known. **Figure 7.9** illustrates the point.

Figure 7.9

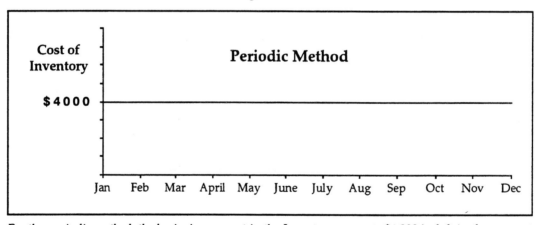

For the periodic method, the beginning amount in the Inventory account, $4,000, is left in the account throughout the year. Changes (purchases and sales) are not included until the end of the year. The inventory is counted and valued, and whatever is gone is assumed to have been sold.

(**Figure 7.9** continued on next page)

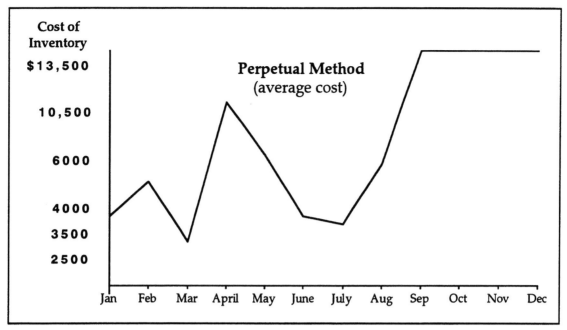

For the perpetual method, as you can see, the purchases and sales throughout the year are kept track of, so that at all times the Inventory account has the correct balance.

EXAMPLE OF INVENTORY VALUATION

In this section, we present a detailed example of the three valuation methods: Average, FIFO, and LIFO. We will calculate both the ending inventory amount and cost of goods sold using the periodic method and the perpetual method. Our firm is Feng's Toys, which buys and sells dolls. Assume at the beginning of the year Feng's Toys has the following:

January 1 inventory: **2,000 dolls for $4,000.**

During the year, purchases and sales occur as shown next.

Date	Units Purchased*	Units Sold	Unit Cost	Total
February 10	2,000		$3	$6,000
April 20		3,000		
May 25	2,000		4	8,000
August 18		2,000		
November 20	2,000		5	10,000

*Be aware that purchase cost consists of purchase price less any discounts, and including all costs of acquiring the units and getting them ready for sale.

• Periodic Inventory Example •

We will use the information given for Feng Toys.

–Periodic average costing–

The easiest method to use is average, often called "weighted" average, for the periodic method because you average the total cost for the period over the total units available. To illustrate, consider the following case.

	units	costs
Beginning inventory	2,000	$4,000
Add: Purchases - Feb 10	2,000	6,000
May 25	2,000	8,000
Nov 20	2,000	10,000
Total available for sale	8,000	$28,000

So, average cost will be: $28,000/8,000 units = $3.50 per unit

The cost of ending inventory will be:

3,000 units left x $3.50 = $10,500

The calculation of cost of goods sold will be:

Costs of units available for sale*	$28,000
Less: Cost of ending inventory	(10,500)
Cost of goods sold	$17,500

Of course, you could also find cost of goods sold by looking at the number of units that must have been sold (8,000 total units less 3,000 units left equals 5,000 units sold) and multiplying that by the average unit cost:

5,000 units sold x $3.50 = $17,500 COGS

and that gives a good figure to check your work. Thus, the Balance Sheet will report an ending inventory valued at $10,500, and the income statement will report a cost of goods sold of $17,500.

–Periodic FIFO costing–

FIFO assumes the first things in are the first sold, so the dolls remaining in ending inventory must be the last in. This flow is sometimes referred to as "last in still there" or LIST.

If the 3,000 dolls left are from the last units purchased, then their value must be:

2,000 units from the Nov 20 purchase at $5 each =	$10,000
1,000 units from the May 25 purchase at $4 each =	4,000
3,000 units in ending inventory at a cost of	$14,000

This was found by looking at the chart of purchases and working backwards from the bottom until you have valued the 3,000 units counted at the end of the year. Cost of goods sold for the year can now be calculated as:

Costs of units available for sale	$28,000
Less: Cost of ending inventory	(14,000)
Cost of goods sold	$14,000

–Periodic LIFO costing–

LIFO assumes the last things in are the first sold, so the dolls in ending inventory must be the first in. This flow is sometimes referred to as "first in still there" or FIST.

If the 3,000 dolls left are from the first units purchased, then their value must be:

2,000 units from the beginning inventory at $2 ea. =	$4,000
1,000 units from the Feb 10 purchase at $3 ea. =	3,000
3,000 units in ending inventory at a cost of	$ 7,000

This was found by looking at the chart of purchases plus the beginning inventory balance, and working down from the top until you have valued the 3,000 units counted at the end of the year. Cost of goods sold for the year can now be calculated as:

Costs of units available for sale	$28,000
Less: Cost of ending inventory	(7,000)
Cost of goods sold	$21,000

• Perpetual Inventory Example •

We will use the example of Feng Toys. Recall that when using the perpetual method, Feng Toys will record the cost of purchases on the purchase dates, and also the cost of goods sold at each sales date.

–Perpetual average costing–

Unlike periodic valuation, the average method for perpetual inventory is probably the most complicated. Why? Because unlike the periodic method in which you find one average cost for the whole period, here you must find a *new* average cost every time goods are purchased because you need an updated figure to cost out at the time of each sale. Hence, the average method for perpetual inventory is often called "moving average" since the average moves over time. **Figure 7.10** summarizes the process.

For Feng's Toys the beginning inventory of 2,000 units costs $4,000, or $2 per unit. On February 10, when they buy another 2,000 units for $6,000, they then have 4,000 units available for sale at a total historical cost of $4,000 + $6,000 = $10,000. This works out to be $10,000/4,000 = $2.50 per unit on average.

Figure 7.10   Perpetual Average Cost

Date	Units Purchased*	Units Sold	Unit Cost	Total
January 1	2,000 beginning inventory		$2.00	$4,000
February 10	2,000		$3.00	6,000
April 20		3,000	(see A)	(7,500)
May 25	2,000		4.00	8,000
August 18		2,000	(see B)	(7,000)
November 20	2,000		5.00	10,000
Ending Inventory	(3,000 units)		(see C)	$13,500
Cost of Goods Sold	(5,000 units)		(see A,B)	14,500

Thus, on April 20, when Feng's Toys sells 3,000 dolls to the Earhardt Preschool System, they figure cost of goods sold as:

Calculation A.
April 20 Cost of Goods Sold:
3,000 dolls x $2.50 = $7,500

Immediately after the sale on April 20 Feng's Toys now has 1,000 units left at an average unit cost of $2.50, or $2,500 of inventory on hand. Feng's Toys now makes another inventory purchase on May 25, this time buying 2,000 units for $8,000. So, immediately after the purchase they have on hand:

1,000 units from before the purchase at $2.50 each =	$ 2,500
2,000 units from the May 25 purchase at $4 each =	8,000
3,000 total units on hand at a cost of	$10,500

and so the average cost per unit after the May 25 purchase will be $10,500/3,000 units = $3.50 per unit. This means that on August 18, when Feng sells 2,000 dolls to the Blowfish Recreation Center, Feng's Toys will report cost of goods sold of:

Calculation B.
August 18 Cost of Goods Sold:
2,000 dolls x $3.50 per doll = $7,000

Feng's Toys will then have 1,000 dolls left at an average unit cost of $3.50 or $3,500 in total. When Feng's Toys makes the final purchase of 2,000 dolls for $10,000, their average unit cost will be ($3,500+$10,000) ÷ (1,000+2,000) = $4.50 and they will have 3,000 units as seen below.

Calculation C.
Ending inventory will then be valued as:
3,000 units x $4.50 = $13,500

Cost of Goods Sold will be reported for the year as:

April 20 sale	$7,500
August 18 sale	7,000
Total cost of goods sold	$14,500

–Perpetual FIFO costing–

FIFO assumes the first things in are the first sold, so the cost of goods sold will be from the first costs in inventory. **Figure 7.11** summarizes the process.

Inventory

Figure 7.11   Perpetual FIFO

Date	Units Purchased	Units Sold	Unit Cost	Total
January 1	2,000 beginning inventory		$2.00	$4,000
February 10	2,000		$3.00	6,000
April 20		3,000	(see D)	(7,000)
May 25	2,000		4.00	8,000
August 18		2,000	(see E)	(7,000)
November 20	2,000		5.00	10,000
Ending Inventory	(3,000 units)		(see F)	$14,000
Cost of Goods Sold	(5,000 units)		(see D,E)	14,000

At the date of the first sale, 3,000 units are sold. The costs of these units must come first from the 2,000 dolls in beginning inventory at $2 each. When beginning inventory is used up Feng's Toys starts selling items from the first purchase, where 1,000 items at $3 each are needed to sell a total of 3,000 on February 10. Thus:

Calculation D.	
April 20 Cost of Goods Sold:	
2,000 units from beginning inventory at $2 =	$4,000
1,000 units from the Feb 10 purchase at $3 each =	3,000
3,000 units sold	$ 7,000

On August 18 when Feng's Toys sells the other 2,000 units, they again go back to the first things in, but of course beginning inventory and half of the February 10 purchase are gone, so the first items they can use for the sale are the remaining 1,000 units from February 10 that cost $3 each. The other 1,000 dolls they need to sell to total 2,000 must come from the May 25 purchase, which had a unit cost of $4 each. Given this, the cost of the second sale will be:

Calculation E.	
August 18 Cost of Goods Sold:	
1,000 units from the 2/10 purchase at $3 each =	$3,000
1,000 units from the 5/25 purchase at $4 each =	4,000
2,000 units sold	$7,000

So you see two things, that the cost of goods sold for the year is the sum of the two costs of sales:

Cost of goods sold for the year:

April 20 sale	$7,000
August 18 sale	7,000
	$14,000

And the ending inventory is comprised of the remaining units on hand as shown below:

Calculation F.

Ending inventory for the year:

From November 20 purchase 2,000 units x $5 =	$10,000
From May 25 purchase 1,000 units x $4 =	4,000
	$14,000

It is _not_ a coincidence that the periodic FIFO and the perpetual FIFO methods give the same answers for the values of inventory and cost of goods sold. In fact, they will _always_ yield the same results, because if you sell from the first things in first, you always sell the same items regardless of the timing of the sale. However, this will not be the case for periodic and perpetual LIFO.

–Perpetual LIFO costing.–

LIFO assumes the last things in are the first sold, so at each sale the dolls sold come from the last batch in _as of that date._ This means that, unlike in periodic LIFO where you assume you sell from the _very_ last batch purchased regardless of the dates of the sales, timing of the sale now becomes important. **Figure 7.12** summarizes the process.

Figure 7.12 Perpetual LIFO

Date	Units Purchased	Units Sold	Unit Cost	Total
January 1	2,000 beginning inventory		$2.00	$4,000
February 10	2,000		$3.00	6,000
April 20		3,000	(see G)	(8,000)
May 25	2,000		4.00	8,000
August 18		2,000	(see H)	(8,000)
November 20	2,000		5.00	10,000
Ending Inventory	(3,000 units)		(see I)	$12,000
Cost of Goods Sold			(see G, H)	16,000

If the 3,000 dolls sold in this example on April 20 come from the last items in inventory to date, then they must have come from the February 10 purchase. Why? Because in the perpetual method you must record cost of goods sold *as of* April 20, and thus you can only use historical information (things that have already happened by April 20) and cannot assume what will happen later in the year.

Calculation G.
April 20 Cost of Goods Sold:
2,000 units from the Feb.10 purchase at $3 each = $6,000
1,000 units from beginning inventory at $2 each = 2,000
3,000 units sold $ 8,000

The cost of goods sold was found by looking at the chart of purchases plus the beginning inventory balance, and, **_starting from April 20,_** working backward in time until you have valued the 3,000 units sold on April 20 as illustrated above.

Likewise, on August 18, the 2,000 units sold must come from the last items in as of that date, which are the 2,000 units purchased on May 25 for $8,000 total as shown below.

Calculation H.
August 18 Cost of Goods Sold:
2,000 units from the May 25 purchase at $4 each = $8,000

So, total cost of goods sold for the year will be $8,000 + $8,000 = $16,000. Now to find ending inventory you look at the units remaining, the 1,000 units not yet sold from beginning inventory and the 2,000 units purchased on November 20, *after* the date of the last sale as shown below.

Calculation I.	
Ending inventory:	
2,000 units from the 11/20 purchase at $5 each =	$10,000
1,000 units from beginning inventory at $2 each =	2,000
3,000 units left	$12,000

–Difference between perpetual and periodic.–

Notice now the major difference between periodic and perpetual LIFO: the periodic method assumes the *very last* things in are the first sold, regardless of the date of the sale. The perpetual method assumes the last things in *at the date of each sale* are the first sold. So, in this example, in the perpetual method we had the 2,000 toys purchased on November 20 still in inventory at the end of the year because there were no subsequent sales. However, in the periodic method we assumed these were the first toys sold, because we ignored the dates of the sales. That is why the numerical answers for periodic and perpetual LIFO differ.

PROBLEMS WITH INVENTORY

• Risks of Holding Inventory •

By holding inventory, we can identify at least three risks a company faces, which are not necesarily mutually exclusive.

1. Risk of obsolescence. The inventory may not be saleable if consumer preferences change rapidly or unexpectedly. For example, a certain toy may be very popular for a few months, and then suddenly lose its popularity. Women's fashions are known to change constantly. If a firm has inventory that has lost its saleability, we say that it is "obsolescent." The toy is still in good condition, and the clothes are still wearable, but they cannot command the price we want to "break even" due to economic reasons.

2. Risk of having too much or too little. If a company has too much inventory, it will not only incur greater storage costs but also encounter the risk of obsolescence. Aging may also be a problem. Certainly, this would be true for perishable goods. If a company has too little inventory, it stands the chance of losing sales.

3. Risk of theft. Inventory is subject to theft. Research shows that for many companies employees are more likely to steal than customers.

• Inventory Errors •

Errors in counting and reporting inventory will affect both the balance sheet and the income statement. Let us examine this assertion in more detail.

Suppose that you make an error in counting or valuing ending inventory for December 31, 1995. Then the value of inventory on the balance sheet will be misstated, and so will the total current assets and total assets. Likewise, the error will affect expenses on the income statement. Further, in December of the following year, even if you correctly count and value the ending inventory for 1996, the erroneous beginning inventory value will affect the periodic method's cost of goods sold calculation (beginning inventory plus purchases less ending inventory) for the 1996 Income Statement.

Here are some numerical examples. Suppose that in 1995 your beginning inventory is correctly stated as $33,000, and net purchases for the year total $560,000. However, from some counting error or math error in the valuation calculations you value ending inventory for 1995 as $45,000, when the actual number is $47,500. Thus, you have *understated* ending inventory by $2,500. If ending inventory is $2,500 understated then current assets and total assets on the balance sheet will also be *understated* by $2,500.

1995	incorrect	correct
Beginning inventory	$ 33,000	$ 33,000
Add: Purchases	560,000	560,000
Available for sale	$593,000	$593,000
Less: Ending inventory	45,000	47,500
Cost of goods sold	$548,000	$545,500

The income statement will report a cost of goods sold that is overstated by $2,500, as seen above. Since the expense is *overstated* (too high), both the gross profit and the net income will be *understated* (too low.)

Here we have assumed the periodic method. With the perpetual method the only difference is that the discrepancy between the $47,500 of inventory you thought you had and the $45,000 of inventory you calculated will be charged to an inventory loss account rather than to cost of goods sold. This would be the "Inventory Over or Short" account described earlier in this chapter. Like cost of goods sold,the inventory loss is still an income statement item, and will still understate net income by $2,500 (net of taxes, of course.) However, it will not affect gross profit.

Now, we carry the erroneous $45,000 of inventory into 1996 because we have adjusted the Inventory account to reflect that amount at the end of 1995. This becomes beginning inventory for 1996.

Suppose the 1996 net purchases total $440,000, and ending inventory is correctly counted and valued at $39,000.

While the inventory, current assets and total assets are correctly stated on the 1996 Balance Sheet, the cost of goods sold (under the periodic method) is still incorrect in 1996:

1996	incorrect	correct
Beginning inventory	$ 45,000	$ 47,500
Add: Purchases	440,000	440,000
Available for sale	$485,000	$487,500
Less: Ending inventory	39,000	39,000
Cost of goods sold	$446,000	$448,500

Cost of goods sold is now _understated_ by $2,500. This error causes both gross profit and income to be _overstated_ by $2,500. Again, in the perpetual method the difference would be a charge (credit) to Inventory Over or Short, and the credit would increase and thus overstate income by $2,500.

Figure 7.13 provides a table to summarize the results of the inventory errors on the financial statements.

Figure 7.13   Effect of Inventory Errors

Financial Statement/Element Affected If:	1995 Ending Inventory Is Overstated	1995 Ending Inventory Is Understated
1995 Inventory (Balance Sheet)	Overstated	Understated
1995 Total Current Assets	Overstated	Understated
1995 Total Assets	Overstated	Understated
1995 Cost Of Goods Sold	Understated	Overstated
1995 Income	Overstated	Understated
1996 Cost Of Goods Sold	Overstated	Understated
1996 Income	Understated	Overstated

• Obsolescent Inventory •

As mentioned earlier, some inventory items lose their popularity and thus their salability long before the seller has estimated this will happen. In such a case, the seller now has *obsolescent* inventory on hand. Toys and games, high technology goods such as computers and calculators, and items with styles and seasons such as clothing and shoes tend to have a high rate of obsolescence.

As an example, suppose a WorkSkoool, a toy manufacturer, produces a toy called Space Guy, modelled after a popular cartoon character.[39] Space Guy costs $3 to manufacture and sells for $10. WorkSkoool, estimating this will be quite popular, manufactures 10,000,000 Space Guy dolls. After 6,400,000 Space Guy dolls have been sold, a new cartoon character becomes popular and sales of Space Guy become sluggish. WorkSkoool reduces its price to $5, then to $3, and finally cannot sell Space Guy for more than $1. At this time WorkSkoool has 2,000,000 Space Guy dolls remaining in inventory. Poor Space Guy has become obsolescent.

–Write down.–

The accounting rule is that WorkSkoool should write down the value of the obsolete toy, given the permanent impairment of value, and report the loss on the income statement just as with lower of cost or market. However, some firms with obsolescent inventory still remain optimistic that the item will again be popular, and they wait to report any losses until the items are sold.

Following the accounting rule, the loss of $4,000,000 (2,000,000 dolls left x [$3 cost - $1 market]) would appear on WorkSkoool's income statement.

Loss Due to Price Decline	4,000,000	
Inventory		4,000,000

WorkSkoool would report the value of the remaining Space Guy dolls as $2,000,000 (calculated equivalently as *either* 2,000,000 dolls left x $1 per doll, *or* dolls with a historical cost of $6,000,000 less the $4,000,000 reduction in value) on the balance sheet.

If WorkSkoool refrained from writing down the value of the obsolescent inventory at this time, claiming perhaps that Space Guy will become popular again when new episodes of the cartoon air, or that the Space Guy popularity is cyclical, how will this affect WorkSkoool's financial statements? Both

---

[39] This is a fictional example, but many toys such as Ninja Turtles, Power Rangers and Barney dolls have been extremely popular when the characters were first introduced, but quickly lost their audience to newer characters. Other character toys, like Mickey Mouse and Snoopy, have always been popular.

the income statement and balance sheet will be overstated by $4,000,000. Is this fraudulent? Not if WorkSkoool really believes the value of Space Guy will increase. However, there is clear evidence to the manufacturer that the toy's value is impaired, since WorkSkoool cannot sell the toy for more than $1. Is this reporting by WorkSkoool ethical? Will it mislead the users of the financial statements? Most likely, not ethical and yes, misleading.

• Inventories and Fraud •

While inventory errors occur by accident, inventory is one of the most common assets used in *fraudulent reporting.* Why? Because while inventory must be counted and verified, sometimes by *external auditors*, at the end of each fiscal year, it is impractical to really count each item on hand. So, techniques are used to perform estimated counts, and these can be manipulated by an unscrupulous firm.

For example, if a manager knows that the auditor will be in one warehouse on Monday, but not in the second warehouse until Tuesday, the manager can move items from the first to the second warehouse during the night on Monday, so the auditor counts the same set of items twice.

–Actual cases–

In a real world case, Accuhealth, which provided home health care and owned several retail drug stores, overstated inventory in two ways during the 1989-92 period. First, it prepared false inventory count sheets for those drug stores in which independent auditors did not oversee the counts. Second, management had employees deliberately double count some expensive drugs by moving them from the warehouse, where the drugs had already been counted in inventory, to one of the drug stores at which the same inventory was then recounted. Accuhealth falsified its accounting records and misrepresented facts to the external auditors, then destroyed all false records to hide the evidence.[40]

Another trick is to stack empty boxes or cartons under full boxes of inventory, or to stack the boxes so they look like a solid cube of boxes when the cube really has a hole in the middle. Also, a firm may misrepresent consignment inventory as their own to overstate inventory value. The CFO and accounting staff of Barton, a corporation that manufactures and sells oil and gas exploration equipment, did just that. In 1989-90 they falsified inventory records by preparing fake invoices to record fictional inventory, they inflated inventory counts, and they told auditors that goods on the premises on consignment were part of their own inventory.[41]

---

[40] From SEC *Accounting and Auditing Enforcement Release No. 589.*

[41] From SEC *Accounting and Auditing Enforcement Release No.538.*

Such acts are unethical, fraudulent and illegal, and of course in each year they are perpetrated they will lead to misstatement of financial statements over two years as explained in the previous section. Overstatement of ending inventory leads to overstatement of asset and of income, which in a fraudulent setting can be intended to fool a creditor into granting a loan or fool potential investors into investing in the firm. This is also what the scenario at the beginning of this chapter was describing; however, the auditor in that story was smart enough to detect the fraud.

• Inventory and Internal Control •

Two other problems that may arise with inventory are inventory loss due to **_damage or theft_**, and **_mishandling_** of the accounting records for fraudulent purposes. To avoid losing and damaging inventory by accident, losing inventory to theft, or misstating the records one may introduce **_internal control_** measures into the firm which are similar to those for cash.

These internal control measures include accounting measures such as **_separation of duties_**. Those employees who physically handle inventory are separate from those who keep the records, and the employees who keep records of inventory purchases are not the same employees who record inventory sales or cost of goods sold.

There are also many **_physical safeguards_** for inventory. For example, inventory may be kept in a locked warehouse or storeroom administered by special inventory handlers. Documents may be needed to remove items from the warehouse, and separate records are kept of what has been removed and by whom.

Some stores also need to safeguard inventory against customers because inventory is readily available on display. These stores use such devices as security cameras and mirrors, security personnel who watch for theft, and magnetized devices implanted in goods that set of alarms if goods are taken out the door without being paid for. While some determined thieves may circumvent these controls, they still reduce theft.

–Actual case–

A breakdown of internal control occurred in Comptronix, a contractor for electronics manufacturers. Starting in 1989 several managers in the firm wrote journal entries transferring costs in cost of goods sold to the inventory accounts, thus overstating inventory and understating cost of goods sold. Later they wrote costs back from inventory to cost of goods sold, and to cover up the transfer also wrote fictitious entries for inventory sales on account (thereby also overstating revenue and assets,) created false shipping documents to support the sales and even made fictitious entries for customer payments on those fictitious accounts receivable. How could this happen? It happened because of poor internal control--one small group of managers had access to the sales, inventory, cost of sales, shipping and accounts receivable records, including the books of accounts and the ability to generate source documents such as shipping bills and fake customer checks.[42]

INVENTORY VALUATION AND FINANCIAL STATEMENT ANALYSIS

• The Financial Statements •

–The balance sheet–

As you have already inferred from the previous discussions, the method one chooses to value inventory will affect both *current* and *total assets* on the balance sheet if purchase prices for merchandise change over time. However, the balance sheet figure must be accompanied by a note disclosing the method used, so the sophisticated user of the financial information understands what the value on the Balance Sheet represents.

That is, in periods of rising prices LIFO assumes the older (and thus less costly) merchandise is still on hand, while FIFO assumes the last purchases (at highest historical cost) are still on hand. (If prices are dropping the LIFO ending inventory will have a higher value, because it is older merchandise, than the FIFO ending inventory.) Based on our calculations of Feng Toys inventory for the periodic method, let us assume the following balance sheets illustrated in **Figure 7.14**.

Figure 7.14   Balance Sheets – Different Inventory Methods (prices rising)

	LIFO	FIFO	AVERAGE
Assets			
Cash	$1,000	$1,000	$1,000
Receivables	4,000	4,000	4,000
Inventory	7,000	14,000	10,500
Fixed assets (net)	115,000	115,000	115,000
TOTAL ASSETS	$127,000	$134,000	$130,500
Liabilities And Stockholders' Equity			
Payables	$3,000	$3,000	$3,000
Long term liabilities	8,000	8,000	8,000
Common stock	5,000	5,000	5,000
Retained earnings*	111,000	118,000	114,500
TOTAL LIABILITIES AND EQUITY	$127,000	$134,000	$130,500

*The retained earnings differ because the different inventory methods create different Cost of Goods Sold; this, in turn, yields different net incomes which are closed into Retained Earnings.

---

[42]From SEC *Accounting and Auditing Enforcement Release No. 543.*

–The income statement–

On the income statement, the inventory value will affect *cost of goods sold* and thus also gross profit and net income. With the valuation method disclosed in the financial statements, the users of that information will understand that firms using LIFO in periods of *rising* inventory purchase prices (FIFO in periods of falling prices) will have the lowest net income of any valuation method, and that it is because the last things purchased at the highest prices (first things purchased at highest prices) are the first things expensed that period.

Based on our calculations of the cost of goods sold for Feng Toys, under the periodic method, we have the income statements shown in **Figure 7.15**. Again, as a user of these income statements it is important to understand that all three amounts of cost of goods sold are "correct," because each method used to derive the cost falls within generally accepted accounting principles (GAAP.) The method of valuation the firm chooses must be used consistently. That is, if the firm uses FIFO to value its product in the first year, it it must use FIFO in all subsequent years unless the firm has a provable valid reason to change.

Figure 7.15   Income Statements – Different Inventory Methods (prices rising)

	LIFO INCOME STATEMENT	FIFO INCOME STATEMENT	AVERAGE INCOME STATEMENT
Sales revenue	$54,000	$54,000	$54,000
Cost of goods sold	21,000	14,000	17,500
Gross profit	$33,000	$40,000	$36,500
Less: Operating expenses	12,000	12,000	12,000
NET INCOME*	$21,000	$28,000	$24,500

*assuming no taxes

Note however that firms with more than one type of inventory, for example a firm that sells chairs, desks and tables, may use a different valuation method for each inventory type as long as it uses the methods consistently and discloses the methods used in the financial statements. That is, this firm could use FIFO for chairs, LIFO for desks and Average for tables as long as this is disclosed and they keep the same methods for chairs, desks and tables over time.

Researchers in accounting have studied issues related to choice of accounting method, such as why a firm chooses one inventory method over another.[43] They also have studied investor response to

---

[43] For example, Michael Granof and Daniel Short, "Why Do Companies Reject LIFO?" *Journal of Accounting, Auditing and Finance*, Summer 1994; Barry Cushing and Marc LeClere, "Evidence on the Determinants of Inventory Accounting Policy Choice," *The Accounting Review*, April 1992;

choice of method, and have found that investors are typically "not fooled" by the results of different methods.[44]

• Financial Ratio Analysis •

–Inventory turnover–

Investors and creditors want to know if the inventory is saleable. The inventory turnover ratio gives some indication of this. It is calculated by dividing Cost of Goods Sold by average Inventory for the period:

$$\frac{\text{Cost of Goods Sold}}{\text{Average Inventory}}$$

The average inventory is calculated as the inventory at the beginning of the period (for which one typically uses ending inventory from the prior period) plus inventory at the end of the period divided by two:

$$\frac{\text{Ending Inventory (from period t-1) + Ending Inventory (from period t)}}{2}$$

Obviously, errors in reporting beginning and ending inventories and in recording cost of goods sold will affect the calculation of inventory turnover.

For Apple Computer Company, for 1997 the information below is relevant to compute the inventory turnover. Finished goods inventory is used because that is what gets sold.

	(in millions)
Cost of sales	$5,713
Finished goods inventory, beginning	406
Finished goods inventory, ending	281

---

[44] For example, Garry Biddle and William Ricks, "Analyst Forecast Errors and Stock Price Behavior Near the Earnings Announcement Dates of LIFO Adopters," *Journal of Accounting Research*, Autumn 1988.

Apple Computer Company

$$\text{Inventory turnover} = \frac{\$5{,}713}{\dfrac{(\$406 + \$281)}{2}}$$

$$= 16.6 \text{ times}$$

On the average, inventory gets "turned over" (sold) 16.6 times in the year.

–Days in inventory–

One may calculate a measure called "days in inventory," which tells us how many days on average for inventory to get sold. This is found by dividing the inventory turnover into 365, the number of days in a year.

For Apple Company, the calculation is: 365/16.6 = 22 days

This means that on the average it takes 22 days for inventory to get sold.

In analyzing a firm one typically looks for a high inventory turnover and low number of days in inventory. However, "high turnover" and "low number of days" are relative to the industry. For example, grocers would want food products to sell quickly, so five days in inventory may be long, while five days may be average for a clothing store and very fast for a bookstore. For Apple Company, 22 days seem to be fast.

If the turnover was slow, say 134 days, then a couple of inferences can be made. One is that the firm is having difficulty selling its products. Second, there may be obsolescent items in its inventory, which should be written off but have not.

SUMMARY OF KEY POINTS

The following key points were discussed in this chapter:

1. Risk of holding inventory. A company must have inventory in stock in order to sell goods to customers in a timely fashion. But having inventory involves risk. We identified three kinds of risk. (a) Obsolescence. This has to do with saleability. (b) Too much inventory is costly in terms of storage costs, and the possibility that they may lose value. Too little inventory is also costly in terms of lost sales when the goods are not available for sale to customers at the time they want them. (c) There is always the chance of theft.

2. Definition of inventory. Inventory is defined as goods or merchandise specifically used to generate sales revenue by giving these goods to customers in exchange for cash or receivables. Such items are considered inventory only when in the control of the selling firm.

3. Physical count of goods. The amount of inventory a firm records at the end of the year must be verified by a physical count of the goods the firm has under its control at the year end date.

4. Valuation of goods. The dollar value of ending inventory depends on whether the firm uses LIFO, FIFO, average or specific identification, but they are all acceptable valuation methods when used consistently. Also, cost flows do not need to match physical flows.

5. LIFO cost flow. The Last In First Out cost flow assumes that the last things purchased are the first sold.

6. FIFO cost flow. The First In First Out cost flow assumes that the first things purchases are the first sold.

7. Average cost flow. The average cost flow assumes that you sell things randomly over the period, so an average of all the different inventory costs are expensed for the period.

8. Specific identification. Specific identification means that you identify the specific inventory items sold each period and thus the specific inventory costs to be expensed in that period.

9. Lower of Cost or Market. Lower of cost or market is a facet of conservatism; if the market price of inventory permanently drops below historical cost, one may record the loss and the decline in inventory value in the period the loss occurs even though the sale has not yet been made.

10. Periodic inventory valuation. Periodic inventory valuation refers to the calculation of cost of goods sold periodically rather than finding cost of goods sold and the reduction in the Inventory account for each sale.

11. Perpetual inventory valuation. Perpetual inventory valuation refers to the method by which cost of goods sold and the inventory accounts are adjusted at the time of each sale.

12. _Inventory errors._ Inventory errors may come from recording or counting mistakes, but are pervasive in the sense that they affect that year's Balance Sheet and that and the subsequent year's Income Statement.

13. _Obsolescent inventory._ This is inventory whose value has dropped because the inventory itself is outdated. Accounting treatment for obsolescent inventory is to reduce its value and report a loss in the period it becomes obsolescent, rather than waiting to sell it for a loss.

14. _Inventory fraud._ Inventory fraud can be perpetrated by the firm most often by miscounting or causing someone else to miscount ending inventory. The effects of fraud on the financial statements are pervasive as are the effects of errors.

15. _Internal control for inventory._ Internal controls for inventory consist of accounting controls such as separation of duties and physical controls that keep employees and customers from absconding with merchandise.

16. _Inventory Turnover and Days in Inventory._ The inventory turnover measures the relative efficiency of the use of inventory, and thus gives us an idea of how "good" (saleable) the inventory is. A firm's turnover must be compared with its industry average to be interpreted. The number of days in inventory may also be calculated to see how quickly inventory is selling. An inventory error will affect turnover for two years, also.

QUESTIONS

1. Explain in your own words the concept of "inventory."

2. How do merchandise inventory and supplies inventory differ?

3. Discuss how merchandise inventory will differ among manufacturing, merchandising and service firms.

4. Explain the difference between an inventory cost and a noninventory cost.

5. Discuss what items you would include in a physical count of inventory.

6. Discuss what items that are physically present in a warehouse would be excluded from an inventory count.

7. Define the following and give an example:

a. "first in first out" inventory flow.

b. "last in first out" inventory flow.

c. "average" inventory flow.

d. "specific identification".

8. How do the different cost flow assumptions affect the financial statements?

9. How does the periodic inventory method differ from the perpetual method? What implications does this have for year end inventory and cost of good sold reporting?

10. What is "Lower of Cost or Market" and why is it used?

11. What effects can overstating the count of ending inventory have on the financial statements? What effects can understating the count have?

12. Discuss some types of inventory fraud to be aware of when studying financial statements.

13. Identify the kinds of risks a company faces by holding inventory.

14. Describe some internal control measures for inventory and discuss why they are used.

EXERCISES

E7-1

Which of the following items are <u>included</u> in Phillip Corporation's physical count of inventory?

a. merchandise on hand, not yet sold

b. supplies

c. goods in transit to a customer, shipped f.o.b. shipping point

d. Phillip's goods on consignment in Angela Company stores

E7-2

Which of the following items are <u>included</u> in Phillip Corporation's physical count of inventory?

a. merchandise ordered on account from but not yet shipped by the supplier

b. the fleet of delivery trucks

c. goods in transit to a customer, shipped f.o.b. destination

d. Angela Company goods on consignment in Phillip's stores

E7-3

Which of these costs are considered inventory costs?

a. purchase cost of merchandise

b. cost of shipping merchandise from the supplier to the firm, paid by the firm.

c. cost of storing the merchandise

d. cost of salespeople's salaries and commissions

E7-4

Which of these costs are considered inventory costs?

a. purchase cost of supplies

b. cost of shipping merchandise from the supplier to the firm, paid by the supplier.

c. cost of shipping merchandise to customers

d. cost of insuring the inventory

E7-5

Which of these costs are considered inventory costs?

a. cost of materials used to manufacture inventory items

b. cost of building the warehouse to house inventory

c. cost of advertising merchandise

d. cost of testing goods before putting them up for sale

E7-6

For each of the following kinds of inventory, state whether you are most likely to use FIFO, LIFO, Average or Specific Identification for the __physical__ flow.

a. books in a rare books store

b. cookies in a bakery

c. nails at a hardware store (from a bin)

d. nails at a hardware store (on shelves in boxes)

E7-7

Assume the following for Dollop Co.

DATE		NUMBER OF UNITS	UNIT COST	SELLING PRICE
May 1	beginning inventory	400	$10	
May 3	purchase	700	10	
May 9	sale	(800)		$15
May 17	purchase	700	11	
May 20	sale	(600)		15

Using the tear-out form in the back of the book, find the (1) Ending Inventory, (2) Cost of Goods Sold, (3) Sales Revenue, and (4) Gross Profit for Dollop for May, assuming they use:

a. periodic average inventory valuation.

b. periodic FIFO inventory valuation.

c. periodic LIFO inventory valuation.

E7-8

Using the information in E7-7 above, find the (1) Cost of Goods Sold, (2) Ending Inventory, (3) Sales Revenue, and (4) Gross Profit for Dollop Co. for May, assuming they use:

a. perpetual FIFO inventory valuation.

b. perpetual LIFO inventory valuation.

Use the tear-out form in back of book.

E7-9

Weevil Motors has two cars in inventory at the beginning of April:

car #3394 with a cost of $10,988

car #3396 with a cost of $11,400

During April the manufacturer ships four more cars to Weevil Motors:

car number	cost
#3401	$8,898
3402	15,489
3403	11,212
3404	9,988

At the end of April Weevil Motors has two cars left: #3394 and #3403.

Find the cost of Weevil's ending inventory and their cost of goods sold for April.

E7-10

For each *independent* case below find the cost of goods sold given the other information:

case	beginning inventory	purchases	purchase returns	freight-in	ending inventory
A	$ 2,000	$25,000	400	$750	$3,200
B	10,400	105,900	1,600	400	8,290
C	700	9,000	–	200	1,400
D	650	12,320	600	–	590

E7-11

Find the missing numbers for each <u>independent</u> case below.

case	beginning inventory	purchases	ending inventory	sales revenue	other expenses	net income
A	$100	$400	$150	$900	$250	?
B	320	1,000	270	?	400	$550
C	?	1,200	300	2,300	440	560
D	700	2,500	?	4,600	1,550	450

E7-12

At year end McGoop Corp has $140,000 in sales and $86,000 in operating expenses. They use the periodic inventory method and find Cost of Goods Sold to be $43,000. However, if they had used the perpetual method they would have had $39,500 recorded in the Cost of Goods Sold account at the end of the year. Explain the discrepancy and discuss how it would be handled in the financial statements.

E7-13

How would Biff, Inc., report the value of inventory on its 1996 Balance Sheet under each of the following <u>independent</u> situations?

a. Cost of ending inventory is $7,800. Market value of the inventory is $8,900.

b. Cost of ending inventory is $7,800. Market value has temporarily dropped to $7,750 but is expected to increase quickly at the beginning of the new fiscal year.

c. Cost of ending inventory is $7,800. Market value has dropped to $7,500. The drop is expected to be permanent.

E7-14

Find Blivit Corporation's gross margin in the following scenarios:

a. Sales revenue is $300,000. Beginning inventory for the period was $7,000. Purchases for the period total $130,000. Ending inventory is counted and valued using LIFO. Its cost is $20,000. Market value of ending inventory is $18,000.

b. Sales revenue is $300,000. Beginning inventory for the period was $18,000. Purchases for the period total $130,000. Ending inventory is counted and valued using LIFO. Its cost is $30,000. Market value of ending inventory is $38,000.

E7-15

Tell whether each of the following will be overstated, understated or not affected if ending inventory for 1995 was erroneusly recorded as $56,000 when it should have been $65,000.

a. 1995 total assets

b. 1995 cost of goods sold

c. 1996 net income

d. 1996 current assets

e. 1995 cash balance

E7-16

Tell whether each of the following will be overstated, understated or not affected if ending inventory for 1995 was erroneusly recorded as $49,000 when it should have been $47,000.

a. 1995 current assets

b. 1995 net income

c. 1996 sales revenue

d. 1996 total assets

e. 1996 cost of goods sold

E7-17

Compute the inventory turnover and days in inventory for a firm with a beginning inventory of $40,000, ending inventory of $55,000, and Cost of Goods Sold totalling $830,000.

E7-18

Journal entries.

Journalize the following inventory transactions assuming the __periodic__ inventory method. Assume this firm has $400 in beginning inventory.

a. Purchase of $4,000 of inventory on account.

b. Sale of $2,000 of inventory for $3,000 in cash.

c. Count of ending inventory reveals $2,300 left. (record cost of goods sold)

E7-19

Journal entries.

Journalize the following inventory transactions assuming the perpetual inventory method. Assume this firm has $400 in beginning inventory.

a. Purchase of $4,000 of inventory on account.

b. Sale of $2,000 of inventory for $3,000 in cash.

c. Count of ending inventory reveals $2,300 left. (record inventory loss)

d. Market value of remaining inventory is $2,140.

E7-20

Fidelwan Stores is a chain of merchandising stores with a warehouse in San Jose, California. For each of the following independent situations, state whether there is a problem with Fidelwan's internal control.

a. Leslie Beam works in the receiving department, handling incoming orders of inventory. Her brother Jim Beam is the accountant in charge of purchases and payments.

b. Min Loo prepares the payroll checks then gives them to Lester Fung to sign. Laurence Parker distributes them, and Sarah Lau records the payroll transactions.

c. Clarence Daly takes customer orders, ships goods to customers and records the sales transactions. Hammond Gee checks the sales receipts against payments received.

CASES

C7-1

The Weaselface, Inc., sells camping equipment and J. Weasel, CEO, wants to include each of the following in his inventory count. For each item state whether it should be included or excluded from the count, and tell why. Also discuss whether J. Weasel's actions are ethical, and the effects including the items that should be excluded will have on the financial statements.

a. 200 jackets Weaselface is selling, marked 40% off.

b. Tents ordered by customers, but not yet shipped by Weaselface.

c. Dried food products Weaselface stocks on consignment from Dryfoods, Inc.

d. A plot of land Weaselface uses to train cross country skiers.

e. Survival kits manufactured by Weaselface, but sold on consignment at grocery stores.

f. Backpacks Weaselface has ordered but not yet received, shipped f.o.b. destination by the manufacturer.

C7-2

Addie Rondack works for The Shoe Guy, a retail shoe store. Addie has taken 20 pairs of shoes home without paying for them, and has left the empty boxes on the shelves in the storeroom so the shoes will not be missed.

a. Discuss the effects this theft will have on cost of goods sold, net income, inventory as reported on the Balance Sheet, and total assets for the Shoe Guy in the year of the theft if it is not detected.

b. Discuss the effects this theft will have on cost of goods sold, net income, inventory as reported on the Balance Sheet, and total assets for The Shoe Guy if it is detected in the same fiscal year the theft occurred. Describe how perpetual and periodic inventory methods would handle the theft differently.

c. Discuss some measures The Shoe Guy could take to prevent such thefts.

C7-3

Refer to the real Balance Sheets at the end of Chapter 2 and the real Income Statements at the end of Chapter 3. Calculate the inventory turnover and days in inventory for each of those firms. Discuss the differing results given they are firms in different industries.

C7-4

Fingerbite Manufacturing Company uses the perpetual inventory method, and has an ending inventory balance in the books of $270,000. The Cost of Goods Sold account contains an ending balance of $1,740,000. After the employees count the inventory, they find its year end cost to be $282,000.

The CEO of Fingerbite tells the accountant to use the $270,000 ending balance because it is lower and therefore more conservative, and the CEO also believes the count was erroneous. The accountant also knows the industry average inventory turnover is 6.6, and Fingerbite must stay at least at that level to obtain an upcoming bank loan.

Instructions:

a. Calculate the inventory turnover using both the recorded and the counted ending inventory values.

b. Comment on any ethical problems you see with the CEO of this firm.

c. Assuming the count is correct, which ending inventory number should they use?

d. If the CEO is correct that the count of inventory is wrong, what further steps should be taken?

C7-5

Goonella Pharmaceuticals owns a series of retail drug stores. They account for inventory using the last in first out cost flow. They started the period with, among other items, 100 bottles of mehrgtin, an expensive prescription pain reliever, for which they had paid $90 per bottle to the manufacturer. During the period they purchased 1,200 more bottles for $120 each, then sold 1,240 bottles during the period.

The bottles of mehrgtin had been selling during the period for $150 each. At the end of the period a competitor came out with a generic substitute for mehrgtin, called glopomyl, which it sold to the public for $100 per bottle. Goonella wants mehrgtin to be competitive, and announces its price will also drop to $100 per bottle.

The CEO of Goonella does not want to write the value of inventory down because they do not want to report any losses this period on the Income Statement. The CEO suggests to the accounting department that they switch inventory valuation methods from LIFO to FIFO just for this period.

Instructions:

Discuss the ethical problems, the effect of switching methods, whether inventory needed to be written down (using LOCOM) and the effect of writing down the inventory on the financial statements. What <u>should</u> the accountants of Goonella do at year end with respect to reporting inventory for the period?

PROBLEMS

P7-1

Idiart Corporation sells clothing. They have the following items on hand at year end. Assuming they have no other inventory, what is the value of their ending inventory?

a. Paper, paper clips and rubber bands valued at $40

b. Men's shirts valued at $5,600

c. Women's gloves and knit hats on consignment from Ann's Knit Shop valued at $1,070.

d. Women's dresses that cost $6,900 but have a market value at year end of $6,220.

P7-2

Mycasa Corporation sells furniture. They have the following items on hand at year end. Assuming they have no other inventory, what is the value of their ending inventory?

a. Tables and chairs with a historical cost of $40,000 and a market value of $56,800.

b. Bedroom sets costing $5,990, already sold to a customer and shipped f.o.b. shipping point.

c. Carved vases and bookends on consignment from Ann's Karvery valued at $1,070.

d. Bookshelves and entertainment centers that cost $6,900 but have a market value at year end of $6,220.

P7-3

Widdle Company has just purchased 2,000 units of inventory and has incurred the following costs. Which costs below should be considered part of the inventory cost, and which are other (operating and financial) expenses?

a. unit cost of the inventory, $4 each.

b. freight-in charges of $700

c. receiving clerk wages of $500.

d. interest charges on the loan used to pay the supplier, $40.

P7-4

(1). Diddle Company has just purchased 2,000 units of inventory and has

incurred the following costs. Which costs below should be considered part of the inventory cost, and which are other (operating and financial) expenses?

a. $3,000 to insure the units of inventory once they are stored in the warehouse

b. $560 to paint the inventory before it can be sold

c. freight-out charges to send the inventory to customers

d. unit cost of inventory, $6 each

(2). Discuss whether the cost of a box use to package a cake at a bakery should be counted as inventory cost or as supplies expense.

P7-5

Consider the following table for Gerip Company:

DATE		NUMBER OF UNITS	UNIT COST	SELLING PRICE
May 1	beginning inventory	400	$10	
May 3	purchase	700	10	
May 9	sale	(800)		$15
May 17	purchase	700	11	
May 20	sale	(800)		15
May 30	purchase	300	12	

Using the tear-out form in the back of the book, find (1) Ending Inventory, (2) Cost of Goods Sold, (3) Sales Revenue and (4) Gross Profit for Gerip, Inc., assuming they use:

a. the periodic FIFO inventory valuation method.

b. the periodic LIFO inventory valuation method.

c. the periodic weighted average inventory valuation method.

P7-6

Using the information in P7-5, find (1) Cost of Goods Sold, (2) Ending Inventory, (3) Sales Revenue and (4) Gross Profit for Gerip, Inc., assuming they use:

a. the perpetual FIFO inventory valuation method.

b. the perpetual LIFO inventory valuation method.

c. the perpetual moving average inventory valuation method.

Use the tear-out form in the back of the book.

P7-7

Consider the following table for Satin Company:

DATE	ITEM	UNITS	UNIT COST	SELLING PRICE
April 1	beginning inventory	100	$5	
April 7	sale	(20)		$10
April 10	purchase	200	5	
April 15	purchase	200	4	
April 20	sale	(300)		10
April 22	purchase	300	6	
April 28	sale	(120)		10
April 30	sale	(120)		11

Using the tear-out form in the back of the book, find (1) Ending Inventory, (2) Cost of Goods Sold, (3) Sales Revenue and (4) Gross Profit for Satin, Inc., assuming they use:

a. periodic FIFO

b. periodic LIFO

c. periodic weighted average

P7-8

Using the information in P7-7 above, find (1) Cost of Goods Sold, (2) Ending Inventory, (3) Sales Revenue and (4) Gross Profit for Satin, Inc., assuming they use

a. perpetual FIFO

b. perpetual LIFO

Use the tear-out form in the back of the book.

P7-9

Refer to P7-7 and P7-8 above and discuss the effects of the different methods on total assets and net income.

P7-10

Lily's Antiques sells antique furniture which they record in inventory by number and historical cost. At the beginning of the period they had numbers 622, 625 and 629, which had costs, respectively, of $400, $67 and $232.

During March, Lily's purchases the following items at the following costs:

item number	item cost
#635	$ 670
636	210
637	100
638	12
639	450

A count of inventory at the end of March reveals these items remaining in the store: #622, #636, #639. Item number 635 is in transit to a customer, shipped f.o.b. destination. What is the value of Lily's ending inventory and cost of goods sold for March?

P7-11

Calculate the periodic cost of goods sold and gross profit for each of the following _independent_ cases.

case	beginning inventory	purchases	purchase returns	freight-in	ending inventory	sales revenue
A	$50,000	$250,000	–	$250	$43,000	$673,900
B	27,400	270,000	$3,000	270	33,900	544,000
C	300	5,000	200	–	650	11,246
D	1,900	16,000	–	16	2,100	36,400
E	75,000	540,000	9,000	540	69,200	800,000

P7-12

Below you see selected year end accounts for M. A. Zing Company, which uses the perpetual inventory method. Given the information below, find the ending inventory, cost of goods sold, gross margin and net income that M. A. Zing will report for the year.

Inventory	Sales Revenue	Cost of Goods Sold	Expenses
540	20,000	7,000	9,000

A count of ending inventory reveals 50 units remaining, with a unit cost of $10.

P7-13

Below you see selected year end accounts for Lorgop Company, which uses the perpetual inventory method. Given the information below, find the ending inventory, cost of goods sold, gross margin and net income that Lorgop will report for the year.

Inventory	Sales Revenue	Cost of Goods Sold	Expenses
7,562	1,032,000	543,000	332,000

A count of ending inventory reveals 198 units remaining, with a unit cost of $40.

P7-14

Willll, Inc. wants to use lower of cost or market, valuing inventory item by item. They have the following four groups of items in ending inventory, with the following sets of costs and market values. What will they report as the dollar value of ending inventory using LOCOM?

item	cost	market value
bags	$2,000	$2,100
logs	7,000	6,920
jags	6,200	6,100
hogs	15,470	20,750

P7-15

Goeble Corp. wants to use lower of cost or market, valuing inventory item by item. They have the following four groups of items in ending inventory, with the following sets of costs and market values. What will they report as the dollar value of ending inventory using LOCOM?

item	cost	market value
cups	$270	$260*
plates	500	660
napkins	133	120
utensils	440	470

* The decline in market price of cups is temporary and expected to be reversed in the following month.

P7-16

If you see the following <u>independent</u> *items in the current asset section of the Balance Sheet, what do they tell you about the firm and its inventory policy?*

a. Inventory (LIFO)	$102,700
Less: Allowance for decline in market value	1,500
	$101,200
b. Inventory (FIFO, at cost)	$720,450
c. Inventory	$693,000
(LIFO; at market, which is below cost)	

P7-17

Discuss the effects of each of the following <u>independent</u> *errors on current year cost of goods sold, net income, and total assets, and on next period's cost of goods sold, net income and total assets.*

a. Ending inventory of $520,900 is mistakenly recorded as $529,000.

b. Ending inventory of $27,300 is miscounted and reported as $26,200.

c. Ending inventory of $13,470 is fraudulently misstated as $43,470.

P7-18

Refer to problem 7-17. Discuss the effect each of those errors would have on Inventory Turnover and days in inventory.

P7-19

Refer to problem 7-17. Discuss how good internal control measures could help prevent the inventory errors in that problem.

WRITING EXERCISES

W7-1

The historical cost principle, the revenue recognition principle and the matching principle all play a part in the way inventory is valued, recorded, and expensed when sold. Write three paragraphs, one for each of the above principles, about this relationship between principle and accounting for inventory .

W7-2

Assume you are the controller of a small firm. The firm's president wants you to report the value of any inventory purchase requisitions as inventory on hand at year end, even if you have not yet paid or received the inventory. Assume you have requisitions totalling $8,335.14 for which you have neither received nor gotten legal title to the inventory. Write a memo explaining to the president why this should be excluded from the Inventory account, and the effect it would have on both the Balance Sheet (Inventory and Total Assets) and the Income Statement (Cost of Goods Sold and Net Income) if it were included.

W7-3

Write a description of the physical safeguards you would use for inventory in a bookstore. Compare that with the safeguards needed for inventory (food) in a restaurant.

W7-4

Your firm has the following inventory records:

		units	unit cost
	beginning inventory	100	$3.00
2/1	purchase	200	4.00
2/26	sale	(250)	
2/28	purchase	100	5.00

Discuss the fact that the perpetual LIFO inventory method will give a different answer than the periodic LIFO method for calculating ending inventory and cost of goods sold for the period. You may use numbers to illustrate your discussion, but use words to compare and contrast the two methods and the reasons for the different inventory values.

KEY ANSWERS TO CERTAIN EXERCISES AND PROBLEMS

E7-7

a. Ending inventory $4,156

   Cost of goods sold $14,546

b. Ending inventory $4,400

   Cost of goods sold $14,300

E7-8

a. Ending inventory $4,400

   Cost of goods sold $14,300

E7-10

A. Cost of goods sold $24,150

D. Cost of goods sold $11,780

P7-2

a. $46,220

P7-5

a. Ending inventory $5,800

   Cost of goods sold $16,500

P7-6

a. Cost of goods sold $16,500

   Ending inventory $5,800

P7-8

b. Gross profit $2,880

P7-11

a. Cost of goods sold $257,250

   Gross profit $416,650

c. Cost of goods sold $4,450

   Gross profit $6,796

GLOSSARY

A

accelerated depreciation this refers to an accounting method that allocates a greater portion of depreciation in the early years of the life of an asset than in the later years.

account a record that keeps track of all the increases, decreases and balances of each asset, liability and owners' equity, including revenues, expenses, gains and losses.

accounting a system that exists in an entity that is concerned with gathering and summarizing selected financial data about the entity and reporting the information to various groups who are interested in the entity for decision-making purposes.

accounting cycle the process by which data are collected, recorded in the journals and ledgers, and reported in the financial statements. The cycle could be monthly, quarterly or yearly, depending on the needs of the entity.

accounts payable the amount owed by a firm to a supplier or vendor for the purchase of goods and services.

accounts receivable the amount owed by customers of a firm due to credit sales made to those customers.

accrual accounting a basis of accounting where revenues are recorded when earned and expenses recorded when incurred, regardless of when cash is received or paid.

accrued expense an expense that is incurred because the firm has used a service but the cash will be paid for it at a future date.

accrued revenue a revenue that has been earned by the firm because it has delivered a product or rendered a service, but the cash will be received at a later date.

accumulated depreciation the total amount of depreciation that has been recorded since the acquisition of the fixed asset.

acid-test ratio same as quick ratio.

allowance for bad debts an account that shows the amount of receivable that is not likely to be collected. On the balance sheet, it is a "contra asset" account, to be deducted from accounts receivable.

allowance for uncollectible accounts same as allowance for bad debts.

amortization the process of allocating a certain amount over a period of time. If the amount to be amortized refers to an intangible asset, then the sum amortized is an expense. If the amount to be amortized refers to the premium of a bond investment (asset), then the sum amortized will reduce the interest revenue. If the amount to be amortized refers to the discount of a bond investment, then the sum amortized will increase the interest revenue. If the amount to be amortized refers to a bond payable (liability), then the sum amortized for a premium will decrease interest expense, and for a discount the sum amortized will increase interest expense.

annuity a series of equal sums of money over equal time periods.

asset turnover the ratio of revenue over the average total assets for a period.

assets economic resources controlled by a firm that will render future services (benefits) for the firm.

audit an examination of a firm's financial statements and underlying records to ensure that proper accounting procedures were used.

audit report an opinion rendered by an auditor (CPA) concerning the fair presentation of the financial statements.

authorized shares the maximum number of shares that a corporation can issue without obtaining approval from the state to amend its corporate charter.

available for sale securities stocks and bonds that a firm has as assets that it can sell but not on an on-going basis. These are securities that do not fit the classifications of trading or held-to-maturity.

B

balance sheet the financial statement that lists the assets, liabilities and owners' equity of a firm as of a particular day.

bank reconciliation a form used to reconcile the cash balance shown on the bank statement with the cash balance shown in the ledger.

bank statement a statement sent by the bank showing all the activities in a firm's account with the bank.

bond a certificate issued by a corporation or governmental unit representing a promise to repay a certain sum of money (principal) and interest in the future.

book value the dollar amount that is reported for a particular account. For a fixed asset, this would be the original cost less accumulated depreciation.

book value per share total stockholders' equity less preferred stock divided by the number of common shares outstanding.

C

capital a general term for money provided to a firm; usually, the resources provided by stockholders; sometimes used as the equivalent to owners' equity.

capital expenditure the amount spent for an asset, either in its purchase/construction or improvement.

capital lease a contract which allows one firm (lessee) to use an asset legally owned by another (lessor) which meets certain criteria established by the FASB, and therefore is considered an asset to the lessee. Almost all the risks and rights of ownership are transferred to the lessee.

capital stock the common stock and preferred stock of a corporation.

capital structure the long-term liabilities plus stockholders' equity of a corporation. This shows the long-term financing arrangement of a company.

cash basis a system of accounting which records revenues only when the related cash is received and records expenses only when the related cash is paid.

cash flow the inflow and outflow of cash for an entity for a given period.

certified public accountant (CPA) the designation given to an accountant who has passed the CPA exam and met other conditions specified by the state.

chart of accounts a list of account titles and their numbers used by an entity in its accounting system.

comprehensive income all revenues, expenses, gains and losses, including unrealized gains and losses.

corporate charter the legal right granted by a state for a corporation to exist.

common stock ownership rights in a corporation represented by certificates.

consolidated financial statements financial statements (income statement, balance sheet, statement of cash flows) of a company (called a parent) that are combined with other companies (subsidiaries) under its conrol.

contingency an existing condition that may have a financial effect (positive or negative) if a future event occurs.

contra account an account that is to be deducted from another account; sometimes referred to as a valuation account.

contributed capital the amount that is invested (contributed) by stockholders into a firm.

convertible bonds bonds that can be converted to stock at a future date.

corporation a form of business organization whose existence is based on a charter received from a state that is considered a separate, legal entity.

cost accounting a system of accounting whose main function is to determine the cost of a company's product.

cost of goods sold the cost of products sold during a given period; it is an expense to be deducted from sales revenue.

coupon rate the rate that is stated on a bond; the nominal rate. Historically, it was the rate stated on a coupon bond, but now the term is used as the stated rate for all kinds of bonds.

creditor an entity to whom a firm owes a sum of money.

credit a bookkeeping term which refers to right side of an account; also the term used when a sale is made and no cash is received by the seller or paid by the buyer until later.

current assets cash or other assets that are expected to be coverted to cash or used within a year of the balance sheet date or operating cycle (if longer than a year).

current liabilities liabilities that are expected to be paid in cash within a year of the balance sheet date or operating cycle (if longer than a year).

current ratio current assets divided by current liabilities.

D

date of record the date used by a corporation to determine which stockholders are to receive a dividend.

debentures bonds which are unsecured, have no collateral.

debit the ~~right~~ *Left* side of an account.

debt to equity ratio total liabilities divided by total stockholders' equity.

deferred charge this refers to an asset that has been purchased and whose cost is expected to be allocated as an expense to future periods. A prepaid expense is a deferred charge.

deferred expense same as deferred charge.

deferred revenue a liability; revenue that has not yet been earned because the firm has not yet delivered the product or rendered the service, but cash has been received. Same as unearned revenue.

deferred tax liability a liability representing the estimate of income taxes which will be paid in the future because of the present difference between net income on the income statement and taxable income on the tax return.

depletion an expense representing the use of a natural resource. The amount of depletion each period is determined by allocating the cost of the natural resource to present and future periods that benefit from the asset.

depreciation an expense representing the use of a fixed asset. The amount of the depreciation each period is determined by allocating the cost of the fixed asset to present and future periods that benefit from the asset.

discontinued operation a major line of business or segment that is dropped and so will no longer provide income to the firm. On the income statement, a special section to disclose this information is shown.

dividend payout ratio total cash dividends for a given period divided by net income for that period.

dividends distributions by a corporation to stockholders, usually in cash, but could be other types of assets or stock of the company.

double-entry bookkeeping a system of recording transactions that follows the accounting equation, Assets = Liabilities + Owners' Equity where there is always a debit and a credit.

E

earnings per share net income available to common stockholders divided by the average number of common shares outstanding.

equity a term used to indicate the ownership element of a firm; often used in place of the term, stockholders' equity.

equity method a method used for investments in stock where a company has significant influence over the investee company. This method requires that the company record its percentage share of the income of the investee.

expense this represents the use of a good or service by a firm to help generate revenue for the current period.

extraordinary item a gain or loss that is due to an event that is unusual in nature and is not expected to occur again in the foreseable future.

F

financial accounting an accounting system in a firm whose objective is to provide useful information to those external to the firm, such as stockholders and creditors.

Financial Accounting Standards Board (FASB) the private-sector entity which formulates and issues accounting standards.

financing activities the activities a firm engages in that relate to obtaining funds from external sources, such as selling the company's own stocks and bonds, and repayment of those funds. Payment of dividends is included.

financial instrument a contract that is both a financial asset for one entity and a financial liability or equity to another. A financial asset is cash or a right to receive cash or financial asset of another entity. A financial liability is an obligation to deliver cash or a financial asset to another entity. Securities, such as stocks and bonds.

financial leverage the existence and use of debt in operating a business to help generate revenues.

financial statements the reports by which the financial information pertaining to a particular firm is communicated to those outside of the firm. The income statement, balance sheet, statement of cash flows, and statement of equity changes.

finished goods this term is applicable to manufacturing firms, and refers to products that are completed and ready for sale.

first-in, first-out (FIFO) a method of inventory valuation which assumes that the flow of products is such that the unit purchased first is the one that is sold first.

fiscal year for accounting purposes, a year that ends other than on December 31.

fixed assets long-term assets which are expected to be used in the operations of the business; property, plant and equipment.

footnotes to financial statements the important explanations that accompany financial statements of various items.

Form 10-K report the annual report that must be filed by a corporation with the SEC.

Form 10-Q the quarterly report that must be filed by a company with the SEC.

future value of a single sum a term which refers to the calculated value in the future when compound interest is considered.

future value of an annuity the term used for the calculated value of a series of sums of money to be receive or paid in the future when compound interest is considered.

G

general journal the book in which transactions are recorded; the book in which transactions are recorded if they are not recorded in a special journal.

general ledger the book in which all the accounts are kept. With the use of computers, it may be in the form of a diskette.

generally accepted accounting principles (GAAP) the various procedures, methods, conventions, rules and practices which are considered appropriate for business firms to use in preparing their financial statements.

generally accepted auditing standards (GAAS) the procedures designated as appropriate by the American Institute of CPAs for use in conducting an audit of a firm.

going concern the assumption that a business firm will continue in business indefinitely.

goodwill an intangible asset which represents superior earning power. It can only be recorded when a company is purchased and the amount is determined as the excess of the cost paid over the market value of the net assets (assets less liabilities).

gross profit the profit derived when deducting cost of goods sold from net sales revenue.

H

held-to-maturity debt securities investments in debt securities in which the investor intends to hold until the maturity date.

I

income statement the financial statement of a company that includes revenues, expenses, gains and losses for a given period.

intangible assets long-term assets that do not possess physical properties, such as goodwill, copyrights, and patents.

interest for a debtor, the cost of borrowing; for a creditor, the return for lending.

internal control the plan and procedures within a firm to safeguard its assets, ensure the accuracy and reliability of its accounting records, and promote efficiency.

inventory turnover a measure of the number of times an average amount of inventory is sold during a given period; cost of goods sold divided by the average amount of inventory.

investing activities activities of a firm which concern the acquisition and disposition of long-term assets.

investors those who invest in a firm by buying its securities or lending money to it; stockholders and creditors.

issued shares the number of shares that have been issued by a corporation.

J

journal a book in which transactions are recorded; see general journal.

L

last-in, first-out (LIFO) an inventory method that assumes the flow of goods is such that the last unit purchased is the first to be sold.

ledger a book of accounts; see general ledger.

leverage the use of debt financing; the existence of debt in the capital structure.

liability obligation of an entity in which it promises to settle it at a future date by conveying assets or rendering services; amount owed to a creditor.

liquidity having enough cash and cash equivalents to pay debts as they become due.

long-term asset an asset on the balance sheet that is expected to be kept for a period of a year or operating cycle whichever is longer.

long-term liability a liability on the balance sheet that is due after a year or operating cycld, whichever is longer.

loss a decrease in owners' equity due to expenses exceeding revenues, or for the sale of an asset when the cost exceeds the selling price.

lower of cost or market a method of valuation in which inventory is priced at cost or market, whichever is lower.

M

management accounting an accounting system which focuses on providing information to managers.

matching an accounting principle underlying accrual accounting in which expenses which helped to create the revenues are "matched" (deducted) from those revenues.

materiality an accounting convention which directs accountants to consider items only that are important; that is, will make a difference in decision-making to users of the financial statements.

maturity date the date when a debt is due.

monetary asset or liability an asset or liability in which the denominated amount is fixed, usually by contract.

mortgage a debt which is secured by an asset.

N

net assets total assets less total liabilities; owners' equity.

net sales gross sales revenues less sales discounts and returns and aloowances.

net income the difference between revenues (+ gains) and expenses (+ losses).

no par stock stock in which there is no specified par value.

nominal interest rate the interest rate that is stated on a bond or note.

nominal account any income statement account; it is temporarily used to determine income for a period, and once the income is determined it is closed out (balanced to zero).

note payable a liability that is evidenced by a signed note.

note receivable an asset that is evidenced by a signed note, usually from a customer.

O

obsolescent when an asset becomes out of date, although it may still be in good technical condition, due to economic reasons.

off-balance-sheet financing when a firm receives an asset without having to record a liability.

operating activities profit-making activities; transactions and events that help to produce income.

operating cycle the average time a firm takes to purchase inventory, sell it, and collect the cash from the sale.

operating lease a lease in which the lessor (owner) has no intention of transferring ownership benefits and risks to the lessee (tenant); therefore, the lessee simply records the rental amounts paid.

owners' equity one of serveral terms used to denote the financial investment in a firm by the owners. The accounting equation, Assets - Liabilities = Owners' Equity, shows the monetary amount of this investment.

P

par value the designated value stated on the stock certificate, and which is agreed upon by the state in which the corporation has its charter. It should not be confused with the market value of the stock.

parent company a corporation which has a controlling interest in another corporation. Usually, control is determined by ownership of the majority of the voting stock.

patent an exclusive right given by the U.S. Patent Office to use or sell a certain product or process. It has a legal life of 17 years.

periodic inventory system an inventory system which does not keep track continuously of all items sold and the correct balance; instead, the items sold and the balance are determined periodically, depending on when the accounting period is.

perpetual inventory system unlike the periodic system, this system keeps track continuously of all items sold so that "perpetually" the correct balance of inventory is known.

physical inventory count the actual counting and costing of the inventory. It is necessary for the periodic inventory system and optional for the perpetual inventory system, although it should be done at least once a year for verification purposes.

pooling of interests a procedure of accounting for a business combination in which at least 90% of the stock of the subsidiary must be acquired by the parent by exchanging voting stock. Book value is recorded.

post-closing trial balance the trial balance after the books have been closed, so that no income statement accounts would be included.

posting a bookkeeping procdure in which the information in the journal is transferred to the ledger.

preferred stock a type of stock which gives the holders certain preferences over common stock holders.

present value the sum of money at the beginning of an investment period, which at a given rate of interest compounded periodically, will produce a certain future value.

present value of an annuity the sum of money at the beginning of an investment period which represents the present value of a series of future equal cash amounts to be received or paid at equal intervals.

price-earnings (PE) ratio the market price of a stock divided by the earnings per share.

principal the sum of money on a note or bond which is to be paid on the date of maturity.

publicly-held corporation a corporation whose stock is owned by investors outside of the company and whose stock is listed on an exchange.

purchase returns and allowances when a firm receives refunds and other allowances from suppliers for merchandise returned to them or merchandise with defects.

Q

quality of earnings a judgment made concerning the earnings reported by a company as to whether accounting methods used resulted in a conservative or inflated amount.

quick ratio quick assets over current liabilities. Quick assets are current assets less those that cannot be converted to cash quickly, which are inventory and prepaid expenses. This ratio gives an indication of how quickly a firm can pay its current liabilities.

R

ratio analysis analyzing a company with respect to financial position and profitability by using relationships of amounts from the financial statements.

real account an account that is on the balance sheet; to be contrasted with temporary account, which is an income statement account and is closed out at the end of the accounting period. A real account, sometimes called a permanent account, is never closed; it is balanced and the amount is forwarded to the next period.

recognition the decision to record an asset, liability, revenue, expense, gain or loss.

relevance when information will make a difference in a decision.

reliability when information can be depended on to represent what it is suppose to represent.

replacement cost the cost of acquiring the best available asset to undertake the function of the asset owned and to be replaced (less depreciation if appropriate).

research and development costs expenditures for discovery, planning, designing, testing and constructing prototypes for a new product or process.

residual value sometimes referred to as salvage value; an estimate of the sales value of an asset at the end of its useful life.

retained earnings the amount of income that is not paid out as dividends but is retained in the business.

revenues the amount received for the sale of goods and services; in a few cases, the amount of the products produced but not yet sold.

S

sales the exchange activities of a firm in which it delivers the product to customers or renders a service to them, and therefore it receives a certain amount of assets.

sales allowance a reduction of the sales price due to a defect in the product.

sales discount when payment is received from a customer by a firm within a specified time, a reduction is given to the customer for prompt payment.

sinking fund a certain amount of cash or other assets set aside for a specific purpose.

solvency ability of a firm to pay its debts and thus remain in business.

stated interest rate the interest rate that is specified on a bond or other debt instrument.

stock dividend when a stockholder receives more stock on a proportional basis as a dividend.

stock split when the number of shares of a company is increased and thus the par value is divided proportionally.

subsidiary a company that is controlled by a "parent" company.

subsidiary ledger a ledger that contains details of a general ledger account; e.g., for accounts receivable, the subsidiary ledger would contain subsidiary accounts of each customer.

T

temporary account an income statement account which is temporarily established for the purpose of determining the details of income.

temporary difference a difference between an item on the income statement and the tax return due to "timing," and which is expected to reverse at a future time.

time value of money the concept that the value of money includes a time dimension, such that money now is worth more than money in the future because money now can be invested and earn interest.

treasury stock a company's own stock which it has purchased in the market.

U

unadjusted trial balance a listing of balances from the ledger in which total debits should equal total credits. This listing is made before adjusting entries are made.

unsecured bonds bonds that do not have collateral to support the principal; debenture bonds.

V

vertical analysis a technique of financial analysis in which a figure is used to represent 100% and all other figures are a percentage of it.

W

working capital current assets less current liabilities.

weighted average of shares number of shares weighted by the time the shares have been outstanding.

work in process for a manufacturing company, products that are not yet complete.

Y

yield the rate of interest that is earned on an investment.

Z

zero-coupon bonds bonds that do not include periodic interest payments. They are issued at below face value and on date of maturity the face value is paid.

INDEX

Index

Index

For **P2-9**

Melvine Company
Balance Sheet
December 31, Year 4
Assets

Current assets:
  Cash $ 35,000
  Marketable securities   17,000
  _____
  _____
  _____
  _____
  _____

  _____   _____
  Total current assets $215,900
Investments:
  _____

Property, plant and equipment:
  Land   20,000

  _____
  _____   _____

  Total property, plant and equipment
Intangible assets:
  _____

  _____   _____
  Total assets $586,900

Liabilities and Stockholders' Equity
Current liabilities:
  Accounts payable $ 14,000

  _____
  _____
  _____

  _____   _____
  Total current liabilities   45,300
Long-term liabilities:
  _____

Stockholders' equity:
  Common stock   240,000

  _____

  _____   _____
  Total stockholders' equity   411,600
  Total liabilities and stockholders' equity $586,900

Form for **P3-2** (fill in blank lines)

Name

Roberts Company
Income Statement
For the Year Ended December 31, Year 14

Sales revenues		$170,000
_____		_____
Gross profit		$116,000
Less operating expenses:		
Wages and salaries expense	$43,000	
_____		
_____	_____	
Total operating expenses		71,000
Income from operations		$
Other items:		
Gain on sale of equipment	8,000	
_____		
_____	_____	
Total		7,300
Income before income taxes		$
Income tax expense		15,000
Net income		$
		=====

Worksheet

_____
Name

Cash

Supplies

Equipment

Building

Accounts Payable

Common Stock

For **E-4-22**

_____
Name

Cash	Merchandise Inventory

Equipment	Accounts Payable

Notes Payable	Common Stock

Wages Expense

Worksheet

For **P4-8** (fill in blanks)

_____
                              Name

Franks's Auto Shop
Balance Sheet
December 31, Year 1

Assets		Liabilities and Capital	
Cash	$ 6,000	Accounts Payable	$ 870
_____		_____	
_____		_____	
_____		_____	
	_____	Jordan, Capital	_____
Total assets	$	Total liabilities and capital	$
	=====		=====

Frank's Auto Shop
Income Statement
For the Year Ended December 31, Year 1

Service Revenues $
Less expenses:

_____

_____

_____

_____

_____

Total expenses

                                                    _____
Income $ 47,170

For **P4-10** (fill in blanks)

Part 2.

Name

Henry Company
Income Statement
For the Year Ended December 31, Year 5

Sales revenue		$250,200
Cost of goods sold		_____
Gross profit		
Less expenses:		
Wages expense	$43,000	
_____		
_____		
_____		
_____		
_____	_____	
Total expenses		_____
Income		$ 59,500

(continue)

For **P6-11**

_____
Name

Effect on Net Accounts Receivable
(specify any relevant amount)

<u>Increase</u>   <u>Decrease</u>   <u>No change</u>

a. Write off $200 bad debt.

b. Write off $9500 abnormal bad debt.

c. Bad debt estimate 10% of Sales.

d. Bad debt estimate 2% of accounts receivable.
   Credit balance of $900 in Allowance account.

e. Bad debt estimate 2% of accounts receivable.
   Credit balance $1500 in Allowance account.

f. Bad debt estimate 2% of accounts receivable.
   Debit balance of $200 in Allowance account.

Calculations:

Worksheet

For **E7-7** (fill in blanks)

_____

Name

Use periodic inventory formula:

Beginning inventory	400 units	$_____
Purchases:		
May 3	700	_____
May 17	700	_____
Total goods available for sale	1,800 units	$_____
		========

Total units available for sale	1,800 units
Less units sold	1,400
Ending inventory	400 units

a. Periodic Average.

First, find average cost per unit:
Total goods available for sale ÷ 1,800 units = $____

(1) Ending Inventory (400 units x cost per unit) $_____

(2) Cost of Goods Sold (1400 units sold x cost per unit)   _____

(3) Sales Revenue (number of units sold x sales price)   _____

(4) Gross Profit (Sales revenue less Cost of goods sold)   _____

b. Periodic FIFO

(1) Ending Inventory:
    (400 units x FIFO per unit cost) = $_____
(2) Cost of Goods Sold:
Total goods available for sale $
Less Ending inventory (answer for (1))   _____
= Cost of Goods Sold
(3) Sales Revenue   _____

(4) Gross Profit (Sales revenue less Cost of goods sold)   _____

c. Periodic LIFO

(1) Ending Inventory:
    400 units in Ending Inventory x LIFO per unit cost $_____
(2) Cost of Goods Sold:
    Total goods available for sale $
    Less Ending inventory (answer for (1))   _____
    = Cost of Goods Sold
(3) Sales Revenue   _____

(4) Gross Profit (Sales revenue less Cost of goods sold)   _____

For **E7-8**   (fill in blanks)

Name _____

Beginning inventory   400 units
Purchases:
  May 3   700
  May 17   <u>700</u>
Total units available for sale 1,800 units
  Less units sold   <u>1,400</u>
  =Ending inventory   <u>400</u> units

a. Perpetual FIFO

(1) Cost of goods sold
    May 9 sale (800 units x FIFO cost) = $_____
    May 20 sale (600 units x FIFO cost) =   _____
    Total Cost of Goods Sold $_____

(2) Ending inventory
    400 units x FIFO cost   _____

(3) Sales revenue
    1400 units sold x sales price   _____

(4) Gross profit
    Sales revenue less Cost of goods sold   _____

b. Perpetual LIFO

(1) Cost of goods sold
    May 9 sale   (800 units x LIFO cost) $_____
    May 20 sale (600 units x LIFO cost)   _____
    Total Cost of Goods Sold   _____

(2) Ending inventory
    400 units x LIFO cost   _____

(3) Sales revenue
    1400 units x sales price   _____

(4) Gross profit
    Sales revenue less Cost of goods sold   _____

Worksheet

For **P7-5** (fill in blanks)

Name _____

Use periodic inventory formula:

Beginning inventory	400 units	$_____
Purchases:		
May 3	700	
May 17	700	_____
May 30	300	_____
Total goods available for sale	2,100 units	$_____
		========

Total units available for sale	2,100 units
Less units sold	1,600
Ending inventory	500 units

a. Periodic FIFO

(1) Ending Inventory:
   (500 units x FIFO per unit cost) = $_____

(2) Cost of Goods Sold:
Total goods available for sale $_____
Less Ending inventory (answer for (1)) _____
= Cost of Goods Sold   _____

(3) Sales Revenue   _____

(4) Gross Profit (Sales revenue less Cost of goods sold) _____

c. Periodic LIFO

(1) Ending Inventory:
   500 units in Ending Inventory x LIFO per unit cost $_____

(2) Cost of Goods Sold:
   Total goods available for sale $_____
   Less Ending inventory (answer for (1)) _____
   = Cost of Goods Sold

(3) Sales Revenue   _____

(4) Gross Profit (Sales revenue less Cost of goods sold) _____

c. Periodic Average.

First, find average cost per unit:

   Total goods available for sale ÷ 2,100 units = $____

(1) Ending Inventory (500 units x cost per unit) $_____

(2) Cost of Goods Sold (2100 units sold x cost per unit) _____

(3) Sales Revenue (number of units sold x sales price) _____

(4) Gross Profit (Sales revenue less Cost of goods sold) _____

For **P7-6** (fill in blanks)

_____

Name

```
Beginning inventory          400 units
Purchases: May 3        +    700
Available for sale           1,100
Sold: May 9             -     800
Available for sale            300
Purchase May 17         +     700
Available for sale           1,000
Sold: May 20            -     800
Available for sale            200
Purchase May 30         +     300
Ending inventory             500 (consisting of two batches of 200 + 300)
```

a. Perpetual FIFO

(1) Cost of goods sold
  May 9 sale (800 units x FIFO cost) = $_____
  May 20 sale (800 units x FIFO cost) =   _____
  Total Cost of Goods Sold $_____

(2) Ending inventory
  200 units x FIFO cost
  300 units x FIFO cost   _____

(3) Sales revenue
  1600 units sold x sales price   _____

(4) Gross profit
  Sales revenue less Cost of goods sold   _____

b. Perpetual LIFO

(1) Cost of goods sold
  May 9 sale   (800 units x LIFO cost) $_____
  May 20 sale (800 units x LIFO cost)   _____
  Total Cost of Goods Sold   _____

(2) Ending inventory
  200 units x LIFO cost
  300 units x LIFO cost   _____

(3) Sales revenue
  1600 units x sales price   _____

(4) Gross profit
  Sales revenue less Cost of goods sold   _____

447

For **P7-6**

(continued)

c. Perpetual Moving Average

(1) Cost of goods sold
May 9 sale (800 units x av. cost per unit) $_____

May 20 sale (800 units x av. cost per unit)   _____

Total Cost of Goods Sold   _____

(2) Ending inventory
500 units x av. moving cost per unit   _____

(3) Sales revenue
1600 units x sales price   _____

(4) Gross profit
Sales revenue less Cost of goods sold   _____

For **P7-7** (fill in blanks)
_____
Name

Use periodic inventory formula:
Beginning inventory 100 units $_____
Purchases:
April 10 200 _____
April 15 200 _____
April 22 300 _____
Total goods available for sale 800 units $_____
========

Total units available for sale 800 units
Less units sold 560
Ending inventory 240 units

a. Periodic FIFO

(1) Ending Inventory:
(240 units x FIFO per unit cost) = $_____
(2) Cost of Goods Sold:
Total goods available for sale $_____
Less Ending inventory (answer for (1)) _____
= Cost of Goods Sold _____
(3) Sales Revenue (units sold x sales price) _____
(4) Gross Profit (Sales revenue less Cost of goods sold) _____

c. Periodic LIFO

(1) Ending Inventory:
240 units in Ending Inventory x LIFO per unit cost $_____
(2) Cost of Goods Sold:
Total goods available for sale $_____
Less Ending inventory (answer for (1)) _____
= Cost of Goods Sold _____
(3) Sales Revenue _____
(4) Gross Profit (Sales revenue less Cost of goods sold) _____

c. Periodic Average.
First, find average cost per unit:
Total goods available for sale ÷ 800 units = $____
(1) Ending Inventory (240 units x cost per unit) $_____
(2) Cost of Goods Sold (560 units sold x cost per unit) _____
(3) Sales Revenue (number of units sold x sales price) _____
(4) Gross Profit (Sales revenue less Cost of goods sold) _____

Worksheet

For **P7-8**   (fill in blanks)

_____

Name

Beginning inventory	100 units
Sale April 7	- 20
Available for sale	80
Purchases:April 10	+ 200
Purchase April 15	+ 200
Available for sale	480
Sale April 20	- 300
Available for sale	180 units

(continued)	
Available for sale	180 units
Purchase April 22	+ 300
Available for sale	480
Sale April 28	- 120
Available for sale	360
Sale April 30	+ 120
Ending inventory	240

(consisting of 2 batches of 120 + 120)

a. Perpetual FIFO

(1) Cost of goods sold
   April 7 sale (20 units x FIFO cost) = $_____
   April 20 sale (300 units x FIFO cost) =   _____
   April 28 sale (120 units x FIFO cost) =   _____
   April 30 sale (120 units x FIFO cost) =   _____
   Total Cost of Goods Sold $_____

(2) Ending inventory
   120 units x FIFO cost
   120 units x FIFO cost   _____

(3) Sales revenue
   units sold x sales price   _____

(4) Gross profit
   Sales revenue less Cost of goods sold   _____

b. Perpetual LIFO

(1) Cost of goods sold
   April 7 sale (20 units x LIFO cost) = $_____
   April 20 sale (300 units x LIFO cost) =   _____

   April 28 sale (120 units x LIFO cost) =   _____
   April 30 sale (120 units x LIFO cost) =   _____
   Total Cost of Goods Sold   _____

(2) Ending inventory
   120 units x LIFO cost
   120 units x LIFO cost   _____

(3) Sales revenue
   units sold x sales price   _____

(4) Gross profit
   Sales revenue less Cost of goods sold   _____